something ABOUT THE AUThOR

SOMETHING ABOUT THE AUTHOR

Facts and Pictures about Authors
and Illustrators of Books for Young People

ANNE COMMIRE

VOLUME 32

GALE RESEARCH COMPANY
BOOK TOWER
DETROIT, MICHIGAN
48226

Editor: Anne Commire

Associate Editors: Agnes Garrett, Helga P. McCue

Assistant Editors: Dianne H. Anderson, Joyce Nakamura, Linda Shedd, Cynthia J. Walker

Sketchwriters: Barbara G. Farnan, Rachel Koenig, Eunice L. Petrini, Michael G. Williston

Researcher: Kathleen Betsko

Editorial Assistants: Carolyn Brudzynski, Lisa Bryon, Susan Pfanner, Elisa Ann Sawchuk

External Production Supervisor: Carol Blanchard

External Production Associates: Cynthia G. La Ferle, Mary Beth Trimper

Internal Senior Production Assistant: Louise Gagné

Text Layout: Vivian Tannenbaum

Art Director: Arthur Chartow

Special acknowledgment is due to the members of the *Contemporary Authors* staff
who assisted in the preparation of this volume.

Frederick G. Ruffner, *Publisher*

James M. Ethridge, *Editorial Director*

Adele Sarkissian, *Senior Editor*

Library of Congress Catalog Card Number 72-27107

Copyright © 1983 by Gale Research Company. All rights reserved.

ISBN 0-8103-0059-1

ISSN 0276-816X

Table of Contents

Introduction

If you had the chance to meet the writer or artist who created your favorite book, what would you like most to discuss? The chances are good that one of your first questions would be "Where do you get your ideas?" That seems to be one of the universally intriguing mysteries of the writer's or artist's profession. Although you may never have the opportunity for such a face-to-face talk, *Something about the Author* can probably tell you about the experiences of your favorite author or illustrator; you may then want to compare what the other famous and near-famous creators of children's literature in the *SATA* series have to say.

Let's take the question of how book ideas are born and see what kinds of answers you'll find in *SATA*. Nathaniel Benchley (Volume 25) spoke for many writers who admit they can't completely answer the question even for themselves: "You ask 'from what experience you derive your material,' and to that I think I can safely reply that you derive your material from everything you do, see, or hear, but beyond that I can't be of much help. . . ." But other writers can take us a bit further.

For some people, like Pearl Buck (Volume 25), ideas seem to flow naturally from a lifetime of experience that seems rather exotic to most of us. In more than forty years of living in China, Buck experienced the upheaval of the Boxer Rebellion in 1900, survived the Nationalists' attack on Nanking in 1927, and carried away a lasting sympathy for the hard lives of the Chinese peasants. That wealth of experience found its way into books like her Pulitzer Prize-winner *The Good Earth.*

But writers often glean their book ideas from the quiet drama and small adventures of more ordinary lives. Witness Judy Blume (Volume 31), who recognized that *Are You There, God? It's Me, Margaret* ". . .came right out of my own sixth-grade life, except for the family situation. Her feelings, her actions, her friends, her concerns—they were all the things we were interested in in the sixth grade." But even Blume reached beyond her own experience when necessary, as she did in *Deenie,* which was ". . .a deliberate idea, to write a book about a child with scoliosis, because I met a kid with scoliosis. That required a lot of research, while all my other books required none. That was a very special experience. . . . I went to the hospital and watched these kids being molded and fitted for body-braces. . . . All the dialogue in [the scene in the plaster-room] is real. I sat in there with a pencil and a paper and wrote down everything the nurse and the doctor said."

E.B. White (Volume 29) is another writer who discovered an important book idea in very ordinary circumstances. White, who wrote all his children's books on his Maine farm, explained: "One day when I was on my way to feed the pig, I began feeling sorry for the pig because, like most pigs, he was doomed to die. This made me sad. So I started thinking of ways to save a pig's life. I had been watching a big, grey spider at her work and was impressed by how clever she was at weaving. Gradually I worked the spider into the story. . . a story of friendship and salvation on a farm." Of course, we now know that story as *Charlotte's Web.*

Still other writers find their inspiration in a special hobby or activity. For Jean Slaughter Doty (Volume 28) raising animals, particularly horses and ponies, has always been a special love. ". . .I have helped mares in labor and raised the foals myself; I have galloped race horses in Phoenix Park just outside Dublin, and had glorious days of fox hunting in England, Ireland, and the United States. I have raised, schooled, ridden, driven and judged show horses and ponies, from little shows in back fields to Madison Square Garden—some pretty rotten horses, and a lot of good ones, and some superb ones, too. . . . These are the adventures I like writing about. . . . The ideas for my books come from incidents and experiences with the animals and people I've known for so many years."

From what many people report in *SATA*, ideas for books can dawn almost anytime and anywhere. Author-illustrator Leonard Weisgard (Volume 30) put it this way: "Books sometimes have grown from the moment of shaving, a moment of pain, a time of listening to children, from out of a dark tunnel, a groping into the past, or a stretching into the future, from amorphic places of the blackness of despair, or the joyousness of the bursting heart. And sometimes, even from the noise of a subway train." Hardy Gramatky (Volume 30) recalled just such an unexpected moment that led to his most famous book: "When I moved to New York I had a studio in a loft overlooking the East River. The boats fascinated me so that I did nothing but make drawings of them all day long. Each one took on a definite personality and soon a story had developed around them, which became Little Toot. . . ."

Even among writers, the old saying often holds true: necessity is the mother of invention. Many writers owe their "inspiration" to the need for a new bedtime story for their own children. Roald Dahl (Volume 26) described his experience this way: "I spent at least twenty years of my life writing nothing but short stories for adults, but then our first child came along. When she was old enough to have stories told to her at bedtime, I made a point of making up a story every single night. . . . Had I not had children of my own, I would have never written books for children, nor would I have been capable of doing so."

People who specialize in particular types of writing seem to have special sources for their ideas. The husband-and-wife team of Sam and Beryl Epstein (Volume 31) are fairly typical of nonfiction writers. They start with a natural curiosity about things in general and stay attuned to people and events around them. According to the Epsteins: "Sometimes we get a book idea from reading about something or someone in a newspaper. We wrote *Who Says You Can't?* after reading reports of a number of determined individuals who decided that it was possible to fight—and defeat—such overpowering adversaries as the automobile industry, the drug industry, powerful government agencies and entrenched political machines."

For specialists like the writers of historical fiction, the idea often grows out of a family story that has been handed down through several generations. Carol Ryrie Brink (Volume 31) noted that her Newbery Award-winner *Caddie Woodlawn* "is my grandmother's story, and I loved hearing it as a child. . . . It was many years later that I remembered these stories of Caddie's childhood, and I said to myself, 'If I loved them so much, perhaps other children would like them, too.'" Another historical novelist, Walter Edmonds (Volume 27), admitted that he couldn't take credit for the idea behind his Newbery Award-winner *The Matchlock Gun:* ". . .You never can tell how a story is going to get started. . . . Thomas Shepherd of Ilion, New York. . .sent me the transcript he had made of this family incident the way it had been told to him with the idea that I might like to see it. . . . So I don't claim credit for the story as a story. It's true, and I just embroidered the actual circumstances here and there to make it look real."

Perhaps the writers of the various forms of fantasy leave us somewhat in awe, unable to follow their flights of fancy back to a starting point. As Madeleine L'Engle (Volume 27) explained it, even the writer may be puzzled: "A writer of fantasy, fairy tale, or myth must inevitably discover that he is not writing out of his own knowledge or experience, but out of something both deeper and wider. I think that fantasy must possess the author and simply use him. I know that this is true of *A Wrinkle in Time.* I can't possibly tell you how I came to write it. It was simply a book I had to write. I had no choice. And it was only *after* it was written that I realized what some of it meant."

As you might expect, the ideas that grew to be books of humor and "nonsense" are themselves somewhat out of the ordinary. Let's consider the example of Theodor Geisel (Volume 28), whom we know better as Dr. Seuss. His zany creatures and situations did indeed have rather bizarre beginnings. As Geisel tells it, his first children's book was purely accidental: "I had no lofty reason whatsoever. In the fall of 1936, while aboard the *S.S. Kungsholm* on a rainy crossing of the Atlantic, I amused myself by putting words to the rhythm of the ship's engine. The words turned out to be *And to Think That I Saw It on Mulberry Street.* Once ashore, I drew the pictures to go with it." Frequently, his later books began as doodles, and verses came later. For example, "I was doodling around with drawing, the way I like to do, and a sketch of an elephant on some transparent paper happened to fall on top of the sketch of a tree. . . . I stopped, dumbfounded. I said to myself, '. . .An elephant in a tree! What's he doing there?' I brooded over it for three or four weeks, and finally I said to myself, 'Of course! He's hatching an egg!' " And so we have *Horton Hatches the Egg.*

As these few samples suggest, *SATA* is well stocked with information about the authors and illustrators of the books you like best. It's all here, waiting for you to sit back, relax, and open the covers. How's that for a good book idea?

What a *SATA* Entry Provides

In every *SATA* entry the editors attempt to give as complete a picture of the person's life and work as possible. In some cases that full range of information may simply be unavailable, or a biographee may choose not to reveal complete personal details. The information that the editors attempt to provide in every entry is arranged in the following categories:

1. The "head" of the entry gives

   —the most complete form of the name,
   —any part of the name not commonly used, included in parentheses,
   —birth and death dates, if known; a (?) indicates a discrepancy in published sources,

—pseudonyms or name variants under which the person has had books published or is publicly known, in parentheses in the second line.

2. "Personal" section gives

—date and place of birth and death,
—parents' names and occupations,
—name of spouse, date of marriage, names of children,
—educational institutions attended, degrees received, and dates,
—religious and political affiliations,
—agent's name and address,
—home and/or office address.

3. "Career" section gives

—name of employer, position, and dates for each career post,
—military service,
—memberships,
—awards and honors.

4. "Writings" section gives

—title, first publisher and date of publication, and illustration information for each book written; revised editions and other significant editions for books with particularly long publishing histories; genre, when known.

5. "Adaptations" section gives

—title, major performers, producer, and date of all known reworkings of an author's material in another medium, like movies, filmstrips, television, recordings, plays, etc.

6. "Sidelights" section gives

—commentary on the life or work of the biographee either directly from the person (and often written specifically for the *SATA* entry), or gathered from biographies, diaries, letters, interviews, or other published sources.

7. "For More Information See" section gives

—books, feature articles, films, plays, and reviews in which the biographee's life or work has been treated.

Other Information Features in *SATA*

Brief Entries, first introduced in Volume 27, are now a regular feature of *SATA*. Brief Entries present essentially the same types of information found in a full sketch, but do so in a capsule form and without illustration. The editors hope that these entries will give you useful and timely information while the more time-consuming process of attempting to compile a full-length sketch continues. Among the Brief Entries in Volume 32 you'll find Paul Fleischman, author of the 1983 Newbery Honor Book *Graven Images;* Harold Gray, creator of the "Little Orphan Annie" cartoon series; Johnny Gruelle, who wrote and illustrated the "Raggedy Ann and Andy" books; Michael Hague, whose illustration of books like Marianne Mayer's *The Unicorn and the Lake* and his own adaptation of H.C. Andersen's *Fairy Tales* have been linked to the work of Rackham and Dulac; and Robin McKinley, author of the 1983 Newbery Honor Book *The Blue Sword.*

Obituaries are another regular feature of *SATA*. An obituary in *SATA* is intended not only as a death notice, but also as a concise view of a person's life and work. Obituaries appear not only for persons listed in *SATA* prior to their death, but also for people who have not yet appeared in the series. Recent deaths noted in Volume 32 include those of Georges Rémi, creator of the Tintin cartoon series, and Lillian H. Smith, a major figure in American and Canadian library service for children and author of the award-winning *The Unreluctant Years.*

Revised entries became a regular element in the *SATA* series with Volume 25. For each succeeding volume the editors select from among the early *SATA* listees those authors and illustrators who remain of interest to today's young readers and who have been active enough to require extensive revision of their earlier entry. The entry for a given biographee may be revised as often as there is substantial new information to provide. In Volume 32 you'll find revised entries for Mabel Esther Allan, Leon Garfield, Mercer Mayer, and J.R.R. Tolkien.

New Format for Author Index

If you are a regular user of *SATA,* you'll notice that the Author Index in this volume has a new look. We hope you'll find, as we have, that the information in each entry can be identified more quickly and easily in the new format.

Highlights of This Volume

These are some of the people in Volume 32 that you may find particularly interesting:

JIM DAVIS......who found that creating a cartoon strip is better the second time around. He knew he couldn't get far with his first creation, "Gnorm the Gnat." (Davis couldn't identify with a bug and, what's more, he knew bugs don't sell.) But Davis found just the right formula in "Garfield," the lovable-hateable cat whose personality was patterned on Davis's grandfather Garfield, "...huge,...stubborn,...opinionated,...cantankerous."

LEON GARFIELD......who is one of Britain's most highly respected and popular writers for children. Books like *Devil-in-the-Fog* and *The Ghost Downstairs* have won a long list of literary awards and have been successfully adapted as TV and motion picture films. Garfield, who is often compared to Charles Dickens, also wrote a highly-acclaimed ending for Dickens's unfinished novel *The Mystery of Edwin Drood.*

ROBERT J. KEESHAN......whose name and face (out of costume) you wouldn't easily connect with "Captain Kangaroo." In almost thirty years in broadcasting Keeshan has witnessed the birth of television and the death of radio. He has guided "Captain Kangaroo" to becoming not only the longest-running children's program on network television, but also a training ground for dozens of producers and executives who have gone on to other programs for children.

MERCER MAYER......the author-illustrator who started to pile up awards with his very first book—*A Boy, a Dog, and a Frog*—and hasn't stopped yet. He concentrates on illustrating his own writings like his "Little Monster" and "Frog" series, but his illustrations have also brought to life John D. Fitzgerald's "Great Brain" series and Jane Yolen's *The Bird of Time.*

J.R.R. TOLKIEN......the young scholar of Latin, Greek, and Gothic who amused himself by inventing his own language and went on to become professor of Anglo-Saxon at Oxford University. That hardly seems the stuff of which children's writers are made. But then it hardly reveals Tolkien's special gift for expressing the deepest human feelings and yearnings within the new mythology of Middle Earth as he portrayed it in *The Hobbit* and "The Lord of the Rings" cycle.

These are only a few of the authors and illustrators that you'll find in this volume. We hope you find all the entries in *SATA* both interesting and useful. Please write and tell us if we can make *SATA* even more helpful for you.

A Partial List of Authors and Illustrators
Who Will Appear in Forthcoming Volumes of
Something about the Author

Abels, Harriette S.
Adrian, Mary
Ahlberg, Allan
Aldridge, Alan   1943(?)-
Allard, Harry
Allen, Agnes B.   1898-1959
Allen, Jeffrey
Anders, Rebecca
Andrist, Ralph K.   1914-
Ardley, Neil (Richard)   1937-
Armitage, Ronda
Armstrong, Louise
Arneson, D.J.   1935-
Arnold, Caroline
Ashley, Bernard   1935-
Austin, R. G.
Axeman, Lois
Ayme, Marcel   1902-1967
Baker, Olaf
Balderson, Margaret   1935-
Bang, Betsy
Barber, Richard   1941-
Barkin, Carol
Barnett, Moneta   1922-1976
Bartlett, Margaret F.   1896-
Batherman, Muriel   1926(?)-
Batson, Larry   1930-
Bauer, Caroline Feller   1935-
Bauer, John Albert   1882-1918
Becker, May Lamberton   1873-1958
Beckman, Delores
Beim, Jerrold   1910-1957
Beim, Lorraine   1909-1951
Bernheim, Evelyne   1935-
Bernheim, Marc   1924-
Birnbaum, Abe   1899-
Blumberg, Rhoda   1917-
Boegehold, Betty   1913-
Boning, Richard A.
Bonners, Susan
Bowden, Joan C.   1925-
Bowen, Gary
Bracken, Carolyn
Brewton, Sara W.
Bridgman, Elizabeth P.   1921-
Broekel, Ray   1923-
Bromley, Dudley   1948-
Bronin, Andrew   1947-
Bronson, Wilfrid   1894-
Brooks, Ron(ald George)   1948-
Brown, Fern G.   1918-
Brown, Roy Frederick   1921-
Brownmiller, Susan   1935-
Buchanan, William   1930-
Buchenholz, Bruce
Budney, Blossom   1921-

Burchard, Marshall
Burke, David   1927-
Burns, Marilyn
Burstein, Chaya
Butler, Dorothy   1925-
Butler, Hal   1913-
Calvert, Patricia
Camps, Luis
Carey, M. V.   1925-
Carley, Wayne
Carlson, Nancy L.
Carmer, Carl   1893-1976
Carrie, Christopher
Carroll, Ruth R.   1899-
Cauley, Lorinda B.
Chang, Florence C.
Charles, Carole
Charles, Donald
Chase, Catherine
Cline, Linda   1941-
Cohen, Joel H.
Cole, Brock
Cole, Joanna
Coleman, William L.   1938-
Coontz, Otto
Cooper, Elizabeth Keyser   1910-
Cooper, Paulette   1944-
Corbett, Grahame
Cosgrove, Margaret   1926-
Coutant, Helen
Craik, Dinah M.   1826-1887
Dabcovich, Lydia
Darley, F(elix) O(ctavius) C(arr)   1822-1888
D'Aulnoy, Marie-Catherine   1650(?)-1705
David, Jay   1929-
Davies, Peter   1937-
Dean, Leigh
Degens, T.
DeGoscinny, Rene
Deguine, Jean-Claude   1943-
Deweese, Gene   1934-
Ditmars, Raymond   1876-1942
Dodd, Lynley
Duggan, Maurice (Noel)   1922-1975
Dumas, Philippe   1940-
East, Ben
Eastman, Philip D.   1909-
Edelson, Edward   1932-
Ehlert, Lois Jane   1934-
Eisenberg, Lisa
Elder, Lauren
Elgin, Kathleen   1923-
Elwood, Roger   1943-
Erwin, Betty K.

Etter, Les   1904-
Everett-Green, Evelyn   1856-1932
Falkner, John Meade   1858-1932
Farmer, Penelope   1939-
Fender, Kay
Filson, Brent
Fischer, Hans Erich   1909-1958
Fisher, Barbara
Flanagan, Geraldine Lux
Folch-Ribas, Jacques   1928-
Ford, Barbara
Fox, Thomas C.
Frame, Paul   1913-
Frascino, Edward
Freschet, Berniece   1927-
Frevert, Patricia D(endtler)   1943-
Gans, Roma   1894-
Garcia-Sanchez, S.L.
Gardner, John Champlin, Jr.   1933-1982
Garrison, Christian   1942-
Gathje, Curtis
Gault, Clare   1925-
Gelman, Rita G.   1937-
Gemme, Leila Boyle   1942-
Gerber, Dan   1940-
Gerson, Corinne
Giff, Patricia R.
Gobbato, Imero   1923-
Goldstein, Nathan   1927-
Gordon, Shirley
Gould, Chester   1900-
Grabianski, Janusz   1929(?)-1976
Graboff, Abner   1919-
Graeber, Charlotte Towner
Gregor, Arthur S.
Gridley, Marion E(leanor)   1906-1974
Gross, Ruth B.
Gutman, Bill
Halacy, Daniel S., Jr.   1919-
Harris, Marilyn   1931-
Hayman, LeRoy   1916-
Healey, Larry
Heine, Helme   1941-
Henty, George Alfred   1832-1902
Herzig, Alison Cragin
Hicks, Clifford B.   1920-
Hill, Douglas Arthur   1935-
Hirshberg, Albert S.   1909-1973
Hollander, Zander   1923-
Hood, Thomas   1779-1845
Horwitz, Elinor L.
Hull, Jessie Redding
Hunt, Clara Whitehill   1871-1958
Ingelow, Jean   1820-1897
Irvine, Georgeanne
Jackson, Anita

Jackson, Kathryn 1907-
Jackson, Robert 1941-
Jacobs, Francine 1935-
James, Elizabeth
Jameson, Cynthia
Janssen, Pierre
Jaspersohn, William
Jewell, Nancy 1940-
Jezard, Alison 1919-
Johnson, Harper
Joyner, Jerry 1938-
Kahl, Virginia 1919-
Kahn, Joan 1914-
Kalan, Robert
Kantrowitz, Mildred
Kasuya, Masahiro 1937-
Keith, Eros 1942-
Kessler, Ethel
Kirn, Ann (Minette) 1910-
Koenig, Marion
Kohl, Herbert
Kohl, Judith
Kraske, Robert
Kredenser, Gail 1936-
Krensky, Stephen 1953-
Kullman, Harry
Kurland, Michael 1938-
Laure, Jason
Lawson, Annetta
Leach, Christopher 1925-
Lebrun, Claude
Leckie, Robert 1920-
Lerner, Carol
LeRoy, Gen
Le-Tan, Pierre 1950-
Levoy, Myron
Lewis, Naomi
Lindblom, Steve
Lindman, Maj (Jan)
Lines, Kathleen
Livermore, Elaine
Lubin, Leonard
MacDonald, George 1824-1905
MacKinstry, Elizabeth (?)-1956
Mali, Jane Lawrence
Manes, Stephen
Marryat, Frederick 1792-1848
Mayakovsky, Vladimir 1894-1930
McCannon, Dindga
McKee, David 1935-
McKim, Audrey Margaret 1909-
McLenighan, Valjean
McLoughlin, John C.
McNaughton, Colin
Melcher, Frederic G. 1879-1963
Mendoza, George 1934-
Mezey, Robert
Molesworth, Maria L. 1839(?)-1921
Molly, Anne S. 1907-
Moore, Lilian
Moore, Patrick 1923-
Morgenroth, Barbara
Murdocca, Sal
Murphy, Shirley Rousseau 1928-
Myers, Elisabeth P. 1918-
Nash, Bruce
Nickl, Peter

Nostlinger, Christine 1936(?)-
Obligado, Lillian Isabel 1931-
Odor, Ruth S. 1926-
O'Hanlon, Jacklyn
Oleksy, Walter 1930-
Oppenheim, Shulamith (Levey) 1930-
Orr, Frank 1936-
Orton, Helen Fuller 1872-1955
Overbeck, Cynthia
Owens, Gail 1939-
Packard, Edward 1931-
Parenteau, Shirley L. 1935-
Parker, Robert Andrew 1927-
Pascal, Francine
Paterson, A(ndrew) B(arton) 1864-1941
Paterson, Diane 1946-
Patterson, Sarah 1959-
Pavey, Peter
Pelgrom, Els
Peretz, Isaac Loeb 1851-1915
Perkins, Lucy Fitch 1865-1937
Peterson, Esther Allen
Peterson, Jeanne Whitehouse 1939-
Phillips, Betty Lou
Plotz, Helen 1913-
Plowden, David 1932-
Plume, Ilse
Poignant, Axel
Pollock, Bruce
Polushkin, Maria
Pope, Elizabeth M. 1917-
Porter, Eleanor Hodgman 1868-1920
Poulsson, Emilie 1853-1939
Powers, Richard M. 1921-
Prager, Arthur
Prather, Ray
Preston, Edna Mitchell
Pursell, Margaret S.
Pursell, Thomas F.
Pyle, Katharine 1863-1938
Rabinowitz, Solomon 1859-1916
Rae, Gwynedd 1892-
Rappoport, Ken 1935-
Rees, David 1936-
Reich, Hanns
Reid, Alistair 1926-
Reidel, Marlene
Reiff, Tana
Reynolds, Marjorie 1903-
Rice, Eve H. 1951-
Rockwell, Anne 1934-
Rockwell, Harlow
Rockwood, Joyce 1947-
Rosier, Lydia
Ross, Pat
Ross, Wilda 1915-
Roughsey, Dick 1921(?)-
Roy, Cal
Roy, Ron
Ruby, Lois 1942-
Rudstrom, Lennart
Ryder, Joanne
Sargent, Sarah
Schneider, Leo 1916-
Schoenherr, John C. 1935-
Sebestyen, Ouida
Seidler, Rosalie

Sewall, Helen 1881-
Sewell, Marcia 1935-
Shea, George
Shreve, Susan
Slater, Jim
Slepian, Jan(ice B.)
Smith, Alison
Smith, Catriona (Mary) 1948-
Smith, Ray(mond Kenneth) 1949-
Smollin, Michael J.
Sobol, Harriet L. 1936-
Spencer, Zane 1935-
Steiner, Charlotte
Steiner, Jorg
Stevens, Leonard A. 1920-
Stevenson, James
Stine, R. Conrad 1937-
Stubbs, Joanna 1940-
Sullivan, Mary Beth
Suteev, Vladimir Grigor'evich
Sutherland, Robert D.
Sweet, Ozzie
Taback, Simms 1932-
Taylor, Ann 1782-1866
Taylor, Jane 1783-1824
Thaler, Mike
Thomas, Ianthe
Thompson, Brenda 1935-
Thurman, Judith 1946-
Timmermans, Gommaar 1930-
Todd, Ruthven 1914-
Tourneur, Dina K. 1934-
Treadgold, Mary 1910-
Van Steenwyk, Elizabeth
Velthuijs, Max 1923-
Villiard, Paul 1910-1974
Waber, Bernard 1924-
Wagner, Jenny
Walker, Charles W.
Walsh, Anne Batterberry
Waterton, Betty
Watson, Aldren A. 1917-
Watts, Franklin 1904-1978
Wayne, Bennett
Wellman, Alice 1900-
Werner, Herma 1926-
Weston, Martha
Whelen, Gloria
White, Wallace 1930-
Whitlock, Ralph 1914-
Wild, Jocelyn
Wild, Robin
Wilson, Edward A. 1886-1970
Winn, Marie
Winter, Paula 1929-
Winterfeld, Henry 1901-
Wolde, Gunilla
Wolf, Bernard
Wong, Herbert H.
Wormser, Richard
Wright, Betty R.
Yagawa, Sumiko
Youldon, Gillian
Zaidenberg, Arthur 1908(?)-
Zelinsky, Paul O.
Zimelman, Nathan
Zistel, Era

In the interest of making *Something about the Author* as responsive as possible to the needs of its readers, the editor welcomes your suggestions for additional authors and illustrators to be included in the series.

GRATEFUL ACKNOWLEDGMENT

is made to the following publishers, authors, and artists for
their kind permission to reproduce copyrighted material.

ABELARD-SCHUMAN. Illustration by Graham Byfield from *Selina's New Family* by Anne Pilgrim. Copyright © 1967 by Anne Pilgrim. Reprinted by permission of Abelard-Schuman.

ADDISON-WESLEY PUBLISHING CO., INC. Illustration by Susanna Natti from *The Downtown Fairy Godmother* by Charlotte Pomerantz. Text copyright © 1978 by Charlotte Pomerantz. Illustrations copyright © 1978 by Susanna Natti./ Illustration by Erik Blegvad from "Monkey Vines" in *Blueberries Lavender* by Nancy Dingman Watson. Text copyright © 1977 by Nancy Dingman Watson. Illustrations copyright © 1977 by Erik Blegvad. Both reprinted by permission of Addison-Wesley Publishing Co., Inc.

GEORGE ALLEN & UNWIN LTD. Illustration by Pauline Baynes from *The Adventures of Tom Bombadil* by J.R.R. Tolkien. Copyright © 1962 by George Allen & Unwin Ltd./ Illustration by Pauline Baynes from *Smith of Wootten Major* by J.R.R. Tolkien. Copyright © 1967 by George Allen & Unwin Ltd. Both reprinted by permission of George Allen & Unwin Ltd.

ATHENEUM PUBLISHERS. Illustration by Charles Robinson from *An Island in a Green Sea* by Mabel Esther Allan. Copyright © 1972 by Mabel Esther Allan./ Illustration by Graham Booth from *The Case of the Missing Kittens* by Mark Taylor. Text copyright © 1978 by Mark Taylor. Illustrations copyright © 1978 by Graham Booth./ Illustration by Gaynor Chapman from *The Luck Child* retold by Gaynor Chapman, based on a story by the Brothers Grimm. Text copyright © 1968 by Hamish Hamilton. Illustrations copyright © 1968 by Gaynor Chapman. All reprinted by permission of Atheneum Publishers.

BALLANTINE BOOKS, INC. Illustration by Jim Davis from *Garfield at Large* by Jim Davis. Copyright © 1980 by United Feature Syndicate, Inc./ Illustration by Jim Davis from *Garfield Weighs In* by Jim Davis. Copyright © 1982 by United Feature Syndicate, Inc. Both reprinted by permission of Ballantine Books, Inc.

BLACK OAK PRESS. Illustration by Adam Laceky from *The Magic Pretzel* by James Magorian. Copyright © 1979 by James Magorian. Reprinted by permission of Black Oak Press.

BLACKIE & SON LTD. Illustration by Gaynor Chapman from *Treasure in Devils' Bay* by Alexis Brown. Reprinted by permission of Blackie & Son Ltd.

THE BODLEY HEAD LTD. Illustration by Donald Crews from *Truck* by Donald Crews. Copyright © 1980 by Donald Crews./ Illustration by Donald Crews from *Freight Train* by Donald Crews. Copyright © 1978 by Donald Crews. Both reprinted by permission of The Bodley Head Ltd.

BONI & LIVERIGHT. Sidelight excerpts from *The Life of Steele MacKaye: Genius of the Theatre in Relation to His Times and Contemporaries, Vol. 1* by Percy MacKaye./ Sidelight excerpts from *The Life of Steele MacKaye: Genius of the Theatre in Relation to His Times and Contemporaries, Vol. 2* by Percy MacKaye. Both reprinted by permission of Boni & Liveright.

DON BOSCO PUBLICATIONS. Illustration from *Stories of Don Bosco* by Peter Lappin. Copyright © 1979 by Salesian Society, Inc. Reprinted by permission of Don Bosco Publications.

BROADMAN PRESS. Illustration by Ron Martin from *The Pattersons and the Goat Man* by Brenda Knight Graham. Copyright © 1981 by Broadman Press. Reprinted by permission of Broadman Press.

CHILDRENS PRESS. Photograph from *Kurt Thomas, International Winner* by Nancy Robison. Photo courtesy of Indiana State University. Copyright © 1980 by Regensteiner Publishing Enterprises, Inc./ Illustration by Gene Holtan from *Old Blue, You Good Dog, You* by Mark Taylor. Text copyright © 1970 by Mark Taylor. Illustrations copyright © 1970 by Gene Holtan. Both reprinted by permission of Childrens Press.

WILLIAM COLLINS & WORLD PUBLISHING CO., INC. Illustration by William Plummer from *Mystery at Saint-Hilaire* by Priscilla Hagon. Text copyright © 1968 by Priscilla Hagon. Illustrations copyright © 1968 by William Plummer./ Illustration by Susanne Suba from *Dancing to Danger* by Priscilla Hagon. Text copyright © 1967 by World Publishing Co. Illustration copyright © 1967 by Susanne Suba. Both reprinted by permission of William Collins & World Publishing Co., Inc.

COWARD, McCANN & GEOGHEGAN, INC. Sidelight excerpts from *The Kneeling Tree, and Other Folktales from the Middle East* by Dorothy Spicer. Copyright © 1971 by Dorothy Gladys Spicer./ Illustration by Sofia from *13 Dragons* by Dorothy Gladys Spicer. Text copyright © 1974 by Dorothy Gladys Spicer. Illustrations copyright © 1974 by Sofia Pelkey./ Illustration by Pat Rotondo from *The Gift of Magic Sleep* by Irwin Shapiro. Text copyright © 1979 by Irwin Shapiro. Illustrations copyright © 1979 by Pat Rotondo. All reprinted by permission of Coward, McCann & Geoghegan, Inc.

COWLES BOOK CO., INC. Illustration by Lee Jack Morton from *Leroy Oops* by Barbara Glasser. Copyright © 1971 by Barbara Glasser. Reprinted by permission of Cowles Book Co., Inc.

CRITERION BOOKS, INC. Illustration by Whitear from *The Dancing Garlands* by Mabel Esther Allan. Copyright © 1968 by Mabel Esther Allan./ Illustration by Howard Simon from "Stretch, Puff and Blazer: A Russian Tale" in *Eurasian Folk and Fairy Tales* by I. F. Bulatkin. Copyright © 1965 by Criterion Books, Inc. Both reprinted by permission of Criterion Books, Inc.

THOMAS Y. CROWELL CO., PUBLISHERS. Illustration by Jacques Hnizdovsky from *The Auk, the Dodo, and the Oryx: Vanished and Vanishing Creatures* by Robert Silverberg. Copyright © 1967 by Robert Silverberg./ Illustration by Arthur Getz from *Mr. Goat's Bad Good Idea* by Marileta Robinson. Text copyright © 1979 by Marileta Robinson. Illustrations copyright © 1979 by Arthur Getz./ Illustration by Dave Ross from *How to Keep Warm in Winter* by Dave Ross. Copyright © 1980 by Dave Ross. All reprinted by permission of Thomas Y. Crowell Co., Publishers.

CROWN PUBLISHERS, INC. Illustration by Susanna Natti from *Frederick's Alligator* by Esther Allen Peterson. Text copyright © 1979 by Esther Allen Peterson. Illustrations copyright © 1979 by Susanna Natti. Reprinted by permission of Crown Publishers, Inc.

DELACORTE PRESS. Sidelight excerpts from *The Education of Little Tree* by Forrest Carter. Copyright © 1976 by Forrest Carter./ Sidelight excerpts from an article "And So It Grows," by Leon Garfield, December, 1968, in *The Horn Book*./ Jacket illustration by Michael Dudash from *Hold Fast* by Kevin Major. Text copyright © 1978 by Kevin Major. Jacket painting copyright © 1980 by Michael Dudash. All reprinted by permission of Delacorte Press.

DELL PUBLISHING CO., INC. Sidelight excerpts from an article "The Captain and the Kids," by Max Wilk in *The Golden Age of Television*. Reprinted by permission of Dell Publishing Co., Inc.

THE DIAL PRESS. Jacket illustration by Michael Hague from *The Unicorn and the Lake* by Marianna Mayer. Text copyright © 1982 by Marianna Mayer. Pictures copyright © 1982 by Michael R. Hague./ Illustration by Mercer Mayer from *The Great Brain at the Academy* by John D. Fitzgerald. Text copyright © 1972 by John D. Fitzgerald. Illustrations copyright © 1972 by Mercer Mayer./ Illustration by Mahiri Fufuka from *Poochie* by Ted Pontiflet. Text copyright © 1978 by Ted Pontiflet. Illustrations copyright © 1978 by Mahiri Fufuka. All reprinted by permission of The Dial Press.

DODD, MEAD & CO. Photograph by Colleen Stanley Bare from *Mule Deer* by Colleen Stanley Bare. Text and photographs copyright © 1981 by Colleen Stanley Bare./ Illustration by Betsy Lewin from *Cat Count* by Betsy Lewin. Copyright © 1981 by Betsy Lewin./ Jacket illustration by Morton Künstler from *Fullback Fury* by Gene Olson. Copyright © 1964 by Gene Olson./ Illustration by Kurt Wiese from *Honk the Moose* by Phil Stong. Copyright 1935 by Phil Stong./ Illustration by Doris Lee from *The Hired Man's Elephant* by Phil Stong. Copyright 1939 by Dodd, Mead and Co. All reprinted by permission of Dodd, Mead & Co.

DOUBLEDAY & CO., INC. Jacket illustration by Raymond Davidson from *The Eclogues and the Georgics of Virgil* by David R. Slavitt./ Sidelight excerpts from *George Washington Carver: An American Biography* by Rackham Holt./ Wood engraving by Stefan Martin from "The Lutin in the Barn," by Natalie Savage Carlson in *Ghosts and Spirits of Many Lands*, edited by Freya Littledale. Copyright © 1956 by Natalie Savage Carlson. Copyright © 1970 by Freya Littledale./ Illustration by Sammis McLean from *Super-Spy K-13 in Outer Space* by Bob Teague. Text copyright © 1980 by Robert L. Teague. Illustrations copyright © 1980 by Sammis McLean./ Illustration by Geoffrey Moss from *Agent K-13, the Super-Spy* by Bob Teague. Text copyright © 1974 by Robert L. Teague. Illustrations copyright © 1974 by Geoffrey Moss. All reprinted by permission of Doubleday & Co., Inc.

DOVER PUBLICATIONS, INC. Sidelight excerpts from *Techniques of Drawing* by Howard Simon. Copyright © 1972 by Dover Publications, Inc. Reprinted by permission of Dover Publications, Inc.

E. P. DUTTON, INC. Illustration by Robin Jacques from *A Book of Enchantments and Curses* by Ruth Manning-Sanders. Copyright © 1976 by Ruth Manning-Sanders./ Illustration by Robin Jacques from *A Book of Monsters* by Ruth Manning-Sanders. Copyright © 1975 by Ruth Manning-Sanders./ Illustration by Robin Jacques from "The Enchanted Candle," in *A Book of Enchantments and Curses* by Ruth Manning-Sanders. Copyright © 1976 by Ruth Manning-Sanders. All reprinted by permission of E. P. Dutton, Inc.

FARRAR, STRAUS & GIROUX, INC. Sidelight excerpts from *Papier Mâché* by Peter Rush. Reprinted by permission of Farrar, Straus & Giroux, Inc.

FOUR WINDS PRESS. Illustrations by Mercer Mayer from *Beauty and the Beast,* retold by Marianna Mayer. Text copyright © 1978 by Marianna Mayer. Illustrations copyright © 1978 by Mercer Mayer./ Illustration by Marianna and Mercer Mayer from *Me and My Flying Machine* by Marianna and Mercer Mayer. Copyright © 1971 by Marianna and Mercer Mayer./ Illustration by Mercer Mayer from *Everyone Knows What a Dragon Looks Like* by Jay Williams. Text copyright © 1976 by Jay Williams. Illustrations copyright © 1976 by Mercer Mayer. All reprinted by permission of Four Winds Press.

GARRARD PUBLISHING CO. Illustration by Paul Frame from *Willie's Whizmobile* by Irwin Shapiro. Text copyright © 1973 by Irwin Shapiro. Illustrations copyright © 1973 by Paul Frame. Reprinted by permission of Garrard Publishing Co.

GREENWILLOW BOOKS. Illustration by Donald Crews from *Freight Train* by Donald Crews. Copyright © 1978 by Donald Crews./ Illustration by Donald Crews from *Truck* by Donald Crews. Copyright © 1980 by Donald Crews. Both reprinted by permission of Greenwillow Books.

HARPER & ROW, PUBLISHERS, INC. Illustration by Jo Polseno from *Swan Cove* by Jane White Canfield. Text copyright © 1978 by Jane White Canfield. Illustrations copyright © 1978 by Jo Polseno./ Illustration by Thomas Di Grazia from *Hold My Hand* by Charlotte Zolotow. Text copyright © 1972 by Charlotte Zolotow. Illustrations copyright © 1972 by Thomas Di Grazia./ Sidelight excerpts from "Leon Garfield Writes," in *A Sense of Story* by John Rowe Townsend. Copyright © 1971 by John Rowe Townsend./ Illustration by John and Ian Schoenherr from *The Fallen Spaceman* by Lee Harding. Text copyright © 1973, 1980 by Lee Harding. Illustrations copyright © 1980 by John and Ian Schoenherr./ Illustration by Howard Simon from *Candita's Choice* by Mina Lewiton. Copyright © 1959 by Mina Lewiton./ Illustration by Howard Simon from *That Bad Carlos* by Mina Lewiton. Text copyright © 1964 by Mina Lewiton. Illustration copyright © 1964 by Howard Simon./ Illustrations by Maurice Sendak from *She Loves Me . . . She Loves Me Not* by Robert Keeshan. Text copyright © 1963 by Robert Keeshan. Illustrations copyright © 1963 by Maurice Sendak. All reprinted by permission of Harper & Row, Publishers, Inc.

HASTINGS HOUSE, PUBLISHERS, INC. Illustration by Barbara Cooney from *Shaun and the Boat* by Anne Molloy. Copyright © 1965 by Anne Molloy and Barbara Cooney./ Illustration by Ingrid Fetz from *Wendy and the Bullies* by Nancy K. Robinson. Text copyright © 1980 by Nancy K. Robinson. Illustrations copyright © 1980 by Scholastic Magazines, Inc. Both reprinted by permission of Hastings House, Publishers, Inc.

WILLIAM HEINEMANN LTD. Jacket painting by Stefen Bernath from *The Apprentices* by Leon Garfield. Reprinted by permission of William Heinemann Ltd.

HOLIDAY HOUSE, INC. Illustration by Edward Gorey from *Treehorn's Treasure* by Florence Parry Heide. Text copyright © 1981 by Florence Parry Heide. Illustrations copyright © 1981 by Edward Gorey. Reprinted by permission of Holiday House, Inc.

THE HORN BOOK, INC. Sidelight excerpts from *Illustrators of Children's Books: 1957-1966,* edited by Lee Kingman and others. Copyright © 1968 by The Horn Book, Inc. Reprinted by permission of The Horn Book, Inc.

HOUGHTON MIFFLIN CO. Sidelight excerpts from *The Letters of J. R. R. Tolkien,* edited by Humphrey Carpenter and Christopher Tolkien./ Sidelight excerpts from *Tolkien: A Biography* by Humphrey Carpenter./ Illustration by J. R. R. Tolkien from *The Hobbit; or, There and Back Again* by J. R. R. Tolkien. Copyright 1937, 1938 by J. R. R. Tolkien./ Illustration by Pauline Diana Baynes from *Farmer Giles of Ham* by J. R. R. Tolkien./ Illustration by Pauline Baynes from *The Adventures of Tom Bombadil* by J. R. R. Tolkien. Copyright © 1962 by George Allen & Unwin Ltd. All reprinted by permission of Houghton Mifflin Co.

KESTREL BOOKS. Sidelight excerpts from "Leon Garfield Writes," in *A Sense of Story* by John Rowe Townsend. Copyright © 1971 by John Rowe Townsend. Reprinted by permission of Kestrel Books.

J. B. LIPPINCOTT CO. Illustration by Katherine Coville from *Sarah's Unicorn* by Bruce Coville. Text copyright © 1979 by Bruce Coville. Illustrations copyright © 1979 by Katherine Coville. Reprinted by permission of J. B. Lippincott Co.

LITTLE, BROWN & CO. Illustration by Glen Rounds from *Jennie Jenkins* by Mark Taylor. Text copyright © 1975 by Mark Taylor. Illustrations copyright © 1975 by Glen Rounds./ Illustration by George and Doris Hauman from *Poems for Youth* by Emily Dickinson. Copyright 1918, 1919, 1924, 1929, 1932, and 1934 by Martha Dickinson Bianchi. Both reprinted by permission of Little, Brown & Co.

LONGMAN GROUP LTD. Illustration by Arvia MacKaye from *Weathergoose-woo!* by Percy MacKaye. Copyright 1929 by Percy MacKaye. Reprinted by permission of Longman Group Ltd.

LOTHROP, LEE & SHEPARD BOOKS. Illustration by Michael Bragg from *King Nimrod's Tower* by Leon Garfield. Text copyright © 1982 by Leon Garfield. Illustrations copyright © 1982 by Michael Bragg./ Jacket illustration by Stan Skardinski from *With a Wave of the Wand* by Mark Jonathan Harris. Copyright © 1980 by Mark Jonathan Harris. Jacket illustration copyright © 1980 by Stan Skardinski./ Illustration by Roy Doty from *Extraordinary Stories Behind the Invention of Ordinary Things* by Don L. Wulffson. Text copyright © 1981 by Don L. Wulffson. Illustrations copyright © 1981 by Roy Doty./ Illustration by Marcia Keegan from *Moonsong Lullaby* by Jamake Highwater. Text copyright © 1981 by Jamake Highwater. Photograph copyright © 1981 by Marcia Keegan. All reprinted by permission of Lothrop, Lee & Shepard Books.

MACMILLAN, INC. Illustration by Stefan Martin from *Ronnie and the Chief's Son* by Elizabeth Coatsworth./ Illustration by Dorothy P. Lathrop from *Stars Tonight: Verses New and Old for Boys and Girls* by Sara Teasdale. Copyright 1930 by Sara Teasdale Filsinger./ Illustration by Dugald Walker from *Rainbow Gold: Poems Old and New Selected for Boys and Girls* by Sara Teasdale. Copyright 1922 by Macmillan Co./ Illustration by Leon Shtainmets from "The Fast" by I. L. Peretz in *The Case against the Wind and Other Stories* by I. L. Peretz, translated and adapted by Esther Hautzig. Copyright © 1975 by Esther Hautzig. Copyright © 1975 by Macmillan Publishing Co., Inc. All reprinted by permission of Macmillan, Inc.

MACMILLAN LONDON LTD. Sidelight excerpts from *Letter from Reachfar* by Jane Duncan. Copyright © 1975 by Jane Duncan. Reprinted by permission of Macmillan London Ltd.

McGRAW-HILL BOOK CO. Illustration by Gail Owens from *Sprout and the Dogsitter* by Jenifer Wayne. Copyright © 1972 by Jenifer Wayne./ Illustration by Gail Owens from *Sprout* by Jenifer Wayne. Copyright © 1970 by Jenifer Wayne. Both reprinted by permission of McGraw-Hill Book Co.

DAVID McKAY CO., INC. Illustration by Asa Battles from *Indian America: A Cultural and Travel Guide* by Jamake Highwater. Copyright © 1975 by Fodor's Modern Guides, Inc. Reprinted by permission of David McKay Co., Inc.

JULIAN MESSNER. Sidelight excerpts from "Author's Note," in *Yankee Thunder: The Legendary Life of Davy Crockett* by Irwin Shapiro. Copyright 1944, © 1971 by Irwin Shapiro./ Illustration by James Daugherty from *Joe Magarac and His U.S.A. Citizen Papers* by Irwin Shapiro. Copyright 1948 by Irwin Shapiro. Both reprinted by permission of Julian Messner.

METHUEN CHILDREN'S BOOKS LTD. Illustration by Michael Bragg from *King Nimrod's Tower* by Leon Garfield. Text copyright © 1982 by Leon Garfield. Illustrations copyright © 1982 by Michael Bragg./ Illustration by Robin Jacques from *A Book of Monsters* by Ruth Manning-Sanders. Copyright © 1975 by Ruth Manning-Sanders./ Illustration by Robin Jacques from "The Enchanted Candle" in *A Book of Enchantments and Curses* by Ruth Manning-Sanders. Copyright © 1976 by Ruth Manning-Sanders. All reprinted by permission of Methuen Children's Books Ltd.

WILLIAM MORROW & CO., INC. Illustration by Gisela Kalow from *Bruno Takes a Trip* by Achim Bröger. Translated by Caroline Gueritz. Copyright © 1978 by K. Thienemanns Verlag. Translation copyright © 1978 by Caroline Gueritz. Reprinted by permission of William Morrow & Co., Inc.

OXFORD UNIVERSITY PRESS. Illustration by Johnny Ross from the "War" in *The New Dragon Book of Verse,* edited by Michael Harrison and Christopher Stuart-Clark. Copyright © 1977 by Oxford University Press./ Sidelight excerpts from an article "On Fairy-Stories," by J. R. R. Tolkien in *Essays Presented to Charles Williams.* Copyright 1947 by Oxford University Press. Both reprinted by permission of Oxford University Press.

PANTHEON BOOKS, INC. Illustration by Anthony Maitland from *Jack Holborn* by Leon Garfield. Copyright © by Leon Garfield. Reprinted by permission of Pantheon Books, Inc.

PENGUIN BOOKS LTD. Illustration by Gunvor Edwards from *Snuffle to the Rescue* by Elisabeth Beresford. Text copyright © 1975 by Elisabeth Beresford. Illustrations copyright © 1975 by Gunvor Edwards./ Sidelight excerpts from *The Thorny Paradise*, edited by Edward Blishen. Both reprinted by permission of Penguin Books Ltd.

PLATT & MUNK. Illustrations by George and Doris Hauman from *The Little Engine That Could*, retold by Watty Piper. Copyright 1930, 1945, 1954, © 1961 by Platt & Munk. Copyright renewed © 1958, 1973, 1982 by Platt & Munk. Reprinted by permission of Platt & Munk.

G. P. PUTNAM'S SONS. Photograph by Scott Barry from *The Kingdom of Wolves* by Scott Barry. Copyright © 1979 by Scott Barry. Reprinted by permission of G. P. Putnam's Sons.

RANDOM HOUSE, INC. Illustration by Harry McNaught from *Baby Animals* by Harry McNaught. Copyright © 1976 by Random House, Inc. Reprinted by permission of Random House, Inc.

ROBSON BOOKS LTD. Illustration by John Astrop from *Arthur and the Great Detective* by Alan Coren. Copyright © 1979 by Alan Coren. Reprinted by permission of Robson Books Ltd.

RAY ROURKE PUBLISHING CO., INC. Illustration by Ralph Steadman from *Emergency Mouse* by Bernard Stone. Text copyright © 1978 by Bernard Stone. Illustrations copyright © 1978 by Ralph Steadman. Copyright © 1982 by Ray Rourke Publishing Co., Inc. Reprinted by permission of Ray Rourke Publishing Co., Inc.

RUNNING PRESS. Illustration by Michael Green and illustrations by Tim Kirk from *The Tolkien Scrapbook*, edited by Alida Becker. Copyright © 1978 by Running Press. Reprinted by permission of Running Press.

ST. MARTIN'S PRESS, INC. Illustration by Victor Ambrus from *Camerons Ahoy!* by Jane Duncan. Text copyright © 1968 by Jane Duncan. Illustrations copyright © 1968 by Macmillan, Inc./ Sidelight excerpts from *Letter from Reachfar* by Jane Duncan. Copyright © 1975 by Jane Duncan./ Illustration by Victor Ambrus from *Camerons at the Castle* by Jane Duncan. Copyright © 1964 by Jane Duncan./ Illustration from *Camerons on the Train* by Jane Duncan. Copyright © 1963 by Jane Duncan. All reprinted by permission of St. Martin's Press, Inc.

ST. MARY'S PRESS. Illustration by Anna Maria Ahl from *Exploring Narrative Poetry* by Howard A. Van Deinse. Copyright © 1971 by St. Mary's Press. Reprinted by permission of St. Mary's Press.

THE SEABURY PRESS, INC. Illustration by Mairi Hedderwick from *Janet Reachfar and Chickabird* by Jane Duncan. Text copyright © 1978 by Jane Duncan. Illustration copyright © 1978 by Mairi Hedderwick. Reprinted by permission of The Seabury Press, Inc.

K. THIENEMANNS VERLAG. Illustration by Gisela Kalow from *Bruno Takes a Trip* by Achim Bröger. Translated by Caroline Gueritz. Copyright © 1978 by K. Thienemanns Verlag. Translation copyright © 1978 by Caroline Gueritz. Reprinted by permission of K. Thienemanns Verlag.

VANGUARD PRESS INC. Illustration from *Drina Dances in Italy* by Jean Estoril. Copyright © 1961 by Jean Estoril. Reprinted by permission of Vanguard Press Inc.

VIKING PENGUIN, INC. Illustration by Asa Battles from *Ritual of the Wind: North American Indian Ceremonies, Music, and Dances* by Jamake Highwater. Copyright © 1977 by Jamake Highwater./ Illustration by Valenti Angelo from *The Animals' Christmas* by Anne Thaxter Eaton. Copyright 1944 by Anne T. Eaton and Valenti Angelo. Copyright renewed © 1972 by Jane E. Molitor, Charles H. Eaton, and Valenti Angelo./ Sidelight excerpts from *Reading with Children* by Anne Thaxter Eaton. Copyright 1940 by Anne Thaxter Eaton. Copyright renewed © 1967 by Anne Thaxter Eaton./ Illustration by Don Freeman from *Mike's House* by Julia L. Sauer. Copyright 1954 by Julia L. Sauer and Don Freeman./ Illustration by Aldren A. Watson from *Tommy's Mommy's Fish* by Nancy Dingman Watson. Text copyright © 1971 by Nancy Dingman Watson. Illustrations copyright © 1971 by Aldren A. Watson. All reprinted by permission of Viking Penguin, Inc.

HENRY Z. WALCK, INC. Illustration by Ruth Hürlimann from *The Cat and the Mouse Who Shared a House*, retold by Ruth Hürlimann. Translated from the German by Anthea Bell. Copyright © 1973 by Atlantis Verlag. English text copyright © 1973 by Longman Young Books Ltd. Reprinted by permission of Henry Z. Walck, Inc.

WEBSTER/McGRAW-HILL BOOK CO. Sidelight excerpts from *Themes in Science Fiction: A Journey into Wonder,* edited by Leo P. Kelley. Copyright © 1972 by Webster/McGraw-Hill Book Co. Reprinted by permission of Webster/McGraw-Hill Book Co.

THE WESTMINSTER PRESS. Illustration by Beth and Joe Krush from *The Pig at 37 Pinecrest Drive* by Susan Fleming. Copyright © 1981 by Susan Fleming. Reprinted by permission of The Westminster Press.

ALBERT WHITMAN & CO. Frontispiece illustration by Joe Krush from *Brillstone Break-In* by Florence Parry Heide and Roxanne Heide. Text copyright © 1977 by Florence Parry Heide and Roxanne Heide. Illustrations copyright © 1977 by Albert Whitman & Co. Reprinted by permission of Albert Whitman & Co.

XEROX PUBLISHING GROUP. Sidelight excerpts from an article "Television Is Ruining Our Folktales," December, 1959, in *Library Journal.* Copyright © 1959 by Xerox Corp. Reprinted by permission of Xerox Publishing Group.

Sidelight excerpts from *To Be an Author: A Short Biography* by Mabel Esther Allan. Copyright © 1982 by Mabel Esther Allan. Reprinted by permission of Mabel Esther Allan./ Sidelight excerpts from an article "The Stylized Woodcuts of Jacques Hnizdovsky," by William Gorman, October, 1978, in *American Artist* magazine (Amended by Hnizdovsky). Copyright © 1978 by Billboard Publications, Inc. Reprinted by permission of *American Artist* magazine./ Sidelight excerpts from an article "Dialogue on Film: Steven Spielberg," September, 1978, in *American Film.* Copyright © 1978 by The American Film Institute. Reprinted by permission of *American Film.*/ Sidelight excerpts from an article "P. W. Interviews: Jim Davis" by John F. Baker, March 13, 1981, in *Publishers Weekly.* Copyright © 1981 by Xerox Corp. Reprinted by permission of R. R. Bowker Co./ Sidelight excerpts from *Annals of an Era: Percy MacKaye and the MacKaye Family, 1826-1922; a Record of Biography and History in Commentaries and Bibliography,* edited by Edwin Osgood Grover. Reprinted by permission of Dartmouth College./ Photographs from *Sara Teasdale: Woman and Poet* by William Drake. Copyright © 1979 by William Drake. Reprinted by permission of William Drake./ Frontispiece illustration by Arthur Rackham from *The Far Familiar: Fifty New Poems* by Percy MacKaye. Reprinted by the kind permission of Mrs. Barbara Edwards./ Sidelight excerpts from an article "Writing for Children: A Challenge and a Vision," December, 1962, in *Elementary English.* Reprinted by permission of *Elementary English.*/ Sidelight excerpts from an article "Sand Castles," by Todd McCarthy, May-June, 1982, in *Film Comment.* Reprinted by permission of *Film Comment.*

Sidelight excerpts from *The Purple Dress: Growing Up in the Thirties* by Jenifer Wayne. Reprinted by permission of David Higham Associates Ltd./ Sidelight excerpts from an article "Wood Engraving: Monmouth Artist Works in Rare Medium at Home Studio," by Michele Molnar, January 22, 1981, in *The Home News.* Reprinted by permission of *The Home News.*/ Sidelight excerpts from *Illustrators at Work* by Robin Jacques. Reprinted by permission of Robin Jacques./ Sidelight excerpts from "Family: Another Name for America," by Robert Keeshan. Reprinted by permission of Robert Keeshan Associates./ Sidelight excerpts from an article "The Father of Christmas Letters," by J. R. R. Tolkien, December, 1976, in *McCall's* magazine. Reprinted by permission of *McCall's.*/ Sidelight excerpts from *If School Keeps* by Phil Stong. Copyright renewed © 1967 by Virginia Stong. Reprinted by permission of Harold Matson Co., Inc./ Sidelight excerpts from an article "And Still No Purple Cow," by S. J. Woolf, January 26, 1941, in *The New York Times Magazine.* Copyright 1941 by The New York Times Co. Reprinted by permission of The New York Times Co./ Sidelight excerpts from an article "It May Seem That Way, but TV Isn't a Surrogate Parent," by Captain Kangaroo, February 10, 1979, in *The New York Times.* Copyright © 1979 by The New York Times Co. Reprinted by permission of The New York Times Co./ Sidelight excerpts from "The Two Faces of Spielberg—Horror vs. Hope," by Michiko Kakutami, May, 1982, in *The New York Times.* Copyright © 1982 by The New York Times Co. Reprinted by permission of The New York Times Co.

Sidelight excerpts from an article "The Prevalence of Hobbits," by Philip Norman, January 15, 1967, in *The New York Times Magazine.* Copyright © 1967 by The New York Times Co. Reprinted by permission of The New York Times Co./ Sidelight excerpts from an article "Bay Area Writer and Photographer Ted Pontiflet," by Ted Pontiflet, June, 1980, in *Oakland Public Library Association Newsletter.* Reprinted by permission of *Oakland Public Library Association Newsletter.*/ Sidelight excerpts from *Sweet Agony* by Gene Olson. Copyright © 1972 by Gene Olson. Reprinted by permission of Gene Olson./ Sidelight excerpts from an article "Penthouse Interview: Steven Spielberg," February, 1978, in *Penthouse* magazine. Reprinted by permission of Penthouse International, Inc.

Sidelight excerpts from an article "Garfield Goes Hollywood—with Jim Davis on His Cattails—for Feline Fame and Fortune," by Mary Vespa, November 1, 1982, in *People* magazine. Reprinted by permission of People Weekly./ Sidelight excerpts from an article "A Call to Excellence," January, 1967, in *The Reading Teacher*. Reprinted by permission of *The Reading Teacher*./ Sidelight excerpts from an article "Excerpts from Letters to a Black Boy," January, 1969, in *Redbook* magazine. Reprinted by permission of *Redbook* magazine./ Sidelight excerpts from an article in *Rolling Stone* by Chris Hodenfield, January 26, 1978. Reprinted by permission of *Rolling Stone* magazine./ Sidelight excerpts from the book jacket of *Jackie Robinson of the Brooklyn Dodgers* by Milton J. Shapiro. Copyright © 1983 by Milton J. Shapiro. Reprinted by permission of Milton J. Shapiro.

Sidelight excerpts from *Cabin on a Ridge* by Howard Simon. Reprinted by permission of Mrs. Howard Simon./ Sidelight excerpts from an article "Steven Spielberg Seminar," edited by Rochelle Reed in *Dialogue on Film*. Copyright © 1974 by The American Film Institute. Reprinted by permission of Steven Spielberg./ Sidelight excerpts from an article "Lovable Monsters Between the Covers," by Susan Yim, October 8, 1979, in *Star Bulletin*. Reprinted by permission of *Star Bulletin*./ Sidelight excerpts from *Sara Teasdale: Woman and Poet* by William Drake. Copyright © 1979 by William Drake. Reprinted by permission of the Estate of Sara Teasdale./ Sidelight excerpts from an article "Steve's Summer Magic," May 31, 1982, in *Time* magazine. Reprinted by permission of Time, Inc./ Sidelight excerpts from "Literature Is . . . Continuous . . . From Childhood Onward," February, 1971, in *The Horn Book* magazine. Reprinted by permission of *Times Literary Supplement*./ Photograph from *Heredity* by Robert E. Dunbar. Copyright © 1978 by United Press International. Reprinted by permission of United Press International./ Sidelight excerpts from an article "TV's Impact on the Movies as a Noted Director Sees It," by Steven Spielberg, November 21, 1977, in *U.S. News and World Report*. Reprinted by permission of *U.S. News and World Report*./ Sidelight excerpts from an article "A Fat Cat Claws His Way to the Top," by Walter Shapiro, February 20, 1983, in *The Sunday Record*. Reprinted by permission of *The Washington Post*.

PHOTOGRAPH CREDITS

Charles L. Berlitz: Joseph di Gennaro; Gelett Burgess: copyright by Marceau; Elizabeth Jane Cameron: Mark Gerson; Forrest Carter: Eleanor Friede; Bruce Coville: Kenneth Tambs; Donald Crews: Chuck Kelton; Raymond Davidson: Luke Di Gesu; Jim Davis: Dale Wittner (*People* Weekly, © 1982 by Time, Inc.,); Anne T. Eaton: Consuelo Kanaga; Susan Fleming: copyright by Frances Antupit, Paul Koby Studio; Mark Jonathan Harris: Susan Harris; Robin Jacques: copyright by J. Schadeberg; Leo P. Kelley: Darrell Flugg; Anne Baker Molloy: Roger Paul Jordan; Milton J. Shapiro: Barbara and Justin Kerr; Sara Teasdale, 1932: E. O. Hoppé (London).

SOMETHING ABOUT THE AUTHOR

ACS, Laszlo (Bela)   1931-

BRIEF ENTRY: Born May 18, 1931, in Budapest, Hungary. A graphic designer and illustrator, Acs received his diploma from the Academy of Fine Arts in Budapest and later attended Hornsey College of Art in London. He began his professional career in England with three years in the advertising field. Later he became head of graphic design for Independent Television News and, finally, a free-lance illustrator of children's books as well as a lecturer in art at Exeter College of Art. In addition to book illustration, Acs has produced various poster designs and has been involved in audio-visual design for foreign language teaching. His work has been exhibited by the National Gallery, Budapest, Leyden University, Holland, and Wakefield and York, England. He has illustrated over twenty books of fiction and nonfiction for children, among them Allan Aldous's *Bushfire,* Walter Shepherd's *Electricity* and *The Story of Man,* Robert J. Unstead's *Living in Pompeii,* William Mayne's *Max's Dream,* and Alexander M. Smith's *The Perfect Hamburger. For More Information See: Illustrators of Children's Books: 1967-1976,* Horn Book, 1978.

AHL, Anna Maria   1926-

PERSONAL: Born March 26, 1926, in Chicago, Ill.; daughter of Bruno (a chef) and Sophie (Clemens) Ahl. *Education:* Mt. St. Joseph, B.A., 1960; University of Notre Dame, M.A., 1968. *Politics:* Independent. *Religion:* Catholic. *Residence:* Colorado Springs, Colo.

CAREER: Taught in elementary and secondary schools in Ohio and Colorado, 1950-70; free-lance illustrator, 1970—.

ANNA MARIA AHL

Paul Revere's Ride
by Henry Wadsworth Longfellow

. . .The people will waken and listen to
hear
The hurrying hoofbeats of that steed,
And the midnight message of Paul Revere.

■ (From *Exploring Narrative Poetry* by Howard A. Van Deinse. Illustrated by Anna Maria Ahl.)

ILLUSTRATOR—All published by St. Mary's College Press, except where indicated: Joan Denise Busch, compiler, *What's So Special about Me?* (anthology, 3 volumes), 1970; Howard A. Van Deinse, *Exploring Narrative Poetry,* 1971; Robert Rotering, editor, *Yesterday, Today and Tomorrow,* 1971; Esther Weir, *The Partners,* McKay, 1972; Andrew Panzarella, *Microcosm,* 1972; Naomi B. Stone, *To Be a Pilgrim,* 1973; A. Panzarella, *Religion and Human Experience,* 1974; Peter Gilmour, *Praying Together,* 1978.

WORK IN PROGRESS: Illustrating a series of books in religious education for use with hearing-impaired children including a First Communion book based on bible history by Mary Dugan.

SIDELIGHTS: "I've always enjoyed illustrating, but only in the last ten years have I had the time to pursue it. I tend to be word-oriented, and therefore work up the illustration in a style and mood to fit the particular story. This results, alas, (or maybe 'hurray') in not having a single recognizable style. One of my projects—an anthology of short selections from contemporary junior high fiction—looks like it was illustrated by at least ten people. Oh, well—that's how I operate.

"I prefer working with dry media—pencil, crayon, chalk, but for production reasons usually end up with pen and ink, or felt tip markers. The only full-color book I've illustrated is not specifically for children. It's a series of inspirational quotes, titled *Yesterday, Today and Tomorrow.* The children's books have been limited to black and white, or two-color.

"I've done many full-color greeting cards for Abbey Press. I enjoy listening to classical music, poetry, creative cooking and baking. I love the out-of-doors, nature in general, animals in particular, and leisurely hiking."

AHLBERG, Janet

BRIEF ENTRY: Author and illustrator of books for children. With her husband Allan Ahlberg, also an author and illustrator, Janet Ahlberg has written and illustrated five picture books for children, including *Burglar Bill, Jeremiah in the Dark Woods, The Vanishment of Thomas Tull, Cops and Robbers,* and *The Ha Ha Bonk Book.* The Ahlbergs have also collaborated as both authors and illustrators of eight other books, including *Each Peach Pear Plum* which was awarded the Kate Greenaway Medal in 1978. The Ahlbergs are known for producing innovative books that provide wry humor and amusing pictures for children from kindergarten through the primary grades. Janet Ahlberg has also illustrated books by other authors, among them *My Growing Up Book* by Bernard Max Garfinkel, *Providence Street* by Ivy Eastwick, and several books written by her husband.

ALLAN, Mabel Esther 1915- (Jean Estoril, Priscilla Hagon, Anne Pilgrim)

PERSONAL: Born February 11, 1915, in Wallasey, Cheshire, England; daughter of James Pemberton (a merchant) and Priscilla (Hagon) Allan. *Education:* Educated at private schools in England. *Home:* Glengarth, 11, Oldfield Way, Heswall, Wirral, Merseyside L60 6R0, England. *Agent:* John Farquharson Ltd., 250 West 57th St., New York, N.Y. 10107.

CAREER: Author. Served as warden of a wartime nursery for children of two-to-five years during World War II. *Military service:* Women's Land Army, two years during World War II. *Member:* Crime Writers Association, Mystery Writers of America. *Awards, honors:* Best children's book of the year award for *Lise en Italie,* France, 1960; Mystery Writers of America award for *Mystery in Wales,* 1971; Boston Globe-Horn Book award for *An Island in a Green Sea,* 1972.

WRITINGS: The Glen Castle Mystery, Warne, 1948; *Adventurous Summer,* Museum Press, 1948; *Wyndhams Went to Wales,* Sylvan Press, 1948; *Cilia of Chiltern's Edge,* Museum Press, 1949; *Mullion,* Hutchinson, 1949; *Trouble at Melville Manor,* Museum Press, 1949.

Chiltern Adventure, Blackie & Son, 1950; *Everyday Island,* Museum Press, 1950; *Holiday at Arnriggs,* Warne, 1950; *Seven in Switzerland,* Blackie & Son, 1950; *Clues to Connemara,* Blackie & Son, 1952; *MacIans of Glen Gillean,* Hutchinson, 1952; *Return to Derrykereen,* Ward, 1952; *School in Danger,* Blackie & Son, 1952; *School on Cloud Ridge,* Hutchinson, 1952; *School on North Barrule,* Museum Press, 1952; *Lucia Comes to School,* Hutchinson, 1953; *Room for the Cuckoo,* Dent, 1953; *Strangers at Brongwerne,* Museum Press, 1953; *Here We Go Round,* Heinemann, 1954; *Margaret Finds a Future,* Hutchinson, 1954; *New Schools for Old,* Hutchinson, 1954; *Summer at Town's End,* Harrap, 1954.

Changes, for the Challoners, Ward, 1955; *Glenvara,* Hutchinson, 1955; *Judith Teaches,* Bodley Head, 1955; *Swiss School,* Hutchinson, 1955; *Adventure in Mayo,* Ward, 1956; *Amber House,* Hutchinson, 1956; *Balconies and Blue Nets,* Harrap, 1956; *Lost Lorrenden,* Blackie & Son, 1956; *Strangers in Skye* (Junior Literary Guild selection), Heinemann, 1956, Criterion, 1958; *Two in the Western Isles,* Hutchinson, 1956; *Vine Clad Hill,* Bodley Head, 1956; *Ann's Alpine Adventure,* Hutchinson,

MABEL ESTHER ALLAN

1957; *At School in Skye,* Blackie & Son, 1957; *Black Forest Summer,* Bodley Head, 1957, Vanguard, 1959; *Sara Goes to Germany,* Hutchinson, 1957; *Summer of Decision,* Abelard, 1957; *Swiss Holiday,* Vanguard, 1957; *Blue Dragon Days,* Heinemann, 1958; *Conch Shells,* Blackie & Son, 1958; *House by the Marsh,* Dent, 1958; *Murder at the Flood* (adult), Paul, 1958; *Rachel Tandy,* Hutchinson, 1958; *Amanda Goes to Italy,* Hutchinson, 1959; *Catrin in Wales,* Bodley Head, 1959, Vanguard, 1961; *A Play to the Festival,* Heinemann, 1959 (published in America as *"On Stage, Flory!"* Watts, 1959).

Shadow Over the Alps, Hutchinson, 1960; *A Summer in Brittany,* Dent, 1960 (published in America as *Hilary's Summer on Her Own,* Watts, 1960); *Tansy of Tring Street,* Heinemann, 1960; *Holiday of Endurance,* Dent, 1961; *Home to the Island,* Dent, 1962, Vanguard, 1966; *Pendron Under the Water,* Harrap, 1962; *Romance in Italy,* Vanguard, 1962; *Schooldays in Skye,* Blackie & Son, 1962; *Signpost to Switzerland,* Heinemann, 1962, Criterion, 1966; *The Ballet Family,* Methuen, 1963, Criterion, 1966; *Kate Comes to England,* Heinemann, 1963; *New York for Nicola,* Vanguard, 1963; *The Sign of the Unicorn,* Criterion, 1963; *It Happened in Arles,* Heinemann, 1964 (published in America as *Mystery in Arles,* Vanguard, 1964); *The Ballet Family Again,* Methuen, 1964, Criterion, 1966; *Fiona on the Fourteenth Floor,* Dent, 1964 (published in America as *Mystery on the Fourteenth Floor,* Criterion, 1965); *The Way Over Windle,* Methuen, 1966; *Skiing to Danger,* Heinemann, 1966; *In Pursuit of Clarinda,* Dent, 1966; *A Summer at Sea,* Dent, 1966, Vanguard, 1967; *Mystery of the Ski Slopes,* Criterion, 1966; *It Started in Madeira,* Heinemann, 1967 (published in America as *The Mystery Started in Madeira* [Junior Literary Guild selection], Criterion, 1967); *Missing in Manhattan,* Dent, 1967 (published in America as *Mystery in Manhattan,* Vanguard, 1968); *The Dancing Garlands,* Criterion, 1968; *The Wood Street Secret* (Child Study Association book list), Methuen, 1968, Abelard, 1970; *Climbing to Dan-*

Pelagia, rising like Ondine, with her hair dark and flattened with water, called sharply: "Tim, don't be an idiot! I can swim!" ■ (From *The Dancing Garlands* by Mabel Esther Allan. Illustrated by Whitear.)

ger, Heinemann, 1969 (published in America as *Mystery in Wales*, Vanguard, 1971); *The Wood Street Group*, Methuen, 1969; *The Kraymer Mystery*, Criterion, 1969.

Dangerous Inheritance, Heinemann, 1970; *The Wood Street Rivals*, Methuen, 1970; *Christmas at Spindle Bottom*, Dent, 1970; *The Secret Dancer*, Dent, 1971; *The May Day Mystery*, Criterion, 1971; *Behind the Blue Gates*, Heinemann, 1972; *Time to Go Back* (Junior Literary Guild selection), Abelard, 1972; *An Island in a Green Sea*, Atheneum, 1972, Dent, 1973; *The Wood Street Helpers*, Methuen, 1973; *Mystery in Rome*, Vanguard, 1973; *A Chill in the Lane* (Junior Literary Guild selection), T. Nelson, 1974; *Ship in Danger* (Junior Literary Guild selection), Criterion, 1974; *The Night Wind* (illustrated by Charles Robinson), Atheneum, 1974; *A Formidable Enemy*, T. Nelson, 1975; *Romansgrove*, Atheneum, 1975; *The Flash Children*, Dodd, 1975; *Bridge of Friendship*, Dodd, 1977; *My Family's Not Forever*, Abelard, 1977; *Trouble in the Glen*, Abelard, 1977; *Pine Street Pageant*, Abelard, 1978; *Tomorrow Is a Lovely Day*, Abelard, 1979 (published in America as *A Lovely Tomorrow* [Junior Literary Guild selection], Dodd, 1980); *Wood Street and Mary Ellen*, Methuen, 1979; *The View Beyond My Father* (Junior Literary Guild selection), Dodd, 1979.

The Mills Down Below, Abelard, 1980, Dodd, 1981; *Pine Street Goes Camping*, Abelard, 1980; *A Strange Enchantment*, Abelard, 1981, Dodd, 1982; *Strangers in Wood Street*, Methuen, 1981; *The Pine Street Problem*, Abelard, 1981; *The Haunted Valley and Other Poems*, Charles Gill & Sons, 1981; *The Horns of Danger*, Dodd, 1981; *Growing Up in Wood Street*, Methuen, 1982; *Goodbye to Pine Street*, Abelard, 1982; *Alone at Pine Street*, Abelard, 1983; *The Crumble Lane Adventure*, Methuen, 1983.

Also author of *To Be an Author: A Short Autobiography*, Charles Gill & Sons, 1982.

As Jean Estoril: *Ballet for Drina*, Hodder & Stoughton, 1957, Vanguard, 1958; *Drina's Dancing Years*, Hodder & Stoughton, 1958; *Drina Dances in Exile*, Hodder & Stoughton, 1959; *Drina Dances in Italy*, Hodder & Stoughton, 1959, Vanguard, 1961; *Drina Dances Again*, Hodder & Stoughton, 1960; *Drina Dances in New York*, Hodder & Stoughton, 1961; *Drina Dances in Paris*, Hodder & Stoughton, 1962; *Drina Dances in Madeira*, Hodder & Stoughton, 1963; *Drina Dances in Switzerland*, Hodder & Stoughton, 1964; *Drina Goes on Tour*, Brockhampton, 1965; *We Danced in Bloomsbury Square*, Heinemann, 1967, Follett, 1970.

As Priscilla Hagon; all published by World Publishing: *Cruising to Danger*, 1966; *Dancing to Danger*, 1967; *Mystery at Saint-Hilaire*, 1968; *Mystery at the Villa Bianca*, 1969; *Mystery of the Secret Square*, 1970.

As Anne Pilgrim; all published by Abelard: *The First Time I Saw Paris*, 1961, *Clare Goes to Holland*, 1962; *A Summer in Provence*, 1963; *Strangers in New York*, 1964; *Selina's New Family*, 1967.

SIDELIGHTS: "I was born on **February 11th, 1915** at 12, Belgrave Street in the Liscard district of Wallasey, Cheshire. It was a very large, dull town on the River Mersey opposite Liverpool. Belgrave Street was a very dull, respectable street of red brick terraced houses, with privet hedges in front and only paved yards behind. We were lucky because, from our back windows, over high brick walls and a grim entry, we looked out on tennis courts.

"In retrospect I might have been regarded as lucky because I grew up not far from a great river and the sea. Wallasey is at the end of the Wirral Peninsula and river and sea are dominant features. In reality the town felt a prison as I grew older, for it was so hard to get away from. The nearest bridge across the River Dee to Wales was miles away, and endless walking was needed to get into the real country.

"When I was very young I was not encouraged to wander far, and I really was a street child, playing hopscotch, marbles and various other games in Belgrave Street and a cul-de-sac we called 'Little Trinity.' Later there was a change of scene when we played in Central Park. It was a very dull park indeed and sometimes it would have been good to see the future. I had no slightest idea that another Central Park, three thousand miles away, would one day become my beloved front garden.

"My sight was so poor that nowadays it is called partially sighted. It was a great tragedy to my parents, who took it badly and very wrongly. The result of their attitude was that I could never speak of my problem. It is true to say that I never discussed it with anyone until I was nearly thirty and my sight miraculously improved. I pretended that I was normal and few people ever really seemed to grasp that I was not. I went to private schools, three of them, where I never remember a teacher seeming aware that I simply couldn't see. I knew then, always, that they thought me stupid, almost beyond hope. I regarded them with scorn and some fear. When they weren't boring they were enemies. I hated school, but stayed there, for no reason that I can now understand, until I was seventeen and a half.

"Basically I was unhappy and I was bored. That is the only reason I have ever been able to find for the fact that I turned to the printed word with such desperate joy. My father was a business man heading for success; he read many newspapers, but he never read a book. My mother, and the Welsh maids, read cheap magazines and romances. I may not have been able to see very well, I read with my nose close to a book, but I don't remember learning to read. It seems I always could. Certainly, I could when I went to school. I went rather late, at well over six-years-old. It was a very stuffy, old-fashioned private school on Martins Lane, Wallasey, called Roslyn House. It was run by three unmarried sisters. I hated it.

"Out of the blue, when I was eight, I said: 'I'm going to be an author when I grow up.' I quite clearly remember saying it. I made the announcement to my parents. Amazingly, they took it quite seriously and often told people: 'Mabel's going to be an author when she grows up.'

"I was desperate to join Wallasey's main library, Earlston Library, that had the children's section in what had been, I believe, Liscard Manor. There was a beautiful reading room, with great high windows and comfortable window seats, and you could ask to have annuals brought to you. Everyone I knew belonged. Permission was always refused by my father on the grounds that the books were dirty. It wasn't true; they were not. He wished to discourage me from reading on account of my sight. The form had to be signed by the householder, but, when my father was away on one of his frequent visits to Lima, Peru, I made my weak mother sign it. After that I was in some kind of heaven. The library and the indoor swimming pool, Guinea Gap in Seacombe, were the only places where I was really happy during the next few years." [Mabel Esther Allan, *To Be an Author: A Short Autobiography*, Charles Gill & Sons, 1982.[1]]

1927. "When I was twelve we moved to the fashionable end of Wallasey, near Harrison Drive. . . . There was an extra room looking out on the garage roof and it was given to me to be my study. My father bought me a large office desk (which I still use every day), a smaller desk and an Underwood Standard typewriter. I taught myself to type and I have typed millions of words, but my fingering is all wrong.

"I was very lucky over that, but I can honestly say I never had any other help of any kind over my writing. I went it alone, hour after hour, from the age of twelve. I wrote in longhand and then typed a very long book called *Teddy and her Chums*. We were very well aware that many books were written to a formula and mine was based on the one we called 'discovery of relationship.' Very common in books of that period. In *Teddy* two sisters, parted in infancy, met, all unknowing, at school. The manuscript is lost, but I remember it quite well. It was a proper book, but not very original. In many ways my imagination was still unawakened, though I already had a clear knowledge of publishers; whether or not I'd like their books. Blackie and Collins I would, maybe Ward, Lock, Humphrey Milford, the Oxford University Press, yes, certainly I would. Nelson, Nisbet . . . I knew them all.

Drina was dreaming that she was Little Clara in the ballet *Casse Noisette*. ■(Cover illustration from *Drina Dances in Italy* by Jean Estoril.)

"When would-be adult authors say to me: 'Oh, I never notice publishers' I'm afraid I give them up at once. A *feeling* for books and their publishers seems to me essential. I knew all that at ten-years-old."[1]

1928. Sent to a private school, St. Hilary's. "St. Hilary's was run by two unmarried sisters and great stress was laid on behaving like 'ladies.' We must always wear hats and gloves, and not eat sweets or ice cream in the street. Always a rebel, I detested such rules and put on my hat and gloves at the gate. But to this day I can't eat in the street without a feeling of guilt. . . .

"St. Hilary's had a graduate staff, mainly married women. . . . They made very little impression on me and didn't manage to teach me much, lost as I was in my own world. I learned enough French to read and write business letters in later life, some Latin and Spanish and was bored with history and geography until I discovered the importance of the first for myself, and the joy of the second through getting to know places. I would never *let* anyone teach me anything to do with English. I would never take notes for compositions or essays and I have taken very few in my whole life. I *make* few notes, too. Bad sight gave me a retentive memory.

"Over anything to do with writing I suppose I was conceited; at any rate untouchable. And I very much doubt if anyone at that school, or any other, could have helped me much. For better or worse, it had to be done my way. Probably that's why I am not a 'great' writer.

"But my mind would have broadened much faster if I had been directed to more positive reading. There were, however, *no* books at St. Hilary's, apart from lesson books. As far as I know the idea of a school library had simply not been born. Though it was supposed to be a good school, 'culture' was non-existent. We were never taken anywhere, except to church on Ash Wednesday. No art, no concerts, no theatre, though Liverpool was alive with them all. . . .''[1]

1930. Wrote second book (''Philomel Follows After'' [unpublished]) at the age of fifteen. ''. . . It was a very long book and the manuscript survives. It is typed in single spacing with a purple ribbon, but it is a real and complicated book. Properly punctuated, correctly spelled and with many characters, most of them based on people I knew. The plot is original, though

We were terribly shy of Isobel, except for the old woman, who was bursting with curiosity. She never took her eyes off our guest. She only drank half a cup of tea because she was concentrating so eagerly on our talk. ■ (From *An Island in a Green Sea* by Mabel Esther Allan. Illustrated by Charles Robinson.)

slightly mad, and my scenic pictures are vivid, though over-written toward the end of the book. The sheer labour of it impresses me now, and the fact that, in some ways, I knew all about writing a book at the age of fifteen.

"The book took well over a year to write. I think it was mainly written at St. Hilary's in school time; of course in longhand. It wasn't until 1944 that I learned to write books straight on to the typewriter. But then the whole thing had to be typed, and it must have been a tremendous task for a young girl who didn't see very well. All those hours shut up alone with my typewriter set a pattern for the rest of my life. If anyone who wants to be an author doesn't like the thought of all that solitude and self discipline, then forget it. Few authors are able to dictate to secretaries. Who'd want to, anyway?

"At St. Hilary's the afternoons, for older girls, were supposed to be spent in doing preparation for next day, or in tennis or high jumping when the weather was fine. I couldn't see the ball, and I couldn't see the rope until I was on top of it, so I expressed a great scorn for sports. The attitude was at first entirely to hide my suffering at being the odd one out, but it soon turned into rock hard opinion. To this day I can't bear to watch any ball game. Swimming was the only sport I ever enjoyed, and I did that moderately well.

"So *Philomel* and the summer term moved toward their close, and the future was a blank. School was, at least, a known problem. I was aware in my heart that I'd never get any kind of ordinary job, say as a librarian. I'd have loved that, but I hadn't a hope. The only thing I *intended* to do was write, yet I couldn't imagine selling anything, getting a start. That would be a huge jump into the real world.''[1]

1930-1939. Wrote several short stories for children and novels. Her first children's book was accepted for publication in 1939, but, because of the threat of war, the book was returned, unpublished. The book was later sold in 1945 and published in 1948 as *The Glen Castle Mystery.*

1940. During World War II, Allan served in the Woman's Land Army. "I was called up for the Land Army just after Christmas, and, in bitter winter weather, I went to Reaseheath Agricultural College in South Cheshire. . . . In *A Strange Enchantment* I give a pretty accurate description of those frozen days at the College, and my experiences on farms in Cheshire and Shropshire have been in that and other books. Of course it's true that nothing is ever lost to an author, but I never dreamed then, alone and scared in the English fields, afraid that we would lose the war, that long, long years later I would be writing about much that happened. Oh, yes, in many ways it would be good to see the future.

"Likewise, sitting in the air raid shelter in Wallasey during some heavy raids, I would have thought anyone mad if they had told me that a book about that would one day, in the far future, be read by German young people. That book was *Time to Go Back.* Things do come full circle if one lives long enough.

"In Cheshire and Shropshire I wrote poetry, much of which was published, but little else. I worked from six in the morning sometimes until ten at night. There was no time for writing long things. But, in the periods when I was home, and mostly in the air raid shelter, I wrote a hundred and twenty thousand word book. It was set in the Outer Isles in the late nineteen twenties. It was strange how my very short breaks in Wallasey nearly always coincided with a raid once the war hotted up. I was there during the December raids of 1940 and on many occasions afterward.

". . . Not very long after the house in Wallasey was bombed. I gave up the Land Army and hoped for the best over a future call up. For my age group had not yet registered."[1]

1941-1944. "In the middle of September I got a job at Bromborough Preparatory School, teaching a class of seventeen four- and five-year-olds. I had never taught anyone to read in my life, but I had many teacher friends and somehow it just happened. Those little children were supposed to *work*, not play. I taught them all to read without difficulty, unbelievable as it may sound, and even a very small child called Amanda, who was nowhere near four, learned to read just by being there. She used to come to tea with me on Saturday afternoons.

". . . I joined Little Sutton Red Cross and went on duty two nights a week. I took Ambulance, Home Nursing and Anti-Gas exams and passed them all, though I had a horror of sickness and loathed anything to do with nursing.

"I still wrote mainly poetry, though I did an occasional five thousand word story for older girls. They still turn up in secondhand book stores, in Blackie's Girls annuals and others.

"I was at the school for over a year, then the war caught up with me again, and I wasn't allowed to stay there. I was directed to become a Nursery Warden and was sent to Bolton in Lancashire for training. . . .

"I finished my training in Liverpool and was then sent to be in charge of the nursery at Gwladys Street School in Walton, close to Anfield Cemetery and Stanley Park. . . . I had forty-eight two-to-five-year-olds and somehow had to keep them occupied from eight-thirty in the morning until five-thirty. In two wholly unsuitable classrooms. The main one had an open fire, protected by an iron guard, but it was always a hazard, and I had to keep them as quiet as possible because of the rest of the school. There were about six classes, with at least fifty in each class. It was an Infant School and there had been a nursery there before the war, but with a trained nursery teacher and of course only for a few hours a day.

"There wasn't much time for writing, except when I sat in their second classroom while the whole forty-eight were supposed to sleep for two hours. Their energy was amazing and they rarely did. Often I sang Hebridean songs to them.

"In **1943** we moved to Heswall, on Deeside, and the journey was rather worse than before.

"By early **1944** I was desperately tired and the last straw was when I was told I had to stay all night at the school once a week for fire watching. The raids on Liverpool had been over for some time, but still a constant watch was kept. In fact, D Day was fast approaching.

"Then a miracle happened to me. . . . Overnight I saw brilliantly for the first time. It was such a shock I almost died. It happened on June 5, the day before D Day, and it finished the war for me.

"I wasn't allowed to do much for some time, and I couldn't read for six months. I spent the rest of that eventful summer lying on a rubber mattress in the garden when the weather was fine, and feeling guilty because of all that was going on in France and elsewhere.

"But oh, the wonder of seeing what seemed to me so brilliantly. Always I had seen the world through a thick yellowish blur. . . . Even as a very young child I was far more afraid of going blind than of dying. Death would have been preferable . . . I always knew that quite clearly. I still feel that way. It would never have been any use to tell me, as of course no one did, as the matter was never discussed, that blind people can do wonderful things. All my pleasures were always visual, which has perhaps been my tragedy. Even music was tied up with ballet.

"I couldn't read because I had not been given new glasses, and I had no focus without them. I wasn't to get them until my sight had settled. But eventually it occurred to me that there was nothing to stop me *typing* things, even if I couldn't read them afterward. So that is how I learned to put my work straight on to the typewriter. One of the blessings in disguise that have come my way.

"I wrote a lot of short stories and sold them all later, when I could make good copies of them. I also wrote a non-fiction account of my Land Army days called *Room for the Cuckoo*. It was rather late in the day, for many women had done it

The sun was hot, the white houses of Kilronan dreamed in the midday glare, and a cuckoo called— . . . . ■ (From *Selina's New Family* by Anne Pilgrim. Illustrated by Graham Byfield.)

. . .Then I gasped, for Marci Mannering—for a split second—was in the wrong place, and had almost cannoned into Elizabeth Grace, who would certainly be furious. ■ (From *Dancing to Danger* by Priscilla Hagon. Illustrated by Susanne Suba.)

before me, but it very nearly sold. In the end the interested publisher backed out because there was fear of libel.

"The war in Europe ended in **May, 1945,** and in the same month I sold my first book. It seemed, then, that I was going to write for young people. I settled down and wrote another book, *The Adventurous Summer*. It was set in the Cotswolds, and I sent it out to the Museum Press in early September, 1945."[1]

1950. Plunged into writing full-time. "The new books sold rapidly and I settled down to write plenty more. They simply poured out of me, as I visited new countries and was frantic to paint pictures of them. For my own pleasure. It has simply been sheer luck that other people liked my books. I took the dangerous road of writing first, always, and hoping to sell. Occasionally I didn't and my path is well strewn with unsold books. But I had to go my own way.

"I had started to get reviews, some quite kind, others scornful. I was regarded as a 'popular author' for young people and the attitude to children's books was changing fast. No longer could boys and girls read for pleasure and escape. The 'social consciousness' thing was beginning, even in the early fifties, but was nothing like as all pervading as it is now.

"After the very early books I have almost always written my own blurbs. The author is the only one who really knows the book. Any that have been written by editors have almost always been wrong in some respect. And I was quick to see that reviewers always fastened on to the wrong thing. This has remained so throughout my writing life.

"So I learned early to take a bad review, or even a very good one, with a pinch of salt. Few reviewers read the whole book. They read the blurb, the beginning and the end and form their own conclusions. Sometimes they don't even bother to read the end and form their own wrong conclusions. An American friend, who did a lot of reviewing, said to me quite blandly: 'Of course I couldn't possibly read them all, but I do get through yours.'

".". . . If I had the power of the evil eye many a reviewer, and many an editor, too, would have suffered. For authors really are abominably treated. They are often the last to learn about the progress of their own book. They may be charmingly treated when it seems necessary, but cast off without a thought when the firm's policy changes, or there is a new editor. Ordinary hardworking authors must be among the worst paid workers in the world and have to wait longest for their money.

"However . . . I was prolific enough to begin to make a moderate amount of money, and I was doing what I wanted to do, even if there were times when I'd have given a lot to go out to an ordinary job and not to have to spend endless hours alone at the typewriter. At least most other people knew they'd get paid at the end of the week or month. I never knew, and still don't, when I would get the money due to me."[1]

1953. Underwent an operation to repair a detached retina. ". . . Since 1944 I had been quite carefree about my sight. The old fear had quite disappeared. I didn't expect trouble, but, while I was attending an authors' meeting at the Midland Hotel in Manchester, there was a kind of slosh in one of my eyes and it was filled with coloured scarves. There was no sensation at all and I had no idea what had happened. I hardly knew I had a retina. I didn't say anything to anyone, but got myself all the long way home by train and bus. I hoped it would go away, whatever it was.

"But it didn't and I had to confess. I found myself rushed into the Lourdes Hospital in Liverpool. I had always been terrified of hospitals and I had never had an operation. After the operation, which I had been warned had only a small chance of success in my kind of eye, I was flat on my back, with no pillow. I was told not to move at all and my eye specialist, who was a wonderful man, took it for granted that I would obey. Later I heard cases of people who had been packed in with sandbags and other devices to keep them immobile.

"I was told not to move and I didn't, hardly a muscle for more than three weeks. That was the way they treated detached retinas then. Both eyes were covered with itchy woollen pads and I was bitterly uncomfortable.

"My martyrdom paid off; the retina went back. But I was told plainly that I could either be a semi invalid or take risks for the rest of my life. But the risks couldn't include anything more energetic than walking. Anything jerky was out forever. So no more dancing or swimming or even flying. The latter was forbidden for twenty years, then allowed, as it was considered that great jets were as steady as any other kind of transport.

"I wasn't allowed to go on buses for six months and had to be driven very quietly in a car. Keeping that darned retina in place dominated my life, but I of course opted to take reasonable risks. . . .

"So, accompanied by fear, I went back gradually to a more or less normal life. I have told this at some length, after a good deal of thought. Oddly enough very few people, apart from my intimate friends, really understood my problems. I have not wanted them to. I'd sooner pass as normal if I can, and mostly I seem to do so. But this eye thing is the key to my life, and if I don't tell a little about it no one else can. Without it I would probably not have turned to writing. That's how I always felt, anyway."[1]

1959. Made first of many trips to New York. "*My* Manhattan was a quiet place. I have a slide-talk called 'My Manhattan,' and when the friend with whom I lived saw my pictures she said: 'You aren't playing fair!' Because I show mostly the lovely quiet and secret places, the dreaming skyscrapers, the gentle reaches of Central Park. But it is quite as 'fair' as the films that show only violence. It is a city of tremendous contrasts, and I don't think I have many illusions about life there, but it has so much beauty, and little flowers *do* grow on the sidewalks.

"So the years passed, with my sailing back and forth across the Atlantic. Loving the outward journey; suffering agonies of pain and nostalgia as I sailed away."[1]

1960-1970. "I wrote a number of books under three pen names, as well as continuing with my own name. I continued with the Drina ballet stories, started in the mid fifties, and I wrote five books as Anne Pilgrim for one New York publisher. These were all issued here, but in very small numbers. I also wrote five mystery-thrillers as Priscilla Hagon (my mother's maiden name) for World, New York. . . . Among other Mabel Esther Allen books I started the Wood Street series. These books were a new departure, more or less, because I had written very little for younger readers since the short story days. I never really understood Liverpool until I had fallen in love with New York. Then I realised that the two cities had some great similarities and I began to enjoy writing about Liverpool.

"Those really were my years of travel. As well as going to America, I visited a lot of other countries, often on ships, as that was the best and safest way for me to travel alone. I could write a whole book about my travel experiences, but it is all there in my fiction. I was always falling in love with countries and cities.

"I worked hard, my books were translated into other languages, and I had what I must call a moderate success. For that is all it was when compared with authors who make an enormous amount of money. But the name of Mabel Esther Allan was certainly spreading around a good part of the world.

"But there were always times when I was scared. Writing was my only source of income and there was nothing else I could do. On occasion, when there was a bad setback and I thought

I was on the third step from the bottom when the old door in front of me gave a protesting creak. Then it opened slowly. . . . ■ (From *Mystery at Saint-Hilaire* by Priscilla Hagon. Illustrated by William Plummer.)

my luck was running out, I would think in panic: 'What'll I do if I can't write?'

"1970 was one of the times when I was vaguely aware that things were changing in publishing, that my books weren't selling so easily. And then I had a terrible shock. As it turned out, it was just what I needed and it had excellent results, but at the time I was very angry and shaken. A friend and publisher in New York attacked me out of the blue one day. What she should have done was to wait for a quiet time and then say: 'Why don't you write me something different? Maybe your books are getting a bit stereotyped.' What she said was: '*I* bet your agent is having trouble selling your books. They've grown so samey. Publishers want something different now.' And a lot more, in very brutal terms.

"I was frantic with anger . . . and fear. For she had only expressed what I had dimly felt myself. And then, after a while I began to think, and I saw that I was released from an unconscious bondage. Things *had* changed. Originally I had wanted to write adult novels, where there would have been no taboos as the years passed. Writing for young people, I had more or less happily accepted the endless taboos, and conventions, except over the school stories, where I had broken away entirely from the old ideas and really expressed some of my views on coeducation and young people's right to run their own affairs. Self discipline, ideally, and not imposed discipline.

"I had written about many countries with love and perhaps the power to create a great deal of atmosphere, but without the faintest political awareness. I have all my life been fairly blank about politics. . . .

"But I can see now that I might at least have asked myself, when I made British girls marry Germans, Italians and other foreigners, what it would mean to them to live in another country for the rest of their lives, especially as women.

"I had never expressed my attitude to religion, or tried to put over the idea, so deeply rooted in me, that people can live bravely and behave as good human beings without supernatural aid.

"Actually, and perhaps odder still, the first book I wrote after that brutal awakening in 1970, was *An Island in a Green Sea*, about a poor Roman Catholic family in the Outer Hebrides in the late nineteen twenties. I can write about Roman Catholicism because I have had a number of Catholic friends and habitually went to Mass in foreign countries. It's really all part of being an author to be able to get into other people's minds.

"I wrote another book in the seventies about friendship between an Irish family and a Jewish family, *Bridge of Friendship*. That was the one set partly in the decaying West Forties of Manhattan.

"In those years I went on with the Wood Street stories and gradually I think they grew better and slightly more related to the real conditions in Liverpool.

"Then I began on what I suppose really was a nostalgic thing. The war, I suddenly realised, was history to present day young people and they liked to read stories about it. So I wrote *Time to Go Back*, set mainly in Wallasey and Liverpool during the German raids of 1941, and I used a lot of the poetry I wrote in the air raid shelter, and out in Cheshire, at the time. I had only rarely put real people in my books, but *Time* was based on a different reality from most others, and real people crept in. The book sold first in the U.S.A., as a Junior Literary Guild choice there, and was in a number of hardback and paperback editions."[1]

1970-1980. Continued to write prolifically. In the United States eleven of Allan's books for young people have been Junior Literary Guild selections. "I'm well aware that I still have my limitations. I'll never get the Carnegie Medal. 'Popular' authors don't. But I honestly feel I have written some very good books during the last ten years or so.

"I don't really regret very much. I have done what I wanted to do. I suppose I would have liked to be a 'great novelist.' It might have been nice to be a best seller and make millions of dollars. But I have survived for a long time in a difficult world. I've pleased myself and I've enjoyed writing most of my books. They brought me travel and contacts and friends in many countries. The latest country is Japan, where I have had twelve books published, including all ten Drina books very recently. . . .

"I write for young people and sometimes young children, but it doesn't mean that I like children. Children are people, and

I don't like all that many people. I *have* liked some children very much, and I am always deeply interested in their problems and I think I understand them as far as one can. . . .

"I wish I had written more about women's rights, and children's rights, too. The older I get the more strongly I feel about such things and there is still a lot that must be done. I grew up as a second class citizen just because I was a girl, and I never even questioned it for a very long time. There were two million surplus women when I was a child, which didn't help matters. My father totally despised women, unless they were the clinging type, then, in a way, he despised them even more. I was never the clinging type and I always fought for what independence I thought due to me. I didn't do too badly and managed to go my own way in the face of great odds, but the idea that a child might have any rights was as remote as the moon. In my work, of course, I have never come up against any discrimination. Authors are sexless as far as payments and royalties are concerned."[1]

1982. Published her autobiography. About her purpose in writing, Allan commented: "I was pleasing myself when I wrote and never thinking of the readers an author must have to survive. But I am glad where I have given pleasure, or have helped. And particularly glad if I have sent people to places I have loved. The first fan letter I ever had said: 'Thank you for writing such a lovely book. It made me very happy.' That made me happy, too, but it was incidental.

"American students sometimes write me earnest letters asking what my purpose is in writing for young people. The truth is that I haven't really a purpose. I am not a do-gooder.

"I am a rather cynical, questioning person, really. I may vote Conservative, but many of my views are way-out for my generation. I am, in many ways, anti the Establishment, and I am not much of a royalist. I was when I was young, but when Edward the Eighth was thrown out it almost broke my heart (I was anti everyone I knew then) and I never took any interest after that.

"Apart from bad sight and an unhappy childhood, maybe the key to my kind of writing is that I have a very long and retentive memory. I can, in fact, remember incidents that happened before I was two. And, more important, I remember exactly how I felt at each age. Most adults, I have found, have totally forgotten.

"But the *spark*, the thing that made me say: 'I'm going to be an author when I grow up!' I cannot explain. My North of Scotland great grandfather, James Allan, is variously described as a compositor, a journalist or a newspaper reporter. One of my great great grandfathers was a ship's master sailing out of Wick. So writing and liking the sea . . . who can say?"[1]

FOR MORE INFORMATION SEE: Junior Literary Guild Catalogue, September, 1972; *Horn Book,* October, 1972, February, 1976; Mabel Esther Allan, *To Be an Author: A Short Autobiography,* Charles Gill & Sons, 1982.

The school system has much to say these days of the virtue of reading widely, and not enough about the virtues of reading less but in depth.

—John Ciardi

ARKIN, Alan (Wolf) 1934-

BRIEF ENTRY: Born March 26, 1934, in New York, N.Y. Actor, director, composer, and author. Arkin began his entertainment career as a folksinger, performing with the musical group "The Tarriers" from 1957 to 1959. He made his stage debut in an off-Broadway production of "Heloise," in 1958, later appearing in other plays, including "From Second City," in 1961, "Enter Laughing," in 1963, and "Luv," in 1964. He has since appeared in such films as "The Russians Are Coming, the Russians Are Coming," 1966, "The Heart Is a Lonely Hunter," 1968, "Last of the Red Hot Lovers," 1972, "Freebie and the Bean," 1974, "The In-Laws," 1979, and "Simon," 1981. Arkin also directed the Broadway play "The Sunshine Boys," 1973, the television drama "Twigs," 1975, and a number of short films. Among his stage and screen awards are the 1967 Golden Globe Award for best Actor in a comedy for his performance in "The Russians Are Coming, the Russians Are Coming," and a 1973 Tony nomination for his direction of "The Sunshine Boys." He has written two books for young people, *Tony's Hard Work Day* and *The Lemming Condition*. He is also the composer of a number of songs which have been recorded on various albums. *Agent:* Robinson & Associates, 132 South Rodeo Dr., Beverly Hills, Calif. 90212. *For More Information See: Current Biography Yearbook, 1967*, H.W. Wilson, 1968; "A Family Portrait—the Arkins" (motion picture), Parents' Magazine Films, 1975; *Notable Names in the American Theatre*, Volume 1, 17th edition, Gale, 1981; *Who's Who in America, 1982-83*, Marquis, 1982.

COLLEEN STANLEY BARE

The mule deer is often called a muley. This is because of its large, burrolike ears, which are two-thirds the length of its head. ■ (From *Mule Deer* by Colleen Stanley Bare. Illustrated with photographs by the author.)

BARE, Colleen Stanley

PERSONAL: Born in Oakland, Calif.; daughter of Carl Jessup (a banker; in feed business) and Harriett (Kirkman) Stanley; married Grant Eugene Bare, June 29, 1947; children: Randall Stanley, Warren Grant. *Education:* Stanford University, A.B., 1946; University of California, Berkeley, M.A., 1950. *Home and office:* 2502 Dorrington Court, Modesto, Calif. 95350.

CAREER: Psychometrist and counselor at public schools in Stanislaus County, Calif., 1946-47; College of Marin, Kentfield, Calif., psychometrist and counselor, 1947-48; free-lance writer, 1959—. Creative writing instructor at public schools in Stanislaus County, 1966-70; chairman of Stanislaus County task force on gifted education and Modesto City Schools Open Enrollment Education Committee, 1974-75, Modesto Culture Commission, vice-chairman, 1975, chairman, 1976—.

MEMBER: National League of American Pen Women (president, Modesto branch, 1964-66), American Association of

University Women, California Writers Club, Stanislaus County Psychological Association, Pi Lambda Theta, Delta Kappa Gamma, California Arts Council Literary Panel, 1981-82, California Federation of Chaparral Poets. *Awards, honors:* Prizes from California Writers Club poetry contests, 1966-81, including first prize, 1974, for "What Is Christmas?" and 1979, for "A Lady's Letter to Santa"; National League of American Pen Women National Contest, 1982, first prize for "Light Verse," and second prize for "Outdoor Books."

WRITINGS—Juvenile; all self-illustrated with photographs: *The Durable Desert Tortoise,* Dodd, 1979; *Ground Squirrels,* Dodd, 1980; *Mule Deer,* Dodd, 1981; *Rabbits and Hares,* Dodd, 1983. Contributor of hundreds of poems and articles to magazines, including *Good Housekeeping, Saturday Evening Post, Ladies' Home Journal, Look, McCall's, Christian Home,* and to newspapers.

WORK IN PROGRESS: Light poems; articles. "I am always working on a book and writing poetry."

SIDELIGHTS: "Writing is my obsession and salvation. Without it life would be much less meaningful. I enjoy the diversity of doing both prose and poetry and am constantly challenged by new directions in my writing. My travels to Egypt, Europe, and the Far East have cultivated my interests in Egyptian and European history; and my travels to areas like the Galapagos Islands have cultivated a new interest in natural and wildlife subjects, particularly for children. My juvenile books reflect this and have given me the opportunity to utilize my lifelong hobby of photography with my writing. Writing is very hard work, and photography is often even harder, so it takes true dedication and motivation to sustain an author."

BARNEY, Maginel Wright   1881-1966

BRIEF ENTRY: Born June 19, 1881, in Weymouth, Mass.; died April 18, 1966, in East Hampton, N.Y. An illustrator, artist, and craftsperson, Barney first learned to draw under the guidance of her older brother, renowned architect Frank Lloyd Wright. After attending the Chicago Art Institute, she worked as a commercial artist for an engraving company and spent several years at an advertising agency before becoming an illustrator. Included among her illustrated books for children are such classical works as Mary Mapes Dodge's *Hans Brinker of the Silver Skates* and Johanna Spyri's *Heidi.* She also illustrated the covers of numerous magazines, including *McClure's, Everybody's, Woman's Home Companion, Ladies' Home Journal, Woman's World,* and others. During the Depression, Barney began creating "long point" landscapes and flower pictures using colored wool. Several exhibitions of her work were held in New York. In the 1940's, she was the designer of jeweled and sequinned shoes which were considered highly stylish. The year before her death, she published her autobiography, *The Valley of the God-Almighty Jones,* which focused on her youthful years in rural Wisconsin as well as her relationship with her famous brother. *For More Information See: Illustrators of Children's Books: 1744-1945,* Horn Book, 1947; *The Illustrator in America: 1900-1960's,* Reinhold, 1966. *Obituaries: New York Times,* April 19, 1966; *Publishers Weekly,* May 9, 1966.

BARRY, Scott   1952-

PERSONAL: Born December 1, 1952, in Flushing, N.Y.; son of Martin and Elayne (Rosenbaum) Barry. *Education:* Attended Hunter College of the City University of New York, 1970-73. *Home:* 79-43 210th St., Oakland Gardens, N.Y. 11364. *Agent:* Bertha Klausner, International Literary Agency, Inc., 71 Park Ave., New York, N.Y. 10016.

CAREER: Photographer of dog shows, 1972-74; free-lance photographer, lecturer, and writer beginning in 1974. Photographs exhibited at Smithsonian Institution, Carnegie Hall, and on television programs, including "Today Show."

WRITINGS: The Kingdom of Wolves (with own photographs), Putnam, 1979. Contributor of articles and photographs to magazines and newspapers, including *Pet News, Nature Canada,* and *National Wildlife.*

Illustrator: Lewis Regenstein, *The Politics of Extinction,* Macmillan, 1975; Dr. Michael Fox, *The Soul of the Wolf,* Little, Brown, 1980.

Scott Barry with "Raven."

The very reasons that make us think that we want to own a wolf are the same reasons why we should not even consider owning one. ■ (From *The Kingdom of Wolves* by Scott Barry. Illustrated with photographs by the author.)

WORK IN PROGRESS: Photo-illustrations for *Canids* (tentative title) by Dr. Randall Lockwood for Indiana University Press; *The Raspberry Wolf* (children's fiction); *The Beasts of Amsterdam* (fiction); *The Legend of Shamone* (adult).

SIDELIGHTS: "In the last ten years I have worked extensively with forty wolves and have observed the behavior of over 100 wolves. This fact seems to amaze people when they learn that I was born and raised in Queens, New York. Yet, I have always felt people in urban areas have a greater need and perhaps a greater appreciation for animals, since their world lacks that which is natural.

"My views of the world are perhaps most closely related to those of the North American Indians—for wolves and the values they represent (intelligence, strength, reasoning, non-aggression, civilized behavior and cooperation with one's own kind, freedom, playfulness, etc.) are more of a personal religion in my life, represented by the silver wolf medallion I wear around my neck. My books, writings, and lectures reflect these views and encourage the growth of our own sensitivities—not just towards wolves and wilderness, but ultimately towards humankind. . . . The preservation of wilderness and wildlife is not merely a campaign slogan of sorts—it is a very real, hard necessity with which we cannot do without.

"In my next children's book, *The Raspberry Wolf*, I try to draw bonds or common grounds between man and beast, and man and nature. . . . In the last ten years of lectures [about wolves], I have reached over two million people and have spoken to all ages."

FOR MORE INFORMATION SEE: St. Louis Post Dispatch, October 8, 1975, May 7, 1979; *St. Louis Globe Democrat*, October 20, 1975; *Toronto Star*, November 13, 1975; *Chicago Tribune*, November 3, 1976; *Waukegan New Sun*, December 17, 1977; *National Star*, June 16, 1978; *Waukegan News*, September 26, 1980; *Cosmopolitan*, January, 1980; *Woodstock Times*, October 22, 1981; *Old Dutch Star*, February 25, 1982.

BATTERBERRY, Michael (Carver) 1932-

PERSONAL: Born April 8, 1932, in Newcastle, England; son of William J. (an executive) and June (Forsman) Batterberry; married Ariane Ruskin (a writer), May 15, 1968. *Education:* Attended Carnegie Institute of Technology (now Carnegie-Mellon University), University of Cincinnati, and Art Students League. *Home:* 1100 Madison Ave., New York, N.Y. 10028.

CAREER: Painter, designer, and writer; co-founder of design agency in Venezuela; editor-in-chief of *International Review of Food and Wine*, 1977—. Co-founder with wife, Ariane, of *International Review*. President of Good Living Media Productions, Inc. President of Batterberry Associates, Inc. Has exhibited work in Europe, South America, and the United States. Appeared on television and radio programs, including "Good Morning America" and "The Joyce Brothers Program." *Awards, honors:* National award for Bonwit Teller window designs.

WRITINGS: Chinese and Oriental Art, McGraw, 1968; *Twentieth Century Art*, McGraw, 1969; (with wife, Ariane Batterberry) *Greek and Roman Art*, McGraw, 1970; *Art of the Early Renaissance*, McGraw, 1970; (with A. Batterberry) *To Picasso with Love*, Abrams, 1971; *Art of the Middle Ages*, McGraw, 1972; (with A. Batterberry) *Primitive Art*, McGraw, 1972; (with A. Batterberry) *Children's Homage to Picasso*, Abrams, 1973; (with A. Batterberry) *On the Town in New York*, Scribner, 1973; (with A. Batterberry) *The Pantheon Story of American Art: For Young People* (Literary Guild selection), Pantheon, 1976; (with A. Batterberry) *The Bloomingdale's Book of Entertaining* (Literary Guild selection), Random House, 1976; (with A. Batterberry) *Vanity Fair*, Holt, 1977; *Mirror, Mirror: A Social History of Fashion*, Holt, 1977 (reissued as *Fashion Mirror of History*, Crown, 1982). Contributor to "The Great Cooks Series," Random House, 1977. Contributor of articles, illustrations, and drawings to popular magazines and newspapers, including *New York, Ladies' Home Journal, Playbill*, and *Travel and Leisure*. Contributing editor of *Harper's Bazaar*, 1972-73; co-author with wife of an art column for *Harper's Bazaar*.

BERLITZ, Charles L. (Frambach) 1913-

PERSONAL: Born November 22, 1913, in New York, N.Y.; son of Charles L. and Melicent (Berlitz) Frambach; Berlitz added to surname at request of grandfather, Maximillian D. Berlitz, founder of first Berlitz school of languages, 1878; married Valeria Ann Seary (now an editor and writer), January 28, 1950; children: Lin Maria, Marc Daniel. *Education:* Riverdale Country School graduate, 1932; Yale University, A.B. (magna cum laude), 1936. *Politics:* Independent. *Religion:* Episcopal. *Home:* Glen Cove, Long Island, N.Y.

CAREER: Berlitz Schools of Languages, New York, N.Y., 1934-67, starting as summer teacher at New York school while student at Yale; became assistant director of Chicago School, 1936; director of Berlitz schools in Brooklyn, N.Y., Baltimore, Md., Boston, Mass., 1936-40; language coordinator in Venezuela, 1941; vice-president and head of Berlitz Publications, Inc., 1946-67. *Military service:* U.S. Army Reserve, twenty-five year's service in Intelligence, Counter Intelligence and Special Warfare; on active duty, 1941-46, 1947-49; became major; now lieutenant colonel. *Member:* Reserve Officers Association, Military Order of World Wars, Yale Club (New York).

WRITINGS—Language books for children; all published by Grosset: *Berlitz Spanish for Children*, Series I, 1959, Series II, 1961, Series III, 1963; *Berlitz French for Children*, Series I, 1959, Series II, 1961, Series III, 1963; *Berlitz Italian for Children*, 1959; *Berlitz German for Children*, Series I, 1960, Series II, 1962; *Berlitz French Alphabet and Numbers for Children*, 1963; *Berlitz French Zoo Animals for Children*, 1963; *Berlitz Spanish Alphabet and Numbers for Children*, 1963; *Berlitz Spanish Zoo Animals for Children*, 1963.

Dictionaries; all published by Grosset, except as noted: *Berlitz Basic German Dictionary*, 1957; *Berlitz Basic Italian Dictionary*, 1957; *Berlitz Basic French Dictionary*, 1957; *Berlitz Basic Spanish Dictionary*, 1957; *Berlitz Diners' Dictionary*, 1961. *Dictionary of Foreign Terms*, Crowell, revised edition (Berlitz was not associated with the original 1934 edition), 1975.

Editor or co-director of compilation with Robert Strumpen-Darrie—"Self-Teacher Courses"; all published by Grosset: *Berlitz Self-Teacher: Spanish*, 1949; *Berlitz Self-Teacher: Italian*, 1950; *Berlitz Self-Teacher: French*, 1950; *El Berlitz sin maestro: Ingles*, 1951; *Berlitz Self-Teacher: Russian*, 1951; *Berlitz Self-Teacher: Portuguese*, 1953; *Berlitz Self-Teacher: Hebrew*, 1953.

Phrase Books, except as noted; all published by Grosset: *Berlitz Spanish for Travelers*, 1954, 2nd edition, 1962; *Berlitz Italian for Travelers*, 1954, 2nd edition, 1962; *Berlitz German for Travelers*, 1954, 2nd edition, 1962; *Berlitz French for Travelers*, 1954, 2nd edition, 1962; *Berlitz Ingles para viajeros*, 1958; *Berlitz Russian for Travelers*, 1959, 2nd edition, 1962; *Berlitz Scandinavian Languages for Travelers*, 1959, 2nd edition, 1962; *Berlitz World-Wide Phrase Book*, 1962; *Berlitz Complete Handbook of Effective English*, 1963; *Berlitz Hebrew Phrase Book*, 1964; *Berlitz Japanese for Travelers*, 1964; *Berlitz Greek for Travelers*, 1966.

"Passport to" series; all published by New American Library, 1974: *Passport to French; . . . Spanish; . . . German; . . . Italian.*

"Step-By-Step" series; all published by Everest House, 1979: *French Step-By-Step; Spanish. . . ; German. . . ; Italian. . . .*

Other: *The Mystery of Atlantis* (fiction), Grosset, 1969; *Mysteries from Forgotten Worlds* (fiction), Doubleday, 1972; *Dive*, Crowell, 1973; *The Bermuda Triangle* (fiction), Doubleday, 1974; *Without A Trace*, Doubleday, 1977; *The Philadelphia Experiment*, Grosset, 1979; *The Roswell Incident*, Grosset, 1980; *Doomsday 1999 A.D.*, Doubleday, 1981; *Native Tongues* (nonfiction), Grosset, 1982.

Also "Berlitz Method Books," some revised, some new editions: *Primer Libro, Segundo Libro*, and *Escuela del Aire* in Spanish; *Primer Livre, Deuxieme Livre*, and *Ecole de l'Air* in French; *Erstes Buch* and *Zweites Buch* in German; *Libro Italiano* in Italian; *First Book* and *Second Book* in English; and books in Afrikaans, Chinese, Greek, Hindi, Hungarian, two languages of Indonesia, Japanese, Korean, Malay, Swahili, Urdu. Prepared training tests and tapes in Amharic, Hausa, Lao, Khmer, Lingala, Somali, Urdu, and Swahili for the U.S. Army.

Also prepared material for self-teaching record courses in French, Spanish, Italian, English (for Spanish-speaking people), and German, verb finders for French, Spanish, Italian, and German, and filmstrip courses in French, Spanish, and German.

Author of *Language 30* (books and tapes for thirty different language courses), published by Dunn Donnelly. Daily column, "Languages in the News," syndicated to seventy newspapers by Associated Press.

WORK IN PROGRESS: A book on the Chinese language.

SIDELIGHTS: Born in New York City in **1913**, Berlitz grew up accustomed to hearing five languages at home. "I just thought that different people spoke in different ways. I didn't know that it was anything unusual." [Taken from an interview by Robert Dahlin in *Publishers Weekly,* June 18, 1982.[1]]

His grandfather, who spoke fifty-eight languages, founded the first Berlitz school to teach foreign languages. Archaeology was another interest which his grandfather passed on to him. "He had a friend, Dr. Max Müller, who was a famous linguist and Egyptologist, and so I used to copy the Egyptian hieroglyphics when I was a child, thinking it was an alphabet just like any other. That's where I got my interest in ancient languages, and then in Oriental languages."[1]

This interest in archaeology prompted Berlitz to write *The Bermuda Triangle* and *The Mystery of Atlantis,* and his latest book, *Native Tongues.* "I've been concerned with languages all my life, but this time I wanted to write a book on language from a human interest point of view. There are some tribes so near a certain element in their lives that have no name for it. The Eskimo has a word for baby walrus, one for two-year-old walrus, other words for mature walrus, large male walrus, tusked walrus, but there is no word for plain walrus, just as there is no special word for snow. The words that apply all address particular kinds of snow or snow patterns.

"Of the world's present languages, 115 are spoken by more than a million people, but there are enough English- and French-style words that are building up a base of 200 to 300 tourist-style words—hotel, taxi, airport, words familiar to everyone—that will form a nucleus of an international language. I travel all the time, going to different countries, and it occurred to me that most books about language don't tell you what to say to make a good impression, what you should say to compliment someone. Also, what's an insult in one country isn't in another. There are so many differences and misunderstandings.

"Did you know that in Russia the word 'red' doesn't mean something revolutionary at all? Red means beautiful. Red Square was always called that. It had nothing to do with the revolution. In China, red is a great association for the sharing of food, it's true, but red is really thought of as the color of life.

"A language like Chinese is something I have to study like Alice in Wonderland—you know, where you have to run as fast as you can just to stay in one place. Because of changes the Communists have made, it's quite different, but at least Chinese spelling has a consistency now. I don't say it's easier, but at least it's easier to pronounce."[1]

Berlitz is fluent in twelve languages. "I speak twelve languages and have twelve more I can use to a larger or lesser degree. When I enlisted in the Army, they always presumed I knew more languages than I did, and so I was always being assigned duties for a linguist. It was a time I had to learn languages very quickly."[1]

During his military career, Berlitz served in Army intelligence in Latin America and Europe. "I did a lot of investigating then, which is obviously what I still like to do. When I researched

CHARLES L. BERLITZ

my books on Atlantis and the Bermuda Triangle I approached them just as an investigator would. I am a diver, so I can explore what's underwater first hand, but only recently have we had enough equipment to actually see much of what's down on the bottom of the ocean. Now we can see underwater plateaus, and we can identify the ruins down there."[1]

Currently, Berlitz does not have any definite work in progress, although tentative plans include a book on the Chinese language. "I don't know what I'll write about next, but I'm always interested in languages. There are only 2800 of them now. Once there were 10,000. They vanish—that of a Siberian tribe in Russia, for example. The last member of one tribe died while the Russians were trying to tape his voice to preserve the language. And for many years in this country, if a young Indian was studying at a mission school, he would get a crack across the knuckles if he spoke his own language instead of English. Now, thank goodness, they're trying to save Indian languages, so much so that you know what they say—The normal Indian family is composed of five people; a mother, a father, a son, a daughter and an anthropologist."[1]

HOBBIES AND OTHER INTERESTS: Underwater exploration, archaeology ethnology, history.

FOR MORE INFORMATION SEE: New York World Telegram, January 5, 1954; *Saturday Evening Post,* August 4, 1956; *New Yorker,* February 22, 1958; *Detroit News,* May 29, 1958; *Time,* June 21, 1963; *Publishers Weekly,* June 18, 1982; *Wall Street Journal,* July 21, 1982.

BJORKLUND, Lorence F.

BRIEF ENTRY: Born in St. Paul, Minn. An illustrator for over fifty years, Bjorklund attended Pratt Institute and has worked in both magazine and advertising illustration. His main interest, however, has always been book illustration, particularly books about the American West. He has illustrated over three hundred books throughout his career, primarily in black-and-white. Using charcoal, graphite and Wolff pencil, he is well-known for pictures that are extremely accurate and meticulous in detail. Many of the books he has illustrated deal with geographical or historical subjects, a reflection of his interest in travel which began at the age of seventeen when he and a friend took a rowboat from St. Paul to New Orleans. He is the author and illustrator of two books, *Faces of the Frontier,* 1967, and, for young readers, *The Bison: The Great American Buffalo,* 1970. His many illustrated works for young readers include Hallie H. Violette's *On the Road to Santa Fe,* 1941, Oliver La Farge's *Cochise of Arizona: The Pipe of Peace Is Broken,* 1953, Clara Judson's *St. Lawrence Seaway,* 1959, Bruce Grant's *American Forts, Yesterday and Today,* 1965, Julian May's *How the Animals Came to North America,* 1974, and *The Warm-Blooded Dinosaurs,* 1978. *Residence:* Croton Falls, N.Y. *For More Information See: Publishers Weekly,* November 6, 1967; *Illustrators of Children's Books: 1957-1966,* Horn Book, 1968; *Illustrators of Books for Young People,* 2nd edition, Scarecrow, 1975.

BOBRITSKY, Vladimir 1898-
(Bobri; Vladimir Bobri)

BRIEF ENTRY: Born May 13, 1898, in Kharkov, Ukraine (now U.S.S.R.). An artist and illustrator, Bobritsky attended the Kharkov Imperial Art School. His career began at an early age in the theater as scene designer for drama and ballet. By age seventeen, he was designing sets for the Great Dramatic Theater at Kharkov. Following the Revolution, he was forced to flee his homeland as a refugee. In the following years, he led a vagabond life during which he played guitar with a band of gypsies, worked with archeologists in Turkey, pressed wine in the Crimea, painted icons in Greece, and designed sets for the Ballet Russe in Constantinople. Saving enough money for passage, he arrived in the United States in 1921 where he became owner and operator of his own textile firm. During the 1930's, he began a successful career as a commercial artist in the advertising field and book illustration.

Bobritsky is the recipient of the Art Directors Award for Distinctive Merit from the Art Directors Club. His illustrated books for children include Blossom Budney's *A Kiss Is Round* which was selected as one of the *New York Times* Choice of Best Illustrated Children's Books of the Year in 1954. Also an accomplished musician, Bobritsky composed "Danza En La" which was performed in New York in 1936. He has also directed radio broadcasts of chamber music and has served as art director and editor of *Guitar Review* magazine for which he received two awards from the American Institute of Graphic Arts. He is the author of two books on music, The *Segovia Technique* and *A Musical Voyage with Two Guitars. Home:* Elting Rd., Rosendale, N.Y. 12472. *For More Information See: Forty Illustrators and How They Work,* Watson-Guptill, 1946; *Illustrators of Children's Books: 1957-1966,* Horn Book, 1968; (under name Vladimir V. Bobri) *Contemporary Authors,* Volume 105, Gale, 1982.

BROCK, C(harles) E(dmond) 1870-1938

BRIEF ENTRY: Born February 5, 1870, in Holloway, London, England; died February 28, 1938, in Cambridge, England. Book illustrator and portrait painter; student of the noted sculptor Henry Wiles. A member of the Royal Institute of Painters in Water Colours, Brock came from a large and well-known family of artists, which included his brothers H(enry) M(atthew), R(ichard) H(enry), and Edmond. C. E. Brock is particularly noted for his depiction of period settings in his book illustrations. Brock illustrated books for both adults and children. His work for children includes *A Christmas Carol* and *The Cricket on the Hearth* both by Charles Dickens, *Gulliver's Travels* by Jonathan Swift, *The Life and Adventures of Robinson Crusoe* by Daniel Defoe, and *Silas Marner* by George Eliot. *For More Information See: Junior Book of Authors,* second editon, H. W. Wilson, 1951; *Who's Who of Children's Literature,* Schocken, 1968; C. M. Kelly, *The Brocks: A Family of Cambridge Artists and Illustrators,* Skilton, 1975.

BURGESS, (Frank) Gelett 1866-1951

PERSONAL: Born January 30, 1866, in Boston, Mass.; died of a heart attack, September 18, 1951, in Carmel, Calif.; buried in Monterey, Calif.; son of Thomas Harvey and Caroline Matilda (Brooks) Burgess; married Estelle Loomis, June 18, 1914 (died October 11, 1947). *Education:* Massachusetts Institute of Technology, B.S., 1887. *Residence:* New York, N.Y.

CAREER: Author and illustrator of books for adults and young people, editor, humorist, and neologist. Southern Pacific Railroad, draftsman, 1887-90; University of California, instructor of topographical drawing, 1891-94; furniture designer in San Francisco, Calif., 1894-95; *Wave* magazine, associate editor, 1894-95; *The Lark* magazine, San Francisco, co-editor, 1895-97; co-editor of *Le Petit Journal des Refusées;* began writing books, 1897; *The Sketch,* London, England, staff member; *Ridgeway's,* associate editor, 1906. Founder, first boys' club in America (San Francisco). *Member:* Bohemian Club (San Francisco), The Players Club (New York City).

WRITINGS—Of special interest to young readers; humorous verse; all published by F. A. Stokes, except as indicated: *The Purple Cow* (poem), W. Doxey, 1895; *To the Readers of "The Lark" Who Have Laughed They Knew Not Why,* William Doxey, 1895; *"Who'll Be the Clerk?" "I," Said the Lark,* W. Doxey, Book I, 1896, Book 2, 1897; *The Nonsense Almanack for 1900,* 1899; *The Lively City O'Ligg: A Cycle of Modern Fairy Tales for City Children* (self-illustrated), 1899.

Goops and How to Be Them: A Manual of Manners for Polite Infants (self-illustrated), 1900, reprinted, Dover, 1968; *The Burgess Nonsense Book* (poems; self-illustrated; also see below), 1901; *A Gage of Youth* (poems), Small, Maynard, 1901; *Nonsense Almanac, 1901,* 1901; *More Goops and How Not to Be Them: A Manual of Manners for Impolite Infants* (self-illustrated), 1903, reprinted, Dover, 1968; *Goop Tales Alphabetically Told* (self-illustrated), 1904, reprinted, Dover, 1973; *The Rubaiyat of Omar Cayenne* (parody), 1904; *Blue Goops and Red* (self-illustrated), 1909; *The Goop Directory of Juvenile Offenders* (self-illustrated), 1913; *Burgess Unabridged* (illustrated by Herb Roth), 1914; *The Goop Encyclopedia* (self-illustrated), 1916; *Why Be a Goop?* (self-illustrated), 1924; *New Goops and How to Know Them* (self-illustrated), Random House, 1951; *The Purple Cow and Other Nonsense* (self-illustrated; selected from *The Burgess Nonsense Book*), Dover, 1961.

Principal novels; all published by Bobbs-Merrill, except as indicated: *Vivette,* Copeland & Day, 1897; *The White Cat* (mystery), 1907; *The Heart Line,* 1907; *Lady Méchante* (farce; self-illustrated), F. A. Stokes, 1909; *Find the Woman,* 1911; *The Master of Mysteries,* 1912, reprinted, Arno, 1976; *Love in a Hurry,* 1913; *Mrs. Hope's Husband,* Century, 1917; *Two O'Clock Courage* (mystery), 1934; *Too Good Looking,* 1936; *Ladies in Boxes* (mystery), Alliance Book, 1942.

Other principal writings: *The Romance of the Commonplace* (essays), Elder & Shephard, 1902, enlarged edition, Bobbs-Merrill, 1916, reprinted, Books for Libraries Press, 1968; (with Will Irwin) *The Reign of Queen Isyl* (short stories), McClure, Phillips, 1903; (with W. Irwin) *The Picaroons* (short stories), McClure, Phillips, 1904; *A Little Sister of Destiny* (short stories), Houghton, 1906; *Are You a Bromide?* (satire; self-illustrated), B. W. Huebsch, 1906, reprinted, Literature House, 1969, revised and reprinted from the original, published as "The Sulphitic Theory" in *The Smart Set,* April, 1906; *The Maxims of Methuselah* (satire), F. A. Stokes, 1907; "The Cave Man" (play; produced in New York City at Fulton Theatre, October 30, 1911); *The Maxims of Noah* (humor), F. A. Stokes, 1913; *War the Creator,* B. W. Huebsch, 1916; (editor) *My Maiden Effort,* Doubleday, 1921, reprinted, Arden Library, 1979; *Have You an Educated Heart?* (humor), Boni and Liv-

GELETT BURGESS

eright, 1923; *Ain't Angie Awful!* (illustrated by Rea Irvin), Dorrance, 1923; *Why Men Hate Women* (illustrated by Herb Roth), Payson & Clarke, 1927; *The Bromide and Other Theories,* Viking, 1933; *Look Eleven Years Younger* (non-fiction), Simon & Shuster, 1937.

Also author of *Short Words Are Words of Might,* 1939. Contributor to periodicals such as *McClure's, Century,* and *Saturday Evening Post.*

ADAPTATIONS—Movies: "The Caveman," Vitagraph Co. of America, 1915, Warner Brothers, starring Marie Prevost and Matt Moore, 1926; "The Two Soul Women," Bluebird Photoplays, 1918; "Two in the Dark," RKO Radio Pictures, starring Walter Abel and Margot Grahame, 1936; "Two O'Clock Courage," RKO Radio Pictures, starring Tom Conway, 1945.

TIDINESS

Little scraps of paper,
   Little crumbs of food,
Make a room untidy,
   Everywhere they're
     strewed.

Do you sharpen pencils,
   Ever, on the floor?
What becomes of orange-
     peels
And your apple-core?

Can you blame your mother
   If she looks severe,
When she says, "It looks
    to me
As if the Goops were
    here"?

(From *Goops and How to Be Them* by Gelett Burgess. Illustrated by the author.)

SIDELIGHTS: Born **January 30, 1866,** in Boston, Massachusetts. Burgess was the son of Thomas Harvey and Caroline Brooks Burgess. His ancestors came to America on the *Mayflower.* He attended Boston public schools and received a Bachelor of Science degree in 1887 from the Massachusetts Institute of Technology where he edited *Tech,* the student magazine.

(From the movie "Two O'Clock Courage," starring Tom Conway and Ann Rutherford. Copyright 1944 by RKO Radio Pictures, Inc.)

(From the movie "Two in the Dark," starring Margot Graham and Walter Abel, based on the novel _Two O'Clock Courage_. Copyright 1935 by RKO Radio Pictures, Inc.)

His first job was as a draftsman on survey work for the Southern Pacific Railway. Here he met picturesque characters of various nationalities which gave him a wonderful insight into human nature. He always carried around a notebook to write down quaint things that he saw.

1891-1893. Instructor in mechnical topographical drawing at the University of California at Berkeley. ''I liked the life at Berkeley very much. I realized a life of teaching and writing were incompatible, and I wanted the latter.'' [Cyril Clemens, ''My Friend Gelett Burgess,'' *Hobbies*, February, 1952.[1]]

1894. Made a radical change in his profession by becoming associate editor of *Wave* magazine.

1895. Led a young San Francisco literary group called *Les Jeunes* and established and edited a small, monthly publication, the *Lark*. This magazine made him well-known as an author and humorist and began his career as a grotesque illustrator. It also featured his pen drawings of the strange, ill-mannered creatures he called ''goops.''

Burgess' ''Purple Cow'' was published in the *Lark*. Burgess became famous for this single rhyme at the expense of other better work and he once said ''I wish that silly bovine had never been born in my imagination! Folks seem to think that is the only thing I ever wrote.''[1]

1896. After two years of commercial designing, Burgess decided to quit and turn to writing for a living. He illustrated his articles and books with his own quaint drawings. ''An author who can illustrate his own work gets much closer to the reader, and wherever the text weakens, the pictures reinvigorate.''[1]

1897. First book, *Vivette,* published to considerable attention. Like many writers, Burgess made a habit of keeping a daily diary. ''For . . . years I have kept my diary scrupulously, without missing a day. . . . There are certain good habits, it would seem, as hard to break as bad ones, and if the practice of keeping a daily journal is a praiseworthy one, it derives no little of its virtue from sheer inertia. The half-filled book tempts one on; there is a pleasure in seeing the progress of the volume, leaf by leaf; like sentimental misers we hoard our store of memories; we end each day with a definite statement of fact or fancy—and it grows harder and harder to abstain from the self-enforced duty. Yet it is seldom a pleasure, when one is fatigued with excitement or work, to transmit our affairs to writing.

''Some, it is true, love it for its own sake, or as a relief for pent-up emotions, but in one way or another most autobiographical journalists consider the occupation as a prudent depositor regards his frugal savings in the bank. Sometime, somehow, they think, those coined memories will prove useful.

''Does this time ever come, I wonder? For me it has not come yet, though I still picture a late reflective age when I shall enjoy recalling the past and live again my old sensations. But life is more strenuous then of yore, and even at seventy or eighty nowadays, no one need consider himself too old for a fresh active interest in the world about him. Your old gentleman of to-day does not sit in his own corner of the fireplace and dote over the lost years, he reads the morning papers and insists upon going to the theatre on wet evenings. Have I, then, been laying up honey for a winter that shall never come? It would be better were this true, I am sure, yet the mania holds me.

''Besides this distrust of my diaries, I am awakening . . . to the fact that, as an autobiography, the books are strangely lacking in interest. They are not convincing. I thought, as I did my clerkly task, that I should always be I, but a cursory glance at these naive pages shows that they were written by a thousand different persons, no one of whom speaks the language of the emotions as I know it to-day. It is true, then, my diary has convinced me, that we do become different persons. . . . Here is written down rage, hate, delight, affection, yearning, no word of which is comprehensible to me now. I am reading the adventures of some one else, not my own. Who was it? I have forgotten the dialect of my youth.

''Ah, indeed the boy is father of the man! I will be indulgent, as a son should, to paternal indiscretions.

''And yet, for the bare skeleton of my history, these volumes are useful enough. The pages which, while still wet with ink and tears, I considered lyric essays, have fallen to a merely utilitarian value. I am thankful, on that account, for them, and for the fact that my bookkeeping was well systematized and indexed. . . .

''The especial event of each day, if the day held anything worthy of remark or remembrance, was boldly noted as the top of the page, over the date. Whirring the leaves, I catch many sugestive pharses [*sic*]: 'Dinner at Madame Qui-Vive's,' (it was there I first tasted champagne!)—'Henry Irving as Shylock' (but it was not the actor who made that night famous— I took Kitty Carmine home in a cab!)—'Broke my arm' (or else I would never have read Marlowe, I fear!)—and 'Met Sally Maynard' (this was an event, it seemed at that time, worthy of being chronicled in red ink!) So they go. They are the chapter headings in the book of my life.

''In the lower left-hand corner of each page I noted the advent of letters, the initials of the writers inscribed in little squares, and in the opposite right hand corner, a complimentary hieroglyph kept account of every letter sent. So, by running over the pages, I can note the fury of my correspondence. . . .

''Perpendiculary, along the inner margin, I wrote the names of those to whom I had been introduced that day, and on the back page I kept a chronological list of the same. . . .

''Besides all this, the books are extra-illustrated in the most significant manner. There is hardly a page that does not contain some trifling memento; here a theatre coupon pasted in, or a clipping from the programme, an engraved card or a penciled note—there a scrap of a photograph worn out in my pocketbook. Somebody's sketched profile, or at rare intervals, a whisp of Someone's hair!. . .

''It gratifies my conceit to chronicle my small happenings, and, somehow, written down in fair script, they seem important.'' [Gelett Burgess, ''The Diary Habit,'' *Overland Monthly,* January-June, 1901.[2]]

1900. Third book, *Goops and How to Be Them,* published and established his fame as an American humorist. ''Some authors consider it a reflection on their work if they can be enjoyed also by children, but I consider it a very high compliment. For children often have a truer sense of humor than their elders.''[1]

Burgess moved to Paris, France and lived there for thirteen years. Upon his return, he married Estelle Loomis and resided

I NEVER SAW A PURPLE COW,   I NEVER HOPE TO SEE ONE;

BUT I CAN TELL YOU, ANYHOW,   I'D RATHER SEE THAN BE ONE!

I never saw a purple cow
I never hope to see one;
But I can tell you anyhow,
I'd rather see than be one.

■ (From *The Purple Cow and Other Nonsense* by Gelett Burgess. Illustrated by the author.)

in New York City, where he became one of America's most popular and productive writers.

Became an inventor of words which he put together in *Burgess Unabridged*, a collection of his neologisms. One new word was "blurb" which designates a short, laudatory comment printed on a book jacket. He defined the word as "self-praise; to make a noise like a publisher." Another word is "bromide— a person who utters platitudes with the air of having just invented them."

An established humorist, he was once described by a *New York Times* reporter as a sad, serious man. On the subject of humor, Burgess commented: "It's hard to discuss humor without being solemn and stodgy. You'd think it was the most serious subject in the world. But the fact is that it is as elusive and as difficult to analyze as love, swing or a young girl's thoughts.

"A lot of people say it is based on cruelty, as when we enjoy seeing a fat man slip on a banana peel. Others contend that it is frustrated expectation, as when a man remarks, 'That's no lady, that's my wife.' Then there is the inversion-of-natural-conditions school—a dowager chasing her hat which for the nonce becomes her master. . . .

"Whatever humor is, it is deeply implanted in human nature as the love of sleep. Like dreams, it is a flight from dull reality and an escape from the doggone rules of reason. It is delightful because it inflates one's ego. When you watch a comedy from

a box seat you are looking down to see 'what fools those mortals be.'

"Humor is dependent upon our egotistic delight in the imperfection of others and our own strange enjoyment of our frustrated expectations. This paradox is similar to our enjoyment of danger. Humor is like skating on thin ice. The pleasure is in victory over peril. Nonsense is a special form of humor which derives its pleasure from precisely the opposite quality. It delights in the catastrophe of reason and logic and finds infantile pleasure in incongruity.

"Humor is the most serious subject in the world and it is almost impossible to discuss it without being solemn." [S. J. Woolf, "And Still No Purple Cow," *New York Times Magazine*, January 26, 1941.[3]]

September 18, 1951. Died of a heart attack in Carmel, California where he had lived for his last two years. "Sometimes I think it would be better to write up my diary in advance to fill in the year's pages with what I would like to do, and attempt to live up to the prophecy. And yet, I have had too many unforseen [*sic*] pleasures in my life for that—I would rather trust Fate and Imagination."[2]

FOR MORE INFORMATION SEE: Overland Monthly, January-June, 1901; Thomas L. Masson, *Our American Humorists,* Dodd, 1931, reprinted, Books for Libraries Press, 1966; Vincent Starrett, *Buried Caesars*, Covici-McGee, 1923, reprinted, Books for Libraries Press, 1968; *New York Times Magazine*, January 26, 1941; Stanley J. Kunitz and Howard Haycraft, editors, *Twentieth-Century Authors*, H. W. Wilson, 1942; *Hobbies*, February, 1952; *Illustrators of Children's Books*, 1946-1956, Horn Book, 1958; Max J. Herzberg, editor, *Readers Encyclopedia of American Literature*, Crowell, 1962.

Obituaries: New York Times, September 19, 1951; *Publishers Weekly*, September 29, 1951; *Life*, October 1, 1951; *Newsweek*, October 1, 1951.

CAGLE, Malcolm W(infield) 1918-

PERSONAL: Born September 26, 1918, in Grand Junction, Colo.; son of Victor Malcolm, and Anna Leila Cagle; married Virginia Lee Power, August 20, 1941; children: Patrick, Mary Winfield, Jane Forrest. *Education:* U.S. Naval Academy, B.S., 1941; graduated from National War College, 1958. *Religion:* Presbyterian. *Office:* Naval Air Station, Pensacola, Fla. 32508.

CAREER: U.S. Navy, 1941—; commissioned ensign in U.S. Navy, 1941; designated naval aviator, 1943; present rank, vice admiral. Served in the Atlantic and Pacific theaters during World War II; served in the Korean War; served in the Vietnam War. Commanding officer, USS *Suribachi*, 1963-64, USS *Franklin D. Roosevelt*, 1964-65; director of aviation programs division, Office of the Deputy Chief of Naval Operations, 1965-68; commander of Carrier Division ONE, 1968-69; director of general planning and programming division, Office of the Chief of Naval Operations, 1969-70; assistant deputy chief of naval operations for air, 1970-71; chief of Naval education and training, Office of the Chief of Naval Operations, 1971—. *Awards, honors:* Navy Cross, Legion of Merit, Distinguished Flying Cross, Air Medal; essay award, U.S. Naval Institute, 1957; Alfred Thayer Mahan award, 1958.

WRITINGS—Juvenile: Flying Ships: Hovercraft and Hydrofoils, Dodd, 1970; *The United States Navy of Tomorrow*, Dodd, 1975.

Other: *Battle Report*, Volume VI: *The War in Korea* (Cagle was not associated with Volumes I-V), edited by Walter Karig and others, Farrar & Rinehart, 1952; (with Frank A. Manson) *The Sea War in Korea*, United States Naval Institute, 1957, reprinted, Arno, 1980; *The Naval Aviator's Guide*, United States Naval Institute, 1963, second edition published as *The Naval Aviation Guide*, United States Naval Institute, 1969; (with C. G. Halpine) *A Pilot's Meteorology*, 3rd edition (Cagle was not associated with earlier editions), Van Nostrand, 1970.

CAMERON, Elizabeth Jane 1910-1976
(Jane Duncan, Janet Sandison)

PERSONAL: Born March 10, 1910, in Dunbartonshire, Scotland; died October 20, 1976, in Scotland; daughter of Duncan and Janet (Sandison) Cameron. *Education:* University of Glasgow, M.A., 1930. *Religion:* Presbyterian. *Agent:* A.M. Heath & Co. Ltd., 40-42 William IV St., London WCZN 4DD, England; and Brandt & Brandt, 101 Park Ave., New York, N.Y. 10017.

ELIZABETH JANE CAMERON

CAREER: Worked as private secretary in Great Britain, 1931-39. *Military service:* Royal Air Force, Women's Auxiliary, 1939-45; became flight officer. *Member:* P.E.N. International.

*WRITINGS—*All published by Grosset: *The Big Book of Real Trains*, 1963; *The Big Book of Real Fire Engines*, 1964; *The Big Book of Real Trucks*, 1970.

Under pseudonym Jane Duncan; "My Friend" series, all originally published by St. Martin's, except as indicated: *My Friends the Miss Boyds*, 1959; *My Friend Muriel*, 1959; . . . *Monica*, 1960; . . . *Annie*, 1961; . . . *Sandy*, Macmillan (London), 1961, St. Martin's, 1962; . . . *Flora*, Macmillan (London), 1962, St. Martin's, 1963; . . . *Martha's Aunt*, 1962; . . . *Madame Zora*, 1963; . . . *Rose*, 1964; . . . *Cousin Emmie*, 1965; *My Friends the Mrs. Millers*, 1965; . . . *My Father*, Macmillan (London), 1966, St. Martin's, 1967; *My Friends from Cairnton*, 1966; *My Friends the Macleans*, 1967; *My Friends the Hungry Generation*, 1968; . . . *the Swallow*, 1970; . . . *Sashie*, 1972; *My Friends the Misses Kindness*, 1974; *My Friends George and Tom*, 1976.

"Camerons" series, all originally published by Macmillan, except as indicated: *Camerons on the Hills*, 1963; . . . *on the Train*, 1963; . . . *at the Castle*, 1965; . . . *Calling*, 1965, St. Martin's, 1966; . . . *Ahoy!*, St. Martin's, 1968.

"Janet Reachfar" series: *Brave Janet Reachfar* (illustrated by Mairi Hedderwick), Seabury, 1975; *Herself and Janet Reachfar*, Macmillan (London), 1975; *Janet Reachfar and the Kelpie*

Inside the oval, Neil and Donald were sitting side by side on stools, holding the broomsticks as if they were oars and, behind them on another stool, sat Professor Grant, also holding a broomstick oar. ■ (From *Camerons Ahoy!* by Jane Duncan. Illustrated by Victor Ambrus.)

(illustrated by M. Hedderwick), Seabury, 1976; *Janet Reachfar and Chickabird* (illustrated by M. Hedderwick), Seabury, 1978.

Letter from Reachfar (a memoir), Macmillan (London), 1975, St. Martin's, 1976.

Under pseudonym Janet Sandison; all orginally published by St. Martin's, except as indicated: "An Apology for the Life of Jean Robertson," Volume I: *Jean in the Morning*, 1964, Volume II: *Jean at Noon; or, Summer's Treasure,* Macmillan (London), 1971, St. Martin's, 1972, Volume III: *Jean in the Twilight; or, the Mists of Autumn,* 1973, Volume IV: *Jean towards Another Day; or, Can Spring Be Far Away?,* 1975.

SIDELIGHTS: **March 10, 1910.** Born in Dunbarton, Scotland; daughter of Duncan and Janet (Sandison) Cameron. "I come of a lawless, cattle-stealing, claymore-waving ancestry but in my father these traits were perforce subdued by his police service. . . .

"My father started his police service in 1899 at the age of twenty-one in the then little town of Helensburgh on the estuary of the Clyde. It was a wealthy place at the time, with the houses of the working-class huddled by the water and the 'big houses' of the wealthy on the hill behind. The young policemen were given most of the night duty and there was much larking about between nine and midnight between them and the servant girls among the rhododendrons of the gardens that surrounded the big villas. But my father did not meet my mother among the rhododendrons. She was lady's-maid-companion to a rich old spinster. . . .

"My father was very much aware of her parental responsibility and especially after the death of our mother he was at great pains to bring up my brother and me to the best of his ability.

"The Colony . . . was my 'real home' as I called it in my mind. This was the origin of my fictional 'Reachfar.' It was the birthplace of my father and of many of my ancestors before him, a small croft on top of a hill in the Black Isle of Ross-shire, to which I was taken for my first holiday at three months old and where I spent all my holidays until I went to England to earn my living at the age of twenty-one.

"It was called 'The Colony' I have been told because once upon a time a colony of weavers lived on that ground, who gradually died off and drifted away, leaving mine as the last surviving family who gradually took over the abandoned sixty acres of marginal arable and the hundred and fifty of moorland. . . .

"The school terms of my life were lived in police stations, usually in the less salubrious environs of Glasgow, for it is in such places that there is the greatest need for the police stations and as a policeman's child, I was always slightly suspect by my fairly lawless contemporaries. This apart, I do not think that I was a very friendly or sociable youngster, for I was an only child until I was ten years old. Quite early, I had turned The Colony into a fantasy world—not the people there but the place itself which was like a private country of the mind—of mental escape during school time and I returned to it in fact every holiday with great joy." [Jane Duncan, *Letter from Reachfar,* St. Martin's Press, 1976.']

1922. "At the age of twelve, I entered the Second Year of the upper school at my good, sound Scottish academy. At this time, my favourite subject was French, which I had begun to learn the year before. The reasons for this preference were, I think, that I liked the language for itself, for its musical fluidity and I liked the mistress who taught it, a dignified lady of great culture, (Edinburgh University and the Sorbonne) as academy mistresses were in those days, who seemed to be able to impart some of her own love of the language to her pupils. The first year of study had been given mainly to vocabulary and grammar. Those were still the days of the 'pen of my aunt' mode of teaching but in spite of this, I never found the lessons dull and I was delighted when, at the beginning of this second year, I was given an actual *book* in French that could be read, along with a dictionary that would help one through the puzzling parts. The book was *Lettres de mon Moulin* by Alphonse Daudet, a collection of short articles and stories sent from the Provencal windmill he had bought to a Paris newspaper and the first little article opens with the words: 'Ce sont les lapins qui ont été étonnés!' I had to look up the word 'lapins' in my dictionary, for rabbits had not figured in my lessons of the year before and when I had gathered the meaning of the sentence I, as well as the rabbits, were astonished.

"'Just imagine,' I thought, 'anybody writing about rabbits!'

"I had been able to read English since the age of three and was 'the nose always in a book' sort of child but most of the reading matter that came my way had been fairy tales, stories of children who lived in nurseries and had a background very different from my own, *Alice's Adventures in Wonderland* which I disbelieved profoundly and which yet terrified me and a few late Victorian and Edwardian novels of high moral tone. In addition to such fiction, we had in our house a copy of *The Pilgrim's Progress,* a large bible bound in dark green boards, a *Chambers Dictionary* of similar size in similar boards and a fascinating eight volumes of *Mysteries of Police and Crime.* . . .

"You will notice that the early reading at my 'away home' was all of high moral tone. The fairy stories ended happily ever after. The picture-book stories about the middle-class nursery children were mostly records of the comeuppance of naughtiness. *The Pilgrim's Progress* was all about the struggle to get to Heaven, all the people in the Bible were good just because they were in the Bible, the dictionary was a very serious affair of great learning and the *Mysteries of Police and Crime* showed very clearly what happened to people who were wicked. (My favourite story in all eight volumes was that of Jack the Ripper, the one who got away.) So, just imagine anybody writing about *rabbits* and getting away with it into solemn print! *I* could write about rabbits, I thought. I could write about rabbits darting into the Bluebell Bank at The Colony.

"So, although at the age of twelve I did not think of putting pen to paper, I am convinced that it was at the age of twelve that I began to write. Those astonished rabbits stayed with me and from then on I could never see the white retreating scut of a rabbit without remembering Daudet's words as he described his arrival at his windmill: '—there were, without a word of a lie, a good twenty, sitting in a ring on the platform busy warming their paws in a moonbeam.' It was a pretty picture and one that I had seen many times at various places on the lands of The Colony.'"[1]

1927. "I was a quiet, solitary, dreamy adolescent, the very type to be an annoyance to my irritable, voluble, opinionated stepmother. I was and still am utterly uncompetitive in every way, would not play games like other girls, did not like parties and did not care if Elsie was the prettiest girl in the school or Mary the star of the hockey field. . . .

"Well, in the final days of my final year at my academy, I did one of my unnatural things. I won the Dux Medal of the school and forgot all about it until my father looked up from the little local newspaper and said: 'Listen to this—'The Dux Medal of Lenzie Academy has been won by Elizabeth Jane Cameron, Police Station, Croy.'" He put the paper down on his knees and asked: 'Is this true?'

"'Yes,' I said. 'I get it on Prize Day.'

"'And you never told us?'. . .

"Being non-competitive, the medal meant nothing to me. What was important to me at the time was that a week or so later, it would be the holidays and The Colony, and that after the holidays I would go to the university. The medal, for me, was the merest incident and eminently forgettable but although my father was still looking puzzled, I could not find the words to explain. Passions were difficult to explain, even when one is quite experienced in life and moderately articulate and at seventeen my passions were The Colony and learning about literature, but I did not recognise them as passions. They were great secret things that were part of me and for which I had no words.'"[1]

. . .There was an absolute shower of black stuff that went all over the men's faces and into their eyes and up their noses and they began to cough and splutter. ■ (From *Camerons on the Train* by Jane Duncan.)

1930. ". . . I went on and up through school and on and up through university in the period now known sometimes as The Roaring Twenties, the time of the Bright Young Things, whose spokesman was Noël Coward, but I did not belong to this gilded group.

"In the last years of this decade, I was reading English Literature and Language at Glasgow University. . . .

"On the whole, I think the most important things I learned from my reading of English Literature and Language were the words 'bore' and 'boredom.' They were words never used in my family circle and when I became aware of them I discovered that boredom was something that existed, apparently, but that it had never happened to me in my whole life.

"Yet I spent a great deal of my time alone. I was extremely shy and made no close friends at the university, merely acquaintances with whom I swopped the frowned-upon books. I travelled about twenty miles from the current police station by bus or train to attend my classes and twenty miles home again afterwards and at home I was still, virtually, an only child. My brother had been born when I was ten but my mother had died shortly afterwards and Baby John had gone to The Colony, into the care of our grandparents and Uncle George. By the time I went to university, my father had re-married but I had little in common with my stepmother and my free time was spent either reading in my room or walking in the hills beyond the town. Yet, I repeat, I never suffered from boredom and at this late date I recognize that this was because the rabbits were always there, astonishing as ever. I still had not put pen to paper because I could not find the words for what was in my mind but I was always aware of a sense of waiting, waiting,

Down in there, . . . was Nink, standing on top-most tiptoe with his arms round the neck of a beautiful white hind whose head rested on the shoulder of his blue jersey. ■ (From *Camerons at the Castle* by Jane Duncan. Illustrated by Victor Ambrus.)

waiting to achieve my degree, waiting to get away from my family and get out into the world, waiting, above all, for the turmoil of observations, impressions, half-formed beliefs and disbeliefs in my mind to take on some sort of coherence, to come out of chaos into order. I was waiting to find myself and to discover the nature of my rabbits.

". . . I achieved my degree but I did not get away from my family, for what became known as the Great Trade Depression had settled over the land and nobody wanted to employ a Master of Arts with good secretarial qualifications. Nobody wanted to employ anybody, so I went home to John, Uncle George, my aunt, my grandparents and The Colony. I would have been happy at The Colony but for the unspoken discontent in the air that a Master of Arts, whose education had cost a considerable amount of money, was milking cows, making butter and doing housework but I think now, that if I had stayed there, the pen would never have reached the paper.

"I happened to read at this time the best-selling American novel *Flaming Youth* by Warner Fabian. The book was presented to me by a friend and I still have it so the quotation that follows is exact but it would have been exact even if I had not been able to check it. The printed word only corroborates what is engraved on my memory.

"I do not claim that *Flaming Youth* is a great work of literature but I am grateful to it for this sentence that was written of one of the female characters: 'The layers of fat were insulating that soft and comfort-enslaved soul.' This was the first intimation to come to me that happy dreaming contentment can smother

and choke the potentiality of a personality, can drug to death the desire to achieve.

"It was not until the early 1930s that my pen reached paper and from then forward pens, ink and paper became a constant problem. I worked . . . as a sort of secretary-companion-general-dog's-body to various women, lived-in and had a salary of twenty-five shillings a week. On this, I was expected to buy clothes for all occasions and clothes suitable for stays in places like Italy, Switzerland and the South of France. When I write of these foreign parts, it may sound as if my life were very interesting indeed but things are not always as they sound and seem. I think it summarises the way of life if I tell you that one employer and I, on our travels by car, chanced to arrive in Salzburg to spend a night during the period of the music festival. We spent the evening in a cinema, watching a film that we had both seen already in London called 'Fire Over England' (starring Errol Flynn), with English sound and German sub-titles.

"It was with this employer that I really learned about boredom. I myself was never bored—one could try to match the German sub-titles to the English sound, for instance—but I saw how my wealthy employer suffered from boredom. The layers of fat had insulated soul, heart and mind to the degree where she could take no interest in anything but moved from moment to moment in effortless passivity, as if the boredom acted like a drug. She always had to have something to 'do,' like sitting through 'Fire Over England' but never did anything that called for the slightest effort or even understanding.

"Repression and frustration have their uses. It is impossible to be bored if you are stuggling all the time against odds and my odds were a dearth of paper, ink and the time to use them. I made most of my own clothes, made over to fit me cast-offs that my employers gave me, economised in every way, bought the cheapest seats at concerts and theatres and bought them at all only when the mental and spiritual wasteland threatened to overwhelm me. From the best seats in theatres, I saw all the farces and musical comedies of the time. But economise as I would, there was never enough money to buy paper to write on or books to read. I wrote on opened-out paper bags, brown paper and opened-out envelopes and on Fridays, when I received my twenty-five shillings for the week, I would spend half-a-crown on white quarto and have a debauch during the night of Friday, Saturday and Sunday. The writing was all done, of course, in secret or during the night for my various employers would not have approved of this absurd activity in 'their' time.

"I had no friends in the real sense of the word because I belonged neither in the drawing-room nor in the servants' hall. I had a string of what are called boy-friends, some of them met in the drawing-rooms, some of them 'picked up' in concert halls or theatres but I was not deeply interested in any of them and as soon as one of them showed signs of moving towards a more intimate relationship, I took flight. They were merely an escape from the drawing-rooms and the current employer.

"Yet, although I found my way of life unsatisfactory in the main, I did not try to escape from it for I could not think of anywhere to go. In spite of the boy-friends, I was still shy, that I did not seem to want what other young women wanted, such as beautiful clothes, a 'good time,' marriage, travel or wealth but I admitted this only to myself. Outwardly, I tried to conform but, inwardly, I truly was neither flesh, fowl nor good red herring, for this is what a writer is, a rogue who is outside any and every group, even the 'group' of writers.''[1]

One morning around Christmas-time, when the snow was very deep, Janet went up to the moor with some corn and found that Chickabird had a very special guest. ■ (From *Janet Reachfar and Chickabird* by Jane Duncan. Illustrated by Mairi Hedderwick.)

1939. Served with the Royal Air Force during World War II. "I found my freedom as a six-digit number, an aircraftwoman in the Women's Auxiliary Air Force, inside a high wire-mesh fence, behind the guarded gates of a Coastal Command station. My shyness, my reticence dissolved like mist in a barrack room shared with twenty-nine other women. I was no longer in the fashionable drawing-room in homemade clothes. I wore a uniform that was identical with the other twenty-nine uniforms but, at five feet nine inches tall and with shoulders broader than my twenty-two inch waist, I wore the uniform better than the other twenty-nine. On my first visit to the barrack square, I became the 'marker' of the two-hundred-strong squad and that evening, in the barrack room, when I elected to lie on my cot and read a book instead of going to the NAAFI with the other twenty-nine, they told me with cheerful frankness that I was a 'queer one' but they implied that they accepted me as I was. I hasten to add that the word 'queer' did not have, in 1939, the connotation that it now has in some circles. It was the first time that I had ever felt that I was accepted as myself and not as part of my family or an insignificant member of a student group or an even more insignificant companion-secretary and in being accepted as myself, the person who for convenience had been given a six-digit number, I accepted myself for the first time and began to feel that I had some particular, individual personal value.

"My astonished rabbits were still at the back of my mind but in that noisy rabbit-warren of a barrack room, it was impossible to write of rabbits or of anything else but when I became corporal in charge of the other twenty-nine, which happened within a few weeks, I thought of my airwomen secretly as my rabbits. I watched them, listened to them, helped them write

their letters home, bullied them to bed when they came in drunk, forced them to wash and mend their underwear, man-handled them apart when they indulged in hair-tearing clawing quarrels and discovered some nine months later, when I was posted to be commissioned as an officer, that I loved them. I left them with my rabbit-warren of a mind stored with the things they had said and done and my heart full of love and admiration for their lusty courageous humanity.

". . . I had never known so much raw, rumbustious uninhibited life, I had made the discovery that I loved it and I was also approaching the discovery that you cannot write about rabbits, people, the Highlands of Scotland or anything else with any true understanding unless you love to write and love, also, the subject you write about."[1]

1948. Moved to Jamaica with common-law husband, Sandy Alexander, who was an engineer and later a manager of a sugar plantation. "The estate, to someone like myself, born and bred among the small fields and barren hills of northern Scotland, was enormous, an ocean of waving sugar-cane enclosed, for seven-eights of its circumference of saucer-like valley, by its surrounding hills, while the last eighth was bounded by a curve of the valley of the Rio d 'Oro. The cane gave way on all sides to the bananas and coconuts of the foothills and these in turn gave way to the lumber forests of the higher ground." [Jane Duncan, *My Friend Martha's Aunt,* St. Martin's Press, 1962.[2]]

1956-1958. "In December of 1956 . . . I decided that the time had come, aged forty-six, to make a real effort to put on paper the material that was stuffing my head. Much of this material had been written down a number of times before between 1931 and 1956 and then destroyed but I was now going to try for the final form. I decided to open with *My Friend Muriel*. . . .

"I had always written on quarto paper when I could afford it but in Jamaica the quarto which was imported was American and a little bigger than the British size, so I scoured the house for a book big enough to act as a backing board and what I found was an atlas, of about foolscap size and an inch thick. I still write with a cushion behind me with this atlas on my knees. Its spine wore out from the grip of my left hand: I repaired it with a five-inch strip of sticky-back plastic and now, I note, the plastic has worn through where my left hand takes its grip. It is little wonder, when I think of it, for this atlas has been on my knees for many hours in the course of nearly twenty years."[1]

1958. First book, *My Friend Muriel*, accepted for publication. "At the time of the acceptance of *My Friend Muriel*, I was a housewife who had no connections whatsoever with the world of writing, and living four thousand miles away from London, the center of British publishing.

"It was thus, then, that I entered the world of writing and by coincidence the post brought me the formal contract with the publishers on the morning of my forty-eighth birthday. An association was formed at that time which has remained for all of us, I think, pleasant and rewarding until the present day. It seems to be a fact of life, though, that moments of unclouded happiness are vary rare. At the time of the arrival of the contract, my husband who had been an invalid for some five years, was seriously ill and six weeks later, he died. It was like the closing of one door and the opening of another into the strange new world of writing and publishing which I found very frightening, alone as I was four thousand miles from home, with very little money and an 'unusual' book going into print which might fail utterly to justify even the advance of one hundred pounds which the signing of the contract had brought me. . . .

". . . I had in my possession the manuscript of six more novels and *My Friend Monica* was despatched to London, followed in July by *My Friend Rose* and what was known at that time as *My Friends the Misses Boyd*."[1]

Cameron once remarked that the "only time of interest" about her as a writer was that "in late 1958 and early 1959 I submitted the manuscripts of [my] first seven novels . . . to Macmillan of London and they were accepted *en bloc*. I am led to believe that this was new in British publishing."

1959. Returned to northern Scotland to reside with her Uncle George. ". . . My Uncle George was the George of the Reachfar novels and a great deal more. Tom of the same novels is another facet of him and Angus the Shepherd in my novels about the Cameron family for young people is yet another. The real George was a man so complex and of such stature that one can put down on paper only little bits of him. Fictional characters are usually made up like those Identikit pictures that the police use, the eyes from the description of one witness, the hair from that of another. For a fictional character, one usually takes a trick of speech from one person, a trick of gesture from another, adds a little something of one's own and welds the lot together. But my Uncle George was and still is, in memory, such a deep quarry, so rich, that it needs only a little bit of him to make a fictional man. To portray the whole real man is away far beyond my powers.

"All my characters arise out of real people I have met and in some cases not even met but merely seen across a hotel lounge, for instance, and sometimes only a few words or a gesture are necessary to sow the seed of a fictional character."[1]

Cameron's books for children, about the Cameron family, were all based on her brother's family. "I like to write books for children and about children because I like children and remember what it was like to be a child. I remember the sense of utter and unjust defeat by the total lack of logic of the adult world."[1]

1975. A memoir, *Letter from Reachfar*, published. "I thought it might be of interest if I sketched the background of my life and placed the novels against it, in an endeavour to show how fiction arises out of fact by some mysterious process that I cannot explain.

". . . The origins of the names I use in my writing may be . . . obvious. My mother's maiden name was Janet Sandison, my father was Duncan Cameron and I was baptised Elizabeth Jane. I took my mother's name for my heroine of the Reachfar series and my own second name added to my father's forename for my pseudonym, by way of a belated tribute to my dead parents."[1]

October 20, 1976. Died at The Colony in Scotland. "My novels are spun like a thread out of some store of material that is inside me, they are part of me and private to me until the moment when I post the typescript to my editor. Then come the anxious days until I am told the thing 'will do' and in that moment the relief is enormous and as if an umbilical cord had been cut, the detachment is complete."[1]

FOR MORE INFORMATION SEE: Best Sellers, November 15, 1967, September 15, 1968; *Books and Bookmen,* August, 1968; *Book World,* September 8, 1968; Jane Duncan, *Letter from Reachfar,* St. Martin's, 1976; *Publishers Weekly,* March 8, 1976; *New York Times Book Review,* October 31, 1976; (obituary) *Publishers Weekly,* November 22, 1976.

CANFIELD, Jane White 1897-

PERSONAL: Born April 29, 1897, in Syracuse, N.Y.; daughter of Ernest Ingersol and Katharine Curtin (maiden name, Sage) White; married Charles F. Fuller, September 9, 1922; children: Jane Sage, Isabel, Blair. *Education:* Attended Art Students League, 1918-20, James Earle & Laura Gardin Fraser Studio, and Borglum School, 1920-22; also studied with A. Bourdelle in Paris. *Home:* Guard Hill Rd., Bedford, N.Y. 10506. *Dealer:* Far Gallery, 20 East 80th St., New York, N.Y. 10021.

CAREER: Sculptor. Executed figures for Paul Mellon estate, Upperville, Va., 1940, Miss Porter's School, Farmington, Conn., 1960, Church of St. John of Lattington, Locust Valley, N.Y., 1963, and Memorial Sanctuary, Fishers Island, N.Y., 1969. Exhibited work in group shows, including the World's Fair, N.Y., 1939, Architectural League, Knoedler Gallery and American Academy, and in one-man shows, including those at American-British Art Gallery, New York City, 1951, County Art Gallery, Westbury, N.Y., 1960, Far Gallery, New York City, 1961, 1965, 1974, and Country Art Gallery, Locust Valley, 1971. Work is represented in permanent collections at Whitney Museum of American Art and Cornell University Mu-

But one day two black-backed gulls attack the cygnets. ■ (From *Swan Cove* by Jane White Canfield. Illustrated by Jo Polseno.)

seum of Art. Board chairman, Bedford-Rippowam School, 1933-38; board member, ARC Arts and Skills, Washington, D.C., 1942-45, Planned Parenthood, 1945-55, International Planned Parenthood, 1955-65, and Margaret Sanger Bureau, 1965—.

WRITINGS—For children: *The Frog Prince: A True Story* (illustrated by Winn Smith), Harper, 1970; *Swan Cove* (illustrated by Jo Polseno), Harper, 1978.

CARTER, Forrest 1927(?)-1979

PERSONAL: Born about 1927, in Tennessee; died June 7, 1979, of a heart attack, in Abilene, Tex.; buried in Georgiana, Ala.; son of Clay W. and Naomi (Wales) Carter; married India Thelma Walker. *Home:* Dallas County, Texas.

CAREER: Author of Western fiction. Worked odd jobs, including ranch hand and wood chopper.

WRITINGS: The Rebel Outlaw: Josey Wales, Whipporwill Publishers, 1973, published as *Gone to Texas,* Delacorte, 1975; *The Education of Little Tree* (autobiography), Delacorte, 1976; *The Vengeance Trail of Josey Wales,* Delacorte, 1976; *Watch for Me on the Mountain,* Delacorte, 1978; *Cry Geronimo,* Dell, 1980.

ADAPTATIONS: "The Outlaw Josey Wales" (motion picture), based on the book *Gone to Texas,* Warner Brothers, 1976.

SIDELIGHTS: Orphaned at the age of ten, the half-Cherokee Indian was raised by his grandfather in the Tennessee hill country. Carter, whose Indian name is "Little Tree," had the urge to write from the time he was a young boy, although he never spent more than six months in a classroom. Instead, Carter learned from his grandfather's homespun tales and from fireside readings of the classics. Years later he could still recite any passage from one of Shakespeare's plays. "Ma lasted a year after Pa was gone. That's how I came to live with Granpa and Granma when I was five years old.

"Twice a week, every Saturday and Sunday nights, Granma lit the coal oil lamp and read to us. Lighting the lamp was a luxury, and I'm sure it was done on account of me. We had to be careful of the coal oil. Once a month, me and Granpa walked to the settlement. . . .

"When we went, we always carried a list of books made out by Granma, and Granpa presented the list to the librarian, and turned in the books that Granma had sent back.

"We kept the dictionary checked out all the time, as I had to learn five words a week, starting at the front, which caused me considerable trouble, since I had to try to make up sentences

FORREST CARTER

in my talk through the week using the words. This is hard, when all the words you learn for the week start with A, or B if you're into the B's.

"But there were other books; one was *The Decline and Fall of the Roman Empire* . . . and there were authors like Shelley and Byron. . . ." [Forrest Carter, *The Education of Little Tree*, Delacorte, 1976.¹]

Carter's grandfather taught him "The Way of the Cherokee." "'It is The Way,' he said softly. 'Take only what ye need. When ye take the deer, do not take the best. Take the smaller and the slower and then the deer will grow stronger and always give you meat. Pa-koh, the panther, knows and so must ye.'

"Granpa lived *with* the game, not *at* it. The white mountain men were a hardy lot and Granpa bore with them well. But they would take their dogs and clatter all over the mountains chasing game this way and that, until everything run for cover. If they saw a dozen turkey, why they killed a dozen turkey, if they could.

"But they respected Granpa as a master woodsman. I could see it in their eyes and the touching of their hat brims when they met him at the crossroads store. They stayed out of Granpa's hollows and mountains with their guns and dogs, whilst they complained a lot about the game getting scarcer and scarcer where they was. Granpa often shook his head at their comments and never said anything. But he told me. They would never understand The Way of the Cherokee.

"If you could be a giant and could look down on its bends and curves, you would know the spring branch is a river of life.

"I was the giant. Being over two feet tall, I squatted, giant-like, to study the little marshes where trickles of the stream eddied off into low places. . . .

"Rock minnows darted to chase musk bugs scuttering across the stream. When you held a musk bug in your hand, it smelled real sweet and thick.

"Granma said I had done right, for when you come on something that is good, first thing to do is share it with who ever you can find; that way, the good spreads out to where no telling it will go. Which is right.

"I got pretty wet, splashing in the spring branch, but Granma never said anything. Cherokees never scolded their children for having anything to do with the woods.

"Granpa said that since whiskey-making was the only trade he knowed, and since I ws five coming on to six, then he reckined I would have to learn that trade. He advised that when I got older, I might want to switch trades but I would know whiskey-making, and could always have a trade to fall back on in times when I was pushed otherwise to make a living.

"Granpa had a mark for his whiskey. It was his maker's mark, scratched on top of every fruit jar lid. Granpa's mark was shaped like a tomahawk, and nobody else in the mountains used it. Each maker had his own mark. Granpa said that when he passed on, which more than likely he would eventually do, I would git the mark handed down to me. He had got it from his Pa. At Mr. Jenkins' store, there was men who come in and would not buy any other whiskey but Granpa's, with his mark.

"Granpa said that as a matter of fact, since me and him was more or less partners now, half of the mark was owned by me at the present time. This was the first time I had ever owned anything, as to call it mine. So I was right proud of our mark, and seen to it, as much as Granpa, that we never turned out no bad whiskey under our mark. Which we didn't.

"I was learning five words a week out of the dictionary, and Granma would explain the meanings, then had me put the words in sentences. I used my sentences considerable on the way to the store. This would get Granpa to stop while he figured out what I was saying. I could catch up and rest with my fruit jars. Sometimes Granpa would totally knock out words, saying I didn't have to use that word no more, which speeded me up considerable in the dictionary.

"Me and Granpa thought Indian. Later people would tell me that this is naive—but I knew—and I remembererd what Granpa said about 'words.' If it is 'naive,' it does not matter, for it is also good. Granpa said it would always carry me through . . . which it has. . . .

"Granpa was half Scot, but he thought Indian. Such seemed to be the case with others, like the great Red Eagle, Bill Weatherford, or Emperor McGilvery or McIntosh. They gave themselves, as the Indian did, to nature, not trying to subdue it, or pervert it, but to live with it. And so they loved the thought, and loving it grew to be it, so that they could not think as the white man.

(From the movie "The Outlaw Josey Wales," starring Chief Dan George and Clint Eastwood, based on the book, *Gone to Texas*. Released by Warner Brothers, 1976.)

"Granpa told me. The Indian brought something to trade and laid it at the white man's feet. If he saw nothing he wanted, he picked up his wares and walked off. The white man, not understanding, called him an 'Indian giver' meaning one who gives and then takes back. This is not so. If the Indian gives a gift, he will make no ceremony of it, but will simply leave it to be found.

"As to folks saying, 'How!' and then laughing when they see an Indian, Granpa said it all come about over a couple of hundred years. He said every time the Indian met a white man, the white man commenced to ask him: *how* are you feeling, or *how* are your people, or *how* are you getting along, or *how* is the game where you come from, and so on. He said the Indian come to believe that the white man's favorite subject was *how;* and so, being polite, when he met the white man, he figured he would just say *how*, and then let the [man] . . . talk about whichever *how* he wanted to. Granpa said people laughing at that was laughing at an Indian who was trying to be courteous and considerate.

"Now I was six. Maybe it was my birthday that reminded Granma time was passing. She lit the lamp nearly every evening and read, and pushed me on my dictionary studying. I was down into the B's, and one of the pages was torn out. Granma said that page was not important, and the next time me and Granpa went to the settlement, he paid for and bought the dictionary from the library. It cost seventy-five cents.

". . . Granma wrote to our kin in the Nations (we always called Oklahoma 'the Nations' for that is what it was supposed to be, until it was taken from the Indians and made a state). . . .

"He had come all through the winter and the spring, once a month, regular as sundown, and spent the night. Sometimes he would stay over with us a day and another night. Mr. Wine was a back peddler.

"He learnt me to tell time. He would twist the hands of the clock around and ask me what time it was, and would laugh when I missed. It didn't take me long before I knew everything.

"Mr. Wine said I was getting a good education. He said there wasn't hardly any young'uns atall at my age that knew about Mr. Macbeth or Mr. Napoleon, or that studied dictionaries. He learnt me figures.

"I could already figure money somewhat, being in the whiskey trade, but Mr. Wine would take out some paper and a little pencil and put figures down. He would show me how to make the figures and how to add them, and take away, and multiply. Granpa said I was might near better than anybody he had ever seen, doing figures.

"Mr. Wine said figuring was important. He said education was a two-part proposition. One part was technical, which was how you moved ahead in your trade. He said he was for getting more modern in that end of education. But, he said, the other part you had better stick to and not change it. He called it valuing.

"Mr. Wine said if you learnt to place a value on being honest and thrifty, on doing your best, and on caring for folks; this was more important than anything. He said if you was not taught these values, then no matter how modern you got about the technical part, you was not going to get anywheres atall.

"Willburn [a friend] asked me what I was going to do when I growed up. I told him I was going to be an Indian like Granpa and Willow John and live in the mountains. . . .

"During the summer I come up to seven years.

"We was to have two more years together; me and Granpa and Granma. Maybe we knew time was getting close, but we didn't speak of it. Granma went everywhere now with me and Granpa. We lived it full. We pointed out things like the reddest of the leaves in the fall, to make sure the others saw it, the bluest violet in the spring, so we all tasted and shared the feelings together."[1]

After his grandmother and grandfather died, Carter at the age of ten, was on his own. "I lasted out the winter; me and Blue Boy and Little Red [his dogs] until spring. Then I went to Hangin' Gap and buried the still's copper pot and worm. I was not much good at it, and had not learned the trade as I had ought to. I knew Granpa would not want anybody else using it to turn out bad wares.

"I took the whiskey trade money that Granma had set out for me and determined I would head west, across the mountains to the Nations, Blue Boy and Little Red went with me. We just closed the cabin door one morning and walked away.

"At the farms I asked for work, if they would not let me keep Blue Boy and Little Red then I would more on. Granpa said a feller owed that much to his hounds. Which is right."[1]

Carter spent most of his life moving from one ranching job to another. He continued his education in small town libraries. "I traveled for most of my life looking for work. I remember going to the back door of a ranch house north of Dallas when I was almost starved to death. I asked the owner if he had work to be done, and he said no. Then he asked me if I was hungry, and when I said yes, he offered me a meal. But I wouldn't take it without working first. The ranch owner was Don Josey. We became great friends through the year."[Dick Davis, "The Little Tree in Forrest," *Writer's Digest,* May, 1977.[2]]

It wasn't until the age of forty that Carter's boyhood dream was realized, when in an effort to raise money for a Creek Indian Settlement, he paid for the printing of his first story. He eventually sent copies to several agents and publishers, and also to Hollywood actors. As a result, the story was published by Delacorte as *Gone to Texas* and movie rights were purchased by Clint Eastwood, who produced and starred in the film version.

Movie fame insured Carter's reputation as an author, and he pursued writing on a full-time basis until his death at the age of fifty-two. Never forgetting his Indian heritage, Carter dedicated each of his books to a different tribe, and donated a significant portion of his earnings to Indian causes. He preferred to dress simply, in blue jeans and an old cowboy hat, and shied away from publicity and the bustle of city life.

"I don't like to make people think I'm looking for publicity on this, because I'm not. It is just the thing to do—and nothing else needs to be said.

"I just write down what I've experienced by living with my granpa and what I studied in small-town libraries. But I do make it as authentic as possible. That's my philosophy on writing, and it's a good one for young writers to follow. Just simply be honest and true. Have a kinship with your readers and try to take them to the place you're writing about.

"Libraries are the most wonderful places in the whole world. I think the greatest honor would be for a man to have a library named after him. That would indicate to me a great man."[2]

Carter's novel *Gone to Texas* has been translated into Italian, French, and Spanish. His autobiography, *The Education of Little Tree,* tells the story of his first ten years, including his insights into Indian culture.

FOR MORE INFORMATION SEE: New York Times Book Review, June 29, 1975, March 18, 1979; *Times Literary Supplement,* November 14, 1975; Forrest Carter, *The Education of Little Tree,* Delacorte, 1976; *Writer's Digest,* May, 1977; (obituary) *Reporter* (Abilene, Tex.), June 9, 1979.

CHAPMAN, Gaynor 1935-

PERSONAL: Born May 28, 1935, in London, England; daughter of Kenneth Martyn (an engineer) and Eva (Harle) Chapman; married Christopher Albert (an advertising director), April 27, 1963 (divorced, 1972); children: Mark, Simon. *Education:* Attended Epsom School of Art, 1951-52; Kingston School of Art, N.D.D., 1955; Royal College of Art, A.R.C.A., 1958. *Politics:* Liberal. *Religion:* "Agnostic?" *Home and office:* 21 Elm Gardens, Claygate, Surrey KT10 0JS, England.

(From *Treasure in Devil's Bay* by Alexis Brown. Illustrated by Gaynor Chapman.)

GAYNOR CHAPMAN

CAREER: Illustrator and graphic designer, 1960—. Newman Neame Ltd., London, England, designer, 1958; Thames and Hudson Ltd., London, England, illustrator, 1958-60; Brighton College of Art, Brighton, England, part-time lecturer, 1958-63; Kingston Polytechnic, part-time lecturer, 1969-70; Brighton Polytechnic, part-time lecturer, 1970-80. *Member:* The 1957 Society, Society of Authors. *Awards, honors: The Luck Child* was runner-up for the Kate Greenaway Medal of Library Association (England), 1968; elected a fellow of the Society of Industrial Artists and Designers, 1979.

WRITINGS—For children; self-illustrated: (Reteller) Brothers Grimm, *The Luck Child*, Atheneum, 1968.

Illustrator: Elfrida Vipont, *The Story of Christianity in Britain*, M. Joseph, 1960; M. Burton and W. Shepherd, *The Wonder Book of Our Earth*, Ward, Lock, 1961; Stuart Piggot, editor, *The Dawn of Civilization* (adult), McGraw, 1961; *Postmen Through the Ages*, H. M. Stationery Office, 1961; Kurt Rowland, editor, *Wealth from the Ground*, Weidenfeld & Nicholson, 1962; Alexis Brown, *Treasure in Devils' Bay*, Blackie, 1962; Edward Bacon, editor, *Vanished Civilizations of the Ancient World* (adult), McGraw, 1963 (published in England as *Vanished Civilizations: Forgotten Peoples of the Ancient World*, Thames & Hudson, 1963); K. Rowland, editor, *Our Living World*, Weidenfeld & Nicolson, 1964; Edward Blishen, editor, *Miscellany Two*, Oxford University Press, 1965; Henry Garnett, *Treasures of Yesterday*, Natural History Press, 1965; Mimoko Ishii, *The Doll's Day for Yoskio*, translated by Yone Mizuta, Oxford University Press, 1965; Mervyn Skipper, *The Fooling of King Alexander*, Atheneum, 1967; Eilis Dillon, *The Wise Man on the Mountain*, Atheneum, 1969; *Aesop's Fables*, Atheneum, 1971; Hans Christian Andersen, *The Jumping Match*, Hamish Hamilton, 1973; Donald Swann, *Around the Piano with Donald Swann*, Bodley Head, 1979.

WORK IN PROGRESS: Four self-illustrated children's books, *Patch, Stripey, Bess,* and *Freda,* about a dog, a cat, a donkey, and a fox.

SIDELIGHTS: "I lived in Merton Park, London as a small child and I started school in 1940, an unfortunate time. I set off each day with my gas mask and specified pack of food. I particularly remember the chocolate coated raisins because I loved them. When we returned home from school many of us were worried that our home might have been bombed. During air-raids lessons were conducted in the air-raid shelters. At home we often used to sleep in an underground shelter made by my father in the garden. I thought that I should like to be a nurse when I grew up.

"My childhood was unsettled, moving from one area and from one school to another. I enjoyed living in Banstead, Surrey because of the surrounding woodlands, and we spent several months living on a farm in Cornwall during the 'Blitz.'

"When the war was over in 1945 we moved to Bookham in Surrey and lived happily in a coverted barn on my aunt and uncle's farm while my parents had a new house built. Much of the wood for the house was provided by my mother's father who was a timber importer. There were ducks, chickens and wild rabbits on the farm which had five acres of woodland. My aunt, Mrs. Frost, told me about a neighbour she used to know who illustrated children's books. This interested me greatly and I decided to become an illustrator. Quite by chance I later

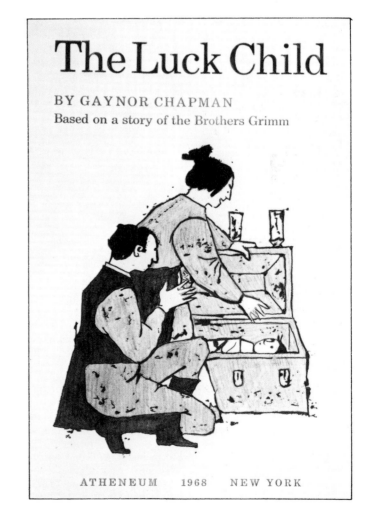

(From *The Luck Child* retold by Gaynor Chapman, based on a story by the Brothers Grimm. Illustrated by Gaynor Chapman.)

discovered that the head of the department at Brighton College of Art where I taught part time, was this aunt's previous neighbour!

"A great deal of my energy since 1970 has gone into bringing up my two sons single-handedly. I don't regret this because it was essential and being creative is not restricted to those who write, paint or compose music. I based my last four books, *Patch, Stripey, Bess,* and *Freda,* on an early book written for my children when they were small. *The Luck Child* was illustrated entirely during the evenings when the children were in bed.

"I think that books should be well considered and designed to last in contrast to magazine illustrations which need to make an immediate impact. . . .

"I like to consider myself as a designer who illustrates because I am interested in the broad aspects of design. For instance a book jacket is really a poster which has to attract the eye and convey to a reader some idea of the contents of the book. I don't like writing about my work per se because I feel that it's impossible to discuss visual elements in literary terms.

"I do find a conflict between the desire to produce work which has value and integrity and the desire to earn money. I think it is appalling that so many talented writers and illustrators in Britain are rewarded so poorly for their work."

In addition to the books Chapman has illustrated, she has done design work for publishers including Heinemann, Hutchinson, Collins, and J. Cape. She has also designed posters for London Transport, covers for *The Radio Times,* brochures for Air France, brochures, a poster, and a window display for Barclay Bank Ltd., a mural for the ship *S.S. Dover* as well as designs for Esso Petroleum Co., Shell Chemicals, American Express and I.C.I. Wallpapers.

Chapman's work has been reproduced in the Swiss *Graphis Annual* five times.

COOPER, Lester (Irving) 1919-

PERSONAL: Born January 20, 1919, in New York, N.Y.; son of Samuel and Clara (Levine) Cooper; married Audrey Rosemary Levey (a writer), July 1, 1949; children: Kim, Elizabeth, Matthew. *Education:* Attended New York University, 1936, and Columbia University, 1936. *Home:* 45 South Morningside Dr., Westport, Conn. 06880. *Office:* ABC News, 7 West 66th St., New York, N.Y. 10023.

CAREER: Television writer and producer. Warner Bros., Inc., Hollywood, Calif., writer, 1937-41; J. Arthur Rank—British National Pictures, London, England, screenwriter, 1945-49; *Esquire* magazine, New York, N.Y., chief copy editor, 1949-50; Lester Cooper Productions, New York, N.Y., writer, 1953-55; Columbia Broadcasting System, New York, N.Y., writer, 1953-55; National Broadcasting System, New York, N.Y., writer, 1955-58; Westinghouse Broadcasting Co., New York, N.Y., supervising producer, head evening writer, 1959-61; "Exploring the Universe" series, PBS-TV, New York, N.Y., producer, 1962-64; ABC News, New York, N.Y., executive producer, 1965—. *Military service:* U.S. Army, 1941-45. *Member:* Directors' Guild of America, Writers' Guild of Amer-

ica. *Awards, honors:* Recipient of Television Journalism Award from the American Medical Association, 1967; Peabody Award, 1968, for "Hemingway's Spain"; Albert Lasker Medical Journalism Award, 1970; Peabody Award, 1971, and Emmy Award from the National Academy of Television Arts and Sciences, 1974, for television series, "Make a Wish"; Emmy Award, 1976, Peabody Award, 1976, Action for Children's Television Award, 1977, 1978, 1979, and Ohio State Award, 1979, for "Animals, Animals, Animals" television series.

WRITINGS—"Animals, Animals, Animals" series; based on ABC television's children's series of the same title; all edited by Julie Duffy; all published by Handel & Co.: *Starring Dogs and Dolphins* (illustrated by Bette Griffin), 1978; *Starring Pelicans, Cats, and Frogs* (illustrated by Ed Cage and Novle Rogers; photographs by H. Michael Stewart), 1978; *Starring Sharks,* 1980; *Starring Snakes,* 1982.

SIDELIGHTS: A native of New York City, Cooper attended Columbia and New York Universities. He and his wife, Audrey, and their three children, currently make their home in Westport, Connecticut.

Cooper began his career as a film writer for Warner Brothers studios in Hollywood in 1937. Drafted in 1941, he spent the next five years in the U.S. Army where he wrote the first joint British-American film on the invasion of a French town.

After the war, Cooper stayed in England writing feature films for J. Arthur Rank and British National Productions.

In 1949, Cooper returned to the United States and started his own film production company. He then joined *Esquire* magazine as chief copywriter and also wrote free-lance magazine pieces.

In 1953, he joined CBS News as a writer on the "Eye on New York" series. He also wrote a CBS News special titled "A Day Called X" and worked as a writer for a series titled "FYI."

Departing from CBS News in 1956, Cooper joined NBC News as a writer for the "Today" show starring Dave Garroway. After several years, he left NBC to become head-writer and supervising producer of "PM," the 90-minute nightly news and talk show with Mike Wallace for Westinghouse Broadcasting Company.

Free-lancing again, Cooper produced a series of eleven shows with Dave Garroway called "Exploring the Universe," which was nominated for an Emmy Award.

Since he joined ABC News as a staff producer in 1964, Cooper has been associated with many outstanding and frequently award-winning news specials. He was named an executive producer with the ABC News Documentary Unit in September, 1967, and in 1971 he was chosen as executive producer and writer of the children's series, "Make a Wish," which he created, and which won Peabody and Emmy Awards.

In 1976, Cooper created the ABC News children's series, "Animals, Animals, Animals," which has been honored with the Emmy, Peabody, Ohio State and ACT Awards and has received the "Award of Excellence" from the Coalition on Children and Television.

Cooper's credits include those of producer, writer and executive producer of the two "National Polling Day" specials and producer, writer and executive producer of "Hemingway's Spain: A Love Affair"; "The Right to Live," a study of Medicare and Medicade; "Can You Hear Me?" the story of the special problems encountered by a child born deaf; "Heart Attack"; and "This Land Is Mine," an examination of some places of great natural beauty still remaining in America.

Cooper also served as executive producer for the ABC News "Summer Focus" series in 1969 and as executive producer of "View from the White House," which featured Mrs. Lyndon B. Johnson.

Other ABC News programs Cooper has been associated with include: "P.O.W."; Next of Kin"; "The Beautiful Blue and Red Danube"; "War in the Skies"; "Southern Accents: Northern Ghettos"; "Marathon: The Story of the Young Drug Users"; "Who in '68"; and "Take a Deep, Deadly Breath."

Since his first ABC News assignment as a writer-producer for the weekly public affairs series, "ABC Scope," he has produced shows which received a total of fourteen Emmy Award nominations, three Peabody Awards and two Emmys.

"If I have discovered anything over the years, it is that inspiration is no substitute for sitting down and doing it."

COREN, Alan   1938-

PERSONAL: Born June 27, 1938, in London, England; son of Samuel (a builder) and Martha (Phelps-Cholmondeley) Coren; married Anne Kasriel (a doctor), October 14, 1963; children: Giles, Victoria. *Education:* Wadham College, Oxford University, B.A., 1960, M.A., 1970; attended University of Minnesota, 1961, Yale University, 1962, and University of California, Berkeley, 1962-63. *Home:* 26 Ranulf Rd., London, England. *Agent:* A.D. Peters & Co. Ltd., 10 Buckingham St., London WC2N 4DD, England: *Office:* Punch Magazine, 23-27 Tudor St., London EC4Y OHR, England.

CAREER: Punch magazine, London, England, assistant editor, 1963-67, literary editor, 1967-69, deputy editor, 1969-77, editor, 1978—. Television critic for *The Times* (London), 1971—; writer of columns, "Alan Coren" for *Daily Mail*, 1972-77, and "Alan Coren's Monday View" for *Evening Standard*, 1977—. Rector of St. Andrew's University, 1973-76.

WRITINGS—Children's fiction; all illustrated by John Astrop; all published by Robson, except as noted: *Buffalo Arthur*, 1976, Little, Brown, 1978; *Arthur the Kid*, 1976, Little, Brown, 1978; *The Lone Arthur*, 1976, Little, Brown, 1978; *Railroad Arthur*, 1977, Little, Brown, 1978; *Klondike Arthur*, 1977, Little, Brown, 1979; *Arthur's Last Stand*, 1977, Little, Brown, 1979; *Arthur and the Great Detective*, 1979, Little, Brown, 1980; *Arthur and the Bellybutton Diamond*, 1979; *Arthur and the Purple Panic*, 1981; *Arthur Versus the Rest*, 1982.

Adult satirical fiction: *The Dog It Was That Died*, Hutchinson, 1965; *All Except the Bastard*, Gollancz, 1969; *The Sainty Inspector*, Robson, 1974, St. Martin's Press, 1975; *The Collected Bulletins of Idi Amin*, Robson, 1974; *The Further Bulletins of Idi Amin*, Robson, 1975; *Golfing for Cats*, Robson, 1975, St. Martin's Press, 1976; *The Lady from Stalingrad Mansions*, St. Martin's Press, 1977; *The Peanut Papers*, St. Martin's Press, 1977; *The Rhinestone as Big as the Ritz*, St. Martin's Press, 1978; *Tissues for Men*, Robson, 1980; *The Cricklewood Diet*, Robson, 1982; *Present Laughter*, Robson, 1982.

ALAN COREN

Television scripts: "That Was the Week That Was," BBC-TV, 1963-64; "Not So Much a Programme," BBC-TV, 1965-66; "At the Eleventh Hour," BBC-TV, 1967; "The Punch Review," BBC-TV, 1976-77; "Every Day in Every Way" (play), BBC-TV, 1977; "Nuts" (situation comedy), Yorkshire-TV, 1977; "The Losers" (series), ATV, 1979.

Radio plays: "The Shelter," BBC-Radio, 1965; "End As a Man," BBC-Radio, 1965; "Black and White and Red All Over," BBC-Radio, 1966.

Documentaries: "The British Hero," BBC-TV, 1972; "A Place in History," Thames-TV, 1974.

Contributor to *Atlantic, Playboy, TV Guide, Harper's, Cosmopolitan*, and *Sunday Times* (London).

WORK IN PROGRESS: A feature filmscript.

SIDELIGHTS: "My greatest pleasure in recent years came from being told, in a *Washington Post* review of *Golfing for Cats*, that I was 'the first transAtlantic humorist since Thurber and Perelman.' That pleasure emanates from the desire throughout my working life to be able to commend myself to both cultures. Educated in both countries, steeped in the literature (particularly the humour) of both countries, and loving both countries equally, I have always wanted to have a part in what one might call the CisAtlantic Tradition. I took the ultimate risk with the

And, taking a firm grip on his stick with one hand and a firm grip on the edge of the canvas with the other, he whipped off the cover.

There, crouched amidships, sat no stowaway but the ship's boatswain! ■ (From *Arthur and the Great Detective* by Alan Coren. Illustrated by John Astrop.)

book, *The Peanut Papers,* ostensibly written by Mrs. Lillian Carter. I doubt that an English humorist has ever stuck his neck out quite so far!

"I am as happy with daily journalism as I am with fiction, drama, TV writing, reviewing, or anything else. To me, it is all writing: I see no point, for me, in exclusivity of area—there are things I wish to say which can't be said in fiction, therefore must be said in journalism, there are things which don't work as drama but will as magazine stories, there's stuff I want to say to kids that I can't say to adults. And it shouldn't be forgotten that variety, for a writer, is the best form of creative regeneration."

HOBBIES AND OTHER INTERESTS: Riding, shooting, collecting English Delft pottery, playing bridge, and rebuilding old motorcars.

FOR MORE INFORMATION SEE: Clive James, *The Metropolitan Critic,* Farber, 1974.

Give a little love to a child, and you get a great deal back.

—John Ruskin

COVILLE, Bruce   1950-

PERSONAL: Born May 16, 1950, in Syracuse, N.Y.; son of Arthur J. (a sales engineer) and Jean (an executive secretary; maiden name, Chase) Coville; married Katherine Dietz (an illustrator), October 11, 1969; children; Orion Sean, Cara Joy. *Education:* Attended Duke University and State University of New York at Binghamton; State University of New York at Oswego, B.A., 1974. *Religion:* "Eclectic." *Residence:* Syracuse, N.Y. 13210. *Agent:* Scott Meredith Literary Agency, Inc., 845 Third Ave., New York, N.Y. 10022.

CAREER: Author and playwright. Wetzel Road Elementary, Liverpool, N.Y., teacher, 1974—. *Seniority* magazine, associate editor, 1983. Worked as camp counselor, grave digger, and toy maker.

WRITINGS—Juvenile; illustrated by wife, Katherine Coville: *The Foolish Giant,* Lippincott, 1978; *Sarah's Unicorn,* Lippincott, 1979; *The Monster's Ring,* Pantheon, 1982. Contributor to *Harper's Bookletter.*

Plays; music by Angela Peterson; produced by Syracuse Musical Theater: "The Dragonslayers," 1981; "Out of the Blue," 1982; (with Barbara Russell) "It's Midnight: Do You Know Where Your Toys Are?," 1983.

WORK IN PROGRESS: "Argyle the Windmaker," a fantasy with mythical undertones; *Sarah and the Dragon,* a sequel to *Sarah's Unicorn.*

SIDELIGHTS: "I was raised in Phoenix, a small town in central New York. Actually, I lived well outside the town, around the corner from my grandparents' dairy farm, which was the site of my happiest childhood times. I still have fond memories of the huge barns with their mows and lofts, mysterious relics, and jostling cattle.

"It was a wonderful place for a child to grow up. In addition to the farm there was a swamp behind my house, and a rambling wood beyond that, both of which were conducive to all kinds of imaginative games.

"Despite this wonderful setting, much of what I remember from that time went on in my head, when I was reading, or thinking and dreaming about what I had read. I was an absolute bookaholic.

"My father had something to do with this. He was a travelling salesman, a gruff but loving man, who never displayed an overwhelming interest in books. But if anyone were to ask me what was the best thing he ever did for me I could reply without hesitation that he read me *Tom Swift in the City of Gold.* Why he happened to read this to me I was never quite certain. But it changed my life. One night after supper he took me into the living room, had me sit in his lap, and opened a thick, ugly brown book (this was the *original* Tom Swift) and proceeded to open a whole new world for me. I was enthralled, listened raptly, waited anxiously for the next night and the next, resented an intrusion, and reread the book several times later on my own. It is the only book I can ever remember him reading to me, but it changed my life. I was hooked on books.

"I think it was sixth grade when I first realized that writing was something that I could do, and wanted to do very much. As it happened, I had spent most of that year making life miserable for my teacher by steadfastly failing to respond to the many creative devices she had to stimulate us to write.

Sarah gave Oakhorn carrots.
And Oakhorn taught Sarah to talk
to the other animals.

(From *Sarah's Unicorn* by Bruce Coville. Illustrated by Katherine Coville.)

BRUCE COVILLE

Then one day she simply (finally!) just let us write—told us that we had a certain amount of time to produce a short story of substance. Freed from writing about topics imposed from without, I cut loose, and over the next several days found that I loved what I was doing.

"This may not have been the first time that I knew I wanted to write, but its the time that I remember.

"I began to write with an eye toward publication when I was seventeen, and when I was nineteen my mother-in-law-to-be gave me a copy of *Winnie the Pooh* to read, and I suddenly knew that what I really wanted to write was children's books— to give to other children the joy that I got from books when I was young.

"This is the key to what I write now. I try, with greater or lesser success, to make my stories the kinds of things that I would have enjoyed myself when I was young; to write the books I wanted to read, but never found. My writing works best when I remember that bookish child who adored reading and gear the work toward him. It falters when I forget him.

"Myth is very important to me. My picture books have firm roots in basic mythic patterns. Hopefully, the patterns do not intrude, but provide a structure and depth that enhances my work.

"I have been deeply influenced in this respect by the work of Robert Graves and Joseph Campbell. The basic mythic pattern, old as man, deep as space, true as the sky, is represented in myriad forms and provides a way to make some sense of this muddled world of ours.

"This 'making sense' is a process that generally takes a lifetime and yet, sadly, it is all too often never even begun. To utilize myth as a guide in this quest one must be familiar with its patterns and structures, a familiarity that is best gained from reading or hearing myth and its reconstructions from earliest childhood on.

"I do not expect a child to read my picture books and suddenly discover the secret of the universe. I do hope that something from my works will tuck itself away in the child's mind, ready to present itself as a piece of the puzzle on some future day when he or she is busy constructing a view of the world that will provide at least a modicum of hope and dignity.

"This may seem like a long-term goal and a minimal result for the work involved, but I am, after all, a teacher. This has always been our lot. We deal with a child for a year, pour our hearts and souls into his development, and then send him on his way with the scant hope that somehow, someday, some little of what we have tried to do may present itself to him when it is needed.

"But this is idle speculation. The first and foremost job in writing is to tell a whacking good story. You just have to hope it might mean something before you're done."

DONALD CREWS

(From *Truck* by Donald Crews. Illustrated by the author.)

CREWS, Donald 1938-

PERSONAL: Born August 30, 1938, in Newark, N.J.; son of Asah (trackman for the railroad) and Marshanna (dressmaker; maiden name, White); married Ann Jonas, January 28, 1963; children: Nina Melissa, Amy Marshanna. *Education:* Attended Cooper Union, 1956-59. *Residence:* New York, N.Y. *Office:* % Greenwillow Books, 105 Madison Ave., New York, N.Y. 10016.

CAREER: Free-lance artist, photographer, and designer. *Dance Magazine*, New York City, assistant art director, 1959-60. *Military service:* U.S. Army, 1961-63. *Awards, honors:* American Institute of Graphic Arts 50 Books of the Year, 1968, for *We Read: A to Z*; chosen by Childrens Book Council for Children's Book Showcase, 1974, for *Eclipse;* American Institute of Graphic Arts Book Show selection, 1979, for *Rain;* Caldecott Honor Book, 1979, for *Freight Train*, 1981, for *Truck*.

WRITINGS—All for children; all self-illustrated: *We Read: A to Z*, Harper, 1967; *Ten Black Dots*, Scribner, 1968; *Freight Train* (ALA Notable Book), Greenwillow Books, 1978; *Truck*, (Junior Literary Guild Selection; ALA Notable Book) Greenwillow Books, 1980; *Light*, Greenwillow Books, 1981; *Harbor*, Greenwillow Books, 1982; *Carousel*, Greenwillow Books, 1982; *Parade*, Greenwillow Books, 1982.

Illustrator: Harry Milgrom, *ABC Science Experiments*, Crowell, 1970; J. Richard Dennis, *Fractions Are Parts of Things*, Crowell, 1971; H. Milgrom, *ABC of Ecology*, Macmillan, 1972; Franklyn M. Branley, *Eclipse: Darkness in Daytime*, Crowell, 1973; Robert Kalan, *Rain*, Greenwillow Books, 1978; R. Kalan, *Blue Sea*, Greenwillow Books, 1979; Dorothy de Wit, editor, *The Talking Stone: An Anthology of Native American Tales and Legends*, Greenwillow Books, 1979.

ADAPTATIONS: ''Freight Train'' (sound filmstrip), Educational Enrichment Material, 1980; ''Truck'' (sound filmstrip), Live Oak Media, 1981.

SIDELIGHTS: Crews attended Arts High School in Newark, New Jersey where he grew up. ''I've drawn and sketched for as long as I can remember. We all did—my older brother and sister, also my younger sister. My mother is an accomplished craftswoman.''

Crews, an artist and illustrator whose work has appeared in the American Institute of Graphic Arts Book Shows and the *Graphis* Annual, has written and illustrated books of his own as well as those of other authors. ''*Freight Train* came out of my past. Summers always began with a train trip to Florida—three days and two nights from Newark to Cottondale, where my mother was born and my grandparents, uncles, cousins, relatives, and assorted acquaintances resided. My grandparents maintained a working farm, small, but complete with cows, chickens, horses, mules, pigs, dogs, corn, peanuts, sweet potatoes, sugarcane, and cotton. We were the summer labor corps.

''As important and exciting as the farm was, [was] the trip down. Diesel and electric trains were used as far south as Washington, D.C. There they were exchanged for steam engines. My grandparents' porch is about 150 yards from the rail line. It was from there that for the next three months we watched trains pass. Freights were frequent and long, counting them a favorite activity. It is from this memory of the summers in Cottondale that *Freight Train* comes.

''All children like to make marks on paper, from scribbles to coloring books. Encouragement can turn casual markings into controlled drawings, and with still more direction and encouragement, drawings can become meaningful forms of self-expression. Introducing new media and new art forms—painting, sculpture, and collage—can stimulate their desire to express themselves from within themselves, and they become artists.

''My training and the process of development is from a designer's point of view. I attempt to isolate an area of interest and to involve my readers in my excitement about that area.

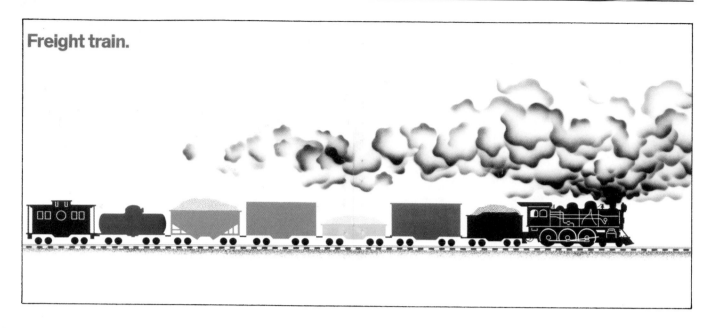

(From *Freight Train* by Donald Crews. Illustrated by the author.)

"Style is less important than effect. Both *Freight Train* and *Truck* for instance are involved primarily with movement. The visualization of that idea is quite different in each. I've even utilized photography in one picture book. The photographs are taken from the same simple, stylized point of view as my graphic images.

"My first children's book *We Read: A to Z* was a design project. I assigned myself the task of creating a broader more involved project for my portfolio. It's purpose was not to be published but to simply convince prospective art directors and editors of my worth as a designer. *We Read* was designed and executed while I was still in the army, the fall of 1962 and spring 1963. It was used as intended until 1967 when it was published by Harper & Row. *Ten Black Dots* (an alphabet primer, number primer) followed as a companion book.

"The people I worked with at Harper & Row prodded me until I admitted to having created a book that no one seemed to want, I had submitted my creation to several German publishers, with no luck.

"Success follows success and I continue to work as long as people continue to respond to the things I do.

"There is tremendous pleasure as a designer/artist in being able to select a topic and have that selection and interpretation appreciated by so many people. Critical acclaim is icing on the cake.

"From my very first book until now I've been working with the same group of wonderful people, editors, art director, friends—'family.' It makes my task much simpler, although the space in between the last effort and the next is always forboding."

Crews' works are included in the Kerlan Collection at the University of Minnesota.

FOR MORE INFORMATION SEE: Lee Kingman and others, compilers, *Illustrators of Children's Books: 1967-1976,* Horn Book, 1978.

DAVIDSON, Raymond   1926-
   (R. Davidson)

PERSONAL: Born August 7, 1926, in Brooklyn, N.Y.; son of Jens Nicholai (a carpenter) and Johanna (Ribaas) Davidson; married Madeleine Violett, August 26, 1955 (divorced, 1965); children: (step-daughter) Maggie Dimond (Mrs. Jon Hale Glick). *Education:* University of San Francisco State College, B.A., 1953; attended Art Students League, New York, N.Y., 1946-47. *Home:* 300 East 33rd St., Apt. 1G, New York, N.Y. 10016. *Office:* Doubleday & Co., Inc., 245 Park Ave., New York, N.Y. 10017.

CAREER: Illustrator. Doubleday & Co., New York, N.Y., book designer and illustrator, 1960—. *Exhibitions*—One man shows: Sagittarius Gallery, New York, N.Y., 1962; Hammerquist Gallery, New York, N.Y., 1982. *Military service:* U.S. Navy, 1944-45.

ILLUSTRATOR: Robert Newton Peck, *The Happy Sadist,* Doubleday, 1962; Jean Dutourd, *The Last of the Redskins,* Doubleday, 1965; Joyce Kissock Lubbhold, *This Half of the Apple Is Mine,* Doubleday, 1965; Ilka Chase, *Second Spring and Two Potatoes,* Doubleday, 1965; Roland Topor, *The Tenant,* Doubleday, 1966; Noel Coward, *Bon Voyage,* Doubleday, 1968; Alfred Andersch, *Efraim's Book,* translated by Ralph Manheim, Doubleday, 1970; David Slavitt, *Anagrams,* Doubleday, 1970; D. Slavitt, *Eclogues of Virgil,* Doubleday, 1971; Yevgeny Yevtushenko, *Stolen Apples,* Doubleday, 1971; Jean Shepherd, *Wanda Hickey's Night of Golden Memories and Other Disasters,* Doubleday, 1971; D. Slavitt, *The Eclogues and Georgics of Virgil,* Doubleday, 1972; Lucien Stryk, *Zen Poems of China and Japan,* Anchor, 1973; Calvin Trillin,

American Fried, Doubleday, 1974; D. Slavitt, *Vital Signs*, Doubleday, 1975; Beverly Keller, *The Genuine, Ingenius, Thrift Shop Genie, Clarissa Mae Bean and Me* (juvenile; Junior Literary Guild selection), Coward, 1977; Barry Tarshis, *What It Costs*, Putnam, 1977; Thomas Boswell, *How Life Imitates the World Series*, Doubleday, 1982; Red Smith, *1947: The Year All Hell Broke Loose in Baseball*, Doubleday, 1982. Illustrations have appeared under the name R. Davidson in the *New Yorker* magazine for the past twenty years.

WORK IN PROGRESS: A novel about the three years spent in Italy by a contemporary American couple with a teen-aged boy entitled, *In Dark Fields Dwelling*.

SIDELIGHTS: "When I was a little boy in Brooklyn I sat drawing a hyacinth in the small garden behind our house. It was a peaceful thing to do and I still feel that way about creating art. I like pen and ink the most and prefer watercolor to oil paint. Reginald Marsh was my teacher at the Art Students League and I remember always doing the opposite of the style he encouraged me to learn. I like clean line—he didn't.

"I live alone and working gives me a feeling of being with others and that's good. Reading books is a pleasure and I've written and illustrated a few books for young people (not yet published). I have lived in Italy—a year in Florence, two in Rome, and speak Italian as well as a little Norwegian. (Both my parents were Norwegian immigrants and I grew up with six sisters and three brothers.) I don't drink, smoke or use drugs. They're okay for others, but I like being alive the most when I know what's going on around me.

"As I sit here writing I see my paintings all around the walls of my studio and wonder if they will hang somewhere else some day. I sometimes think I paint too much, have added clutter to the walls of the world, but I don't think I will stop yet.

(From *The Eclogues and the Georgics of Virgil* by David R. Slavitt. Cover illustration by Raymond Davidson.)

"During the summer of 1982 I spent a lot of time doing watercolors of baseball games at Shea Stadium in Flushing, N.Y. About forty of them now hang in the offices of the Mets team at the Stadium. There's a lot of art to see on a baseball field."

Raymond Davidson against the skyline of New York City.

DAVIS, James Robert 1945-
(Jim Davis)

PERSONAL: Born July 28, 1945, in Marion, Ind.; son of James William (a farmer) and Anna C. (Carter) Davis; married Carolyn Alterkruse (in public relations), July 26, 1969; children: one son, Alex. *Education:* Attended Ball State University, 1963-67. *Politics:* Republican. *Religion:* Protestant. *Residence:* Muncie, Indiana.

CAREER: Free-lance advertising artist, 1969-78; assistant to author of "Tumbleweeds" cartoon strip, 1969-78; writer and cartoonist, under name Jim Davis, of "Garfield" cartoon strip, syndicated internationally by United Feature Syndicate, 1978—. Muncie Civic Theatre (member, 1970—; board member, 1974-76). *Member:* National Cartoonists Society. *Awards, honors:* Outstanding Young Men of America Award, 1972; Reuben award, 1981, for best humor comic strip; named to the American Hall of Fame, 1983.

"Garfield" with Jim Davis.

(From *Garfield at Large* by Jim Davis. Illustrated by the author.)

WRITINGS—All self-illustrated: *Garfield at Large*, Ballantine, 1980; *Garfield Gains Weight*, Ballantine, 1982; *Garfield Bigger Than Life: His Third Book*, Ballantine, 1981; *Garfield Weighs In*, Ballantine, 1982; *The Garfield Treasury*, Ballentine, 1982; *Garfield the Knight in Shining Armor*, Random, 1982; *Garfield Takes the Cake*, Ballantine, 1982; *Garfield Mix and Match Storybook*, Random, 1982.

Illustrator; all published by Random House: Shep Steneman, *Garfield: The Complete Cat Book*, 1981; Emily P. Kingsley, *Garfield the Pirate*, 1982.

SIDELIGHTS: **July 28, 1945.** Born in Marion, Indiana. "It was an incredibly happy childhood. All I remember is sunshine and pets and running around." [Mary Vespa, "Garfield Goes Hollywood—with Jim Davis on His Cattails—for Feline Fame and Fortune," *People*, November 1, 1982.[1]]

Illness during his early youth kept Davis inside a great deal. "You have to do something when you're lying in bed. So you play with your mind. [Mother's] the one who got me started. She'd give me a paper and pencil and make me try to draw. I'd draw someone, and as soon as I learned to spell, I'd have them saying something. Then I started drawing boxes and in second or third grade, it was cartooning."[1]

1969. Married Carolyn Alterkruse. Soon after, Davis began working as an assistant to Tom Ryan who created the comic strip "Tumbleweeds." "I always loved the cartoons, but I never seriously thought I could do it for a living until I started with Tom. I learned the discipline and how to maintain a strip."[1]

Encouraged by Ryan, Davis created "Gnorm the Gnat." "I took a go at a bug strip for a while but I couldn't identify with a bug." [John F. Baker, "PW Interviews: Jim Davis," *Publishers Weekly*, March 13, 1981.[2]]

"It was almost five years before I accepted the bitter reality that bugs don't sell." ["The Market Is Going to the Cats as the Fur Flies Over Retailing Millions," *People*, November 17, 1980.[3]]

"I started getting the idea from all the rejection slips that bugs weren't marketable. I took a long, hard look at the comics. I saw there were a lot of dogs doing very well—Snoopy, Marmaduke . . . I didn't know of any cats."[1]

1976. Created "Garfield." "Garfield's" personality was inspired by Davis' grandfather of the same name. "He had a huge lap. I remember looking up his nostrils most of the time. He was a huge man. . . . A very stubborn man. A very opinionated man. And cantankerous."[1]

"Garfield" underwent a few changes before arriving at his present form. "His eyes got larger to get more expression; so did his mouth. His body got a little smaller just so I could get him around easier. His limbs got longer to make him more animated and his ears got a little shorter because I didn't need them. He's always had this thing against *cute*. He says, 'Cute rots the intellect.' "[1]

1978. "Garfield" became syndicated. "Carolyn never doubted I would get syndicated. She provided a great home life and a lot of support. It was blind faith on her part. Quite frankly, at 32, I was getting a little nervous."[1]

"That's the dream of every comic strip artist, to be syndicated, and I'd been submitting for eight years before I came up with Garfield.

"It was a terrific moment, because they only take on one or two new ones a year. Old comic strips keep on going, even after their original creators have died, and every time there's a strike, or a newsprint shortage, the comic page is the first to shrink, and somehow they never grow back."[2]

"It was like semiretiring."[1]

1980. The publication of *Garfield at Large* was ". . . my single biggest break toward national recognition."[2]

"One reason Garfield is interesting for cat lovers, is that he confirms what they've always suspected about cats. In Garfield they see his human aspects—his refusal to diet, his inability to walk through a room without knocking things over, and his total pursuit of warm places to curl up and sleep. He champions a lot of unpopular causes, like anti-jogging, and what's more, he doesn't apologize for them."[3]

Garfield has "his own head with things. He's a real prima donna.

"He's a little bit of Archie Bunker and Morris the Cat tossed together.

(From *Garfield Weighs In* by Jim Davis. Illustrated by the author.)

"He's a very calculating cat. He's a very believable cat.

"There is a simple line in the expression and gestures."[1]

"Way down deep, we're all motivated by the same urges. Cats have the courage to live by them—that's what Garfield is all about." [J.D. Reed, "Those Catty Cartoonists," *Time*, December 7, 1981.[4]]

Part of Garfield's universal success stems from the conscious efforts of Davis to keep the strip free from cultural events or popular slang. "It's a conscious effort to include everyone as readers. If you were to mention the football strike, you're going to be excluding everyone else in the world that doesn't watch pro football. Garfield is an international character. Therefore, I don't even use seasons. The only holiday I recognize is Christmas. I don't use rhyming gags, plays on words, colloquialisms, in an effort to make Garfield apply to virtually any society where he may appear. In an effort to keep the gags broad, the humor general and applicable to everyone, I deal mainly with eating and sleeping. That applies to everyone, anywhere.

"The Garfield art is very, very simple. Usually there's a tabletop. Nothing distracts the eye. Hopefully they see the characters, the expression. There's as few words as possible. Garfield's expressions are very carefully drawn. There's not much space. We've only got about 3 inches by 7 inches.

"There are a lot better artists than I am. . . . I've never been much at drawing. Which, I'm sure, is another reason that the

simplicity in the strip is very helpful. Long after they've forgotten the artwork or the particular punch line, they remember the character. The predictability of the personality of the character in the long run helps to maintain the comic strip.

". . . By virtue of being a cat, Garfield's not black, white, male or female, young or old, or a particular nationality. He's not going to step on anyone's feet if these thoughts are coming from an animal. So that was my first theory.

"Secondly, it was doing all the writing myself. I think the personality in the long run was going to be the real payoff. So I set out to design the character with some texture. I knew it would have been easy to go the cute-cat route, but that wouldn't have been true to my humor, either. I felt a selfish, cynical, lazy type of character with a little soft underbelly would endure." [Walter Shapiro, "A Fat Cat Claws His Way to the Top," *The Sunday Record* (New Jersey), February 20, 1983.[5]]

"Garfield has all the attributes and attitudes people are supposed to suppress in themselves. He's militant about his right to oversleep and overeat.

". . . And he appeals both to people who love cats and those who hate them; both sides see themselves vindicated in Garfield.

"Wherever [my mind] goes, it's him—and I never know in advance what he's going to do. Sometimes I feel as though

I've created a monster, and that I have less and less to do with the strip.

"I simply respect the mood in which I wrote it.

"Comic strips are off the wall anyway. If they made sense they'd become predictable and people would lose interest.

"For a start, by far the majority [of readers] are adults, not kids. Their average age is 18 to 43, and they're above-average intelligence, many with education beyond high school. After all, readers of a comic have to make an effort of imagination to extrapolate from a tiny two-dimensional drawing.

"Few people have any idea of just how a cartoonist works.

"I have to feel funny, so I write on funny days.

"On a good funny day I can come up with maybe two or three weeks of gags, so you can see I only need two or three of them a month.

"I sometimes work 60-80 hours a week [much of his time is spent answering fan mail]. It's still a young strip, and I feel I have to pay attention to my readers, find out what they enjoy. It's good feedback and helps build rapport."[2]

"A lot of hopeful cartoonists take the work too seriously. The more fun you have with it, the more fun people have reading it. The fewer the words, the better the timing. Ta Da Ta Da Boom!. . . . Drawing a strip is like telling a joke. It *is* telling a joke."[1]

And Davis feels that it should produce "the kind of laugh that leaves you feeling a little better.

"I stop short of being a workaholic, although sometimes it's hard to tell the difference."[1]

"My philosophy for my work is to entertain. While humor and editorial comment are obviously not mutually exclusive, I write strictly for humorous content. Any editorial comment in 'Garfield' is there to serve a humorous end.

"When writing a gag for a humor strip, I simply imagine my character in a funny situation; then I back up three frames and cut it off."[1]

"Here Comes Garfield," an animated television special, was aired on CBS-TV in 1982. The books and various "Garfield" products, marketed by Davis' company, Paws, Inc., have earned between fifty and sixty million dollars. "We design Garfields for each and every product. The thought of rubber-stamping them isn't for me. I have a real conscience about licensing."[1]

When asked if he worried about running out of ideas, Davis replied: "I guess all cartoonists do, and there are all sorts of tricks you can do to tide you over the bad spots. But in the end the process of inspiration is like walking into a dark closet and taking gags off the shelf. Who knows how big the closet is?"[2]

Although Davis could live anywhere, he prefers to stay in Indiana, where he was born and raised. "I like to visit friends. I like to fish. I like to work, primarily. Just the business of getting on with life is just very easy here. There are no hassles. Whereas in New York—I find it hard to believe people actually ride a train an hour and a half each way each day.

"We probably have a better balance as far as being in touch with the pulse of American society here. It formulated my writing style, and my opinions. It's solid. We have to have a sense of humor to live here. If you don't bowl, there's precious little to do here in the winter time."[5]

"My wife and I are family people, so we'll probably continue to live in the Midwest near our families."[1]

Davis doesn't have a cat because his wife is allergic to them. "But this way I don't have to be true to one cat's foibles, I can use the foibles of all of catdom." [Edwin McDowell, "Battle of the Cats," *New York Times Book Review*, July 27, 1980.[6]]

1983. Seven cartoon collections of Garfield were simultaneously on the *New York Times* trade-paperback best-seller list.

"Everything I did cannot erase the fact that I am an Indiana farm boy. Except for the media attention, precious little has changed.

"I look forward to a long and fruitful relationship with Garfield. Garfield is famous. I am not."[1]

HOBBIES AND OTHER INTERESTS: "I like tennis, chess, and hamburgers. My favorite humor strip is 'B.C.'"

"[From Charles Schulz's 'Peanuts'] I think 'Snoopy and the Red Baron' is probably the greatest sequence of strips that was ever done."[1]

FOR MORE INFORMATION SEE: Chicago Sun-Times, November 2, 1978; *Fort Wayne Journal Gazette*, November 2, 1978; *Editor and Publisher*, November 18, 1978; *Cartoonist Profiles*, December, 1978; *New York Times Book Review*, July 27, 1980; *People*, November 17, 1980, November 1, 1982; *Publishers Weekly*, March 13, 1981; *Time*, December 7, 1981; *The Hartford Courant*, January 23, 1983; *Senior Weekly Reader*, Volume 37, January 28, 1983; *The Sunday Record* (New Jersey), February 20, 1983.

THOMAS DI GRAZIA

(From *Hold My Hand* by Charlotte Zolotow. Illustrated by Thomas Di Grazia.)

DI GRAZIA, Thomas   (?)-1983

PERSONAL: Born in New Jersey; died March 10, 1983. *Education:* Graduated from Cooper Union Art School; further study at Academy of Fine Arts in Rome, Italy. *Residence:* New York, N.Y.

CAREER: Designer, painter, and book illustrator.

ILLUSTRATOR—All for children: Natalie S. Carlson, *The Half Sisters,* Harper, 1970; *There's Love All Day,* Hallmark, 1971; Andrew C. Andry and Suzanne Kratka, *Hi, New Baby,* Simon & Schuster, 1970; Arthur Geisert, *The Orange Scarf,* Simon & Schuster, 1970; Ned O'Gorman, *The Blue Butterfly,* Harper, 1971; N. Carlson, *Luvvy and the Girls,* Harper, 1971; Charlotte Zolotow, *Hold My Hand,* Harper, 1972; Peggy Mann, *The Lost Doll,* Random House, 1972; Ianthe Thomas, *Lordy, Aunt Hattie,* Harper, 1973; I. Thomas, *Walk Home Tired, Billy Jenkins,* Harper, 1974; Yuri Suhl, *The Merrymaker,* Scholastic Book Services, 1975; Fran Manushkin, *Swinging and Swinging,* Harper, 1976; Lucille Clifton, *Amifika,* Dutton, 1977; Aleza Shevrin, compiler and translator, *Holiday Tales of Sholom Aleichem,* Scribner, 1979; L. Clifton, *My Friend Jacob* (Junior Literary Guild selection), Dutton, 1980.

FOR MORE INFORMATION SEE: Martha E. Ward and Dorothy A. Marquardt, *Illustrators of Books for Young People,* Scarecrow Press, 1975; Lee Kingman and others, compilers, *Illustrators of Children's Books: 1967-1976,* Horn Book, 1978.

DUCHESNE, Janet   1930-

BRIEF ENTRY: Born May 11, 1930, in London, England. Painter, illustrator, and author. Duchesne attended Bromley College of Art and Royal Academy Schools in London. An accomplished painter of landscapes and portraits, she has written and illustrated several books for children, including *Two-to-Five Books, Richard Goes Sailing, Peach Pudding,* and *The Amazing Pet.* Duchesne has also illustrated the works of numerous authors, such as *The Big Show* by Pamela Rogers, *Pilgrim's Way* by Joan Smith, *Cup Final for Charlie* by Joy Allen, and *Dinner Ladies Don't Count* by Bernard Ashley. *For More Information See:* Bertha Mahony Miller and others, compilers, *Illustrators of Children's Books: 1957-1966,* Horn Book, 1968.

Know you what it is to be a child? It is to be something very different from the man of today. It is to have a spirit yet streaming from the waters of baptism; it is to believe in love, to believe in loveliness, to believe in belief; it is to be so little that the elves can reach to whisper in your ear; it is to turn pumpkins into coaches, and mice into horses, lowness into loftiness, and nothing into everything, for each child has its fairy godmother in its soul.

—Francis Thompson

DUNBAR, Robert E(verett)   1926-

PERSONAL: Born November 24, 1926, in Quincy, Mass.; son of Charles Wheeler and Eva Emma (Duquette) Dunbar; married Sally Arseneault (a teacher and artist), June 26, 1954; children: Yvette Maria, Jesse Robert. *Education:* Marietta College, B.A., 1951; Northwestern University, M.S., 1954. *Religion:* Roman Catholic. *Home and office address:* Dunbairn, East Neck Rd., Nobleboro, Maine 04555. *Agent:* Janet A. Loranger, P.O. Box 113, West Redding, Conn. 06896.

CAREER: Continental Assurance Co., Chicago, Ill., assistant editor of publications, 1954-57; Junior Achievement, Chicago, director of public relations, 1957-58; *Selling Sporting Goods,* Chicago, editor, 1958-67; American Society of Anesthesiologists, Park Ridge, Ill., director of communications, 1967-70; American Fund for Dental Education and Health, Chicago, director of Public Information Division, 1970-74; free-lance writer, 1975—. Partner, Dunbar Art and Editorial, Dunbairn Gallery, Nobleboro, Maine. Adjunct assistant professor at University of Health Sciences, Chicago Medical School, 1973-75. *Military service:* U.S. Naval Reserve, active duty, 1944-45.

MEMBER: American Medical Writers Association (fellow; co-chairman of national education committee, 1970-74; president, Chicago chapter, 1970-71; founding member, New England chapter, 1976), Authors Guild, Authors League of America, Saint Andrew's Society of Maine, Nobleboro Historical Society. *Awards, honors:* Beth Fonda Award for Excellence in medical feature writing from American Medical Writers Association, 1974, for *Learning to Cope with Arthritis, Rheumatism, and Gout.*

WRITINGS: Learning to Cope with Arthritis, Rheumatism, and Gout, Budlong, 1973; *A Man's Sexual Health,* Budlong, 1976; *Zoology Careers* (young adult), F. Watts, 1977; *Heredity* (juvenile), F. Watts, 1978; *Mental Retardation* (juvenile), F. Watts, 1978; *Into Jupiter's World,* (young adult science fiction novel), F. Watts, 1981. Contributor to magazines and newspapers, including *Down East* and *Maine Life.* Former contributing editor of *Dental Economics.*

WORK IN PROGRESS: A science project book on the heart for high school students to be published by F. Watts; a juvenile adventure to be published by Knopf; an adult science fiction novel.

SIDELIGHTS: "I have wanted to be a writer from early childhood, with the desire mounting through my college years. I have written poetry, short stories, and essays, and now I am strongly into nonfiction as well as fiction in the juvenile and young adult fields. I have a universal interest in all subjects and feel I could write about almost any subject for general readership.

"I have reached the fortunate stage in my career wherein I can survive economically as a fulltime free-lance writer. I have enough 'bread and butter' income from writing public service columns to help keep the wolf from the door. For the past couple of years I have been providing these columns in eleven areas (five are medical; among others are insurance, law, and energy conservation) for a client in Massachusetts who markets them nationally. The columns provide important factual information as a service to readers and also serve as advertisements. This effort takes about half of my work week, leaving the other half for other writing efforts, which include non-fiction and fiction books.

ROBERT E. DUNBAR

"When I am not writing, I am usually reading, most of the time for information (research) and sometimes for pleasure. Getting to a writing task is not as easy as it should be. In fact, I find I spend more time *thinking* about a project and reading over material I have written than in actual work at my typewriter (there may be a word-processor machine in my future but I haven't thought seriously about it yet). I am probably typical of many writers who find easy distractions and diversions to keep myself away from the typewriter. But once I get started, I like to stay with it for several hours. Not being an 'early morning person,' I don't really get rolling till late morning; but I can go on well into the night and have done so many times. Knowing I have a deadline to meet (either set by myself or the publisher) is just the prod I need to finish a writing project.

"Usually I write a manuscript three times before I send it off to a publisher. The first effort is a 'rough draft.' Then I study it, making whatever changes I think will improve it and then type it again. After one more close reading, and usually many minor changes, I proceed with the final typing and send it off. Once the publisher gets it, of course, the editor there will probably want lots of changes, too! So there will be at least two more revisions before the manuscript is published.

"My writing style has had many influences—in fact, everything I read influences me to some extent. I try to get lots of variety into my sentences. Some are short, some are long. But I try to make them all flow together as pleasantly as possible, and, when the occasion calls for it, with a certain amount of dramatic emphasis.

"I am very conscious of the rhythm or flow of words and sentences. Sound is important to me also, as well as the mean-

This albino raccoon, found in Illinois in 1975, is the only such mutation ever found. ■ (From *Heredity* by Robert E. Dunbar. Photograph courtesy of United Press International.)

ing of words, and when I have a choice in word-meaning, I usually select the word whose sound has the most appeal and the most appropriateness from my point of view.

"When I read or write, I like to do it with as much quietness as possible and with no interruptions or distractions. At this point in my career I don't feel the need for the approval or encouragement of friend or family for anything I write.

"When I finish a column, chapter, or section of a book, I don't give it to a friend or family to read (though they are always welcome to read it, if they want to, and often do). I have enough confidence in what I write to do my very best and then wait for the publisher's or editor's response and suggestions. I know that there are three people I have to please: myself, the publisher, and the reader. When I write, I write with them in mind.

"For many years I was a very shy person, especially when meeting new people. This is no longer true, although I do tend to be somewhat subdued in my relations with people until I get to know them well.

"I am a creature of many moods. Sometimes I am quiet and prefer quiet hours alone, working or reading. Other times I like to let go and enjoy myself with friends to the full. My wife and I are avid bridge players (though never tournament-

bent) and are always ready to play with friends at a moment's notice. We enjoy theater very much, too. I am also an opera buff and enjoy classical music—but I like all kinds of music, including pop and folk music.

"I have never been a very good athlete, though I enjoy golf. I am also interested in gardening, both vegetable and flower, and enjoy this when time permits. I also like to cook. My interests are broad, and I do not consider myself any kind of specialist, though science and medicine have high appeal for me. So does travel. There is so much of the world I would like to see and savor."

EATON, Anne T(haxter)   1881-1971

PERSONAL: Born May 8, 1881 (some sources cite May 3), in Beverly Farms, Mass.; died May 3, 1971, in New York, N.Y.; daughter of Charles Henry and Jane M. Eaton. *Education:* Smith College, B.A., circa 1905; New York State Library School, Albany, B.L.S., 1906, M.S., circa 1926. *Residence:* New York, N.Y.

CAREER: Pruyn Library, Albany, N.Y., librarian, 1906-10; University of Tennessee, Knoxville, assistant librarian, 1910-17; Columbia University, Lincoln School of the Teachers College, New York, N.Y., librarian, 1917-46. *New York Times Book Review*, children's books department, reviewer, 1932-46, co-editor, 1935-46; St. Luke's School Library, volunteer, 1952-71. Also taught children's literature at St. John's University and was a member of Books Across the Sea Committee for the English Speaking Union. *Awards, honors:* Recipient of James Terry White medal, 1941, for *Reading with Children*.

WRITINGS: (With Lucy E. Fay) *Instruction in the Use of Books and Libraries: A Textbook for Normal Schools and Colleges*, Boston Book Co., 1915, 3rd revised edition, Faxon, 1928; *School Library Service*, American Library Association, 1923; (compiler, with Helen F. Daringer) *The Poet's Craft* (juvenile; illustrated by Helene Carter), World Book Co., 1935, reprinted, Books for Libraries. 1972; *Reading With Children*, Viking, 1940, reprinted, 1963; (compiler) *The Animals' Christmas: Poems, Carols, and Stories* (juvenile; illustrated by Valenti Angelo), Viking, 1944, reprinted, 1966; *Treasure for the Taking: A Book List for Boys and Girls* (juvenile), Viking, 1946; (compiler, with Dorothy E. Cook and Dorothy H. West) *Standard Catalog for High School Libraries: A Selected Catalog of 4,555 Books*, two volumes, H. W. Wilson, 1947; (compiler) *Welcome Christmas!: A Garland of Poems* (juvenile; illustrated by Angelo), Viking, 1955, reprinted, 1966; (compiler and author of foreword) Louisa May Alcott, *A Round Dozen: Stories* (juvenile; illustrated by Tasha Tudor), Viking, 1963.

Contributor of articles to anthologies, including *A Critical History of Children's Literature*, edited by Cornelia L. Meigs, Macmillan, 1953, and *Essays Presented to Anne Carroll Moore*, edited by Frances L. Spain, New York Public Library, 1956. Contributor of articles to periodicals, including *Horn Book, Parents' Magazine, Library Journal, Wilson Library Bulletin*, and *Commonweal*.

SIDELIGHTS: Although born in Massachusetts, Eaton was raised in New York and remained a life-long resident of New York City. Her father, a minister, gave his daughter free access to his extensive library, where she spent numerous hours reading.

Eaton graduated from Smith College and received her library training at the New York State Library School in Albany. Her first job as a librarian was at Pruyn Library in Albany. From there, she accepted a position as assistant librarian at the University of Tennessee in Knoxville, where she worked for seven years. When Lincoln School of Teachers' College at Columbia University was founded in 1917, Eaton became its first school librarian, a position she held until her retirement in 1946.

Throughout her career she also worked as a reviewer of children's books and, later, as a co-editor of the children's department of the *New York Times*. Through her writing, which included articles, book reviews, and textbooks, and her compilation of reading lists and anthologies, she influenced the reading tastes of children, parents, educators, and children's librarians for many years. "The sense of power that comes from the ability to read printed words and tell a story gives satisfaction to a child; so does the finding of books which exactly suit his individual taste. But, in addition, there is an intrinsic joy-giving quality in the best books written for children, a quality that comes from the delight that the author has felt in making his book. This joy in the writing, which in turn makes for joy in the reading, is the touchstone to distinguish real literature in books for boys and girls. It follows naturally that those who cannot read a really good book for children with something of a child's enjoyment should never undertake to criticize children's books or to direct children's reading.

"The more keenly parents, teachers, librarians, and book reviewers recognize this truth, the finer and more genuinely imaginative will be our literature for children and the wiser will be our judgment of the books written for them. . . .

ANNE T. EATON

"Nowadays people and things come crowding into a child's life long before childhood is past, and solitude, which should be a blissful part of everyone's growing up, is no more. Today the best aid to possess the world and one's own soul is given by association with books and great literature. Adults who realize this have a responsibility toward young people to help them make the same discovery in their turn. We can make imaginative literature available, we can put it where it will be fairly stumbled over, we can suggest tactfully, we can sympathize and share our own favorites when we are granted the opportunity.

"No one can go into the children's room of a public library without being glad at heart for the children who are finding it a gateway to a world they would not otherwise know. On the other hand, how discouraging it is to listen to the individual who says: 'Oh, no, I never buy books any more, they take up so much room and are so hard to move one can't carry them around, so I just get all I want from the public library or the circulating library.' And though the conditions of modern life seem to make it more and more difficult to grow up in a household which contains a well-stocked library, it is well for us to remember, even those of us who must live in apartments, that an individual library of six well-chosen books, all his own, will give a child more of a sense of the value, companionship, and individuality of books than sixty volumes hastily read and returned to the public library.

"The home library should be supplemented by the school library and the public library. It is, in fact, valuable for children who have plenty of books at home to use the public library from time to time for the sake of the experience, but it should never be forgotten that the personally owned books, the little library built up gradually, with its associations—this volume

a gift from some favorite elder, that perhaps representing some small self-denial—is a precious possession to a child and a possession that outlasts its actual and material existence.

"This tendency to disregard one of the pleasures to be enjoyed within the four walls of the home may be one of the causes contributing to the restlessness of youth today; of youth that craves the motion picture, the going somewhere, anywhere, instead of enjoying the quiet good time at home. Home, if it is a real home, is after all the best place for the development of children; they are kept there by keeping their interests there. One of the ways of doing this is through a child's own well-selected library.

"It is not a simple task, this bringing children and books together. It means knowing books so thoroughly that we may help the dreamer to see the wonder and romance of the world about him, and the matter-of-fact child to enter the realm of imaginative literature. It means making that spirit of the past which is so real that it still survives for us today in Hector and Odysseus, King Arthur, Robin Hood, Rosalind, and Hamlet, a reality in the lives of all children and thus help them, as they grow older, to interpret the problems of their life today.

"To do this in any degree, we must know both books and children. We must do more: we must be constantly finding out for and feeling for ourselves the points of contact between books and life. We must be so alive to the world around us that its qualities of beauty and reality, whether in books or men or nature, cannot escape us.

"We must have retained or we must recapture for ourselves something of the child's own attitude toward life and the world. . . ." [Anne Thaxter Eaton, *Reading with Children*, Viking, 1940.]

The Royal Camels were about to receive their bath and this was a ceremony always performed in public. ■ (From *The Animals' Christmas* by Ann Thaxter Eaton. Illustrated by Valenti Angelo.)

Following her retirement, Eaton served until her death as a volunteer at St. Luke's School Library. She also taught children's literature at St. John's University. She died at her home in New York City on May 3, 1971, five days before her ninetieth birthday.

HOBBIES AND OTHER INTERESTS: Theater, ballet, folk music, collecting music boxes, and travel.

FOR MORE INFORMATION SEE: New York Times Book Review, March 24, 1935, April 28, 1940, April 14, 1946; Anne Thaxter Eaton, *Reading with Children,* Viking, 1940; *Publishers Weekly,* April 20, 1940; *Catholic World,* October, 1940; *New York Herald Tribune Books,* May 19, 1940; *Elementary School Journal,* June, 1946; *New York Herald Tribune Weekly Book Review,* April 7, 1946; *Saturday Review of Literature,* April 20, 1946; Frances Clark Sayers, *Summoned by Books,* Viking, 1965. *Obituaries—New York Times,* May 9, 1971; *AB Bookman's Weekly,* May 17, 1971.

EDWARDS, Gunvor

PERSONAL: Born in Uppsala, Sweden; married Peter Edwards; children: six. *Education:* Attended Gun Zetterdahls School of Painting, Stockholm, Sweden, and Regent Street Polytechnic, London, England. *Residence:* London, England.

CAREER: Illustrator.

*WRITINGS—*Of interest to young readers: (Translator) Edith Unnerstad, *Larry Makes Music* (illustrated by Ylva Kaellstroem), Oliver & Boyd, 1967; *Cat Samson* (self-illustrated), Abelard, 1978; (translator from the Danish) Stig Weimar, *Norway Is Like This,* Kaye & Ward, 1979.

Illustrator; for young readers: David Thomson, *Danny Fox,* Penguin, 1966; Barbara Softly, *Magic People: A Book to Begin On,* Oliver & Boyd, 1966, Holt, 1967; Johanna B. Olsen, *Stray Dog,* translated from the Norwegian by Evelyn Ramsden, Constable, 1966, Criterion, 1968; Ursula M. Williams, *The Cruise of the 'Happy-Go-Gay',* Hamish Hamilton, 1967, Hawthorn, 1968; D. Thomson, *Danny Fox Meets a Stranger,* Penguin, 1968; Gerard Bell, *The Smallest King in the World,* Oliver & Boyd, 1968; B. Softly, *More Magic People,* Chatto & Windus, 1969.

Charles E. Loveman, *La Douce France,* Thomas Nelson, 1971; C. E. Loveman, *Mystère à Cherbourg,* Thomas Nelson, 1971; Felicia Law, *Something to Make,* Penguin, 1971; Rony Robinson and W. T. Cunningham, *Action in English,* Thomas Nelson, Book I, 1972, Book II, 1972, Book III, 1973, Leavers' Book, 1973; (with husband, Peter Edwards) Wilbert Awdry, *Tramway Engines,* Kaye & Ward, 1972; Anne-Catharina Vestly, *Hallo Aurora!,* translated from the Norwegian by Eileen Amos, Longman, 1973; U. M. Williams, *Tiger-Nanny,* Brockhampton Press, 1973, Thomas Nelson, 1974; C. E. Loveman, *Vas-y gaiement!,* Thomas Nelson, Book I, 1973, Book II, 1973, Book III, 1974; A. Vestly, *Aurora and the Little Blue Car,* translated from the Norwegian by E. Amos, Longman, 1974; Molly C. Ibbotson, *Daniel's Shed,* Brockhampton Press, 1974; Barbara Sleigh, *Ninety-Nine Dragons,* Brockhampton Press, 1974; Frederick Grice, *Tales and Beliefs,* Thomas Nelson, 1974.

A. Vestly, *Aurora and Socrates,* translated from the Norwegian by E. Amos, Kestrel Books, 1974; Louisa May Alcott, *Little Women,* retold by Lysbeth Glibbery, Oxford University Press, 1975; D. Paling and M. E. Wardle, *Oxford Comprehensive Mathematics: A Secondary Course for Mixed Abilities,* Oxford University Press, Book II, 1975, C. S. Banwell and K. D. Saunders, Book III, 1975; Elisabeth Beresford, *Snuffle to the Rescue,* Puffin, 1975, Penguin, 1976; D. Thomson, *Danny Fox at the Palace,* Puffin, 1976; Frances Lindsay, *Mr. Bits and Pieces,* Hodder & Stoughton, 1976; Margaret E. Mountjoy, *German through Reading,* Heinemann, Book I: *Das Haus im Baum,* 1977, Book III: *Alarm bei Nacht,* 1977; Graeme Kent, *English Everywhere,* A. Wheaton, Book II: *Out and About,* 1978; W. Awdry, *Duke and the Lost Engine,* Kaye & Ward, 1980; F. Law, *Going to School,* Octopus, 1980; Margaret S. Barry, *Maggie Gumption Flies High,* Hutchinson, 1981.

For adults: (With Kay Marshall) Elizabeth M. Matterson, *Play with a Purpose for Under-Sevens,* Penguin, 1975; Robina B. Willson, *Musical Merry-Go-Round: Musical Activities for the Very Young,* Heinemann, 1977.

SIDELIGHTS: Edwards grew up in Sweden. She attended art school in England where she met her husband. They live with their six children in London, where she illustrates books for young people. "I have lots of thoughts about art, but no ideas. I find it very mysterious! To me, illustration is writing with pictures." [Lee Kingman and others, compilers, *Illustrators of Children's Books: 1967-1976,* Horn Book, 1978.]

FOR MORE INFORMATION SEE: Times Literary Supplement, November 23, 1973; Lee Kingman and others, compilers, *Illustrators of Children's Books: 1967-1976,* Horn Book, 1978.

Suddenly a large hand came down and picked up Kim. ▪ (From *Snuffle to the Rescue* by Elisabeth Beresford. Illustrated by Gunvor Edwards.)

FEYDY, Anne Lindbergh   1940-

BRIEF ENTRY: Born in 1940. Novelist. Anne Lindbergh Feydy is the daughter of the celebrated aviator, Charles Lindbergh, and the noted author and poet, Anne Morrow Lindbergh. She attended Radcliffe College and has written a novel for young readers entitled *Osprey Island*, a story of magic and adventure set in Paris, France where she resides with her husband. She has also contributed stories to periodicals, including *Vogue* and *Redbook*.

FLEISCHMAN, Paul

BRIEF ENTRY: Born in Monterey, Calif. Author. Fleischman attended the University of California at Berkeley and the University of New Mexico. The son of Sid Fleischman, award-winning author of adventure stories for children, he has won reviewers' praise in his own right as an author of books for children and young readers. He has written two mystery books for young readers, both of which have received awards. *The Half-a-Moon Inn* (Harper, 1980), illustrated by Kathy Jacobi, was a Golden Kite Award Honor Book, 1981, and *Graven Images: Three Stories* (Harper, 1982), illustrated by Andrew Glass, was a Newbery Honor Book, 1983. A writer in the style of Poe and Hawthorne, Fleischman is credited with creating an atmosphere of frightening suspense while leading his readers to a fast-paced conclusion with a surprising twist. *Horn Book* called his writing "unusual in our day . . . timeless, elegant . . . fashioned with fluency and skill." For children, he has also written *The Birthday Tree* (Harper 1979), and *Animal Hedge*, a forthcoming book from Dutton. *Residence:* California.

FLEISHMAN, Seymour   1918-

BRIEF ENTRY: Born January 29, 1918, in Chicago, Ill. Artist; author and illustrator of children's books. Fleishman, who attended the School of the Art Institute of Chicago, is married and the father of two daughters. Although he has worked extensively in advertising, he has devoted a major part of his career to book illustration. Among the books he has illustrated are several that he also wrote: *Where's Kit?*, *Four Cheers for Camping*, *Gumbel, the Fire-Breathing Dragon*, and *Too Hot in Potzburg*. Fleishman has also illustrated the writings of numerous children's authors, including Muriel Stanek's *One, Two, Three for Fun*, Carl Carmer's *The Drummer Boy of Vincennes*, Jane Thayer's "Gus" stories, and many of Florence Heide's mystery stories. *Home:* 5331 North Magnolia St., Chicago, Ill. 60640. *For More Information See:* Bertha Mahony Miller and others, compilers, *Illustrators of Children's Books: 1957-1966*, Horn Book, 1968.

SUSAN FLEMING

FLEMING, Susan 1932-

PERSONAL: Born June 12, 1932, in Eliot, Maine; daughter of Maynard F. (a rural mail carrier) and Marjorie (Fernald) Douglas; married Donald Fleming, Jr. (an administrative assistant), April 17, 1965; children: Eric, Gregory. *Education:* Emerson College, A.B. (high honors), 1953; Harvard University, Ed.M., 1960; Boston University, certificate in reading, 1966. *Home:* 22 Morton St., Needham, Mass. 02194.

CAREER: Teacher at state school in Wrentham, Mass., 1953-54, and at public elementary schools in Ossining, N.Y., 1955-57, Lexington, Mass., 1957-58, and Arlington, Mass., 1958-65; editor in elementary reading department, Houghton Mifflin Co., Boston, Mass., 1966-67; free-lance writer, 1967—. Reporter for *Needham Reporter,* 1975.

WRITINGS: Trapped on the Golden Flyer (illustrated by Alex Stein; Junior Literary Guild selection), Westminster, 1978; *The Pig at 37 Pinecrest Drive* (illustrated by Beth and Joe Krush), Westminster, 1981; *Countdown at 37 Pinecrest Drive,* Westminster, 1982. Contributor to magazines and newspapers, including *American Baby, Instructor, Christian Home,* and *Boston Herald-American.*

WORK IN PROGRESS: Another book for young people.

SIDELIGHTS: "The best part of my childhood was the space I had. Now, living in a small, suburban lot in a compact, three-bedroom house, I realize how rich we were. Not rich in the usual sense. My father had to juggle two jobs (mail carrier and farmer) to make ends meet, and I still remember with stomach cramps, the way he cried, 'I don't know where the money is coming from,' when the bills rolled in. But we were rich in space.

"We lived in a rambling farmhouse where there was always a private place to curl up undisturbed with a book. And there were wonderful places to play: the attic, the musty, cobweb-filled cellar, the shed which had an upstairs chamber for a hired man (whom we could never afford to hire!), and the outbuildings—the deserted bull house, the garage for keeping farm machinery, the chicken coop (an excellent playhouse when it wasn't occupied by chickens).

"And all around were acres and acres of land to explore—an orchard, a pasture, a field, woods. Since my two sisters and my brother were too old to be playmates, I played alone a great deal. But I don't remember being lonely or bored. I invented companions and we had death-defying adventures as I roamed the length and breadth of our property.

"We rarely traveled more than ten or fifteen miles away from home. I was always in rebellion against the restrictions of farm life. I dreamed of being an opera star, traveling triumphantly to all the capitals of the world. Yet, practical and hard-working as they were, my parents never squashed my romantic dreams.

"All this imaginative play helped me to grow into a writer. But I did little writing as a child; I was too busy planning my career as an opera singer. No wonder. My parents were ardent music lovers, who sang in the church choir, took me to every local musical event, and every Saturday afternoon tuned into the Metropolitan Opera on the Air. My father had a rich bar-

. . .We found Olivia in Cadillac's pen, dressed in her red tights and a red tutu, with a whistle in her mouth. She was holding a pink hoop in one hand and a piece of stale bread in the other. ■ (From *The Pig at 37 Pinecrest Drive* by Susan Fleming. Illustrated by Beth and Joe Krush.)

itone voice and was a popular soloist. He always sang as he went about his chores in the barn and often he took me on his lap to sing to me about 'the green-eyed dragon with thirteen tails. He'll feed with greed on little boys, puppy dogs, and big fat snails.'

"My parents were book lovers as well as music lovers. Our house was over-flowing with reading material. Mother took me to the library as soon as I could walk and she never failed to read me a bedtime story. I became a voracious reader, yet I only casually considered being a writer. Instead, I decided next to become an actress. Wisely my mother steered me to a college where I could major in both English and acting.

"Since more jobs were available in education than in the theatre, I became a teacher.

"Only after I married and had little children did I start writing professionally. *Trapped on the Golden Flyer* grew out of my desire to write a different kind of train story for my two boys who are both railroad enthusiasts.

"My sons are still my best sources for ideas. Many situations and much of the conversation in *The Pig at 37 Pinecrest Drive* and *Countdown at 37 Pinecrest Drive* where suggested by watching and listening to them. They are my best critics, too, never hesitating to tell me when something I write is 'boring!'

"I don't know how anyone can get through this world without books. I hide behind them when I need to escape, I lean on them when I need inspiration. For many years I enjoyed teaching children to read. Now I enjoy even more the process of writing a book for them. I love to read tales of triumphant struggle or the little person who wins the big prize. I suspect that these themes will appear in my books as long as I continue to write."

FRASER, Antonia (Pakenham) 1932-

BRIEF ENTRY: Born August 27, 1932, in London, England. Author of the acclaimed biography, *Mary, Queen of Scots,* Fraser is the product of a literary and politically oriented family. Her father, the seventh Earl of Longford, is an Oxford historian while her mother is an award-winning author of biographies, under the name Elizabeth Longford. Fraser received her B.A. in history from Oxford University in 1953. For three years, she worked as an editor for the publishing firm of Weidenfeld & Nicholson before her marriage to Hugh Fraser in 1956. In the following years, Antonia Fraser became known as a trend setter and hostess of lavish parties in the glamorous world of the "Beautiful People." Her subsequent divorce from her husband in 1976 received a great deal of publicity in the society columns, as did her relationship with well-known playwright Harold Pinter, whom she married in 1980.

With the publication of *Mary, Queen of Scots* in 1969, Fraser shed her 'jet-set'' image and replaced it with that of a knowledgeable and thorough historical biographer. That same year, she was the recipient of the James Tait Black prize for biography. She is the author of three additional biographies, *Cromwell, the Lord Protector,* 1973, *King James VI of Scotland, I of England,* 1974, and *Royal Charles: Charles II and the Restoration,* 1979, all of which intensified her reputation as an accomplished writer. Prior to writing her biographies, Fraser wrote two books for children, *King Arthur and the Knights of*

the Round Table, 1954, and *Robin Hood,* 1957. She is also the author of a series of mystery novels, short stories, and plays for radio and television. *For More Information See: Current Biography 1974,* H. W. Wilson, 1975; *New York Times Biographical Service,* November, 1979; *Contemporary Authors,* Volumes 85-88, Gale, 1980.

GAL, Laszlo 1933-

BRIEF ENTRY: Born February 18, 1933, in Budapest, Hungary. Graphic designer and children's book illustrator. Gal began his career as a graphic designer for the Canadian Broadcasting Company (CBC) in 1958 and remained there until 1965. He then went to Verona, Italy, where he was an illustrator at Arnoldo Mondadori Editore until 1969. Returning to Toronto in 1969, Gal worked as a free-lance illustrator until 1977. He has since been employed as a graphic designer at the CBC in Toronto. Three books which Gal illustrated have been cited by the Imperial Order of the Daughters of the Empire as Best Children's Books of the Year: Ronald Melzack's *Why the Man in the Moon Is Happy* and Marian Engel's *My Name Is Not Odessa Yarker,* both in 1978; and Janet Lunn's *The Twelve Dancing Princesses,* in 1979. Gal's illustrated work for young people also includes *Raven, Creator of the World: Eskimo Legends* retold by Melzack, *How the Chipmunk Got His Stripes* by Nancy Cleaver, and *The Moon Painters, and Other Estonian Folk Takes* retold by Selve Maas. *Office:* 101 Mutual St., Toronto. Ontario, Canada M5B 2B2. *For More Information See: Who's Who in America, 1982-83,* Marquis, 1982.

GARFIELD, Leon 1921-

PERSONAL: Born July 14, 1931, in Brighton, Sussex, England; son of David Kalman (a businessman) and Rose (Blaustein) Garfield; married Vivien Dolores Alcock (an artist), October 23, 1948; children: Jane Angela. *Education:* Attended grammar school in Brighton, England. *Politics:* "Somewhere between Labour and Liberal." *Religion:* Jewish. *Home:* 59 Wood Lane, Highgate, London N.6, England. *Agent:* Jo Stewart, 201 East 66th St., New York, N.Y. 10021; Winant, Towers Ltd., Clerkenwell House, 45-47 Clerkenwell Green, London, ECIR OHT, England.

CAREER: Whittington Hospital, London, England, biochemical technician, 1946-66; part-time biochemical technician in a hospital in London, England, 1966; novelist, 1966—. *Military service:* British Army, Medical Corps, 1940-46; served in Belgium and Germany. *Member:* International P.E.N. *Awards, honors:* Gold medal from Boys' Clubs of America for *Jack Holborn;* first *Guardian* Award for children's fiction, 1967, for *Devil-In-the-Fog;* runner-up for the Carnegie Medal, 1967, for *Smith,* 1968, for *Black Jack,* 1970, for *The Drummer Boy;* Arts Council of Great Britain Award for the best book for older children, 1967, for *Smith;* Carnegie Medal for the most outstanding book of the year, 1970, for *The God Beneath the Sea;* Child Study Association Children's Book of the Year, 1976, for *The House of Hanover: England in the Eighteenth Century;* Whitbread Literary Award, 1980, for *John Diamond.*

*WRITINGS—*Novels: *Jack Holborn* (illustrated by Antony Maitland), Constable, 1964, Pantheon, 1965; *Devil-In-the-Fog* (illustrated by A. Maitland), Pantheon, 1966; *Smith* (illustrated by A. Maitland; ALA Notable Book), Pantheon, 1967; *Mr.*

He must have released his hold above to free himself from me—for I remember no more than his roar of sharp pain—then both of us, my teeth still in him, crashing to the deck below. ■ (From *Jack Holborn* by Leon Garfield. Illustrated by Antony Maitland.)

Corbett's Ghost (illustrated by Alan E. Cober), Pantheon, 1968; *The Restless Ghost: Three Stories by Leon Garfield* (illustrated by Saul Lambert), Pantheon, 1969; *Black Jack* (illustrated by A. Maitland; *Horn Book* honor list), Longman, 1968, Pantheon, 1969; *Mister Corbett's Ghost, and Other Stories*, Longman, 1969; *The Boy and the Monkey* (short stories; illustrated by Trevor Ridley), Heinemann, 1969, Watts, 1970.

(Reteller with Edward Blishen) *The God Beneath the Sea* (illustrated by Charles Keeping), Longman, 1970 (American edition illustrated by Zevi Blum), Pantheon, 1971; *The Drummer Boy* (illustrated by A. Maitland), Pantheon, 1970; *The Ghost Downstairs* (illustrated by A. Maitland; ALA Notable Book), Longman, 1970, Pantheon, 1972; *The Strange Affair of Adelaide Harris* (illustrated by Fritz Wegner), Pantheon, 1971; *The Captain's Watch*, Heinemann, 1971; (with David Proctor) *Child O'War: The True Story of a Sailor Boy in Nelson's Navy* (illustrated by A. Maitland), Holt, 1972; (editor) *Baker's Dozen*, Ward, Lock, 1973, Lothrop, 1974; *Lucifer Wilkins*, Heinemann, 1973; (reteller with E. Blishen) *The Golden Shadow*

(illustrated by C. Keeping), Pantheon, 1973; (editor) *Strange Fish and Other Stories*, Lothrop, 1974; (with E. Blishen) *The Sound of Coaches* (illustrated by John Lawrence; Literary Guild selection), Viking, 1974; *The Prisoners of September*, Viking, 1975; *The House of Hanover: England in the Eighteenth Century*, Seabury, 1976; *The Pleasure Garden*, Viking, 1976; *The Book Lovers*, Ward, Lock, 1977, Avon, 1978; (editor) *A Swag of Stories* (illustrated by Caroline Harrison), Ward, Lock, 1978; *The Apprentices* (illustrated by A. Maitland), Viking, 1978; *The Confidence Man*, Kestrel, 1978, Viking, 1979; *The Night of the Comet: A Comedy of Courtship Featuring Bostock and Harris*, Delacorte, 1979.

Footsteps: A Novel, Delacorte, 1980; *John Diamond* (illustrated by A. Maitland), Kestrel, 1980; *The Mystery of Edwin Drood* (completion of the novel begun by Charles Dickens), Deutsch, 1980, Pantheon, 1981; *King Nimrod's Tower* (illustrated by Michael Bragg), Lothrop, 1982; *Fair's Fair*, Doubleday, 1982; *The Writing on the Wall*, Methuen, 1982, Lothrop, 1983; *The House of Cards*, Bodley Head, 1982, St. Martin's Press, 1983; *Tales from Shakespeare*, Gollancz, 1984.

Apprentices series; all published by Heinemann: *The Lamplighter's Funeral*, 1976; *Mirror, Mirror*, 1976; *Moss and Blister* (illustrated by Faith Jaques), 1976; *The Cloak* (illustrated by F. Jaques), 1976; *The Valentine* (illustrated by F. Jaques), 1977; *Labour in Vain* (illustrated by F. Jaques), 1977; *The Fool* (illustrated by F. Jaques), 1977; *Rosy Starling* (illustrated by F. Jaques), 1977; *The Dumb Cake* (illustrated by F. Jaques), 1977; *Tom Titmarsh's Devil* (illustrated by F. Jaques), 1977; *The Enemy*, 1978; *The Filthy Beast*, 1978.

Author of short stories, "The Questioners" in *Winter's Tales for Children, 4*, Macmillan, 1968 and the title story in *The Restless Ghost and Other Encounters and Experiences*, edited by Susan Dickinson, Collins, 1970.

Plays: (With Patrick Hardy) "The Cabbage and the Rose," published in *Miscellany Four*, edited by Edward Blishen, Oxford University Press, 1967.

ADAPTATIONS: Several of Garfields books have been dramatized for film and television. *Devil-In-the Fog, Smith* and *The Strange Affair of Adelaide Harris* have been adapted as television serials for British TV. *Black Jack* was made into a full-length feature film, produced by Tony Garnett and directed by Ken Loach, and won the International Jury Award at the Cannes Film Festival in 1979. *John Diamond* was made into a television film and broadcast on BBC-TV in 1981. *Jack Holborn* was made into a full-length film by Taurus Film and shown on German TV, 1982. *The Ghost Downstairs* and *The Restless Ghost* were both dramatized for TV in 1982 and 1983, respectively.

SIDELIGHTS: **July 14, 1921.** Born in Brighton, Sussex, England. ". . . My childhood was spent in a very eighteenth-century town, Brighton. . . . I had a rather Dickensian background, with the constant warfare between mother and father that occurs in most families. . . . My father was very like Mr. Treet in *Devil-In-Fog*, a very flamboyant man who always created an enormous impression, although one always had the sneaking suspicion that there was very little behind it. It was a gift for being enormously liked by everyone except my mother, who became rather tired of it. She went to the other extreme—excessively careful and neurotic, being driven to it by a most erratic and irresponsible husband, who at the same time presented a facade of enormous solidity.'' [Justin Wintle and Emma Fisher, *The Pied Pipers*, Paddington, 1974.[1]]

Garfield's interest in writing began at an early age. ''The beginnings are hard to remember. I always wanted to write. I do recall soggy stories á la Tolstoy . . . weird tales á la Poe . . . and then drifting towards farcical thrillers. Then to Lewis-Carroll-like efforts, then to Hans Andersen. . . . It all seems to have been rather like a pendulum—swinging and scratching wildly from side to side till at last it settled somewhere in the middle.'' [John Rowe Townsend, *A Sense of Story*, Lippincott, 1971.[2]]

''. . . Unlike most writers I never turned to poetry—or at least not since I was about eleven, when one wrote elaborate narrative verse. But after that my interest was essentially in narrative prose, but in the most high-flown manner possible. One was trying to draw the line between prose and poetry, when of course there is no such line that really exists.''[1]

1940-1946. World War II interrupted Garfield's art studies. ''Colourful incidents have been rather lacking in my life. My war service was distinguished by a steady adherence to the rank of private in the Medical Corps. Yet those marvellously boring five years did have moments on which I've drawn repeatedly: incidents in my brief period of 'war crimes investigation'; incidents comic and bloody in the work of a busy hospital. . . .''[2]

1946. After the war, Garfield worked as a hospital biochemist, writing in his spare time.

1946. Five years' research of the eighteenth century resulted in his first novel, *Jack Holborn*. ''. . . I was contemplating a story set in the eighteenth century and taking place partly at sea. . . . At once the whole thing seemed impossible; I knew absolutely nothing of either subject. But the story still had possibilities and continued to haunt me with odd scenes and ironical twists of fate. At last I looked into Swift and Defoe for some appropriate nautical information. They were both very strong in it, and they appeared to get their effects from vivid personal experience. I was very depressed . . . until I discovered that both had got their information straight out of an old sailing manual from which, in places, they had copied word for word. They knew no more about the sea than I did. . . . It was the most encouraging discovery I have ever made. From there on though it was never plain sailing, it was at least navigable.'' [Leon Garfield, ''And So It Grows,'' *Horn Book*, December, 1968.[3]]

''. . . All the maritime details were absolutely accurate, even to the time it took to cover certain distances by boat in those days. I worked from sixteenth-century maps of that part of Africa—such maps as would have been available. Things like the value of money. The social detail of the time was accurate. This was all necessary because I couldn't believe in what I wrote unless I could believe in the solidity of the research.''[1]

''The historical details were, oddly enough, far less troublesome than the sea. The reason was that, having decided to tell the story in the first person, I had only to worry about such details as were unusual enough to be noticed and remarked on, which cut out all eighteenth-century politics and most social customs. After all, if one writes a contemporary novel, one does not go into details of garbage collection, the price of dustbins, or what a doctor wears. Nor does one worry over political events—unless it is a political novel. People rarely

LEON GARFIELD

remember striking incidents in their own lives in relation to international events. They may not even recall who was president, king, or prime minister. Though I remember very clearly first meeting my wife in Belgium during the war, I cannot say where our troops were then—or even which way they were facing.

''Naturally, many of my discoveries about the period came from voluminous reading of diaries and letters to find out such things as the cost of a journey from Weymouth to London, the price of slaves, the situation of the Law Courts. I discovered all sorts of fascinating trifles, many of which were usable. But nobody ever thought it important to mention who was King or with whom the country was currently at war. . . .

''What has emerged from all this is, I hope, that at no time did I ever think of writing for any particular audience, children or otherwise. I do not believe anybody ever does. . . . One does not write *for* children. One writes so that children can understand. Which means writing as clearly, vividly, and truthfully as possible. Adults might put up with occasional lapses; children are far less tolerant. They must never be bored; not for an instant. Words must live for them; so must people. That is what really matters, and it entails believing entirely in what one writes and having a real urgency to convince the reader that it is absolutely, utterly true.''[3]

''. . . I really became involved in the writing. . . . I sent it to an agent, to whom I had been recommended, and she submitted it as an adult book, because that's what she thought it was. It was turned down by Heinemann after three or four agonizing months, when they said they couldn't quite decide whether it

(From *The Apprentices* by Leon Garfield. Jacket painting by Stefen Bernath.)

was adult or junior. It was at a time when there was no such thing as the young or teenage novel—1964, when it was scarcely beginning. It was then sent to Grace Hogarth at Constable, where they were in fact just beginning a large juvenile list. She suggested that, if I would be willing to cut it, then she'd publish it as a juvenile book. And of course, though I'd vowed I'd never alter a word, once the possibility of its being published became real, I cut it in about one week.''[1]

1967. Second novel, *Devil-In-the-Fog* won the first *Guardian* Award for children's fiction and was runner-up for the Carnegie Medal. Garfield has often been compared to Charles Dickens. Like Dickens, he enjoys the theatrical and melodramatic nature of events, loves eccentric characters, and constructs a strong narrative. ''To me, a novel that is suitable for children is the most demanding and absorbing variety of fiction there is. . . .''[3]

''I seemed to drift to writing for children; or rather, I drifted to the sort of writing I like—which can have wildly exciting adventures *and* something of character and morality.

''I use the quest for identity, which seems to occur pretty often, because I have a passion for secrets and mystery. And the secret and mystery of another individual seems to me the only mystery one can unravel endlessly—and still be uncertain. As for good and evil: I suppose I use large moral issues (in which I feel justified in taking sides) as a sort skeleton of the work: something to which I can relate varied incidents and thus give

them a certain unity. I *think* I do this by making my central character aware of the issue embedded in the incident. But of course if it doesn't fit it has to go—perhaps to be used again elsewhere.

''I suppose my earlier writings were invariably based on literary experience. But from *Jack Holborn* onward I used direct experience, however much transcribed. For my African jungle, I remember, I went several times to Kew Gardens and Epping Forest. For my seafaring I went once to Jersey and a dozen times to Greenwich. Just so long as I had something to go on—something to remember, as it were—I was all right.''[2]

''. . . One cannot really invent outside one's own memory. And it was in *Jack Holborn* that I discovered that really one can use one's own experience. For sheer physical sensation it's essential.''[1]

''. . . I started by pinching ideas from other books until I was able to recognize the sort of idea that was capable of being expanded into a whole book of my own. Today I find such ideas more directly . . . even in television or the cinema, to say nothing of the city streets. It doesn't really matter. One picks up bits of ideas, like an inky magpie, and threads them together until they make something that looks, at first sight, new. It isn't new, of course; nothing is.

He brought a queer smell into the shop with him, damp and heavy: an undertaker perhaps?
■ (From *Mister Corbett's Ghost* by Leon Garfield. Illustrated by Alan E. Cober.)

". . . I try to work by analogy. I rely on the phenomenon that the commonplace is rendered sharper by being placed in unexpected surroundings.

". . . I try to approach my subject from within and work my way outwards. I can't abide that type of historical novel that superimposes an observer (usually an accident-prone boy) on a great event for no other purpose than to comment, with merciless detail, on things and people on whom he has no more effect than a boy of glass.

". . . I'd only write about an event that seemed to me to have some contemporary point; and far from touching too closely on actual historical figures, whose course is well know, I'd try to bring out of the shadows—ourselves.

". . . If history has any value beyond providing a livelihood for historians, it is to enlarge the imagination, to provide more acres for the mind to grow in. . . ." [Edward Blishen, editor, *The Thorny Paradise,* Kestrel Books, 1975.[4]]

1980. Completed an unfinished Charles Dickens' novel, *The Mystery of Edwin Drood.* Several attempts by other writers have been made since Dickens' death in 1870, including two motion pictures based on the uncompleted mystery.

Garfield's books have won numerous awards, including the Carnegie Medal (1970) for *The God Beneath the Sea,* written with Edward Blishen. Although much of his work is categorized as "juvenile," his books are intended for all ages. "The

suggestion that writing for chilren always requires a smaller mental effort than other kinds is surely most careless. We don't wish to make pompous claims for children's books; but what worries us about the sweeping nature of [the] statement is that it is part and parcel of a very common tendency to disparage this field of literature—into which, especially today, at its best, a great deal of effort and talent enters. And the trouble with these hasty and mildly scornful attitudes to children's books is that they make it more difficult for us all to recognize a surely essential truth: that no good comes from thinking of literature as divided into a negligible junior field, and senior field that is alone worth considering seriously. Surely literature is a continuous matter, from childhood onward? With children's books, readers are created for all books whatever. A nursery is not an unimportant part of the house." [Literature Is . . . Continuous . . . from Childhood Onward," *Horn Book,* February, 1971.[5]]

1981. Nominated as the British entry for the Hans Christian Andersen award. Selected as one of two children's writers to be included in the Book Marketing Council's selection of top twenty British authors for the "Best of British" promotion camgaign in 1982.

HOBBIES AND OTHER INTERESTS: Eighteenth century music, collecting paintings and china, watching films, and going to the theater (especially Shakespeare).

FOR MORE INFORMATION SEE: Young Readers' Review, April, 1966; *New Statesman,* May 26, 1967, November 1968; *Times Literary Supplement,* May 25, 1967; *Books and Book-*

(From *King Nimrod's Tower* by Leon Garfield. Illustrated by Michael Bragg.)

men, June, 1967; *Christian Science Monitor*, November 2, 1967; *Children's Book World*, November 5, 1967; *Commonweal*, November 10, 1967; *New York Times Book Review*, November 26, 1967; *National Observer*, January 15, 1968; *The Writer*, April, 1969; *Variety*, March 19, 1969; Brian Doyle, *The Who's Who of Children's Literature*, Schocken Books, 1968; *Horn Book*, December, 1968, February, 1971, February, 1972, October, 1974; John Rowe Townsend, *A Sense of Story*, Lippincott, 1971; *The Guardian*, June 9, 1971; Justin Wintle and Emma Fisher, *The Pied Pipers*, Paddington, 1974; Margery Fisher, *Who's Who in Children's Books*, Holt, 1975; Edward Blishen, editor, *The Thorny Paradise*, Kestrel Books, 1975; Doris de Montreville and Elizabeth D. Crawford, editors, *Fourth Book of Junior Authors and Illustrators*, H. W. Wilson, 1978; *Children's Literature in Education*, Winter, 1978; *Time*, October, 27, 1980.

Films: Penguin Books, ''Leon Garfield,'' Conn Films, Inc., 1969.

GEER, Charles 1922-

BRIEF ENTRY: Born August 25, 1922, on Long Island, N.Y. Author and free-lance illustrator of children's books. Geer attended Dartmouth College for two and a half years, before leaving to serve in the Navy during World War II. He resumed his education following the war, at which time he entered Pratt Institute, attending there for a year and a half. Since that time, Geer has been a full-time free-lance illustrator. He also wrote two books for young people, *Dexter and the Deer Lake Mystery* (Norton, 1965) and *Soot Devil* (Grosset, 1971). Geer has illustrated more than 80 books for young people, including *Clear the Track: True Stories of Railroading* by Louis Wolfe, *The Trouble with Toby* by Molly Cone, *Kristy's Courage* by Babbis Friis Baastad, *Just Plain Betsy* by Helen Fern Daringer, *The Magnificent Mongrel* by Anthony Fon Eisen, and *Miss Pickerell Tackles the Energy Crisis* by Ellen MacGregor and Dora Pantell. *For More Information See: Illustrators of Books for Young People*, Scarecrow, 1975; *Illustrators of Children's Books: 1967-1976*, Horn Book, 1978.

GEHR, Mary

PERSONAL: Born in Chicago, Ill.; daughter of Francis Lycett and Ruth Nettie (Mead) Gehr; married Bert Ray (a designer), October, 1950 (deceased, 1969); children: Virginia Riggle (stepdaughter). *Education:* Attended Smith College, 1930, Chicago Art Institute, 1946-53, and Illinois Institute of Technology. *Home:* 1829 North Orleans St., Chicago, Ill. 60614. *Dealer:* Joseph Faulkner, Main Street Gallery, 620 North Michigan Ave., Chicago, Ill.

CAREER: Painter, printmaker, and illustrator of children's books. Worked with theater and ballet companies, 1933-41. Commissioned by International Graphic Arts Society to produce a membership edition of etchings, entitled ''Golden Santorini,'' 1967. Group exhibitions include: Society of Contemporary American Art, Art Institute of Chicago, 1955-75; San Francisco Art Museum, 1960; Ringling Museum, Sarasota, Fla., 1960; Brooklyn Museum, New York, N.Y. 1960-66; Smithsonian Institute, Washington, D.C., 1966; Boston Museum of Fine Art, 1967; New Horizons, Chicago, Ill., 1970-72. One-woman shows include: Main Street Galleries, Chicago, 1964, 1965, 1967, 1969, 1970; Hellenic American Union, Athens, Greece,

MARY GEHR

1971; United States Information Service, Thessaloniki, Greece, 1971; Art Institute of Chicago, 1972; Jacques Baruch Gallery, Chicago, 1973, 1975. Print exhibitions include: Philadelphia, 1958-68; New Canaan, Conn., 1958, 1966, 1968; Schwarzer Gallery, Vienna, Austria, 1975. Work is represented in numerous permanent collections, including: Philadelphia Museum of Fine Art; Art Institute of Chicago; Free Library, Philadelphia; Library of Congress; Nelson Rockefeller Collection; and various corporate and private collections. *Member:* Archaeological Institute of America, Society of Typographic Arts, Arts Club (Chicago), Print Club (Philadelphia). *Awards, honors:* Recipient of lithograph award from Philadelphia Print Fair, 1960; received first prize from Artist Guild Print Exhibition, Chicago, 1972; received an award for graphics from the Old Orchard Festival, Chicago.

*WRITINGS—*Self-illustrated: *The Littlest Circus Seal* (juvenile), Children's Press, 1952; *Leaves from South Pacific and Asian Sketchbooks*, privately printed, 1981.

Illustrator; all for young people: Caroline H. Mallon, *The Story of the Sandman*, Follet, 1945; C. H. Mallon, *Happy Gingerbread Boy, a Modern Version*, Children's Co., 1946; Sylvestre C. Watkins, compiler, *My First Mother Goose*, Wilcox & Follett, 1946; Marion M. Dryer, *Snoopy Gets a Name*, Children's Co., 1946; C. H. Mallon, *The Story of the Man in the Moon*, Children's Co., 1946; William B. Levenson, *Steve Sears, Ace Announcer*, King Co., 1948; Gertrude C. Warner, *Surprise Island*, Scott, Foresman, 1949.

Frances E. Wood and F. Dorothy Wood, *First Picture Word Book*, Whitman Publishing, 1950; Alene Dalton, *Fluffy and Bluffy*, Children's Press, 1951; Betty Russell, *Funny Boots*, A. Whitman, 1951; Charles W. Holloway, *Little Tweet*, Whitman Publishing, 1951; B. Russell, *Run Sheep, Run*, A. Whitman, 1952; Dorothy Aldis, *We're Going to Town*, Bobbs-Merrill, 1952; Donalda M. Copeland, *The True Book of Little Eskimos*, Children's Press, 1953; G. C. Warner, *The Yellow House Mystery*, A. Whitman, 1953; Olive V. Haynes, *The True Book of Health*, Children's Press, 1954; Illa Podendorf,

The True Book of Pebbles and Shells, Children's Press, 1954, reprinted as *My Easy-to-Read True Book of Pebbles and Shells*, Grosset, 1960; B. Russell, *Big Store, Funny Door*, A. Whitman, 1955; I. Podendorf, *The True Book of Seasons*, Children's Press, 1955, reprinted, 1972; I. Podendorf, *The True Book of Weeds and Wild Flowers*, Children's Press, 1955, reprinted, 1972; William J. Small, *Mary Jane Ellen McCling*, A. Whitman, 1956; Janet Konkle, *Tabby's Kittens*, Children's Press, 1956; Paul A. Witty, *The True Book of Freedom and Our U.S. Family*, Children's Press, 1956; Ray Broekel, *You and the Sciences of Mankind*, Children's Press, 1956; Carla Greene, *I Want to Be a Telephone Operator*, Children's Press, 1958; Thomas Chandler, *Learn to Read by Seeing Sound*, Children's Press, 1958; Katharine Carter, *The True Book of Oceans*, Children's Press, 1958; C. Greene, *I Want to Be a Ballet Dancer*, Children's Press, 1959; C. Greene, *I Want to Be a Mechanic*, Children's Press, 1959.

Benjamin Elkin, *The True Book of Money*, Children's Press, 1960; Margaret Friskey, *Cave Man to Space Man: Picture History of Transportation*, Children's Press, 1961; Elsa Posell, *The True Book of Whales and Other Sea Mammals*, Children's Press, 1963; Philip B. Carona, *The True Book of Numbers*, Children's Press, 1964; Philip E. Cleator, *Exploring the World of Archaeology*, Children's Press, 1966 (Mary Gehr was not associated with earlier edition published as *The True Book about Archaeology*); Ruth Lee, *Exploring the World of Pottery*, Children's Press, 1967; M. Friskey, *Three Sides and the Round One*, Children's Press, 1973; M. Friskey, *What Is the Color of the Wide, Wide World?*, Children's Press, 1973.

SIDELIGHTS: Gehr, whose works may be found in many museums as well as in private collections, has taken walks "on the wild side" all over the world. Wherever she travels, she takes her sketchbook and camera in hand, capturing her impressions. Her latest travels were in newly opened Sikkim, where she trekked through forests and over wild mountain cataracts, climbing 14,000 feet to view the 28,000 foot high Kanchenjunga Range.

Gehr's works are included in the Kerlan Collection at the University of Minnesota. Her art proofs are in the Print and Drawing Department of the Chicago Art Institute, Newberry Library, and in the special collection at the Northwestern University Library.

FOR MORE INFORMATION SEE: Chicago Schools Journal, May, 1951; *Art News*, September, 1954; *Art in America*, 1961; T. J. Carbol, editor, *The Printmaker in Illinois*, Illinois Art Education Association, 1971-72.

GRAHAM, Brenda Knight 1942-

PERSONAL: Born September 17, 1942, in Clarkesville, Ga.; daughter of Floyd S. (an artist) and Eula (Gibbs) Knight; married Charles Graham (a veterinarian), December 20, 1965; children: William Stacey, Julie Victoria. *Education:* Young Harris College, A.A., 1963; University of Georgia, A.B.J., 1965. *Religion:* Baptist. *Home:* 1280 South Broad St., Cairo, Ga. 31728.

CAREER: Writer for children and adults, 1970—. Elementary school teacher in Habersham County, Ga., 1965; secretary in department of housing, University of Georgia, Athens, 1966-

68; preschool teacher, First Baptist Church Kindergarten, Cairo, Georgia, 1972-73. Volunteer worker, teacher in adult literacy program, and speaker in children's classrooms. *Member:* American Veterinary Medical Association Auxiliary. *Awards, honors:* Scholar of Dixie Writers Conference, 1963; first prize from *Baptist Student* poetry contest, 1964, for "Sympathy."

WRITINGS—Of interest to young people: *Stone Gables* (nonfiction), Broadman, 1978; *The Pattersons at Turkey Hill House* (fiction), Broadman, 1979; *The Pattersons and the Mysterious Airplane* (fiction), Broadman, 1980; *The Pattersons and the Goat Man* (fiction), Broadman, 1981; *Juliana of Clover Hill*, Zondervan, in press; *The Buried House*, Broadman, in press.

Work represented in anthologies, including *Yearbook of Modern Poetry*, 1971. Contributor to magazines, including *Home Life*, *Grit*, and *Baptist Student*, and newspapers.

WORK IN PROGRESS: Janie, a story of a girl moving with her family from England to America in the mid-nineteenth century.

SIDELIGHTS: "I have wanted to write almost as long as I've been able to hold a pencil. When I was about seven, I wrote a story nearly as long as this paragraph and took it to my teenage brother to read. He glanced at it and said, 'That's good; you'll be a writer someday.' Now I know he was only trying to get rid of me, but then I took him seriously and from then on it was settled as far as I was concerned: I would be a writer."

BRENDA KNIGHT GRAHAM

"As I grew up one of the activities that I enjoyed was writing and typing and printing a family newspaper, subscription rates $1.00 a year. With nine brothers and sisters and many pets and wild creatures on a 150-acre forested home there were never-ending things to write about. One older brother brought me a worn-out (almost!) printing press from a restaurant where he worked, and a sister brought me her tiny typewriter when she graduated from college and got a new one.

"It was not until I was grown and had children of my own that I realized I wanted to write for children. In fact, it was after I had written my first book. That book, *Stone Gables,* is the true story of my family, particularly the youngest five, as we grew up at Pinedale and were taught totally at home by our parents.

"My father, a retired artist, began at the age of forty-two to teach his children at home rather than send them to public school. There ended up being ten of us, and none of us, except the oldest two, had any schoolteachers through the elementary grades other than Mom and Dad. Most of us had no other teachers until we went to college. Our life on a northern Georgia tree farm was unusual and most wonderful. . . .

"When *Stone Gables* came out in the summer of 1978 I began to hear comments from the other nine like: 'That's really not the way it happened, you know,' or 'Let me tell you how it actually was.' I decided after that I wanted to write some fiction about which no one could argue. Being a child at heart, I slipped easily into relating tales about an imaginary family of children doing the things I enjoyed plus many more that never happened to us—such as rescuing someone from a burning plane, sheltering a tramp in the woods, or defending a Goat Man when everyone else said he was guilty of kidnapping.

"I enjoy writing about things that can happen in our everyday lives, real life situations with a mysterious turn to them. I hope when my readers lay down a book they will have a happy feeling, having made new friends and having experienced a little bit more of life through them.

"Sometimes I go on after-office calls with my veterinarian husband. We run into more interesting stories than I'll ever be able to write! My own children are a constant source of ideas. We have a good time on our mini-farm where we have four steers, an Irish setter, and a Heinz 57 kitten. One of my favorite times of the week is that spent with a small group of third and fourth grade girls called Girls in Action. We visit shut-ins, study mission work around the world, and have a good time together.

"My motivation is basically that of a songbird's: he sings because he *must* sing, I write because I *must* write. God has given me this talent as He gave the bird his song, and it is my joy to exercise it.

"My desire is to put wholesome, family-oriented literature into the hands of young and old alike. I believe that stable loving homes are one of America's biggest strengths. I also believe it is important for the education of our children that they *enjoy* reading; therefore, one of my biggest aims is to give them a good time!

"People tell me they like my descriptions most. I dearly love to make my readers aware of the beauty around them, whether it be shifting sun circles on a sandy brook bottom, or a bare tree silhouetted against an evening sky.

"Well, Sonny, I've got me a nice setup here. A place fer me animals to crop a little grass and git a drink of water an' fer me t'stretch my legs out fer a few days." ■ (From *The Pattersons and the Goat Man* by Brenda Knight Graham. Illustrated by Ron Martin.)

"Some of my favorite things to do are baking bread, making jelly, going fishing or crabbing, tent camping, crewel embroidering, reading (children's mysteries are among my favorites), playing badminton (my son always beats me), knitting, travelling (in 1980 our family went out west as far as Grand Canyon and in 1981 we took our first jet flight—all the way to England!), and photography on a very snap-happy scale."

Books are the treasured wealth of the world and the fit inheritance of generations and nations . . . . Their authors are a natural and irresistible aristocracy in every society, and, more than kings or emperors, exert an influence on mankind.

—Henry David Thoreau

Read not to contradict and confute, nor yet to believe and take for granted, nor to find talk and discourse, but to weigh and consider.

—Francis Bacon

GRAY, Harold (Lincoln)   1894-1968

BRIEF ENTRY: Born January 20, 1894, in Kankakee, Ill.; died of cancer May 9, 1968, in La Jolla, Calif. Cartoonist and author. Creator of the popular comic strip "Little Orphan Annie," Gray graduated from Purdue University in 1917 and that same year began his career as a reporter and artist for the *Chicago Tribune.* After a year in the U.S. Army, he returned to his position at the *Tribune* only to leave again in 1920 to establish his own commercial art studio. From 1921 to 1924, he was assistant draftsman on Sidney Smith's comic strip "Andy Gump."

Taking her name from a James Whitcomb Riley poem, "Little Orphant Annie" made her debut in the August 5, 1924 edition of the *New York Daily News.* Three months later, "Annie" was appearing in the Sunday editions of both the *Daily News* and the *Chicago Tribune.* For the following forty-five years, Gray personally drew the adventures of the curly-haired girl with the vacuous eyes for more than 400 newspapers through syndication. The comic strip became known for its political outspokeness as Gray employed it as a vehicle to expose the subversive elements of American society. Annie, her dog Sandy, and Daddy Warbucks also appeared in over a dozen books, including *Little Orphan Annie,* 1926, *Little Orphan Annie Shipwrecked,* 1931, *Little Orphan Annie and the Gooneyville Mystery,* 1947, *Arf!: The Life and Hard Times of Little Orphan Annie, 1935-1945,* 1970, and *Little Orphan Annie in the Great Depression,* 1979. A musical play based on the comic strip was produced on Broadway in 1977 followed by a movie version in 1982. In addition to "Annie," Gray was the creator of the comic strips "Private Lives," 1931, and "Maw Green," 1933, as well as assistant creator of "Little Joe," 1933. *For More Information See: World Encyclopedia of Comics,* Volume I, Chelsea House, 1976; *Contemporary Authors,* Volume 107, Gale, 1983. *Obituaries: New York Times,* May 10, 1968; *Time,* May 17, 1968; *Editor & Publisher,* May 18, 1968; *Newsweek,* May 20, 1968.

GRUELLE, John (Barton)   1880-1938
(Johnny Gruelle)

BRIEF ENTRY: Born December 24, 1880, in Arcola, Ill.; died January 9, 1938, in Miami Springs, Fla. Cartoonist, author and illustrator. Gruelle was the creator of one of the best-loved characters in children's books, Raggedy Ann. He began his career as a cartoonist for newspapers, including several in Indianapolis, 1899-1902, the *Cleveland Press,* 1905, and the *New York Herald,* 1913-21. In 1910, he originated the comic strip, "Brutus," and that same year won a *New York Herald* contest for a new Sunday page comic, "Mr. Twee Deedle." *Raggedy Ann Stories* was published in 1918, the first of over forty books written and illustrated by Gruelle featuring the button-eyed rag doll and her little brother, Raggedy Andy. The stories were based on an actual doll made by Gruelle's grandmother for his mother as a child. By 1938 over three million copies of the book had been sold, and it was subsequently adapted into several motion pictures, including an animated version in 1977. Numerous authors have continued the Raggedy Ann saga in emulated works.

In addition to the "Raggedy Ann" series, Gruelle wrote and illustrated fifteen other books for children, among them *Orphant Annie Story Book,* 1921, *Beloved Belindy,* 1926, *Wooden Willy,* 1927, *Marcella Stories,* 1929, and *The Camel with the Wrinkled Knees,* 1941. He also wrote and illustrated for nu-

merous periodicals, including *Good Housekeeping, Judge, Life,* and others. *For More Information See: Indiana Authors and Their Books, 1816-1916,* Wabash College Press, 1949. *Obituaries: Publishers Weekly,* January 29, 1938; *Wilson Bulletin,* February, 1938.

HAGUE, Michael (R.)

BRIEF ENTRY: Born in Los Angeles, Calif. An author and illustrator of books for children, Hague graduated with honors from the Art Center College of Design in Los Angeles. He has illustrated over fifteen children's books, including Jane Yolen's *Dream Weaver* which was selected as one of the American Institute of Graphic Arts Fifty Books of the Year, 1980. Together with his wife, Kathleen, he has written adaptations of two Norwegian tales, *East of the Sun and West of the Moon,* 1980, and *The Man Who Kept House,* 1981. He has also written his own adaptation of classic fairy tales entitled *Michael Hague's Favorite Hans Christian Andersen Fairy Tales,* 1981. Hague's style of employing lavish detail and rich, brilliant color in his pictures has been called reminiscent of both Rackham and Dulac. Dealing mainly with subject matters of fantasy and fairyland, he has produced pictures that are, according to *School Library Journal,* ". . . sure to enchant most children." Among his illustrated works are such timeless favorites as Moore's *The Night before Christmas,* Grahame's *The Wind in the Willows,* and Baum's *The Wizard of Oz.* His other works include *A Mouse Called Junction* by Julia Cunningham, Lee B. Hopkin's *Moments: Poems about the Seasons,* Marianne Mayer's *The Unicorn and the Lake,* and *The Dragon Kite* by Nancy Luen. He has also illustrated several calendars, including a series based on C. S. Lewis's *Chronicles of Narnia. Residence:* Colorado Springs, Colo.

HARDING, Lee   1937-
(Harold G. Nye)

PERSONAL: Born February 19, 1937, in Colac, Victoria, Australia. *Home:* 17 Burwash Rd., Plumstead SE18 7QY, London, England. *Agent:* Leslie Flood, Carnell Agency, Rowenybury Bungalow, Sawbridgeworth CM20 2EX, Essex, England.

CAREER: Writer and editor of science fiction for adults and young people. *Member:* Fellowship of Australian Writers, Science Fiction Writers of America. *Awards, honors:* Ditmar Trophy for best Australian science fiction story of the year, 1970, for "Dancing Gerontius," and 1972, for "The Fallen Spaceman."

WRITINGS—All science fiction; all for young people: *The Fallen Spaceman* (first published in *If* magazine, 1971; illustrated by Lee Walsh), Cassell (Melbourne), 1973, American edition illustrated by John and Ian Schoenherr, Harper, 1980; (editor) Ursula K. Le Guin and others, *The Altered I: An Encounter with Science Fiction* (anthology), Nostrilia Press, 1976, Berkley Publishing, 1978; *The Frozen Sky,* Cassell, 1976; *The Children of Atlantis,* Cassell, 1977; *Return to Tomorrow,* Cassell, 1977; *Displaced Person* (first published in *Science Fantasy* magazine, 1961), Hyland House, 1979, published as *Misplaced Persons,* Harper, 1979.

Other: *A World of Shadows* (novel), R. Hale, 1975; (editor; foreward by Isaac Asimov) *Beyond Tomorrow: An Anthology*

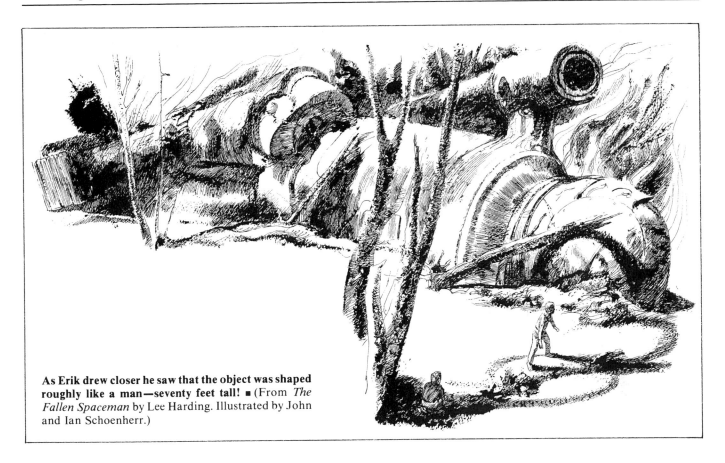

As Erik drew closer he saw that the object was shaped roughly like a man—seventy feet tall! ■ (From *The Fallen Spaceman* by Lee Harding. Illustrated by John and Ian Schoenherr.)

of Modern Science Fiction, Wren, 1976; *Future Sanctuary,* Laser, 1976; *The Gift of Time,* Laser, 1977; *The Weeping Sky* (novel), Cassell, 1977; (editor) *Rooms of Paradise* (anthology), St. Martin's, 1979; *The Web of Time,* Cassell, 1980.

Contributor of numerous stories to periodicals, including *New Writings in Science Fiction* and *If,* some under the pseudonym Harold G. Nye.

mation See: Brian Doyle, *The Who's Who of Children's Literature,* Schocken Books, 1968; Elinor W. Field, *Horn Book Reflections,* Horn Book, 1969; Doris de Montreville and Donna Hill, editors, *Third Book of Junior Authors,* Wilson, 1972; *Contemporary Authors Permanent Series,* Volume I, Gale, 1975; D. L. Kirkpatrick, editor, *Who's Who of Children's Writers,* St. Martin's, 1978. *Obituaries: The Junior Bookshelf,* February, 1982.

HARNETT, Cynthia (Mary)   1893-1981

OBITUARY NOTICE—See sketch in *SATA* Volume 5: Born June 22, 1893, in London, England; died in 1981. Author and illustrator of children's books; considered one of the pioneers of the modern historical story for young people. Instead of recreating history in the traditional manner through the stories of famous and powerful people, Harnett depicted the lives of ordinary people in her books—from the children of the seventeenth-century architect in her first book, *The Great House* (Methuen, 1949), to a fifteenth-century English schoolboy caught in the political intrigues of the War of the Roses in her last book, *The Writing on the Hearth* (Methuen, 1971, Viking, 1973). Harnett won the 1951 Carnegie Medal for the outstanding British children's book of the year for *The Wool-Pack* (published in America as *Nicholas and the Woolpack*), the story of a fifteenth-century wool merchant, whose son uncovers a plot to ruin his father's business. Harnett's other books include *Ring Out Bow Bells* (published in America as *The Drawbridge Gate*), *Stars of Fortune,* and *The Load of Unicorn* (published in America as *Caxton's Challenge*). She also wrote and illustrated books with G. Vernon Stokes, including *Junk, the Puppy, Mudlarks, Bob-tail Pup,* and *Pets Limited. For More Infor-*

HARRIS, Mark Jonathan   1941-

PERSONAL: Born October 28, 1941 in Scranton, Pa; son of Norman (a lawyer) and Ruth (Bialosky) Harris; married Susan Popky (a clinical psychologist), June 9, 1963; children: Laura, Jordan. *Education:* Harvard University, B.A., 1963. *Home and office:* 1043 Point View St., Los Angeles, Calif. 90035. *Agent:* Barbara Lowenstein, 250 West 57th St., New York, N.Y. 10019.

CAREER: Associated Press, Chicago, Ill., reporter, 1963-64; documentary and educational filmmaker, 1964-75; University of Southern California, Los Angeles, senior lecturer in cinema, 1975—. Professor at California Institute of Arts, 1976—. *Member:* Writers Guild of America, Society of Children's Book Writers, Southern California Council on Literature for Children and Young People. *Awards, honors:* Regional Emmy Award from Academy of Television Arts and Sciences, 1965, for "The Golden Calf"; Academy Award for short documentary film from Motion Picture Academy of Arts and Sciences, 1968, for "The Redwoods"; Golden Eagle from Council on International Nontheatrical Events, 1968, for "The Redwoods"; special award from Leipzig International Film Festival, 1968, for "Huelga!";

With a Wave of the Wand was a children's choice selection of International Reading Association, 1981; *The Last Run* was awarded The Golden Spur of the Western Writers of America for the Best Western Juvenile Fiction of 1981; fellowship in writing for children for the 1982 Bread Loaf Writers' Conference in Middlebury, Vt.

WRITINGS: With a Wave of the Wand (juvenile), Lothrop, 1980; *The Last Run* (juvenile), Lothrop, 1981.

Films: "The Golden Calf," KGW-TV (Portland, Ore.), 1965; "Huelga!," King Screen Productions, 1967; "The Redwoods," King Screen Productions, 1968; "The Foreigners," King Screen Productions, 1969.

Contributor to magazines and newspapers, including *Prime Time, TV Guide, Washington Post, Los Angeles Times,* and *Newsday.* Past contributing editor of *New West.*

WORK IN PROGRESS: A juvenile novel, tentatively entitled *Starring Margaret O'Brien Muldaur;* an adult novel, *The Messiah of Palm Springs;* "The American Homefront," a documentary film on the social and economic efforts of World War II on the United States for PBS-TV.

SIDELIGHTS: "I began my career as a wire service reporter, then switched to making educational and documentary films during the politically turbulent 1960's. 'Huelga!' documented the first year of the Delano grape strike. 'The Redwoods' was made to help the Sierra Club establish a Redwood National Park. 'The Foreigners' examined a group of Peace Corps volunteers battling poverty and powerlessness in Colombia. In the 1970's, when the money for political films began running out, I turned to teaching and journalism.

"As I've grown older I've found I'm much more interested in creating my own characters than in reporting about real ones. I began with a twelve-year-old protagonist in *With a Wave of the Wand* and moved up to a fourteen-year-old hero in *The Last Run,* reliving my own childhood and gradually working my way up to adulthood. Soon I expect to be able to write about thirty-year-olds.

"I am particularly interested in writing for children because children value feelings, honesty, and hope in the books they read and so do I. As long as children continue to seek these values in their reading, I will continue writing novels with youthful heroes and heroines.

"So you have rabbits, too," I smiled.

"Of course," he chuckled again. "What's a magician without a rabbit? . . ."

By the time I finished, Mr. Tomaro had reappeared in a top hat and long black coat, carrying a magic wand. ■ (From *With a Wave of the Wand* by Mark Jonathan Harris. Jacket illustration by Stan Skardinski.)

MARK JONATHAN HARRIS

"If there has been a common concern in all my work, it is how people respond to the critical social problems of our society. Whether it is an impoverished farm worker striking for the right to unionize, or a confused twelve-year-old trying to cope with the turmoil of middle-class divorce. I have tried to explore the struggle that occurs when individuals confront the crucial social forces that shape their lives."

HAUMAN, Doris 1898-

PERSONAL: Born August 29, 1898, in West Somerville, Mass.; daughter of Charles Edward (a businessman) and Caroline (Muller) Holt; married George Hauman (an artist and book illustrator), May 14, 1924 (died, 1961); children: Guy R. *Education:* Graduated from Massachusetts Normal Art School, 1920. *Politics:* Republican. *Religion:* Protestant. *Home:* 10 Dickens Row, Third Cliff, Scituate, Mass. 02066.

CAREER: Author of books for children, free-lance illustrator. Derby Academy, Hingham, Mass., art instructor, 1962-76.

WRITINGS—All for children; all written and illustrated with husband, George Hauman; all published by Macmillan: *Bread and Cheese*, 1934; *Buttons: Six Gay Stories with Pictures*, 1936; *Happy Harbor: a Seashore Story*, 1938; *Surprise for Timmy*, 1946.

Illustrator; all with G. Hauman: Marjorie Hayes, *The Little House on Wheels*, Little, Brown, 1934; Emily Dickinson, *Poems for Youth*, Alfred L. Hampson, editor, Little, Brown, 1934; Helena Carus, *Artemis, Fare Thee Well*, Little, Brown, 1935; Dorothy W. Baruch, *I Know a Surprise*, Lothrop, 1935; Rhoda Morris, *Susan and Arabella, Pioneers*, Little, Brown, 1935; Edna H. L. Turpin, *Three Circus Days*, Macmillan, 1935; Barbara F. Fleury, *Luckypiece*, Macmillan, 1936; Henry B. Lent, *Air Pilot*, Macmillan, 1937; H. B. Lent, *Storekeeper*, Macmillan, 1937; Beryl Parker and Paul McKee, *Highways and Byways* (textbook reader), Houghton, 1938; Genevieve M. Fox, *Border Girl*, Little, Brown, 1939; M. Hayes, *The Little House on Runners*, Little, Brown, 1939.

H. B. Lent, *Flight Seventeen*, Macmillan, 1940; R. Morris, *Susan and Little Bird Lost*, Little, Brown, 1941; Hans Christian Andersen, *The Snow Queen*, Macmillan, 1942; Anne S. B. Molloy, *Decky's Secret*, Houghton, 1944; Miriam E. Mason, *Little Jonathan*, Macmillan, 1944, reprinted, 1966; Catherine

Sellew (Hinchman), *Adventures with the Gods*, Little, Brown, 1945; M. Mason, *Happy Jack*, Macmillan, 1945; Nila B. Smith, *Over Hill and Plain*, included in *Learning to Read: A Basic Reading Program*, Silver Burdett, 1945; Thomas M. Longstreth, *Hide-Out*, Macmillan, 1947; T. M. Longstreth, *The Great Venture*, Macmillan, 1948; M. Mason, *Herman, The Brave Pig*, Macmillan, 1949; T. M. Longstreth, *Mounty in a Jeep*, Macmillan, 1949.

George MacDonald, *At the Back of the North Wind*, Macmillan, 1950; M. E. Mason, *Hominy and His Blunt-Nosed Arrow*, Macmillan, 1950, reissue, 1967; Elizabeth J. Coatsworth, *Dollar for Luck*, Macmillan, 1951; Margarite Vaygouny, *Peter the Stork*, Macmillan, 1951; Cornelia L. Meigs, *The Dutch Colt*, Macmillan, 1952; Watty Piper, editor, *Stories That Never Grow Old*, Platt, 1952; H. C. Andersen, *Fairy Tales and Stories*, Signe Toksvig, editor, Macmillan, 1953; W. Piper, reteller, *The Little Engine That Could*, Platt, 1961. Also illustrator of stories for magazines, titles, music books and *ABC Book* published by Platt.

SIDELIGHTS: "When I was quite young my parents moved to Lexington, Massachusetts. My happy summers were spent in Scituate in a cottage beside the ocean. I cannot remember a time, even as a very young child, that I did not yearn to be an artist. I had very little help until I was sent to Sea Pines Boarding School for Girls in Brewster on Cape Cod. There my ambition was helped by an understanding art teacher, and I spent every minute that could be spared from my other classes in the art room, drawing.

"After I graduated, I managed to pass the exams to enter Normal Art School in Boston. There I spent most of the next

Nature is what we know
But have no art to say . . .

■ (From *Poems for Youth* by Emily Dickinson. Illustrated by George and Doris Hauman.)

Puff, puff, chug, chug, went the Little Blue Engine. "I think I can—I think I can—I think I can—I think I can—. . . ." ■ (From *The Little Engine That Could,* retold by Watty Piper. Illustrated by George and Doris Hauman.)

four years drawing in charcoal from the live model. Our fine arts class was very small, for most of the pupils were there to study for the teaching profession.

"After completing my education, I wanted to freelance, and that would mean a studio in Boston so that I could be near the customers. But my father said no, not until I could pay for it myself. It was one of the wisest things he ever did for me, although at the time I did not appreciate it. I started out, my portfolio of drawings under my arm, tramping from publisher to advertising agency to printer—day after day.

"Gradually, I managed to find enough work to pay the rent for a room on Tremont Street. My father approved the location, so I bought some secondhand furniture and moved in. I worked hard to keep up my rent payments, taking drawing home with me at night when necessary. Then the building was sold and I had to move.

"I found a better studio which had a big bay window overlooking Boylston Street. To be sure, it was a third floor walk-up, but it was big and not far from the Public Gardens. Best of all, a good friend that had graduated with me from art school occupied the room next to mine. There were three young men

sharing a studio on the floor below us. They seemed to have plenty of work, but also time to be friendly. One or the other was always ready to walk with me across the Common and down to the North Station, where I had to catch the six o'clock train home every evening. They told us of new places to look for work and were fun, too.

"And that was the way I met my husband-to-be. We were married and he moved his drawing table up to my studio. We bought a small house in Lexington and were soon both working for the same customers and on the same drawings. All work, from then on, was signed Doris and George Hauman.

"When the old building on Boylston Street was sold, we moved our studio into a room on Newbury Street. By this time we were illustrating only for publishers of children's books and music—no more drawing for ads.

"Then our son was born, and I had to stay home and work in our studio there.

"I started to write for children, too, which was something I had always wanted to do. George helped me, and we worked together on the illustrations. Now much of our work was being done by mail to New York, and it seemed wiser and easier for us to be working together at home. Our summers were spent in Scituate at my parents' summer house, where we had a studio on the third floor—cool and spacious. We always took one day a week to sketch out-of-doors in nearby country towns.

"There was plenty of work—hundreds of titles and illustrations for Gustave Schirmer of the Boston and Willis Music Companies and always illustrations for publishers in Boston and New York. There was no more time wasted in commuting. After my parents died and the Lexington houses were sold, we had the cottage taken down and had our new home built there, with a studio overlooking the ocean.

"My husband died in 1961. I was left to work alone. I finished a few illustrations, started and finished a few more, but we had been too close—I couldn't take it. I applied for a position of art instructor at Derby Academy in Hingham, a nearby town, was accepted, and taught there for fourteen years, loving every minute working with children.

"Then, I enjoyed working in my studio beside the ocean—writing more, drawing, carving and making furniture for a fisherman's doll house, lobster pots, sea gulls, and all—just having fun."

"Perhaps the best-loved book that George and I illustrated is *The Little Engine That Could*. Every child I knew loved it. We illustrated Hans Christian Andersen's *The Snow Queen* in full color, and a copy of it is in the Andersen Museum at Odense, Denmark. We did illustrations for many of his stories in *Fairy*

Tales and Stories. Every drawing was a joy to do. I am so fond of Andersen's tales that I have embroidered a large silver-gray linen cloth in white, showing his portrait, many of his sayings, and illustrations of his stories. Another book that we especially enjoyed doing was *Poems for Youth* by Emily Dickinson."

Now, Hauman is legally blind and unable to do any artwork, but keeps busy knitting lap robes for veterans.

FOR MORE INFORMATION SEE: B. M. Miller and others, compilers, *Illustrators of Children's Books: 1946-1956*, Horn Book, 1958.

HAUMAN, George 1890-1961

PERSONAL: Born May 19, 1890, in Revere, Massachusetts; son of George and Minnie (Sullivan) Hauman; married Doris Holt (an illustrator), May 14, 1924; children: Guy R. *Education:* Eric Pape School of Illustration, Boston School of Painting, and Fenway School of Illustration. *Residence:* Scituate, Mass.

CAREER: Free-lance commercial artist and illustrator and author of children's books.

WRITINGS—All for children; all written and illustrated with wife, Doris Hauman; all published by Macmillan: *Bread and Cheese*, 1934; *Buttons: Six Gay Stories with Pictures*, 1936;

And off he rumbled to the roundhouse chugging, "I can not. I can not. I can not." ▪ (From *The Little Engine That Could*, retold by Watty Piper. Illustrated by George and Doris Hauman.)

Happy Harbor: A Seashore Story, 1938; *Surprise for Timmy*, 1946.

Illustrator; all with D. Hauman: Marjorie Hayes, *The Little House on Wheels*, Little, Brown, 1934; Emily Dickinson, *Poems for Youth*, Alfred L. Hampson, editor, Little, Brown, 1934; Helena Carus, *Artemis, Fare Thee Well*, Little, Brown, 1935; Dorothy W. Baruch, *I Know a Surprise*, Lothrop, 1935; Rhoda Morris, *Susan and Arabella, Pioneers*, Little, Brown, 1935; Edna H. L. Turpin, *Three Circus Days*, Macmillan, 1935; Barbara F. Fleury, *Luckypiece*, Macmillan, 1936; Henry B. Lent, *Air Pilot*, Macmillan, 1937; H. B. Lent, *Storekeeper*, Macmillan, 1937; Beryl Parker and Paul McKee, *Highways and Byways* (textbook reader), Houghton, 1938; Genevieve M. Fox, *Border Girl*, Little Brown, 1939; M. Hayes, *The Little House on Runners*, Little, Brown, 1939.

H. B. Lent, *Flight Seventeen*, Macmillan, 1940; R. Morris, *Susan and Little Bird Lost*, Little, Brown, 1941; Hans Christian Andersen, *The Snow Queen*, Macmillan, 1942; Anne S. B. Molloy, *Decky's Secret*, Houghton, 1944; Miriam E. Mason, *Little Jonathan*, Macmillan, 1944, reprinted, 1966; Catharine Sellew (Hinchman), *Adventures with the Gods*, Little, Brown, 1945; M. Mason, *Happy Jack*, Macmillan, 1945; Nila B. Smith, *Over Hill and Plain*, included in *Learning to Read: A Basic Reading Program*, Silver Burdette, 1945; Thomas M. Longstreth, *Hide-Out*, Macmillan, 1947; T. M. Longstreth, *The Great Venture*, Macmillan, 1948; M. Mason, *Herman, the Brave Pig*, Macmillan, 1949; T. M. Longstreth, *Mounty in a Jeep*, Macmillan, 1949.

George MacDonald, *At the Back of the North Wind*, Macmillan, 1950; M. Mason, *Hominy and His Blunt-Nosed Arrow*, Macmillan, 1950, reissue, 1967; Elizabeth J. Coatsworth, *Dollar for Luck*, Macmillan, 1951; Margarite Vaygouny, *Peter the Stork*, Macmillan, 1951; Cornelia L. Meigs, *The Dutch Colt*, Macmillan, 1952; Watty Piper, editor, *Stories That Never Grow Old*, Platt, 1952; H. C. Andersen, *Fairy Tales and Stories*, Signe Toksvig, editor, Macmillan, 1953; W. Piper, reteller, *The Little Engine That Could*, Platt, 1961. Also illustrator of stories for magazines, titles and music books.

SIDELIGHTS: Hauman showed an early interest in drawing. He attended children's classes at the Pape School for three years. Following graduation from high school he attended art schools, worked at the Forbes Lithograph Company and in commercial art studios. He also did free-lance commercial art while he attended night school.

When he met fellow artist, Doris Holt, he found that they shared a common interest in children's illustrations. Following their marriage, the couple collaborated on illustrations for children's books, music books, and commercial art work. Their home and studio overlooked the ocean in Scituate, Massachusetts.

FOR MORE INFORMATION SEE: B. M. Miller and others, compilers, *Illustrators of Children's Books: 1946-1956*, Horn Book, 1958.

Grown-ups never understand anything for themselves, and it is tiresome for children to be always and forever explaining things to them.

—Antoine de Saint-Exupéry

HEIDE, Florence Parry 1919-
(Alex B. Allen, Jamie McDonald)

PERSONAL: Surname is pronounced *High-dee;* born February 27, 1919, in Pittsburgh, Pa.; daughter of David W. (a banker) and Florence (a columnist and drama critic; maiden name Fisher) Parry; married Donald C. Heide (a lawyer), November 27, 1943; children: Christen, Roxanne, Judith, David, Parry. *Education:* Attended Wilson College; University of California, Los Angeles, B.A., 1939. *Politics:* Republican. *Religion:* Protestant. *Home:* 6910 Third Ave., Kenosha, Wis., 53140. *Agent:* Curtis Brown, 575 Madison Ave., New York, N.Y. 10022.

CAREER: Author of children's books, 1967—. Associated with Radio-Keith-Orpheum in New York City; worked at advertising and public relations agencies in New York City; Pittsburgh Playhouse, Pittsburgh, Pa., public relations director.

MEMBER: International Board on Books for Young People, American Society of Composers, Authors, and Publishers (AS-CAP), Authors Guild, National League of American Pen Women, Society of Children's Book Writers, Council for Wisconsin Writers, Children's Reading Round Table. *Awards, honors:* Children's Books of the Year Award from the Child Study Association of America, 1970, for *Sound of Sunshine, Sound of Rain*, and 1972, for *My Castle;* American Institute of Graphic Arts selection as one of the fifty best books of the year, 1971, American Institute of Graphic Arts Children's Book Show selection, 1971-72, *New York Times*, "Best Illustrated Children's Book" Citation, 1971, Children's Book Showcase selection, 1972, Jugendbuchpreis for best children's book in Germany, 1977, Graphic Arts Prize from Bologna Book Fair, 1977, Hans Christian Andersen honor list, 1979, all for *The Shrinking of Treehorn;* runner-up for juvenile fiction from Council for Wisconsin Writers and selected by Children's Book Council as notable children's trade book in field of social studies, both 1975, both for *When the Sad One Comes to Stay;* cited as an honor book for The Golden Kite award from Society of Children's Book Writers, and first prize for juvenile fiction from Council for Wisconsin Writers, both 1976, both for *Growing Anyway Up;* Golden Archer awards, 1976; Litt.D. from Carthage College, 1979; Charlie May Simon award, 1980, for *Banana Twist;* first prize from Council for Wisconsin Writers, 1982, for *Treehorn's Treasure.*

WRITINGS: Benjamin Budge and Barnaby Ball (illustrated by Sally Mathews), Four Winds Press, 1967; (under pseudonym Jamie McDonald; with Anne Theiss and others) *Hannibal* (illustrated by Anne and Walter Theiss), Funk, 1968; *Maximilian Becomes Famous* (illustrated by Ed Renfro), Funk, 1969.

Alphabet Zoop (illustrated by S. Mathews), McCall Publishing, 1970; *Giants Are Very Brave People* (illustrated by Charles Robinson), Parents' Magazine Press, 1970; *The Little One* (illustrated by Ken Longtemps), Lion Press, 1970; *Sound of Sunshine, Sound of Rain* (illustrated by K. Longtemps), Parents' Magazine Press, 1970; *The Key* (illustrated by Ati Forberg), Atheneum, 1971; *Look! Look! A Story Book* (illustrated by Carol Nicklaus), McCall Publishing, 1971; *The Shrinking of Treehorn* (illustrated by Edward Gorey; *Junior Literary Guild* selection; ALA Notable Book), Holiday House, 1971; *Some Things Are Scary*, Scholastic Book Services, 1971; *Who Needs Me?* (illustrated by S. Mathews), Augsburg, 1971; *My Castle* (illustrated by Symeon Shimin), McGraw, 1972; (with brother, David Fisher Parry) *No Roads for the Wind* (textbook), Macmillan, 1974; *God and Me* (illustrated by Ted Smith), Concordia, 1975; *When the Sad One Comes to Stay*, Lippincott, 1975; *You and Me* (illustrated by T. Smith), Concordia, 1975;

FLORENCE PARRY HEIDE

Treehorn was going to write his book report on THE HEADLESS HORROR. The teacher hadn't *said* they could write a book report on a comic book, but she hadn't said they *couldn't*, either. ■ (From *Treehorn's Treasure* by Florence Parry Heide. Illustrated by Edward Gorey.)

Growing Anyway Up, Lippincott, 1976; *Banana Twist* (ALA Notable Book), Holiday House, 1978; *Changes*, Concordia, 1978; *Secret Dreamer, Secret Dreams*, Lippincott, 1978; *Who Taught Me?*, Concordia, 1978; *By the Time You Count to Ten*, Concordia, 1979.

Treehorn's Treasure (illustrated by E. Gorey; ALA Notable Book), Holiday House, 1981; *The Problems with Pulcifer* (illustrated by Judy Glasser), Lippincott, 1982; *The Wendy Puzzle* (Junior Literary Guild selection), Holiday House, 1982; *Time's Up* (illustrated by Marylin Hafner, ALA Notable Book), Holiday House, 1982; *Banana Blitz*, Holiday House, 1983; *I Am*, Concordia, 1983.

All with Sylvia W. Van Clief: *Maximilian* (illustrated by E. Renfro), Funk, 1967; *The Day It Snowed in Summer* (illustrated by K. Longtemps), Funk, 1968; *How Big Am I* (illustrated by George Suyeoka), Follett, 1968; *It Never Is Dark* (illustrated by Don Almquist), Follett, 1968; *Sebastian* (illustrated by Betty Fraser), Funk, 1968; *That's What Friends Are For* (illustrated by Brinton Turkle), Four Winds Press, 1968; *The New Neighbor* (illustrated by Jerry Warshaw), Follett, 1970; (lyricist) *Songs to Sing About Things You Think About* (illustrated by Rosalie Schmidt), Day, 1971; (lyricist) *Christmas Bells and Snowflakes* (songbook), Southern Music Publishing, 1971; (lyricist) *Holidays! Holidays!* (songbook), Southern Music Publishing, 1971; *The Mystery of the Missing Suitcase* (illustrated by Seymour Fleishman), A. Whitman, 1972; *The Mystery of the Silver Tag* (illustrated by S. Fleishman), A. Whitman, 1972; *The Hidden Box Mystery* (illustrated by S. Fleishman), A. Whitman, 1973; *Mystery at MacAdoo Zoo* (illustrated by S. Fleishman), A. Whitman, 1973; *Mystery of the Whispering Voice* (illustrated by S. Fleishman), A. Whitman, 1974; *Who Can?* (primer), Macmillan, 1974; *Lost and Found* (primer), Macmillan, 1974; *Hats and Bears* (primer), Macmillan, 1974; *Fables You Shouldn't Pay Any Attention To* (illustrated by Victoria Chess), Lippincott, 1978.

All with daughter, Roxanne Heide; all published by A. Whitman, except as noted: *Lost!* (textbook), Holt, 1973; *I See America Smiling* (textbook), Holt, 1973; *Tell About Someone You Love* (textbook), Macmillan, 1974; *Mystery of the Melting Snowman* (illustrated by S. Fleishman), 1974; *Mystery of the Vanishing Visitor* (illustrated by S. Fleishman), 1975; *Mystery of the Bewitched Bookmobile* (illustrated by S. Fleishman), 1975; *Mystery of the Lonely Lantern* (illustrated by S. Fleishman), 1976; *Mystery at Keyhole Carnival* (illustrated by S. Fleishman), 1977; *Brillstone Break-In* (illustrated by Beth and Joe Krush), 1977; *Mystery of the Midnight Message* (illustrated by S. Fleishman), 1977; *The Face at the Brillstone Window*, 1978; *Fear at Brillstone* (illustrated by J. Krush), 1978; *Mystery at Southport Cinema* (illustrated by S. Fleishman), 1978; *I Love Every-People* (illustrated by John Sanford), Concordia, 1978; *Body in the Brillstone Garage* (illustrated by J. Krush), 1979; *Mystery of the Mummy Mask* (illustrated by S. Fleishman), 1979; *Mystery of the Forgotten Island* (illustrated by S. Fleishman), 1979; *A Monster Is Coming! A Monster Is Coming!*, Watts, 1980; *Black Magic at Brillstone* (illustrated by J. Krush), 1981; *Time Bomb at Brillstone* (illustrated by J. Krush), 1982.

Under pseudonym Alex B. Allen; all with S. W. Van Clief, except as noted; all published by A. Whitman: *Basketball Toss Up* (illustrated by Kevin Royt), 1972; *No Place for Baseball* (illustrated by K. Royt), 1973; *Danger on Broken Arrow Trail* (illustrated by Michael Norman), 1974; *Fifth Down* (illustrated by Dan Siculan), 1974; (with son, David Heide) *The Tennis Menace* (illustrated by Timothy Jones), 1975. Contributor of stories to *Cricket* magazine.

ADAPTATIONS: "It Never Is Dark" (filmstrip with cassette or record), BFA Educational Media, 1975.

WORK IN PROGRESS: Juvenile novels; an adult thriller; several mystery novels in collaboration with daughter, Roxanne Heide.

SIDELIGHTS: "I didn't start writing until our five children had started school. It hadn't occurred to me that I *could* write—weren't authors those people who started scribbling stories when they were still in their cribs, weren't authors those glamorous, bright, beautiful, talented, *IN* people? I'd never even heard of a sort of *homemade* writer.

"And now I am one! And I love it.

"Drifting into writing for children aimlessly, first writing lyrics for music which a friend composed, then attempting picture books so a song might accompany the text, I found myself making a wonderful discovery: I could put words together to create a story, a character, a mood, a memory, an idea. It was a heady experience and one from which I have not yet recovered. Knowing that something I dream can land on paper, can appear as a book that is read by children I have never seen, knowing that part of me therefore becomes part of them, is a source of great joy and pride, and I am in a constant state of pleased surprise.

"What do I want to write, now that I have access to the ears, the eyes, the heads, of many children? So much to say, so many directions to take, so many possibilities. Should I try to amuse? instruct? entertain? challenge? puzzle? reassure?

"I have tried various kinds of books: serious novels and funny ones, mysteries and introspective books, picture books, textbook stories; a variety of books as I test the variety of ideas

"Not again!" Liza exclaimed. "If this car isn't stalling or smoking or making strange noises, then the doors won't open or the windows won't shut."

"Why don't you just junk it and start over with a bike?" ▪ (From *Brillstone Break-In* by Florence Parry Heide and Roxanne Heide. Illustrated by Joe Krush.)

that I now have that seemed never to occur to me before. I am not a fact person, so I write fiction; I am not an adult person, so I write juveniles. Although many of my books have been published, I know that I am a beginner.

"I grew up with the sound of the typewriter and the sound of many exciting conversations: words were important. My mother, widowed very young, was a business woman and a writer, and for nearly thirty years wrote a daily column for the *Pittsburgh Press* and a thrice a week column as well, as drama critic. Being a writer, she would tell me, is the most exciting thing in the world. And all you need is your own head—and a typewriter, or a pencil and paper. Well, I thought—that's fine for HER to say, she's a WRITER, but I'm not. Certainly *I* didn't know anything about politics, or books, or news, or ideas, or the theatre. What could *I* ever write? Nothing. But words, spoken and written, were in the air, and perhaps I absorbed them or the excitement of using them. And it's true what she always said, and what I keep telling my own children: writing is the best of all worlds."

Heide's sense of accomplishment is knowing children read and enjoy her books. "Writing for young people is the most exciting and rewarding thing I've done, and I hope to continue happily ever after." *The Shrinking of Treehorn* and *Treehorn's Treasure* have been published in England and translated into German, Swedish, Spanish and French. Many of Heide's works, including *Sound of Sunshine, Sound of Rain, That's What Friends Are For*, and *The Shrinking of Treehorn*, have been reprinted in textbook readers. "That's nice, because I know that more and more children are READING Them!"

FOR MORE INFORMATION SEE: Book World, December 31, 1967; *Library Journal*, February 15, 1972; *Horn Book*, February, 1972, April and June, 1976; *School Library Journal*, February, 1976; *Vilas County News-Review*, June 3, 1976; *Kenosha News*, December 10, 1976, May 15, 1979; Doris de Montreville and Elizabeth D. Crawford, editors, *Fourth Book of Junior Authors and Illustrators*, H. W. Wilson, 1978; Martha E. Ward and Dorothy A. Marquardt, editors, *Authors of Books for Young People*, 2nd edition, supplement, Scarecrow, 1979; *Pittsburgh Post Gazette*, April 26, 1979.

HIGHWATER, Jamake 1942-
(J Marks; J Marks-Highwater)

PERSONAL: Given name is pronounced juh-MAH-kuh; born February 14, 1942, in Glacier County, Mont.; son of Jamie (a stuntman) and Amana (Bonneville) Highwater. *Agent:* Alfred Hart, Fox Chase Agency, 419 East 57th St., New York, N.Y. 10022.

CAREER: Writer and lecturer on world cultures, particularly the American Indian. Consultant on American Indians to New York State Council on the Arts, 1975—; founder, host, narrator, and writer of television series "Songs of the Thunderbirds," PBS-TV (Miami affiliate), 1977—; appointed to Task Panel, President's Commission on Mental Health, 1977-78; appointed lecturer, School of Continuing Education of New York University, 1979—; artist-in-residence for Swiss government, Zurich, Switzerland, 1974-82; New York State Council on the Arts, appointed to Task Force on the Individual Artist, 1981-82 and to Literature Panel, 1982—. *Member:* White Buffalo Council of American Indians, Authors League of America, Dramatists Guild, American Federation of Television and Radio Artists, Business Music, Inc., New York Arts Council's American Indian Community House (founding member, past president 1976-78), Board of the American Indian Arts Foundation (founding member), PEN, National Congress of American Indians, Authors Guild. *Awards, honors:* Newbery Honor Book Award and American Library Association Best Book for Young Adults, both 1978, for *Anpao: An American Indian Odyssey;* Jane Addams Book Award from the Women's International League for Peace and Freedom and the Jane Addams Peace Association, 1979, for *Many Smokes, Many Moons;* Cleveland Foundation's Anisfield-Wolf Award, 1981, for *Song from the Earth: North American Indian Painting.* Named honorary citizen of Oklahoma, 1977; named colonel aide-de-camp on staff of governor of New Mexico; given honorary name, Piitai Sahkomaapii ("Eagle Son"), from the Blood Band of the Blackfeet Nations, 1979.

WRITINGS: (Under pseudonym, J Marks) *Rock and Other Four Letter Words* (novel), Bantam, 1969; *Europe Under Twenty-Five: A Young Person's Guide*, Fodor's, 1972; (under J Marks-Highwater) *Mick Jagger: The Singer Not the Song* (novel),

JAMAKE HIGHWATER

Curtis Books, 1973; *Indian America: A Cultural and Travel Guide*, McKay, 1974; *Song from the Earth: North American Indian Painting* (Literary Guild Book Club selection), Little, Brown, 1976; *Ritual of the Wind: North American Indian Ceremonies, Music, and Dances*, Viking, 1976; *Anpao: An American Indian Odyssey* (juvenile novel; illustrated by Fritz Scholder; *Horn Book* honor book), Lippincott, 1977; *Many Smokes, Many Moons: A Chronology of American Indian History Through Indian Art* (juvenile), Lippincott, 1978; *Dance: Ritual of Experience*, A & W Publications, 1978; *Journey to the Sky: Stephens and Catherwood Rediscover the Maya* (novel), Crowell, 1978; *Masterpieces of American Indian Painting*, 8 volumes, Folio/Bell Editions, 1979-83; *The Sun, He Dies: The End of the Aztec World* (novel), Harper, 1980; *The Sweet Grass Lives On: Fifty Contemporary North American Indian Artist*, Harper, 1980; *The Primal Mind: Vision and Reality in Indian America*, Harper, 1981; *Moonsong Lullaby* (juvenile; illustrated by Marcia Keegan), Lothrop, 1981; *Eyes of Darkness*, Morrow, 1983; *Leaves from the Sacred Tree: Arts of the Indian Americas*, Harper, 1983.

Ghost Horse Trilogy: *Legend Days*, Harper, 1984; *I Wear the Morning Star*, Harper, 1985; *Kill Hole*, Harper, 1986.

Author of Introduction: Burton Supree and Ann Ross, *Bear's Heart*, Lippincott, 1976; Charles Eastman, *Indian Boyhood*, Rio Grande Press, 1976; Arthur Silberman, *One Hundred Years of American Indian Painting*, Oklahoma Museum of Art, 1977; Susan Peterson, *Master Pueblo Potters*, ACA Galleries (New York), 1980.

Senior editor of "Fodor Travel Guides," 1970-75. Writer and producer of radio and television scripts; narrator of Olaf Baker's "Where the Buffaloes Begin," Miller-Brody, 1982.

Contributor to popular magazines, sometimes under pseudonym J Marks, including *Smithsonian, Diversion, Esquire, Look, Saturday Review, Vogue, Horizon, American Heritage, Harper's Bazaar,* and *Dance,* and to newspapers. Contributing editor of *Stereo Review,* 1969-80; classical music editor of *Soho Weekly News,* 1975-79; contributing editor of *New York Arts Journal,* 1978—.

ADAPTATIONS: "Anpao: An American Indian Odyssey" (filmstrip and cassette; narrated by the author), Random House, 1978, (recording by author), Folkways Records, 1978; "Song from the Earth: North American Indian Painting" (filmstrip), Random House, 1984. "The Primal Mind," a special for PBS-TV, 1984.

WORK IN PROGRESS: "Indian America: Past, Present and Future," a filmstrip and PBS-TV documentary; "Native Land: Sagas of the Indian Americas," a filmstrip for PBS-TV; dramatization with music of his novel *The Sun, He Dies; Words in the Blood: An Anthology of Native American Literature,* for New American Library; projects in the communications field.

SIDELIGHTS: "My mother, despite her complex blend of French Canadian and Blackfeet (Blood) ancestry, somehow managed to retain much of the special inclusivity which I identify with the heart of Indian people. She rarely expressed intolerance toward anything or anyone, and she was always capable of sustaining utter faith in the most contradictory realities—which is doubtlessly how she managed to keep alive her innermost identity as an Indian despite all the events that took her farther and farther from her origins.

"Although my mother's mother and father apparently died of starvation and she and her sister were passed from one foster home to another, she was completely untouched by loathing for the self-righteousness of her various and numerous guardians and their evangelistic intentions. Though I suspect my

**The night is shelter
for those who weep.**

■ (From *Moonsong Lullaby* by Jamake Highwater. Photograph by Marcia Keegan.)

...The people gathered on the beach were amazed to see a great floating island emerging from the edge of the world with tall, leafless trees spred with vast white wings. ∎ (From *Indian America: A Cultural and Travel Guide* by Jamake Highwater. Illustrated by Asa Battles.)

mother had been christened, she retained an unperturbable faith in her tribal realities which she passed along to me in a strong and constant voice. Her vivid teachings were my access to the Indian world, for I grew up constantly on the move and never had the advantage of the extended family life which had marked the training of my ancestors.

"Though my mother could neither read nor write, she spun her recollections of Blackfeet and French and her faltering English into a rare and enlightened acceptance of the whole world and all the myriad people and events which we encountered during our travels on the rodeo and pow-wow trail. From my disinherited mother I learned to stay alive by dreaming myself into existence—no matter how many influences and forces attempted to negate or to confine my sense of identity. From her I learned that *everything* is real. It was a lesson of enormous value to me, especially during these days of Indian nationalism when the authenticity of urban Indians is constantly under scrutiny by Indians and non-Indians alike.

"My father was not a traditional Indian. I am not even certain if both of his parents were Native people. He was a renegade and an alcoholic—a marvelous, energetic man who helped to organize the American Indian Rodeo Association back in the 1930s and 40s. He called himself by many names during his career in circuses, carnivals, and rodeos, but by the time he met my then sixteen-year-old mother somewhere in the American Northwest his name was Jamie Highwater. He came from Virginia, Tennessee, or North Carolina, depending on his memory and his mood, and he knew very little about his Eastern Cherokee heritage despite his intense pride in being an Indian.

"He was a very dark, tall and handsome man with great athletic abilities. Eventually he became a rodeo clown, and traveled around the pow-wow circuit. Then producers on locations in Montana, Wyoming, the Dakotas, and down in Arizona's Mon-

ument Valley began using my father as a stuntman in western films, which prompted a new career and brought about much traveling and extended visits to Southern California for my family.

"Jamie Highwater died hundreds of times for John Wayne. Then, when I was about ten years old, he died for the last time in an automobile collision. I was adopted by my father's closest friend—a castabout, sometimes actor in films, and an ex-circus aerialist; and I spent my adolescence in his San Fernando Valley home and became 'J Marks.'

"Since those difficult days of living between two cultures I have reclaimed my own name and I have also traveled the arduous journey back to my cultural identity. The grand climax of my professional and personal life took place on March 29, 1979, at Lethbridge University in Alberta, Canada, when Ed Calf Robe, Elder of the Blood Reserve of Blackfeet Indians, a member of the Horns Society, and a descendant of the famous chief Calf Robe, conferred a new name upon me to honor my achievements in behalf of my people. It is a ceremony usually reserved for *minipoka*, 'favored children' of the Blackfeet Nations. This name-ceremony was the vindication of my mother's constant efforts to keep my heritage alive within me. Sadly, she had passed away and could not see the embrace of my people for which she had longed all her life."

Highwater has in what he calls "my Indian sensibility," a strong sense of heritage and a purely Indian concept of reality and identity. "I just happen to be an Indian person. . . . Indians are separate out of choice—not out of demand or necessity. Around reservations, like in Oklahoma, there are a lot of people who don't like Indians, but that isn't the crux of it. The fact is that Indians have decided and determined with great tenacity to remain apart.

"To the Indian mentality, dead people walk and things go backward and forward in time, and these are absolutely real and vivid ideas to my head, our heads. And more than that, the Indian world is one of the few worlds where human identity is not a major issue. In this society, you're not permitted any kind of personal transformation. In ours, it is expected. We can even change gender if we want. So, you see, I still have to fight with people who will say, 'The characters aren't really fully developed' or 'The book isn't really a novel.' To us, it is." ["Jamake Highwater," *Publishers Weekly*, November 6, 1979.¹]

"Educationally I am the product of a wide and complex interplay of university and traditional Indian training. I am disinclined to talk about my education and many other personal details of my life because I feel they have no relationship to my writing. I often quote W. B. Yeats: 'Art is the public act of a private person.' Besides, I spent my adolescence and college days as an adopted child, and I feel it my responsibility to protect the privacy of my adoptive family, whose legal name was not 'Marks' though I used that name professionally.

"The most significant influences of my childhood from the standpoint of my work as a writer were those of Ruth (my adoptive sister), Alta Black (my grammar school teacher), and a family of exceptional people who befriended me as a child (Frederick and Virginia Dorr and Frances Grigsby.) What made these people so exceedingly important to me as a child and what has kept them close friends throughout my life is their willingness and unique capacity to grasp my reality and confirm my existence in two drastically different realities, rather than attempting to change, correct, or Anglicize my world-view.

"During the 1960s I spent most of my time founding and administering an arts foundation in San Francisco. The San Francisco Contemporary Theatre produced some remarkable people, and I was very fortunate to be closely associated with them. I also found an ideal outlet for my own theatrical activities and creations at the theatre, which flourished as an important arts center in the West for more than a decade.

"Touring with the San Francisco theatre group gave me an unusual access to the U.S. and Canada and awakened in me a desire to travel widely. During the 1960s I visited most of the contemporary Indian reservations and all the great centers of ancient American civilizations.

"Meanwhile I witnessed the rise of a counter-culture in San Francisco which struck me as remarkably similar to Native American values in some of its viewpoints and visions. The result of that encounter with the Hippie and Rock movement was a series of articles for various 'underground' newspapers which were being founded at the time, as well as two experimental books: *Rock and Other Four Letter Words* and *Mick Jagger: The Singer Not the Song*.

"But with 1969 and the Indian invasion of Alcatraz Island in the San Francisco Bay, my thoughts—like those of hundreds of young Indians—turned dramatically toward my own heritage. There had always been in everything I did—the dances and stage works I choreographed, the articles and books I wrote—a distinctive ritual premise. But with the Alcatraz takeover I was fired with a sense of visibility and courage as an Indian person. It was in 1969 that I began work on my first 'Indian' book which would bear my real name, Jamake Highwater. It was called *Indian America: A Cultural and Travel Guide* which I researched and wrote for four years for Eugene Fodor whose travel books have won very wide regard.

"Fodor not only gave me my first chance to write about my own heritage, he also gave me the marvelous opportunity to see myself in relationship to the peoples of the whole world. He appointed me editor and writer of a student guide to Europe which gave me virtually unlimited access to the entire world, all expenses paid!

"During much of the 1970s I resided in Europe, with homes in Paris, Brussels, Zurich, and the little fishing village of Kusadasi in Turkey.

"I now live in New York City, and make frequent trips to Canada, Alaska, Mexico, Central and South America. I lecture

(From *Ritual of the Wind: North American Indian Ceremonies, Music, and Dances* by Jamake Highwater. Illustration by Asa Battles.)

widely on the arts as well as American Indian cultures, and I have organized and moderated a seminar at the Aspen Institute entitled 'Indian America: Past, Present and Future'—a project which will be the basis of a sound filmstrip, a series of PBS television documentaries, and an anthology. Also in the field of television, I am featured in six half-hour PBS programs entitled 'Red, White, and Black: Ethnic Dance in America'; a pilot program on mythology featuring the work of Joseph Campbell; and in a six-hour, six-part series produced by Bill Moyers for PBS entitled 'Six Great Ideas.'

"About half of my lectures are given at the invitation of Native American Studies Programs at various universities. I am also a very regular guest-speaker for the American Library Association and the Association of American Art Educators—organizations which have been exceedingly helpful to my career. Though heavily committed to book publishers, I continue to write on music, art, dance, and theatre for various national magazines and newspapers."

Highwater's book about Mick Jagger has been translated into French, Dutch, German, Italian, and Portuguese.

FOR MORE INFORMATION SEE: Contemporary Authors, Volumes 65-68, Gale, 1977; "Jamake Highwater," *Publishers Weekly,* November 6, 1979; "Meet the Newbery Author: Jamake Highwater" (filmstrip and cassette), Random House, 1980.

HNIZDOVSKY, Jacques   1915-

PERSONAL: Born January 27, 1915, in Pylypcze, Ukraine (now part of U.S.S.R.); naturalized U.S. citizen in 1954; son of Yakiv (a farmer) and Martha (Kubej) Hnizdovsky; married Stephania Kouzan, February 16, 1957; children: Mary-Martha. *Education:* Attended Academy of Fine Arts, Warsaw, Poland, and Academy of Fine Arts, Zagreb, Yugoslavia. *Home:* 5270 Post Rd., Riverdale, N.Y. 10471. *Dealers:* Associated American Artists, 663 Fifth Ave., New York, N.Y. 10017. Tahir Gallery, 823 Chartres St., New Orleans, LA 70116; Lumley-Cazalet Ltd., 24 Davies St., London W.1., England.

CAREER: Painter, printmaker, and illustrator. Work has appeared in one-man shows at Lumley-Cazalet, London, England, 1969, 1972; Associated American Artists, "Ten Years of Woodcuts," New York, N.Y., 1971, and in the Hnizdovsky-Woodcuts of the Seventies, 1979; Long Beach Museum of Art, Long Beach, Calif., 1977; and Yale University, New Haven, Conn., 1977. Group exhibitions include Boston Printmakers Annual, Museum of Fine Arts, Boston, Mass., 1961; Contemporary U.S. Graphic Arts, U.S.S.R., 1963; Trienalle International dellaxilogratia Contemporanea, Carpi, Italy, 1972; Contemporary U.S. Printmakers, Tokyo, Japan, 1967. Work is represented in permanent collections of various museums, including Museum of Fine Arts, Boston, Mass., Philadelphia Museum of Art, Philadelphia, Pa., Cleveland Museum, Cleveland, Ohio, Library of Congress, The White House, the Nelson Rockefeller collection and many others. *Member:* Society of American Graphic Artists, Audubon Artists, Boston Printmakers. *Awards, honors:* First prize for woodcut from Boston Museum of Fine Arts, 1962; MacDowell Colony fellowship, 1963; Virginia Center for the Creative Arts (fellowship), 1979.

ILLUSTRATOR: Poems of John Keats (juvenile), edited by Stanley Kunitz, Crowell, 1964; Ivan Rudchenko and Maria Lukiyanenko, *Ukranian Folk Tales* (juvenile), edited and trans-

lated by Marie Halun Bloch, Coward, 1964; Robert Silverberg, *The Auk, the Dodo, and the Oryx* (juvenile), Crowell, 1967, (reprinted in England as *The Dodo, the Auk, and the Oryx: Vanished and Vanishing Creatures,* Puffin, 1973); *Poems of Samuel Taylor Coleridge* (juvenile), edited by Babette Deutsch, Crowell, 1967.

M. M. Graff, *Tree Tails in Central Park,* Greenswood Foundation, 1970; Gordon P. DeWolf, *Flora Exotica: A Collection of Flowering Plants* (adult), David R. Godine, 1972; (contributor) *Portfolio: Jacques Hnizdovsky: Twelve Birds* (adult), Associated American Artists, 1975; Ivan Drach, *Orchard Lamps* (adult; poetry), edited by S. Kunitz, Sheep Meadow Press, 1978; Thomas Hardy, *Poems by Thomas Hardy,* edited by Trevor Johnson, Folio, 1979; Robert Frost, *The Poetry of Robert Frost,* Franklin Library, 1982; William Jay Smith, *The Traveler's Tree* (poems), Persea Books, 1981; Aleksis Rannit, *Signum et Verbum* (poems), Stamperia Valdonega (Italy), 1981; W. J. Smith, compiler, *A Green Place: Modern Poems* (juvenile), Delacorte, 1982; A. Rannit, *The Violin of Monsieur Ingres* (poems), Adolf Hürlimann (Switzerland), 1983.

SIDELIGHTS: Hnizdovsky was born in the Ukraine in 1915. Before the Nazi invasion of Poland in 1939, he was a student at the Academy of Fine Arts in Warsaw. When the Germans invaded Poland, he was in Yugoslavia and unable to return to

...None is more awesome than the rukh, or roc, of the *Thousand and One Nights.* That long-suffering sailor, Sinbad, encountered that mighty bird on his second voyage. ■(From *The Auk, the Dodo, and the Oryx: Vanished and Vanishing Creatures* by Robert Silverberg. Illustrated by Jacques Hnizdovsky.)

JACQUES HNIZDOVSKY

his home. Separated from his family, he continued to study at the Academy of Fine Arts in Zagreb, Yugoslavia, where he supported himself as a free-lance designer. After the war he found himself in Western Europe and, ultimately, emigrated to the United States in 1949, becoming a U.S. citizen in 1954.

His first American position was as a designer in the Minnesota firm of Brown and Bigelow, which published calendars. "For the first time I received a salary, and for the first time I began to pay taxes. After many difficult years in Europe, during and after the War, I was really happy to begin living a stable life." [William Gorman, "The Stylized Woodcuts of Jacques Hnizdovsky," *American Artist,* October, 1978. Amended by Hnizdovsky. [1]]

After gaining local recognition for his prize-winning works, Hnizdovsky decided to resign his designer's job and move to New York City as an independent artist. "It did not take me long to discover my complete innocence, and to understand exactly what my St. Paul colleagues had meant when they commended me on my idealism and courage. New York was neither interested in my Minneapolis newspaper clippings nor in my paintings and prints. In the Twin Cities, having your work receive recognition by judges as important as Kuniyoshi

and A. Hyatt Mayor of the Metropolitan Museum of Art, one would think it would open doors for an artist. In New York, a city with one of the world's largest artist populations, I was just one more artist."[1]

It wasn't long before his meager savings were depleted and he struggled to survive by doing whatever free-lance projects came his way. Finally, in 1958, after he had married, his paintings began to sell and he was able to return to his specialty, wood-cutting. His first woodcut, in his tree series, *Fir Trees,* received the Purchase Award from the Associated American Artists Gallery. *Fir Trees* marked a departure from his traditional woodcuts—only the sides were bordered; the top and bottom were left open, thus producing a sense of freedom. "Only in 1969 did I finally have the courage to eliminate the border completely. Now I put a border on a woodcut not from habit, but only when there is some justification for it."[1]

Today Hnizdovsky's work hangs in numerous museums including: the Museum of Fine Arts in Boston; the Philadelphia Museum of Art; the New York Public Library; the Library of Congress; the Winnepeg Art Gallery in Canada; and in several universities and private collections. He has had fellowships from the Tiffany Foundation and MacDowell Art Colony.

Hnizdovsky and his wife and daughter live in Riverdale, N.Y., where he does all of his drawing, blockcutting and painting in his second-floor studio, which overlooks Van Cortlandt Park, a favorite source for his models. His work is included in the Kerlan Collection at the University of Minnesota. *The Yearbook, 1981-82* of the American Society of Bookplate Collectors and Designers has devoted twenty pages to his bookplates, with eighteen reproductions and a photo. A ten-minute documentary film, ''Sheep in Wood,'' has been made by Slavko Nowytski about Hnizdovsky's woodcutting process. The film was awarded first prize by the American Film Festival in New York, 1971.

FOR MORE INFORMATION SEE: Abe M. Tahir, Jr., *Hnizdovsky Woodcuts, 1944-1975: A Catalogue Raisonné*, Pelican, 1976; *American Artist*, October, 1978.

HOLT, Margaret Van Vechten (Saunders) 1899-1963 (Rackham Holt)

PERSONAL: Born March 5, 1899, in Denver, Colo.; died February 4, 1963; daughter of William Lincoln and Ella Marie (Plank) Saunders; married Guy Holt (a publisher), September 6, 1923 (died, 1934); children: Margaret Van Vechten Wood (died, 1947). *Education:* Attended Columbia University. *Residence:* Long Island, N.Y.

CAREER: Daily News, Chicago, Ill., book reviewer, 1921-22; *Book List,* Albany, N.Y., assistant editor, 1922-23; G.P. Putnam's Sons, New York, N.Y., editorial staff, 1925-33; freelance writer, 1933-63. Worked in the Chicago Public Library, 1919-21, and the New York Public Library, 1923-25.

WRITINGS—Under name Rackham Holt: *George Washington Carver: An American Biography* (young adult), Doubleday, Doran, 1943, revised edition, Doubleday, 1963; *Mary McLeod Bethune: A Biography*, Doubleday, 1964. Contributed articles to periodicals, and worked as a ghost-writer on several biographies.

SIDELIGHTS: Holt, a grandniece of Henry Wadsworth Longfellow, was born March 5, 1899, in Denver, Colorado. As a child she enjoyed *St. Nicholas* magazine and began writing at the age of nine. She edited the school magazine, and after high school graduation, attended Columbia University.

Holt worked in libraries, as a book reviewer and editor until she began ''independent writing.'' She wrote many articles under her pen name for periodicals and ghosted three biographies, including Margaret Sanger's *Autobiography* and *An American Doctor's Odyssey*.

An admirer of George Washington Carver, Holt wrote the first authentic story of his life. ''I am deeply grateful for the privilege of having known Dr. Carver through the daily communications we had over many months. As we talked together and as I read through his scrapbooks, each day brought stronger confirmation of his true greatness. His sweetness and humor, his wisdom and understanding will be sadly missed by all of us, at Tuskegee and in the larger world, who were ever associated with him. We could work better with him at our side.

''. . . I am deeply sensible of the honor of being the instrument through which his life has been recorded. If [my] book does anything to hold up a mirror and thereby help make others of his race better understood by white men who seldom look beyond the color of their skins to the living human being, our joint purpose will have been achieved, and George Washington Carver can rest in peace.'' [Rackham Holt, *George Washington Carver: An American Biography,* Doubleday, 1943.]

HOBBIES AND OTHER INTERESTS: Bullfights, hockey, six-day bike-races and ''playing house—in the kitchen or garden.''

FOR MORE INFORMATION SEE: Rackham Holt, *George Washington Carver: An American Biography,* Doubleday, 1943; (obituary) *Publishers Weekly,* February 18, 1963.

HOOPLE, Cheryl G.

BRIEF ENTRY: Author. Hoople graduated from the University of Kansas and later received her M.A. from the University of Hawaii. She has been employed as an administrator for the Girl Scouts and has contributed written work to the *Pensacola News-Journal.* Considered an expert in the crafts field, she published her first book, for children, in 1975. Entitled *The Heritage Sampler: A Book of Colonial Crafts,* the book explores the historical need for crafts produced by the early American colonists and provides modern readers with the opportunity to duplicate their procedures. In 1978, Hoople published *As I Saw It: Women Who Lived the American Dream,* a collection of excerpts from diaries, letters and journals of women living in America from 1600 to 1900.

HUDSON, (Margaret) Kirsty 1947- (Kirsty McLeod)

PERSONAL: Born December 23, 1947, in Colombo, Ceylon (now Sri Lanka); daughter of Alexander Drummond (a merchant) and Elizabeth Margaret Davidson McLeod; married Christopher John Hudson (a journalist and author), March 10, 1978. *Education:* Attended St. Leonard's School, 1960-65; St. Anne's College, Oxford, M.A. 1969. *Religion:* Church of England. *Home:* 3A Cheyne Pl., London S.W.3, England. *Agent:* Toby Eady, 1234 Madison Ave., New York, N.Y. 10028.

CAREER: Writer. I.P.C. Magazines Ltd., London, England, feature writer, 1970-72; Fontana Paperbacks, London, fiction editor, 1973-75.

WRITINGS—All published under name Kirsty McLeod: *The Wives of Downing Street* (biography), Collins, 1976; *Drums and Trumpets: The House of Stuart* (juvenile), Seabury Press, 1977. Author of monthly book review column for *Yorkshire Post* and *Country Life.*

WORK IN PROGRESS: The Last Summer, a social history of the summer of 1914, to be published by Holt; a BBC documentary on Philip Gibbs for a radio series on famous war correspondents.

HOBBIES AND OTHER INTERESTS: History (especially World War I), antiques (especially of the Regency period), architectural history, travel, cooking, skiing.

HUMPHREYS, Graham   1945-

BRIEF ENTRY: Born October 30, 1945, in Solihull, Warwickshire, England. Illustrator of books for both adults and young people. Humphreys began his career in 1967 by dividing his time between teaching in a London grammar school and illustrating books on a free-lance basis. Since 1969 he has been able to devote his full time to illustration. A specialist in depicting historical subjects, Humphreys has illustrated more than thirty books for young readers, including *The Intruder* by John Rowe Townsend, *The Mirrored Shield* by Violet Bibby, *Echo in the Wilderness* by H. F. Brinsmead, *The Black Pearl* by Scott O'Dell, *Heracles the Strong* by Ian Serraillier, and *The Discovery of America* by J.R.L. Anderson. *For More Information See: Illustrators of Children's Books: 1967-1976.* Horn Book, 1978.

HÜRLIMANN, Ruth   1939-

PERSONAL: Born September 22, 1939, in Zug, Switzerland; daughter of Hans (a teacher) and Josefina (Steiner) Hürlimann. *Education:* Graduated from Kunstgewerbeschule, Lucerne, Switzerland, 1955-60. *Residence:* Goult, France.

CAREER: Author and illustrator of books for children. Worked in advertising agencies as a designer, Zurich, Switzerland, 1960-63, Paris, France, 1963-68; free-lance illustrator and painter, 1968—. Work has been exhibited in Switzerland and abroad. *Awards, honors:* Gold medal, Biennale of Illustrations Bratislava Exhibition, 1971; recipient of prize for design at International Children's Book Fair, Bologna, Italy, 1972; Association of Jewish Libraries award, 1976, and Mildred L.

There was once a cat who was tired of doing her own housework every day, so she made friends with a mouse. ■ (From *The Cat and the Mouse Who Shared a House,* retold by Ruth Hürlimann. Illustrated by the author.)

RUTH HÜRLIMANN

Batchelder Award, American Library Association, 1976, both for *The Cat and the Mouse Who Shared a House.*

WRITINGS—All for children; all self-illustrated: (Reteller) *Stadtmaus und Landmaus*, Atlantis-Verlag, 1971, translation published as *The Mouse with the Daisy Hat*, David White, 1971; (reteller) *Der Fuchs und der Rabe*, Atlantis-Verlag, 1972, translation and adaptation by Brian Alderson published as *The Fox and the Raven*, Longman Young Books, 1972; (reteller) *Katze und Maus in Gesellschaft*, Atlantis-Verlag, 1973, translation by Anthea Bell published as *The Cat and the Mouse Who Shared a House*, Longman Young Books, 1973, Walck, 1974; (reteller) *Der stolze weisse Kater*, Atlantis-Verlag, 1977, translation by A. Bell published as *The Proud White Cat*, Morrow, 1977; (reteller) *The Golden Goose*, Nord-Süd Verlag, 1984.

Also author of *Quaki der Frosch, Der alte Baum, Der Elefant und das Chameleon, Hase Schnuppernase, Herr Rosenkäfer, Die Raupe, Mathilda das Zirkushuhn, Die Eule und der Mond, Das Eichhörnchen und die verlorenen Nüsschen,* and *Der kleine Herr August.*

SIDELIGHTS: "When I started to discover the world, I found in my father a strict teacher and a story teller. I wanted to listen to *Town-Mouse and Country-Mouse, The Fox and the Raven,* and *Cat and Mouse Who Shared a House,* over and over again.

"Later, when I could read and write myself, I discovered the world of the fairy-tales and the wonders of old fables. At school I was a dreamer. Apart from natural science and history, only drawing lessons interested me. Instead of doing arithmetic I was drawing, changing the numbers into flowers and birds. I was often punished because of this, but it did not impress me enough to give it up.

"The best times at school were the holidays, which I spent mostly on a beautiful farm with my relatives. I did not like school very much, but decided to go back when I was sixteen. The arts and crafts school in Lucerne was a real pleasure for me. I ignored my parents' advice to learn a 'proper profession' and began taking a one year's preparatory course. I attended for four more years and received a diploma for an art-graphic-designer. In school we learned to float in the world of art instead of walking on the actual ground of commercial art. I gained much experience while working in Zürich and Paris. In 1969 I gave up commercial art and started working as a free-lance graphic-artist and painter.

"I especially liked the books for children and this surely was no coincidence. I have read and reread Grimms fairy-tales trying to find new meaning told to me by my father. I could show what I once had felt and experienced while I was a child. I have made a children's dream come true and learned a lot while working on it. And I am still making my children's dreams come true. I want children to get pleasure and want to help children capture something which most adults have lost."

ISADORA, Rachel

BRIEF ENTRY: Author and illustrator of children's books, ballet dancer. Isadora attended the American School of Ballet for seven years. She was performing professionally at the age of 11, and by the time she was 17, was asked to sign a contract with the New York City Ballet. While still a novice ballerina, Isadora began drawing, in private, as a release from the tensions of dancing. She has since written and illustrated several books for children, including *Max* (Macmillan, 1976; cited as an ALA Notable Book in 1979), *Willaby* (Macmillan, 1977), *Ben's Trumpet* (Greenwillow, 1979; cited as a 1980 Caldecott Honor Book), *My Ballet Class* (Greenwillow, 1980), *Jesse & Abe* (Greenwillow, 1981), and *City Seen from A to Z* (Greenwillow, 1983). Isadora is married to Robert Maiorano, who is also a dancer and an author of children's books. Together they wrote *Backstage* (Greenwillow, 1978). Isadora has illustrated two books by Maiorano, *Francisco* (Macmillan, 1978) and *A Little Interlude* (Coward, 1980), as well as Elizabeth Shub's *Seeing Is Believing* (Greenwillow, 1979) and *The White Stallion* (Greenwillow, 1982). *Residence:* New York, N.Y. *For More Information See: New York Times Book Review,* March 1, 1981; *Publishers Weekly,* February 27, 1981.

All that mankind has done, thought, gained or been: it is lying as in magic preservation in the pages of books.

—Thomas Carlyle

Books, like proverbs, receive their chief value from the stamp and esteem of ages through which they have passed.

—Sir William Temple

JACQUES, Robin 1920-

PERSONAL: Surname rhymes with "cakes"; born March 27, 1920, in London, England; son of Robin (World War I pilot) and Mary (Thorn) Jacques; children: John Paul. *Home:* 5 Abbots Place, London NW6, England.

CAREER: Illustrator. Began his career in an advertising agency, working as a junior designer, 1935-39; free-lance illustrator, 1945—; *Strand* Magazine, London, England, art editor, 1948-52; Central Office of Information, art director, 1950-51; Harrow College of Art, London, England, teacher, 1973-76; Canterbury Art College and Wimbledon Art College, lecturer, 1975-79. *Exhibitions:* Art Council Travelling Exhibition, throughout the United Kingdom, 1979; many mixed exhibitions in London and overseas. *Military service:* British Army, war service, 1941-45, served in Royal Artillery and Engineers in France and Germany. *Member:* British Society of Industrial Artists (fellow), Chelsea Arts Club. *Awards, honors:* Illustration medal from Bratislava Biennale, 1969, for *A Book of Ghosts and Goblins.*

WRITINGS: Illustrators at Work, Studio Books, 1963.

Illustrator; of interest to young people, except where noted: John Keir Cross, *The Angry Planet,* Lunn, 1945, Coward, 1946; J. K. Cross, reteller, *The Owl and the Pussycat,* Lunn, 1946, published in America as *The Other Side of Green Hills,* Coward, 1947; Patrick De Heriz, *Fairy Tales with a Twist,* Lunn, 1946; Hugh Anderson, editor, *Selected Tales from the Arabian Nights,* Lunn, 1947; Miguel De Cervantes S., *Don Quixote,* Lunn, 1947; Walter de la Mare, *Collected Stories for Children,* Faber, 1947.

Hans Christian Andersen, *Forty-Two Stories,* Faber, 1953; J. K. Cross, *Red Journey Back,* Coward, 1954; Jonathan Swift, *Gulliver's Travels,* Oxford University Press, 1955; James Joyce, *Dubliners* (adult), Cape, 1955; J. Joyce, *Portrait of the Artist as a Young Man* (adult), Cape, 1956.

Rudyard Kipling, *Kim* (adult), Limited Editions Club, 1960; Ann Thwaite, *The House in Turner Square,* Constable, 1960, Harcourt, 1961; Margaret J. Miller, *The Queen's Music,* Verry, 1961; Audrey W. Beyer, *The Sapphire Pendant,* Knopf, 1961; M. J. Miller, *The Powers of the Sapphire,* Brockhampton, 1962; Cecilia Viets Jamison, *Lady Jane,* Hart-Davis, 1963, Delacorte, 1969; William Makepeace Thackeray, *Vanity Fair* (adult), Folio Society, 1963; Joan Aiken, *Black Hearts in Battersea* (Junior Literary Guild selection), Doubleday, 1964; M. J. Miller, *Doctor Boomer,* Verry, 1964; Oscar Wilde, *Three Short Stories,* Macmillan (London), 1964; Helen Cresswell, *The White Sea Horse,* Oliver & Boyd, 1964, Lippincott, 1965; Jules Verne, *Around the World in Eighty Days,* Doubleday, 1964; Basil Davidson, *A Guide to African History,* revised and edited by Haskel Frankel, Doubleday, 1965, 2nd edition, 1971; Elizabeth Coatsworth, *The Hand of Apollo,* Viking, 1965; Rosalie K. Fry, *Promise of the Rainbow,* Bell Books, 1965; Andre Norton, *Steel Magic,* World, 1965.

Hilda Van Stockum, *Mogo's Flute,* Viking, 1966; J. Aiken, *Nightbirds on Nantucket* (Junior Literary Guild selection), Doubleday, 1966; Rita Ritchie, *Pirates of Samarkand,* Norton, 1967; William Cole, editor, *The Sea, Ships, and Sailors: Poems, Songs, and Shanties,* Viking, 1967; Desmond Skirrow, *The Case of the Silver Egg,* Doubleday, 1968; Gerald M. Durrell, *The Donkey Rustlers,* Viking, 1968; Anne S. Molloy, *Five Kidnapped Indians,* Hastings House, 1968; Hester Burton, *The Flood at Reedsmere,* World, 1968; R. K. Fry, *Whistler in the*

ROBIN JACQUES

Mist, Farrar, Straus, 1968; John Hampden, adaptor, *The Gypsy Fiddle, and Other Tales Told by the Gypsies,* World, 1969; John M. Langstaff, editor, *Hi! Ho! The Rattlin' Bog, and Other Folk Songs for Group Singing,* (ALA Notable Book), Harcourt, 1969; Phyllis La Farge, *Jane's Silver Chair,* Knopf, 1969; Janet Frame, *Mona Minim and the Smell of the Sun,* Braziller, 1969.

S. Forst, *Pipkin,* Delacorte, 1970; Jan Wahl, *The Prince Who Was a Fish,* Simon & Schuster, 1970; R. K. Fry, *Snowed Up,* Farrar, Straus, 1970; W. B. Yeats, *Collected Poems of W. B. Yeats* (adult), Limited Editions Club, 1970; Ruth Manning-Sanders, *A Choice of Magic,* Dutton, 1971; A Norton, *Exiles of the Stars,* Viking, 1971; Stanley George Watts, *Number 21,* Transworld, 1971; Martha S. Bacon, *The Third Road,* Little, Brown, 1971; Beverley Nichols, *The Wickedest Witch in the World: A Story for Children of All Ages,* W. H. Allen, 1971; A. Norton, *Dragon Magic,* Crowell, 1972; Ian Kellam, *The First Summer Year,* Oxford University Press, 1972, Crowell, 1974; George Eliot, *Middlemarch* (adult), Folio Society, 1972; Gordon Cooper, *A Time in a City,* Oxford University Press, 1972, Dutton, 1975; Sheena Porter, *The Hospital,* Oxford University Press, 1973; Daniel Defoe, *Robinson Crusoe,* Penguin Education, 1973; G. Cooper, *A Second Springtime,* Oxford University Press, 1973.

Feenie Zinger, *The Duck of Billingsgate Market,* Four Winds, 1974; R. Manning-Sanders, *Granddad and the Magic Barrel,* Methuen, 1974; G. Cooper, *Hester's Summer,* Oxford University Press, 1974; R. Manning-Sanders, *Ram and Goat,* Methuen, 1974; Paul Binding, *Robert Louis Stevenson* (biography), Oxford University Press, 1974; Judith St. John, *Where the Saints Have Trod,* Oxford University Press, 1974; G. Cooper, *A Certain Courage,* Oxford University Press, 1975; Ruth Tomalin, *A Stranger Thing,* Faber, 1975; H. C. Andersen, *Favorite Tales of Hans Christian Andersen,* translated by M. R. James, Faber, 1978; R. Manning-Sanders, *Folk and Fairy Tales,* Methuen, 1978; Lynn Reid Banks, *The Indian in the Cupboard,* Dent, 1980; M. M. Kaye, *The Ordinary Princess,* Kestrel, 1980, *Shakespeare Stories,* Hamish Hamilton, 1982; Henry James, *The Europeans* (adult), Folio Society, 1982.

"A Book of" series; all by Ruth Manning-Sanders: *A Book of Giants,* Methuen, 1962, Dutton, 1963; . . . *Dwarfs,* Methuen, 1963, Dutton, 1964; . . . *Dragons,* Methuen, 1964, Dutton, 1965; . . . *Witches,* Methuen, 1965, Dutton, 1966; . . . *Wizards,* Methuen, 1966, Dutton, 1967; . . . *Mermaids,* Methuen, 1967, Dutton, 1968; . . . *Ghosts and Goblins,* Methuen, 1968, Dutton, 1969; . . . *Princes and Princesses,* Methuen, 1969, Dutton, 1970; . . . *Devils and Demons,* Dutton, 1970; . . . *Charms and Changelings,* Methuen, 1971, Dutton, 1972; . . . *Ogres and Trolls,* Methuen, 1972, Dutton, 1973; . . . *Sorcerers and Spells,* Methuen, 1973, Dutton, 1974; . . . *Magic Animals,* Methuen, 1974, Dutton, 1975; . . . *Monsters,* Dutton, 1975; . . . *Enchantments and Curses,* Methuen, 1976, Dutton, 1977; . . . *Kings and Queens,* Methuen, 1977, Dutton, 1978; . . . *Marvels and Magic,* Methuen, 1978; . . . *Spooks and Spectres,* Dutton, 1979; . . . *Heroes and Heroines,* Methuen, 1981; . . . *Cats and Creatures,* Methuen, 1981; . . . *Magic Adventures,* Methuen, 1983.

Also illustrator of Washington Irving's *Alhambra Tales* for Lunn and *Plays of Labiche* (8 volumes), Club de L'Honnente Homme, 1969-72. Contributor to *Radio Times.*

WORK IN PROGRESS: Illustrations for Eleanor Farjeon's *Kings and Queens* to be published by Dent.

(From "The Enchanted Candle" in *A Book of Enchantments and Curses* by Ruth Manning-Sanders. Illustrated by Robin Jacques.)

SIDELIGHTS: Jacques was born in London, England, where he spent his early childhood. He was educated at the Royal Masonic Schools in Hertfordshire. As a young adult his interest in books—reading, drawing and painting—developed. Although he had no formal art training, he enjoyed drawing and used anatomy books, objects in the Victoria-Albert Museum, and his surroundings for his instruction. "After a conventional education at a provincial school I began to make a tentative beginning as a designer, taking on gratefully whatever came my way. After a year or two, I found my way into an advertising agency where I stayed until the outbreak of war.

"Then for four years I soldiered in the Royal Artillery and the Engineers and was invalided from the British Army in 1945. During one of my leaves I had been lucky enough to meet a young publisher of children's books for whom I began to work, and through him I came to illustrate many children's books in the immediately post-war years." [Bertha M. Miller and others, compilers, *Illustrators of Children's Books: 1946-1956,* Horn Book, 1958.[1]]

"I then began to illustrate books on a free-lance basis, and with the exception of a short phase as art director of two magazines, I have continued ever since. The main advantage of this way of work is that . . . I have been free to live and work in the countries of [my] choice." [Lee Kingman and others, compilers, *Illustrators of Children's Books: 1957-1966,* Horn Book, 1968.[2]]

". . . In 1952 . . . I went to Mexico, drawing and painting for six months and came back to Europe by way of the southern part of the United States. My work seems to me to have been very directly affected by an early love of the English Romantic movement in poetry and drawing. The engravings of Bewick and William Blake and the Victorian illustrators of the sixties and seventies were my particular study."

About today's illustrators, Jacques commented: "Illustrators set about their work in many different ways. The professional black-and-white illustrators . . . are highly individual performers in a very competitive field and, like actors, are required to undertake engagements on a number of different levels. Books, magazines, advertising and more recently television, are some of the media in which they are invited to work. . . .

"Nobody can foresee what new opportunities the future will bring to black-and-white artists. Most of us will be well content to continue working hopefully on the levels already available to us and will be ready, given the chance, to push on into fresh territory.

". . . There is no royal road to success in illustration, no ordered progression that ensures acceptance. Some artists, it is true, seem to leap blithely over the wall at the first bound, but for most it is long, hard climb. . . .

"Illustration is something other than superlative drawing or a display of technical know-how. Unlike painting and sculpture, an illustration has a direct function, sometimes persuasive as in the case of an advertising drawing, sometimes falling into a literary or journalistic context. Illustration can never be a private exercise in graphic experiment unrelated to a specific purpose. Where it becomes this, it may be in itself enormously interesting but it will, by definition, no longer be illustration.

"Nothing is more conducive to *angst,* self-searching and a sense of remoteness from life than the nature of the illustrator's work, the prolonged scratching away in isolation at his draw-

The widow grasped his tail, Monster Horisto gave it a twitch and swung her out of the swamp. ■
(From *A Book of Monsters* by Ruth Manning-Sanders. Illustrated by Robin Jacques.)

ing-board. I am sometimes surprised that more of us don't opt out, take up market-gardening or something really forward-looking like market-research.

"One of the hazards that the free-lance artist most constantly face is the period of time that so often passes before he is paid for his work. . . . For all but the very few, the illustrator . . . is usually obliged to supplement his income by other means, usually teaching. . . ." [Robin Jacques, *Illustrators at Work*, Studio Books, 1963.[3]]

"My illustration work has been split between adult and children's books and magazine drawings of many kinds. My preference is for children's books of the more imaginative and fanciful kind since these leave greater scope for illustrative invention, where I feel most at home. Thus, my work with Ruth Manning-Sanders has proved most satisfying and the twenty-five books we have done together contain much of the work that I feel personally happiest with. There was a time

when I hankered to illustrate the great literary classics, but opportunities of this sort rarely come one's way and as time passed I came to realize that I responded best to material that released my own imaginative capacity. Thus, dragons, ogres, trolls and sorcerers rather than Pantagruel and Anna Karenina!

"At the same time, like most English illustrators, I have worked in many other areas, all of which have their particular interest. I remember, with special pleasure, working as an art editor in the years 1948-52 and trying to find suitable new young artists for the many and varied stories that appeared in the *Strand* magazine, which was famous for having printed the Sherlock Holmes stories many years earlier.

"I had a very happy and interesting period of work during the sixties which I spent in Provence in Southern France. My diligent agent in New York, Hans Fybel, sent me a constant flow of work for many publishers there, to which I added a number of assignments from French editors. Eight years in the

Oh horror, what did she find? A hideous old hag standing amidst a heap of torn lace and cut up cloth — yes, all the fine work of the ladies lay in tattered heaps about the old hag's feet. ■ (From *A Book of Enchantments and Curses* by Ruth Manning-Sanders. Illustrated by Robin Jacques.)

southern sun did much to make up for the loneliness of the illustrator's metier, which has to be carried out in isolation, unlike the earlier period on the *Strand* magazine with one's editorial colleagues in and out of one's office and a constant flow of aspirant illustrators waiting to show their work.

"This isolation is also the reason why, on returning to Britain in 1973, I began to mix my free-lance work with a few days art school teaching each week. Teaching and lecturing help to concentrate the mind, so that the accumulated experience of thirty years work can be canalised into useful advice and guidance. At the same time, the talent and enthusiasm of students helped to confirm and sustain my own belief in our common metier."

HOBBIES AND OTHER INTERESTS: Travel, modern painting, music, especially jazz, poetry, and special study of the habits and backgrounds of the people in the countries he has lived in.

FOR MORE INFORMATION SEE: Bertha M. Miller and others, compilers, *Illustrators of Children's Books: 1946-1956,* Horn Book, 1958; John Ryder, *Artists of a Certain Line: A Selection of Illustrators for Children's Books,* Bodley Head, 1960; Robin Jacques, *Illustrators at Work,* Studio Books, 1963;

Diana Klemin, *The Art of Art for Children's Books,* Clarkson Potter, 1966; Lee Kingman and others, compilers, *Illustrators of Children's Books: 1957-1966,* Horn Book, 1968; Doris de Montreville and Donna Hill, editors, *Third Book of Junior Authors,* H. W. Wilson, 1972; Martha E. Ward and Dorothy A. Marquardt, *Illustrators of Books for Young People,* Scarecrow, 1975; Lee Kingman and others, compilers, *Illustrators of Children's Books: 1967-1976,* Horn Book, 1978.

KALOW, Gisela   1946-

PERSONAL: Born October 23, 1946, in Jever, West Germany; daughter of Heinrich and Gretchen (Brauer) Behrends; married Volker Kalow (an assessor), December 20, 1968; children: Tjark, Behrend. *Education:* Attended Staatliche Kunstschule, Bremen, West Germany. *Home:* Homburger Landstr. 6, 6370 Oberursel/Taunus, West Germany.

CAREER: Artist and illustrator of books for children. Early in career worked as an apprentice at a textbook company.

ILLUSTRATOR—All for children; all written by Achim Bröger: *Guten Tag, lieber Wal,* Thienemanns, 1974, translation by Elizabeth Shub published as *Good Morning, Whale,* Macmillan, 1974; *Das wunderbare Bettmobil,* Thienemanns, 1975, translation by Caroline Gueritz published as *The Wonderful Bedmobile,* Hamish Hamilton, 1976; *Bruno verreist,* Thienemanns, 1978, translation by C. Gueritz published as *Bruno Takes a Trip,* 1978 (published in England as *Bruno's Journey,*

GISELA KALOW

. . .Bruno put his legs through the hole in the bottom of the box. He closed the front door of his house, carefully hiding the key under the doormat. . . . ▪ (From *Bruno Takes a Trip* by Achim Bröger. Illustrated by Gisela Kalow.)

Hamish Hamilton, 1978); *Ich War Einmal,* Thienemanns, 1980, translation by Olive Jones published as *The Happy Dragon,* Methuen, 1981; *Bruno und das Telefon,* Thienemanns, 1983.

SIDELIGHTS: About her collaboration with author Achim Bröger, Kalow commented: "Achim Bröger is an old and very good friend of mine. We met in 1967 in Braunschweig when we both worked for a textbook company. In 1970 Achim Bröger asked me to illustrate some of his children's stories. At that time my husband had finished his studies, we were living near Stuttgart, and I was expecting my first child. I enjoyed working with text and letters and had enough work, so I told him, 'I can't do that!'

"Later in 1970 we moved to Oberursel, my husband got a job in Frankfurt, and my first son was born. By that time I wanted to try drawing. At first it was frightful. There were lots of wonderful pictures in my head, but none on paper. I worked for a year until I was satisfied. Finally, the first picture book, *Guten Tag, lieber Wal,* was finished and we found a publisher!

"Since that time I have been making picture books—stories full of friendship, truth, and little delights—with Achim. It gives me great pleasure. We are a good team, I think. We have a similar sense of humor.

"And so we work together. Maybe there is a story from Achim that I choose; perhaps there is an idea of a good dragon in our heads. The idea grows and grows until we decide to make a book. After I finish all the pictures, Achim writes the text. I like his text very much, particularly the highlights he is able to give the pictures. We complement each other.

"My husband and my children enjoy my profession as well as I do, which makes me grateful."

HOBBIES AND OTHER INTERESTS: "I enjoy reading and if there is enough time, I sketch with my pencil. We live in an old house, which requires work and paint. There are two cats and two birds, which I think is enough!"

ANNE BERNAYS KAPLAN

KAPLAN, Anne Bernays 1930-
(Anne Bernays)

PERSONAL: Born September 14, 1930, in New York, N.Y.; daughter of Edward L. and Doris (Fleischman) Bernays; married Justin D. Kaplan (a writer), 1954; children: Susanna Bernays, Hester Margaret, Polly Anne. *Education:* Wellesley College, student, 1948-50; Barnard College, B.A., 1952. *Home and office:* 16 Francis Ave., Cambridge, Mass. 02138.

CAREER: Discovery, New York, N.Y., managing editor, 1952-54; Houghton Mifflin Co., New York, N.Y., editorial assistant, 1955-57; author, 1960—; Emerson College, Boston, Mass., prose writer-in-residence, 1976-77, 1980-81; Harvard Extension Program, teacher, 1977-82. *Awards, honors:* Edward Lewis Wallant Memorial Book Award for *Growing Up Rich,* 1976.

WRITINGS—All under name Anne Bernays: *Short Pleasures,* Doubleday, 1962; *The New York Ride,* Trident, 1965; *Prudence, Indeed,* Trident, 1966; *The First to Know,* Popular Library, 1975; *Growing Up Rich* (young adult), Little, Brown, 1975; *The School Book,* Harper, 1980; *See Through,* Little, Brown, 1984. Contributor of articles to journals.

KEESHAN, Robert J. 1927-
(Captain Kangaroo)

PERSONAL: Born June 27, 1927, in Lynbrook, Long Island, New York; son of Joseph (a chain grocery supervisor) and Margaret (Conroy) Keeshan; married Anne Jeanne Laurie (formerly a speech therapist and television studio receptionist), December 30, 1950; children: Michael Derek, Laurie Margaret, Maeve Jeanne. *Education:* Attended Fordham University, 1947-50. *Agent:* ICM, 40 West 57th St., New York, N.Y. 10019. *Office:* Robert Keeshan Associates, Inc., 555 West 57th St., New York, N.Y. 10028.

CAREER: National Broadcasting Corp. television, New York, City, page, 1944-47, "Clarabelle the Clown" on "Howdy Doody" show, 1947-52; American Broadcasting Corp. television, New York City, "Corny the Clown" on "Time for Fun" show, 1953-55; Columbia Broadcasting System television, New York City, star of "Captain Kangaroo" show, 1955—; President of Robert Keeshan Associates, New York City. Appeared as "Tinker" on "Tinker's Workshop," American Broadcasting Corp. television, 1954-55; creator and star of "Mr. Mayor" show, Columbia Broadcasting System television, 1964-65; commentator on "Subject is Young People," Columbia Broadcasting Sytem radio, 1980-82; commentator on "Up to the Minute" produced by CBS News, 1981-82. Member of West Islip (New York) board of education, 1953-58; president of Suffolk County Hearing and Speech Center, 1966-71; member of board of directors of United Fund (Long Island), 1967-68, the National Association of Hearing and Speech Agencies, 1969-71; director of Suffolk Child Development Center, 1974-75; Good Samaritan Hospital, West Islip, N.Y., member of board of directors, 1969-78, president, 1978-79, chairman of the executive committee, 1979-80; chairman of the board of trustees of the College of New Rochelle (New York), 1974-80; chairman of Committee of Correspondence for Independent Higher Education in New York, 1976-80; board member of Long Island Philharmonic, 1979-80. Named honorary chairman of The American Heart Association (Suffolk County Chapter) and honorary chairperson of Save the Children. *Military service:* U.S. Marine Corps Reserve, 1945-46.

MEMBER: Long Island Yacht Club (commodore, 1964-65), Friars (New York City), Southward Ho Country Club (Bay Shore, N.Y.). *Awards, honors:* Sylvania Award, 1956, Peabody Award for outstanding television program for children, 1958, 1972, 1979, "Emmy" Award from Academy of Television Arts and Sciences for Outstanding Children's Entertainment Series, 1978, 1981, 1982, and for Outstanding Performer in Children's Programming, 1982, and recommendations from National Audience Board and National Congress of Parents and Teachers, all for "Captain Kangaroo"; Ursula Laurus award from the College of New Rochelle, 1958; Junior Membership award from California Federation of Women's Clubs, 1961, 1962; Freedoms Foundation award, 1962, 1972; Page One Award in radio and television from the Newspaper Guild of New York, 1965, for "unfailing devotion to the development of the minds and hearts of our children"; named "Man of the Year" by the National Association of Television Programs Executives, 1967.

Ohio State Award, 1972; Gabriel Award, 1974, certificate of merit, 1978, 1981; DeWitt Carter Reddick Award from University of Texas, 1978; Sadie Award from University of Alabama, 1978; American Education Award from Education Industries Association, 1978; Distinguished Achievement award from Georgia Radio and Television Institute, 1978; named TV "Father of the Year," 1980; Distinguished Service to Children Award from Parents Without Partners, 1981; Humanitarian Award from Telephone Pioneers, 1981; James E. Allen Memorial Award for distinguished service to education from Albany, N.Y., 1981; National Education Association award for the advancement of learning through broadcasting, 1982; special award from Massachusetts Society for Prevention of Cruelty to Children, 1982; award for contribution to children's television from Suffolk Early Childhood Education Council, 1982; Gabriel Award for Outstanding Personal Achievement, 1982; The Abe Lincoln Distinguished Communications Recognition Award from the Southern Baptist Radio and Television Commission, 1983; recipient of honorary degrees from eleven colleges and universities.

WRITINGS—Juvenile: She Loves Me, She Loves Me Not (illustrated by Maurice Sendak), Harper, 1963; (editor) *Captain Kangaroo's Storybook,* Random House, 1963. Former author of monthly column in *McCall's* (magazine). Contributor to magazines and newspapers, including *New York Herald Tribune, Good Housekeeping,* and *Parade.*

SIDELIGHTS: **June 27, 1927.** Born in Lynbrook, New York and spent his childhood in Forest Hills, New York. During his high school years Keeshan worked after school as a network page boy. He joined the U.S. Marines following graduation.

1946. Following his discharge, Keeshan returned to his job as a page at NBC, working days and attending night school at Fordham University. "In those days, there was no television at all, it was radio. The whole NBC building was devoted to radio, but by 1947 there was a little office up on the sixth floor where a few men were involved in television. The executive in charge was an ex-vaudeville booker named Warren Wade, and he had Owen Davis, Jr., with him, plus a staff of four or five—and they were the entire department. In 1947 nobody at RCA believed that television would ever become a major force for a long time to come—their most optimistic projection was 1956 or so." [Max Wilk, "The Captain and the Kids," *The Golden Age of Television,* Dell, 1976.[1]]

January 3, 1948. Made his television debut on the "Howdy Doody" show. By March, Keeshan was given a costume suit-

ROBERT J. KEESHAN

able to the character he was playing, "Clarabelle the Clown." At first his new career offered little financial reward. "Every day, Bob Smith [of "Howdy Doody"] would slip me a five-dollar bill out of his own pay. But eventually Bob got tired of putting out his own money each day, and persuaded NBC to give me a deal. Warren Wade agreed to put me on salary—$35 a week—but he insisted that for that much money, I'd have to become a film editor and learn to edit film as well! I balked at that—what did I know about editing film? They said, 'You'll learn—you'll learn!' I refused—I had enough to do without that! Finally they reluctantly made the deal with me—and I was a salaried TV performer."[1]

1950. "Howdy Doody" was a major television attraction and its audience increased beyond original estimates. "By that time, everyone was saying, 'Maybe we were wrong, this medium is really taking off.' In 1950 there must have been between 15 and 18 million sets out in the country, and the growth was incredible. We had a union now, AFTRA (American Federation of Television and Radio Artists), actors were coming into the medium, there was money to be made, and radio was rapidly dying. . . ."[1]

1952. Following a dispute with the show's management, Keeshan was discharged from "Howdy Doody." He resumed another clown character for ABC-TV called "Corny the Clown" on the "Time for Fun" show. "I did that show for two years, another clown character—this time a very gentle non-slapstick sort of a guy who sat on a park bench with his cocker spaniel and talked to the kids. He was called 'Corny the Clown.' He was very popular—I still get mail from people who remember Corny. But I was convinced that there was an audience early

He loves me.

He loves me not.

■(From *She Loves Me . . . She Loves Me Not* by Robert Keeshan. Illustrated by Maurice Sendak.)

in the morning from seven to nine that would want a kids' show.''[1]

1954. Started a morning program for children called ''Tinker's Workshop.'' ''[The ABC program manager] . . . called—it was on a Friday morning—and asked me if I still wanted to do the show. I said sure, and he said, 'Okay, you've got the hour eight to nine.' I asked him when. He said, 'This coming Monday morning.'

''We started with nothing, literally nothing. But we worked all weekend, designed a set, had one built. I had a producer friend working with me, and we ran down to Brooks Costume and got some costumes, spent the weekend picking up props and writing material, and Monday morning we were on the air with a show called 'Tinker's Workshop.' Five days a week, eight to nine!

''We were on opposite 'Today' and CBS had Jack Paar on a 'Morning Show,' and yet in eight weeks we were showing double their rating in New York. That was when CBS began to notice us, I guess; and when Jack Paar began to get restless in the spring of 1955, they approached us about coming over to do another show for them, from eight to nine.''[1]

October 3, 1955. Debut of the ''Captain Kangaroo'' show on CBS-TV, with Keeshan as the Captain. ''We went on the air . . . with substantially the same show we do today. Lumpy Brannum is Mr. Greenjeans, Gus Allegretti, who plays most of the animal characters—Peter Birch, was our original director. We've turned over producers in the past twenty years, but not that often. As for staff, well, we've trained dozens of people in the course of working on the show. Our production people came in as clerk-typists, or production assistants, or whatever, and as they learn their jobs, we move them on up to become associate producers, producers, and even executives. . . .''

''In those early days when I was on live I'd be out of my house in Babylon, Long Island, to make the 4:20 A.M. train—every day, because we had to be in the studio by six in the morning. That is something you never get used to, believe me. Unless you were a farm boy, or an insomniac—and that I was not. I always lived in terror of oversleeping. For five years I used to have three alarm clocks, plus a telephone service that would wake me up. The real problem was getting to bed. If you're getting up at 3:30 in the morning, what time do you get to bed? You're always up before dawn. . . . I'd get in here, do the show at eight, then in forty seconds we'd turn around and repeat the whole show again, for the midwest. Then off the air by ten—two hours of live programming, *six* days a week, from Monday to Saturday. And always that nightmare . . . if I don't get in, who'll do the show? Without the Captain, there *was* no show.

''It was a tough grind. I'd stay around here until two, rehearsing the next day's show, then I'd have conferences, then I'd go home and take a nap. But remember, in those days I was much younger; I was only twenty-eight when I started as the Captain. I don't think I'd be able to do that today.''[1]

''Captain Kangaroo'' continued its five-day-a-week broadcasts without interruption for twenty-six-years, making it the longest-running children's program on network television. Throughout the years, the staff of Keeshan's show have been considered members of a long-term television school for children's programming. Many of the people on Keeshan's staff left to initiate their own children's programs on Public Broadcasting, for which Keeshan is inordinately proud. ''. . . Jon Stone, who's the executive producer at Children's Television Workshop, started here as a production assistant. Sam Gibbon, who created 'Electric Company,' started here as an assistant director; and David Connell, who's their vice-president in charge of production, started here in 1955 as a clerk-typist. We have

(Bunny Rabbit ✓nd the Captain. From the daily children's television program "Captain Kangaroo" which premiered on CBS-TV, October 3, 1955.)

(Dancing Bear, Mr. Moose, Bunny Rabbit, the Captain, Mr. Green Jeans, and Cosmo on the set of the television program "Captain Kangaroo." Photo courtesy of CBS-TV.)

almost twenty people who have gone over there from 'Captain Kangaroo.'

"None of our people are ever out of work. It's great training. There's no other show I know of in television that can take a production assistant and teach him everything—because we do everything here. We do everything in a technical sense; we do everything in a program sense. We're a variety show with guest stars, we do some dramatic scenes, there's always some comedy—and in the technical department, with visual material and film, and trick-shot effects, a production assistant gets to learn to work on everything that's available in the medium."[1]

Although the philosophy of the show remained unchanged throughout the years, its technology changed with modern improvements. "Today's children are more mature—they've been exposed to so much more around them, and on TV, and they're quicker to learn *because* of the medium. So our technology has changed and become more complex than in the early days. Every so often, just for the fun of it, we'll run an old kinescope of one of the shows we did back in 1956, before electronic tape recording came along, and it's always a shock how different the show looks.

"In 1956, I would chat with Bunny Rabbit, at the desk (he was played by Gus Allegretti), then I'd go to the garden to talk to Mr. Moose—also Gus. I had to stand there and 'pad'—fill in time—until Gus had gotten up from the desk, around

the back of the set, into the garden, and climbed into his Moose outfit, and then was ready to talk to me. I'd be out there alone for maybe thirty to forty-five seconds. Today I can talk to him in one place, then go to the Moose in the garden, split-second timing, all done on tape and edited later. Today we do a show in the studio, and what with the taping of all the various segments, it may take us three hours to do what used to be done in one hour, live.

"But, in terms of the philosophy of the show, and our approach to the kids, we haven't changed that at all. Nor do we ever intend to."[1]

September 28, 1981. "Wake Up with the Captain," a half-hour program for pre-schoolers and school-age children premiered.

January 18, 1982. "Captain Kangaroo" was reinstated on morning television. Keeshan has devoted his career to ensuring quality programming for children. "In broadcasting, we exploit children, we ignore children. We rarely care for children or use our great power to develop and nurture emotionally and culturally those who will be our nation's future. Children are the seed corn of the republic. In broadcasting, in almost every area of society, we are poisoning our seed corn.

"What fools we mortals be." [Robert Keeshan, "Our Kids: At the Mercy of the Marketplace?" *Access*, September, 1982.[2]]

Although devoted to producing quality children's programming, he has strongly warned against using television as a surrogate parent. "Television, used well, can provide enriching experiences for our young people, but we must use it with some discretion. When the carpet is clean, we turn off the vacuum cleaner. When the dishes are clean, the dishwasher turns itself off.

"Not so the television, which is on from the sun in the morning to the moon at night and beyond!

"Parents must exercise some control and show some concern about the cultural influence on the child when a program not intended for that child is viewed. Parents need to intervene. Nonintervention may be a laudable policy in international affairs, but the results of parental nonintervention will not be applauded at the United Nations or anywhere else.

"A child's television viewing should not be filling the vacuum created by a parent's neglect.

"A child needs to be listened to and talked to at 3 and 4 and 5 years of age. Parents should not wait for the sophisticated conversation of a teen-ager. By then, communication will be impossible because love will have passed both parent and child by. An hour or two of high-quality time, given consistently, will be a daily bouquet of love—and a message well received by a real human being." [Captain Kangaroo, "It May Seem That Way, but TV Isn't a Surrogate Parent," *New York Times*, February 10, 1979.³]

Keeshan advocates the return of strong family life to promote the growth of responsible American citizens. "As surely as we need clean air and clean water we need the environment provided for the young by a strong American family.

"As a communicator working with young people for over thirty years I am greatly concerned about changes in our society which are impinging on our ability to respond to the emotional, intellectual and cultural needs of our young. If we continue in the same direction, at the same rate, by the turn of the century our young people may be on the endangered species list.

"America owes much of its greatness to the strong family unit where its talents and genius were bred in a climate of dedication to excellence and high moral standards. The strong family unit continued to function in most segments of our society until a quarter century ago. Then the very technology, which was often our proudest boast, began to provide miracle after miracle, to make our lives easier, to provide us with comforts and luxuries, to give us more time, in effect to change our lives and to change the structure of the American family and our society for all time.

"Our great new society with its mobility, its flexibility, its sociability has destroyed our ability to relate to our children. Parents are so beaten down by today's society that they are too tired to talk to their young people. A four-year-old waits for hours in great anticipation for the arrival home of a parent to relate some small, but to her important, sandbox experience. The parent, blue collar or white, so often says: 'Later, I'm tired.' Later of course never comes and we wonder why our teenagers don't relate to us. We must find time for our children, in the morning at breakfast table, before our commercial or academic or bureaucratic day begins, and in the evening, in the comfort of our homes.

"Parents have the power to provide the strong family. Let us all proclaim: hurray for parent power!" [Robert Keeshan, "Family: Another Name for America," Robert Keeshan Associates, n.d.⁴]

In addition to his television and literary endeavors, Keeshan also dabbles in music. Recordings he has made, under his own name and as "Captain Kangaroo" for the Golden Records and Columbia Records labels, introduce children to different types of music, from classical to jazz. He also appears at children's concerts throughout the country, promoting good music as both educational and entertaining.

HOBBIES AND OTHER INTERESTS: Photography, fishing, sailing, gardening, boating.

FOR MORE INFORMATION SEE: The Reporter, October 2, 1958; *Coronet*, October, 1960; *McCall's*, August, 1961; *Christian Science Monitor*, February 7, 1963; *New York Times Book Review*, May 12, 1963; *New York Herald Tribune*, May 12, 1963; *New York Post*, August 16, 1964; *Philadelphia Inquirer*, October 4, 1974; Max Wilk, *The Golden Age of Television*, Dell, 1976; *People*, November 5, 1978, February 1, 1982; *New York Times*, February 10, 1979; Les Brown, *Les Brown's Encyclopedia of Television*, New York Zoetrope, 1982; *Access*, September, 1982.

KELLEY, Leo P(atrick)   1928-

PERSONAL: Born September 10, 1928, in Wilkes Barre, Pa.; son of Leo A. and Regina (Caffrey) Kelley. *Education:* New School for Social Research, B.A., 1957.

CAREER: McGraw-Hill Book Co., 1959-69, began as copywriter, became advertising manager; free-lance writer, beginning 1969—. *Member:* Science Fiction Writers of America, Mystery Writers of America, Mensa. *Awards, honors:* Short story, "The Traveling Man," was nominated for a Nebula Award.

WRITINGS—All for young people: (Editor) *Themes in Science Fiction: A Journey into Wonder*, McGraw-Hill, 1972; (editor) *Fantasy: The Literature of the Marvelous*, McGraw-Hill, 1973; (editor) *The Supernatural in Fiction*, McGraw-Hill, 1973; *The Time Trap: Pacesetters*, Children's Press, 1978; *Star Gold*, Children's Press, 1979; *Backward in Time*, Pitman Learning, 1979; *Dead Moon*, Fearon, 1979; *Death Sentence*, Pitman Learning, 1979; *Earth Two*, Pitman Learning, 1979; *Goodby to Earth*, Fearon, 1979; *King of the Stars*, Fearon, 1979; *Night of Fire and Blood* (illustrated by Ed Diffenderfer), Fearon, 1979; *On the Red World*, Fearon, 1979; *Prison Satellite*, Pitman Learning, 1979; *Sunworld*, Fearon, 1979; *Vacation in Space*, Fearon, 1979; *Where No Sun Shines*, Fearon, 1979; *Worlds Apart*, Fearon, 1979.

Science fiction: *The Counterfeits*, Belmont Books, 1967; *Odyssey to Earthdeath*, Belmont Books, 1968; *The Accidental Earth*, Belmont Books, 1970; *Time Rogue*, Lancer, 1970; *Brother John* (based on a screenplay by Ernest Kinoy), Avon, 1971; *The Coins of Murph*, Berkley Publishing, 1971; *Mindmix*, Fawcett, 1972; *Time: 110100*, Walker & Co., 1972 (published in England as *The Man from Maybe*, Coronet, 1974); *Deadlocked*, Fawcett, 1973; *The Earth Tripper*, Fawcett, 1973; *Mythmaster*, Dell, 1973. Contributor of stories and poetry to periodicals, including *Worlds of If* and *Commonweal*.

LEO P. KELLEY

SIDELIGHTS: Kelley, the author of numerous science fiction novels and short stories, is also the editor of two textbooks for high school students on science fiction. "Science-fiction authors have always been very much concerned with tomorrow. But, as authors, their concern encompasses an additional dimension not always shared by everyone, at least not to the same degree. They are deeply concerned with the events that may result from actions taken by men today. Such authors observe the behavior of men in the world today and they speculate on how that behavior may determine the nature and character of the not too distant future. . . .

"Science-fiction authors may be called dreamers. They look about them and they see that we are and have been polluting our air, to use one example of a pressing problem facing mankind today. They ask themselves what might happen in our world as a result. One writer may decide to deal with the subject in fictional terms by depicting a world in which the uncontrolled growth of cities has so thoroughly destroyed all oxygen-emitting plants that men and other species are rapidly dying. Another writer may postulate a future criminal justice system in which the destruction of a tree or living plant by a human being is a capital crime.

"Both authors in this hypothetical example have considered the problem of air pollution. Both have focused on the same aspect of the problem—the need for sufficient oxygen in the air to maintain life. But each has created a different story although both have started from the same premise after thinking about the same problem.

"The possibilities for such stories are almost infinite. What is important is the fact that science-fiction stories are stories writ-

ten by men and women who are concerned not only about conditions as they currently exist but also about what those conditions may imply about future conditions.

"A computer, for example, may someday be constructed that possesses what could literally be called a mind. It may eventually be possible for people to travel in time as well as in space. It might be commonplace at some future date to vacation on Venus.

"Such subjects are the province of the science-fiction author. The fact that the events and beings he portrays may not now exist in no way negates the value of his stories. The principal value of such stories as literature lies in the insight into the human condition which the authors display and the skill with which they express the insight. In this regard, science-fiction does not differ from general fiction. Science-fiction writers, like other serious writers, are interested in basic questions that affect mankind. What is a man? How should life be lived? These are but two of the questions writers—science-fiction writers definitely included—ask themselves.

"Their stories are their answers.

"Science-fiction stories are not necessarily written to predict the future although many such stories have predicted it with surprising accuracy. Instead, the science-fiction story attempts to portray the writer's vision of such subjects as interstellar travel or war in the future. *Vision* is the key word here.

"Just as literature in general reflects life, so does science fiction reflect it but in its own way and on its own terms. Science-fiction authors deal with talents not yet documented, talents that mystify us at the moment but may be proven to exist someday.

"One criticism occasionally leveled at science fiction as a literary form is the accusation that all such stories are about bug-eyed monsters and Martians. Such remarks are occasionally made by critics who may be less than fully informed concerning the stylistic and contextual range of science fiction.

"A reader hearing such criticism might choose to counter it by citing examples of stories that meet high literary standards. . . . He might ask such a critic to read Philip K. Dick's 'The Father-thing,' explaining that it is about a monster, but asking the critic if he finds flaws with the carefully constructed suspense or the development of the characters and their conflicts as they seek to solve the deadly problem facing them.

"All art is subject to criticism, of course. Students of science fiction should develop their own critical faculties so that they will be equipped to debate critical judgments made by others with which they do not agree and to establish their own standards. To be able to do this intelligently and effectively, they should read these stories . . . with their minds attuned to the differences in style, technique, and structure in each story.

"No story succeeds that does not affect its readers. To be affected by a story means simply that the reader's thoughts and emotions must be stirred. It is this stirring of thoughts and emotions that encourages readers to turn to literature for a sharpened insight into life." [Leo P. Kelley, editor, *Themes in Science Fiction: A Journey into Wonder*, McGraw, 1972.]

FOR MORE INFORMATION SEE: Leo P. Kelley, editor, *Themes in Science Fiction: A Journey into Wonder*, McGraw, 1972; *The Science Fiction Encyclopedia*, Doubleday, 1979.

LAPPIN, Peter   1911-

PERSONAL: Born April 29, 1911, in Ireland; son of John (a railroad employee) and Sarah (Barrett) Lappin. *Education:* Fordham University, M.A., 1953; also attended Salesian Studentate, Hong Kong; International School of Theology, Shanghai; Belfast School of Technology; Salesian College, Cowley, Oxford, England; Pallaskenry College; and Columbia School of Writing. *Home and office:* Marian Shrine, Filors Lane, West Haverstraw, N.Y. 10993.

CAREER: Ordained Roman Catholic priest; Marian Shrine, West Haverstraw, N.Y., editorial board member of *Biographic Memoirs of St. John Bosco,* and editor of *Salesian Bulletin.* Lecturer on the Far East, South America, and other topics. *Member:* Catholic Press Association, Ancient Order of Hibernians, International Order of the Alhambra, Knights of Columbus, Cambridge Society of Biographers. *Awards, honors:* Received Venice Festival awards, Catholic Family Club award, two Catholic Literary Foundation awards, and awards for service to various organizations.

WRITINGS: General Mickey, Salesiana Publishers (New Rochelle, N.Y.), 1952; *Bible Stories,* Doubleday, 1953; *Land of Cain,* Doubleday, 1954; *Dominic Savio: Teenage Saint,* Bruce, 1955; *Conquistador!,* Salesiana Publishers, 1957, reprinted, Don Bosco, 1968; *Stories of Don Bosco,* Irish Press, 1958; *Mighty Samson* (juvenile), [Garden City, N.Y.], 1961; *The*

PETER LAPPIN

(From *Stories of Don Bosco* by Peter Lappin.)

Wine in the Chalice, Don Basco, 1961; *Bury Me Deep,* Our Sunday Visitor, 1974; *Give Me Souls!,* Our Sunday Visitor, 1977; *Halfway to Heaven,* Patron Book, 1981; *Challenge of Mornese,* F.M.A. Publications (New Jersey), 1982; *The Falcon and the Dove,* Patron Book, 1982.

WORK IN PROGRESS: Biography of Artemides Joaquin Desiderio Maria Zatti of Viedma Rio Negro Province, Argentina; a popular history of the devotion to the Virgin Mary.

SIDELIGHTS: "To write for the young is both exciting and rewarding. It is exciting for you know that you are moving the hearts and the heads of so many! It is rewarding because you also know that you are helping them solve some of the difficulties they face at this stage. I wish that authors of juvenile books would offer them less froth, even if it does sell, and more of what can help them. Young people, perhaps now more than ever before, need books which, while making pleasant reading clothed in style, also offer them guidance and encouragement.

"Generally speaking, the state of the art of writing is apallingly low. Part of this is due to those who are expected to uphold its standards. If one were to believe the reviews of the best-sellers, one would think that this or that book is a classic. On reading it, one finds that it is not even second rate. Many books get on the bestseller list simply because it makes respectable the reading of pornography. This means that the reviewers and critics, with some notable exceptions, have sold their souls, have betrayed their trust. Some day someone is going to stand up and cry out, 'The emperor has no clothes!'"

At present Lappin is assisting in the creation and production of several religious television programs in Fort Lauderdale, Florida.

HOBBIES AND OTHER INTERESTS: Travel, lecturing, giving retreats, conferences.

LEWIN, Betsy 1937-

PERSONAL: Born May 12, 1937, in Pennsylvania; daughter of John K. (in insurance sales) and Winifred (a teacher; maiden name, Dowler) Reilly; married Ted B. Lewin (a writer and illustrator), 1963. *Education:* Pratt Institute of Art, B.F.A., 1959. *Home and office:* 152 Willoughby Ave., Brooklyn, N.Y. 11025.

CAREER: Free-lance writer and illustrator.

WRITINGS—Self-illustrated: Animal Snackers, Dodd, 1980; *Cat Count,* Dodd, 1981; *Hip, Hippo, Hooray,* Dodd, 1982.

WORK IN PROGRESS: Ghost story involving cats; rhymes about African animals; black and white brush drawings for

Helen Kronberg Olson's *Oliver Wendell Iscovitch,* to be published by Dodd.

SIDELIGHTS: "Drawing and painting have always been my main interests, and there was never a doubt in my mind when I was a child that I would be anything but an artist. But writing seems to me to be a natural accompaniment to visual language. It's an exciting combination of creative energies.

"Sometimes a drawing will inspire an idea for a story, but more often it's the other way around—an idea for a picture book will grow from a single word or combination of words that intrigue me, or from an observation or a particular incident.

"I'm not really sure why I write for children. I suppose it's because writers and illustrators of children's material have influenced me the most. A. A. Milne and Ernest Shepard were the most magical team.

"There's a lot of freedom in writing for children. You can be as fanciful or as practical as you wish. The only absolute requirement is honesty.

"An especially nice thing about writing and illustrating for children is that often it will have adult appeal, too. It's very satisfying to see smiles on the faces of both children and adults as they look through my picture books.

"My books combine my love of drawing, the sounds of words, and the touching humor in much animal behavior. I observe and draw animals and wildlife and paint flowers in watercolors. I have viewed game in East Africa, backpacked in Hawaii's Haleakala Crater, canoed in the Everglades, watched whales off the coast of Baja California, and visited the Pribilof Islands and Alaska."

My cousin has five.
Five cats; jive cats,
Very much alive cats,
Count them!

+5

■ (From *Cat Count* by Betsy Lewin. Illustrated by the author.)

BETSY LEWIN

LEWIS, Alfred E.   1912-1968

BRIEF ENTRY: Born in 1912, in Boston, Mass.; died March 28, 1968, in N.Y. Editor and author. Lewis attended the University of California and was editor of various magazines, including *Research and Engineering, Sugar, Brazil,* and *International Management,* beginning in 1957. He joined the staff of *National Petroleum News* in 1963, later becoming operations and equipment editor. In addition to writing numerous technical and scientific articles, he was the author of seven books for young readers, among them *Treasure in the Andes, Clean the Air!: Fighting Smoke, Smog, and Smaze Across the Country, This Thirsty World: Water Supply and Problems Ahead, The New World of Computers,* and *The New World of Petroleum. Obituaries: New York Times,* March 29, 1968.

MacKAYE, Percy (Wallace)   1875-1956

PERSONAL: Surname rhymes with "high"; born March 16, 1875, in New York, N.Y.; died August 31, 1956, in Cornish, N.H.; son of Steele (an actor, producer, and playwright) and Mary Keith (a dramatist; maiden name, Medbery) Mackaye; married Marion Homer Morse (a writer), October 8, 1898

(died, 1939); children: Robert Keith, Arvia, Christy Loring. *Education:* Harvard University, A.B. (cum laude), 1897; graduate study, University of Leipzig, 1899-1900. *Politics:* Independent. *Residence:* Cornish, N.H.

CAREER: Playwright and poet. Craigie School for Boys, New York, N.Y., teacher, 1900-1904; in 1904 he joined a literary colony in Cornish, N.H., which was the beginning of his career as a full-time writer of literary and dramatic works. Was commissioned to write and deliver commemorative poems and dramas on numerous leaders and public events beginning in 1903, including a commission by the U.S. Government to write a national festival drama commemorating the bicentennial of George Washington's birth, 1931; lecturer on the theatre at various universities, including Harvard, Yale, and Columbia, 1906-1913; instructor in poetry and folk-backgrounds, Rollins College, winters, 1929-31; member, board of governors, Cambridge School of Drama, Harvard University, 1930; visiting professor of creative drama, Sweet Briar College, 1932-33; director of folktales, White Top Mountain Folk Festival, 1933; research on folk materials, Appalachian Mountains, 1933-35, Switzerland, England, Scotland, and Ireland, 1936-37.

MEMBER: National Institute of Arts and Letters, Poetry Society of America, Dramatists' Guild of Authors' League of America, Society of American Dramatists and Composers, International P.E.N., Pan-American Poets' League of North America (president, 1943), Society of Mayflower Descendents, National Economic League, Phi Beta Kappa Society (honorary), Players Club, Harvard Club (New York), MacDowell Club (New York), Cosmos Club (Washington, D.C.), Garrick of London Club (honorary), Everglades Club (Palm Beach). *Awards, honors:* M.A., Dartmouth College, 1914; awarded the first American fellowship in poetry and drama, Miami University, Oxford, Ohio, 1920; D. Litt., Miami University, Oxford, Ohio, 1924; Shelley Memorial Award for Poetry, 1942; Fellowship Award of the Academy of American Poets, 1948, for *The Mystery of Hamlet, King of Denmark: or, What We Will;* the Harvard College Library established the Marion and Percy MacKaye Collection, 1955.

WRITINGS—Of interest to young readers: *Poems,* Macmillan, 1909, reprinted as *The Sistine Eve, and Other Poems,* 1915; *The Present Hour: A Book of Poems,* Macmillan, 1914; *Sinbad the Sailor: His Adventures with Beauty and the Peacock Lady in the Castle of the Forty Thieves* (three-act opera), Houghton, 1917; *Rip Van Winkle* (three-act folk opera; music by Reginald de Koven), G. Schirmer, 1919; *The Skippers of Nancy Gloucester* (poem), E. B. Hackett, 1924; *Tall Tales of the Kentucky Mountains* (decorations by E. MacKinstry), George H. Doran, 1926, reprinted, Greenwood Press, 1973; *Kinfolk of Robin Hood* (four-act play; performed in 1901 under the title "Inhabitants of Carlyale"), Samuel French, 1926; *Young Washington at Mt. Vernon* (three scenes selected from *Washington, the Man Who Made Us: A Ballad Play* [also see below]) Samuel French, 1927; *Washington and Betsy Ross* (two scenes selected from *Washington, the Man Who Made Us: A Ballad Play* [also see below,]), Samuel French, 1927; *The Gobbler of God: A Poem of the Southern Appalachians* (illustrated by daughter, Arvia MacKaye), Longmans, Green, 1928; *Weathergoose-woo!* (folktales; illustrated by A. MacKaye), Longmans, Green, 1929; *The Far Familiar: Fifty New Poems* (decoration by Arthur Rackham), Richards, 1938; *Poog's Pasture: The Mythology of a Child, a Vista of Autobiography* (also see below), B. Wheelwright, 1951, reprinted, 1976; *Poog and the Caboose Man: The Mythology of a Child, a Vista of Autobiography* (sequel to *Poog's Pasture*), B. Wheelwright, 1952, reprinted, 1976.

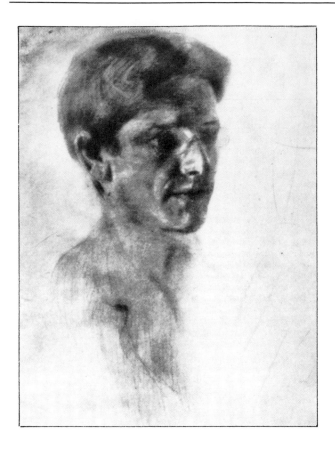

MacKaye in the 1920s. Portrait by Kahlil Gibran.

Other works; poems: *Johnny Crimson: A Legend of Hollis Hall*, Kiley, 1895; (translator) *Canterbury Tales of Geoffrey Chaucer: Modern Rendering into Prose*, Duffield, 1904; *Ode on the Centenary of Abraham Lincoln*, Macmillan, 1909; *Uriel, and other Poems*, Houghton, 1912; (translator with John S. P. Tatlock) *The Modern Reader's Chaucer: The Complete Poetical Works of Geoffrey Chaucer, Now First Put into Modern English*, Macmillan, 1912, reprinted, Free Press, 1966; *Poems and Plays*, two volumes, Macmillan, 1916; *Dogtown Common: A Narrative Poem of Old New England*, Macmillan, 1921; *Moments en Voyage: Nine Poems for the Harvard Class of 1897*, Pioneer Press, 1932; (translator with Albert Steffen) *In Another Land*, Verlag für schone wissenschaften, 1937; *Poesia Religio*, Imprimerie J. Brinkman, 1939; *Poem-Leaflets in Remembrance of Marion Morse MacKaye* (contains *Wedding Song, The Ride to Rheims, Her Pilgrim: Ode to an Italian Fountain, Three Statues of St. Germain*, and *Camerado!*), privately printed, [Dornach, Switzerland], 1939; *My Lady Dear, Arise!: Songs and Sonnets in Rememberance of Marion Morse MacKaye*, Macmillan, 1940, reprinted, B. Wheelwright, 1976; *What Is She?: A Sonnet to Marion Morse MacKaye* (also see below), Minute Man Press, 1943; *Rememberings: 1895-1945*, [North Montpelier, Vermont], 1945; *The Sequestered Shrine* (includes *What Is She?*), privately printed, 1950; *Discoveries and Inventions: Victories of the American Spirit*, Warner Press, 1950.

Plays: (With Evelyn Greenleaf Sutherland and Emma Sheridan-Fry) *Po' White Trash, and Other One-Act Dramas*, H. S. Stone, 1900, reprinted, Core Collection Books, 1977; *The Canterbury Pilgrims: A Comedy* (first produced in Savannah, Ga., by the Coburn Players, April 30, 1909), Macmillan, 1903, reprinted as *The Canterbury Pilgrims: An Opera* (music by

Reginald de Koven; first produced on Broadway at the Metropolitan Opera, 1917), Macmillan, 1916; *Fenris, the Wolf: A Tragedy*, Macmillan, 1905; *Jeanne d'Arc: A Drama* (first produced in Philadelphia by the Sothern-Marlowe Co., October 15, 1906), Macmillan, 1906; *Sappho and Phaon: A Tragedy* (first produced in New York at the Lyric Theatre, 1907), Macmillan, 1907; *Mater: An American Study in Comedy* (first produced in New York at the Savoy Theatre, September, 1908), Macmillan, 1908; *The Scarecrow; or, The Glass of Truth: A Tragedy of the Ludicrous* (adaptation of *Feathertop*, by Nathaniel Hawthorne; first produced by the Harvard Dramatic Club in Cambridge, Mass., December 7, 1909), Macmillan, 1908; *A Garland to Sylvia: A Dramatic Reverie*, Macmillan, 1910; *Anti-Matrimony: A Satirical Comedy* (produced by Garrick Theatre, September 22, 1910), F. A. Stokes, 1910; *Tomorrow* (three-act; first produced at Little Theatre, Philadelphia, October 31, 1913), F. A. Stokes, 1912; *Yankee Fantasies* (five one-act plays; contains "Chuck: An Orchard Fantasy" [first produced by the Coburn Players at Miami University, Oxford, Ohio, July 17, 1912], "Gettysburg: A Woodshed Commentary" [first produced at Bijou Theatre, Boston, January 8, 1912], "The Antick: A Wayside Sketch," "The Cat-Boat: A Fantasy for Music," and "Sam Average: A Silhouette"), Duffield, 1912, new and revised edition, Samuel French, 1928; *Saint Louis: A Civic Masque* (self-produced in St. Louis, 1914), Doubleday, Page, 1914; *A Thousand Years Ago: A Romance of the Orient*, Doubleday, Page, 1914; *Sanctuary: A Bird Masque*, prelude by Arvia MacKaye, F. A. Stokes, 1914, new edition, Samuel French, 1933.

The Immigrants: A Lyric Drama (first produced in Boston at the Boston Opera House), B. W. Huebsch, 1915; *Caliban by the Yellow Sands* (masque; first produced in New York, May 24, 1916), Doubleday, Page, 1916; *The Evergreen Tree* (masque), D. Appleton, 1917; *The Roll Call: A Masque of the Red Cross*, American Red Cross, 1918; (with Harry Barnhart) *The Will of Song: A Dramatic Service of Community Singing*, Boni & Liveright, 1919; *Washington, the Man Who Made Us: A Ballad Play* (three-act; self-produced, 1918; includes *Young Washington at Mt. Vernon* and *Washington and Betsy Ross*), Knopf, 1919, reprinted as *George Washington: A Dramatic Action with a Prologue*, 1920; *The Pilgrim and the Book*, American Bible Society, 1920, reprinted, Samuel French, 1922; *This Fine-Pretty World: A Comedy of the Kentucky Mountains*, Macmillan, 1924; *Kentucky Mountain Fantasies: Three Short Plays for an Appalachian Theatre*, Longmans, Green, 1928; *The Sphinx* (comedy), Row, 1929; *Wakefield: A Folk-Masque of America, Being a Mid-Winternight's Dream of the Birth of Washington* (first produced in Washington, D.C., at Constitution Hall, February 21, 1932), George Washington Bicentennial Commission, 1932; *The Mystery of Hamlet, King of Denmark; or, What We Will* (tetralogy; first produced in Pasadena at the Pasadena Playhouse, 1949), B. Wheelwright, 1950, reprinted, 1976.

Nonfiction: *The Playhouse and the Play, and Other Addresses Concerning the Theatre and Democracy in America*, Macmillan, 1909, reprinted, Johnson Reprint, 1970; *The Civic Theatre in Relation to the Redemption of Leisure: A Book of Suggestions*, M. Kennerley, 1912; *The New Citizenship: A Civic Ritual Devised for Places of Public Meeting in America*, Macmillan, 1915; *A Substitute for War*, Macmillan, 1915; *Community Drama: Its Motive and Method of Neighborliness*, Houghton, 1917; *Epoch: The Life of Steele MacKaye, Genius of the Theatre, in Relation to His Time and Contemporaries: A Memoir*, two volumes, Boni & Liveright, 1927, reprinted, Scholarly Press, 1968; (editor and author of introduction) William Vaughn Moody, *Letters to Harriet*, Houghton, 1935; (editor and author of introduction) written by father, Steele MacKaye, *An Arrant Knave, and Other Plays,* Princeton University Press, 1941, reprinted, Indiana University Press, 1963.

Also author of the play "Napolean Crossing the Rockies," 1927, and the poems "American Consecration Hymn," 1917, "James Russell Lowell Centenary Poem," 1919, "April Fire," 1925, "Winged Victory," 1927, "William Vaughn Moody: Twenty Years After," 1930, and, written with wife, Marion Morse MacKaye, "Untamed American," 1926. Contributor of articles and poems to various magazines, including *Scribner's, Century, Forum, Nation,* and *Outlook.* Advisory editor of *Folk-Say* (national magazine of American Folklore), 1929.

SIDELIGHTS: **March 16, 1875.** Born in New York, New York. "About six weeks after my birth, owing to risk of ill health in the Tenth Street house, my father decided to move, post-haste, with his family to the country. The place suggested . . . was a region of . . . Vermont, amid the Connecticut Valley, in the township of Battleboro, Vermont, of which my father's old teacher in art, William Morris Hunt, had also been a native. Accordingly, in late April, the family exodus occurred, and en route, sitting in the compartment of a parlour car, while crossing the Connecticut River, my father named his latest-born son after an old school friend, Percy Wallace." [Percy MacKaye, *Epoch: The Life of Steele MacKaye, Genius of the Theatre, in Relation to His Times and Contemporaries: A Memoir,* Volume 1, Boni & Liveright, 1927.¹]

Christmas, 1882. "My father had given me a child's drum—a large, fine one, and had set about teaching me just how to hold the drumsticks, in order to tap rhythmically a light and rapid roll-call. He himself had learned how, he told me, from a drummer of the Seventh Regiment, in Civil War times. The sticks, however, that came with my drum from the store, were clumsily made and ill balanced. This troubled him; and he immediately hunted up two pieces of seasoned black walnut, took out his jackknife, sat down beside me on the floor, near the coal grate-fire, and began to whittle me two new drumsticks, of a proper shape.

"In the midst of this careful work, Christmas dinner was announced. But he was too absorbed to take notice. Many guests and relatives were assembled, ready to file off with the family to the dining-room. Again the announcement; but my father did not hear. He was transported far away, in a heaven of whittling—an artist's 'paradise lost' unsought by all present except himself and me, to whom he confided the mysteries of form, balance, finish, and rhythmic line, which his deft fingers were carefully seeking with that sharp knife-blade in the grain of dark wood.

"My mother touched his shoulder. He looked up—sighting one half-closed eye along the half-finished drumstick.

"'My dear—dinner!—the company!'

"'Yes, yes—just a minute. I'll follow you.'

"A despairing glance from the hostess, as she leads the large Christmas party beyond the view. And now 'mine host' is alone on the sitting-room floor, with only small 'me,' beside him, holding one finished drumstick. Silence, then, and rapt whittling. Murmurs and tinkle of dishes from the dining-room. Whittling: only whittling. The job begun must be done—and *rightly* done. And now a boy-delegate (one of my brothers) on tiptoe:

"'The turkey—it's ready to carve!'

(From the stage production of "The Scarecrow," starring Edmund Breese and Fola La Follette, which opened in New York at the Garrick Theatre in 1911.)

(From *The Far Familiar: Fifty New Poems* by Percy MacKaye. Frontispiece by Arthur Rackham.)

"'Yes, yes—in a minute.'

"Silence, again: intense, rapturous whittling. Cycles of time-less *perfecting,* till he held in his hand the smooth pair, beautifully turned and matched. Then another boy-delegate, and the awful whisper:

"'Papa, it's dessert! You and Percy have lost the turkey!'

"'No!—have we, my boy? Never mine! We've saved the drumsticks!'

"He sprang up; snatched the toy-drum, as I followed him; and a long, deep, rippling roll-call announced our arrival—at dessert."[1]

MacKaye's father, Steele MacKaye, was a prominent author, director, inventor and actor in the theater. "One of my earliest recollections of my father is of sitting with my mother in a box at the Madison Square Theatre, and watching a rehearsal of 'Hazel Kirke,' in which my father played Dunstan. I was five years old, and my attention was distracted from the play by the physical discomfort of the distance between the floor and my tiptoes. Another vivid, later recollection, when I was about thirteen, is of going into my father's dressing room at the old Standard Theatre (now the Manhattan), and making up

my face as the villain Duroc in 'Paul Kauvar,' while my father was absent on the stage enacting the title rôle. When he came back, he did not at first know me. He imagined I was one of the supers that acted in a mob of French Revolutionists in the play, and he said: 'You've made a mistake in the room, my boy.' Discovering his mistake, however, we had a hearty laugh together.

"Other recollections made a still stronger impression. Our walks and talks in New York and in country New England. Our long drives together about Washington and he unfolded his plans to me. And I remember his inquiring aspects when I showed him my first play in verse, which he listened to carefully and toward which he showed a tolerant spirit.

"'But why blank verse?' he asked.

"I told him, doubtless very immaturely, that the vehicle depended upon the idea of the play; that some ideas required the poetic dress, and that verse seemed to me the most beautiful form.

"'But is it the natural form?' he insisted.

"'That depends on the nature of the dramatic theme,' I persisted." [Ada Patterson, "Percy MacKaye—An Interview," *The Theatre,* December, 1907.[2]]

". . . Walking home from school one day with a class-mate, I recall my boy-comrade's astonishment when I asked him casually: 'When does your father read his play to you?'

"'What on earth are you talking about?' he answered.

"Then it first dawned on my imagination that every boy's father was not necessarily a dramatist, who normally read aloud his plays to the family after supper, or rehearsed their scenes day and night, Sundays, in the back parlour, or (what was quite as home-like) on the stage of 'our own' Theatre, the Lyceum. Such glimpses of my boyhood I touch upon, because my father, in his work and play, his ideas, ambitions and hopes, was so comradely a part of the life of his children that these boyish memories and their aftermath are integral with his biography. As his affectionate interest and teeming imagination inter-penetrated all our home life, so our lives were imaginatively fused with his, often in actual labours and always in dreams." [Percy MacKaye, *Epoch: The Life of Steele MacKaye, Genius of the Theatre, in Relation to His Times and Contemporaries: A Memoir,* Volume 2, Boni & Liveright, 1927.[3]]

1890. Wrote first poem which was published in 1921.

1892. MacKaye was asked to collaborate with his father. ". . . While I sat playing cards with my father till gray of dawn, he told me of . . . [his] plans, in which he eagerly wanted my assistance—not merely now as errand boy—but as dramatic poet! For, in his scenario, he wished to embody immediately the words of some completed choral-songs, expressive of the meanings of the action, at several great 'musical moments' of the drama, in order to present to [Antonín] Dvořák as definitely vivid an impression as possible of the varied musical elements involved in the production.

"This sudden appeal to me, was, of course, a spurring call to a lad of seventeen, who already, for two or three years, had been teasing his Muse and testing his hand in the writing and directing of 'poetic drama,' with incidental music, for local community productions in his New England 'home-town.'"[3]

1897. Graduated from Harvard University. During his college years MacKaye began serious writing, some of which was published. The prolific outpouring of works was to continue for the rest of his life.

MacKaye was much respected and admired by famous contemporaries such as the poet Vachel Lindsay, who said: ". . . I know of no man whose friendship I covet more. I want to deserve and keep your interest, and you shall hear of me again." [Edwin Osgood Grover, editor, *Annals of an Era: Percy MacKaye and the MacKaye Family, 1826-1922; a Record of Biography and History in Commentaries and Bibliography,* Pioneer Press, 1932.⁴]

1898. Married Marion Homer Morse. Lived abroad for two years.

1907. Speaking of his writing habits MacKaye said in an interview: "I seldom write more than two or three hours a day. I cannot do more and do it well, but I am constantly thinking of my work and my research may consume all the remainder of the day. No one can estimate the amount of work done by the subconsciousness. I am not at all sure that it is not the best work we do.

". . . *Sappho and Phaon* is, I think, my best work thus far, but I hope to do much better work. The work that is finished is the work a man forgets. It is a completed task. All his energy and interest go to the task in hand and to the work to come. 'Sappho and Phaon' required a year in the writing, although I had been thinking of it longer than that."²

1917. "Soon after our country entered the war, my son Rob (then in Exeter) and I registered together at the same booth in New York, but his class was too young and mine too old to be called into service. So my war work consisted of contributing a Masque *(The Roll Call)* for the Red Cross, a Christmas Masque *(The Evergreen Tree)* for army camps and communities, and my play 'Washington, the Man Who Made Us,' having for its theme the still-living leadership of our first president. . . ." [Percy MacKaye, "A Sketch of His Life, with Bibliography of His Works," reprinted from the *Twenty-fifth Anniversary Report of the Class of 1897,* Harvard College, 1922.⁵]

1925. For MacKaye's fiftieth birthday, Sara Teasdale, the famous American poetess, wrote: "Percy MacKaye has put poetry literally upon the lips of more Americans than any other poet, living or dead. Anyone who has seen one of his civic masques, as I did in 1914, when his lyrical drama, 'Saint Louis,' was given, knows that he can make poetry burn suddenly like a great fire in the hearts of multitudes."⁴

Although *Tall Tales of the Kentucky Mountains* reproduced the Appalachian dialect, many of MacKaye's works were written in verse, which he justified by saying: "Reasoning by analogy we have a right to expect the public to enjoy the drama in verse. The audiences that fill the theatres in the United States are persons of a higher intelligence and wider knowledge than the crowds of the Athenian and Elizabethan ages; yet twenty thousand persons would sit from dawn till sunset to watch the poetic drama of Greece, and in the Elizabethan age ten thousand sat contentedly for six and seven hours to see the plays of Shakespeare and his contemporaries which were spoken in blank verse.

"We cannot expect the public taste in amusements to improve until we give it concretely a higher standard."²

Singin' Willie. ■(From *Weathergoose—woo!* by Percy MacKaye. Illustrated by Arvia MacKaye.)

1949. MacKaye published what many considered his greatest work, certainly his most ambitious one, a tetralogy entitled *The Mystery of Hamlet, King of Denmark,* consisting of four full-length plays.

1951-1952. Published *Poog's Pasture* and *Poog and the Caboose Man.* These two books were a combination of child mythology and autobiography—"Poog" is MacKaye's brother Will who died in his twenties.

August 31, 1956. Died in Cornish, New Hampshire. In 1925, Robert Frost wrote of Percy MacKaye: ". . . [He] has spent precious time trying to make the world an easier place to write poetry in. Everybody knows how he has spread himself over the country, as with two very large wings, to get his fellow poets all fellowships at the universities. . . . It is angelic of him to wish all poets a livelihood and a beauty of life that shall be poetry, without being worked up into poetry. That is why many think of him as an angel before they think of him as a poet. He is none the less a poet, one of the truest."⁴

FOR MORE INFORMATION SEE: The Theatre, December, 1907; *The National Cyclopaedia of American Biography,* Volume XIV, James T. White, 1910, reprinted, University Microfilms, 1967; *Twenty-fifth Anniversary Report of the Class of 1897,* Harvard College, 1922; *Playwrights of the American Theatre,* Macmillan, 1925, reprinted, Scholarly Press, 1972; Edwin Osgood Grover, editor, *Annals of an Era: Percy MacKaye and the MacKaye Family, 1862-1922; a Record of Biography and History in Commentaries and Bibliography,* Pioneer Press, 1932; Fred B. Millett, *Contemporary American Authors,* Har-

PERCY MacKAYE

court, 1940, reprinted, AMS Press, 1970; Stanley J. Kunitz and Howard Haycraft, editors, *Twentieth Century Authors,* H. W. Wilson, 1942, supplement, 1969; Miriam Blanton Huber, *Story and Verse for Children,* 3rd edition, Macmillan, 1965; *Who Was Who in America,* Volume 3, Marquis, 1966.

Obituaries: *New York Times,* September 1, 1956; *Newsweek,* September 10, 1956; *Time,* September 10, 1956; *Publishers Weekly,* October 15, 1956; *Wilson Library Bulletin,* October, 1956; *Americana Annual,* 1957; *Britannica Book of the Year,* 1957.

MAGORIAN, James   1942-

PERSONAL: Born April 24, 1942, in Palisade, Neb.; son of Jack and Dorothy (Gorthey) Magorian. *Education:* University of Nebraska, B.S., 1965; Illinois State University, M.S., 1969; attended Oxford University, 1971, and Harvard University, 1973. *Residence:* Helena, Mont. *Office:* 1225 North 46th St., Lincoln, Neb. 68503.

CAREER: Writer.

WRITINGS—Children's books: *School Daze,* Peradam Publishing House, 1978; *Seventeen Percent,* Black Oak Press,

1978; *The Magic Pretzel,* Black Oak Press, 1979; *Ketchup Bottles,* Peradam Publishing House, 1979; *Imaginary Radishes,* Black Oak Press, 1979; *Plucked Chickens,* Black Oak Press, 1980; *Fimperings and Torples,* Black Oak Press, 1981; *Floyd,* Black Oak Press, 1982; *The Three Diminutive Pigs,* Black Oak Press, 1982.

Books of Poems: *Almost Noon,* Ibis Press, 1969; *Ambushes and Apologies,* Ibis Press, 1970; *The Garden of Epicurus,* Ibis Press, 1971; *The Last Reel of the Late Movie,* Third Eye Press, 1972; *Distances,* Ibis Press, 1972; *Mandrake Root Beer,* Cosmic Wheelbarrow Chapbooks, 1973; *The Red, White, and Blue Bus,* Samisdat Press, 1975; *Bosnia and Herzegovina,* Third Eye Press, 1976; *Alphabetical Order,* Amphion Press, 1976; *Two Hundred Push-Ups at the Y.M.C.A.,* Specific Gravity Publications, 1977; *The Ghost of Hamlet's Father,* Peradam Publishing House, 1977; *Safe Passage,* Stone Country Press, 1977; *Notes to the Milkman,* Black Oak Press, 1978; *Phases of the Moon,* Black Oak Press, 1978; *Piano Tuning at Midnight,* Laughing Bear Press, 1979; *Revenge,* Samisdat Press, 1979; *The Night Shift at the Poetry Factory,* Broken Whisker Studio Press, 1979; *The Edge of the Forest,* New Earth Publication, 1980; *Spiritual Rodeo,* Toothpaste Press, 1980; *Ideas for a Bridal Shower,* Black Oak Press, 1980; *Tap Dancing on a Tightrope,* Laughing Bear Press, 1981; *Training at Home to Be a Locksmith,* Black Oak Press, 1981; *The Great Injun Car-*

As the Lurffins entered
Snurling City, they saw
a careless Skurmal that
was not brushing its
teeth after every meal.

■ (From *The Magic Pretzel* by James Magorian. Illustrated by Adam Laceky.)

JAMES MAGORIAN

nival, Black Oak Press, 1982; *Taxidermy Lessons*, Black Oak Press, 1982.

Contributor of poems to more than one hundred fifty literary magazines, including *American Poet, Ararat, Bitterroot Journal, Haiku Journal, Kansas Quarterly, New Earth Review*, and *Spoon River Quarterly*.

WORK IN PROGRESS: Two nonsense stories of children—one about witches and the other about Ground-Hog Day.

SIDELIGHTS: "I deal in whimsy. Eccentric characters and dadaistic relationships are bread and butter to me. I like to concoct gently bizarre stories. If I don't have fun writing a story, I throw it away and start another one. I seldom start a children's book with a clear goal or moral in mind. I write mostly nonsense stories in which I let situations and crazy creatures move in a manner and at a pace that they would move if they really existed. I am tolerant of these creatures and their obsessions, and I don't mind losing control over them and allowing things to happen that I never thought about until the moment I write them. Nonsense has a progression, but it is according to its own weird logic. If a reader can anticipate what's coming on the next page, then I've failed as a writer. My stories for young people are solely for enjoyment. I reserve social ills, politics, violence, etc. as topics for my poetry and leave them out of my children's stories. My children's-story creatures are usually guilty of nothing more than simple foolishness."

MAJOR, Kevin   1949-

PERSONAL: Born September 12, 1949, in Stephenville, Newfoundland, Canada; son of Edward (a fisherman) and Jessie (Headge) Major; married Anne Crawford, July 3, 1982. *Education:* Memorial University of Newfoundland, B.Sc., 1972. *Home address:* Sandy Cove, Bonavista Bay, Newfoundland,

Canada AOG 1Z0. *Agent:* Nancy Colbert, 303 Davenport Rd., Toronto, Ontario M5R 1K5, Canada.

CAREER: Eastport Central High School, Eastport, Newfoundland, teacher of special education and biology, 1974-76; writer, 1976—. Substitute teacher, 1976—. Guest on television and radio programs. *Member:* Writers' Union of Canada. *Awards, honors:* Children's Literature Award from Canada Council, Book-of-the-Year Award from Canadian Association of Children's Librarians, and Ruth Schwartz Children's Book Award from Ruth Schwartz Charitable Foundation and Ontario Arts Council, all 1979, all for *Hold Fast; Hold Fast* was named Best Book of the Year, 1980, by *School Library Journal*, and placed on the Hans Christian Andersen Honor List, 1980; *Far from Shore* received the Canadian Young Adult Book Award, 1980, and named Best Book of the Year, 1981, by *School Library Journal*.

WRITINGS—For young people: (Editor) *Doryloads*, Breakwater Books, 1974; *Hold Fast* (novel), Clarke, Irwin, 1978, Delacorte, 1980; *Far from Shore* (novel), Clarke, Irwin, 1980.

WORK IN PROGRESS: A third novel, with the main characters being young adults.

It had stopped snowing and I could feel it turning milder. What was on the ground probably wouldn't last long. ■ (Cover illustration from *Hold Fast* by Kevin Major. Jacket painting by Michael Dudash.)

KEVIN MAJOR

SIDELIGHTS: ''I had the good fortune to be born in New-foundland, a province with a fascinating history and a way of life that sets it apart from other regions of North America. I was born in its year of Confederation with Canada and have seen the clash between its traditional way of life and the wave of new ideas, attitudes and values that swept in as Newfound-land came out of its long period of relative isolation. The changes that have resulted, particularly as reflected in the lives of its young people, is perhaps the central theme of my writing.

''I can remember having an interest in writing during my youth. I even remember one high school teacher saying that he thought one day I would write a book. I guess that stuck with me, although when I left home to go to university I did so with the intention of becoming a doctor. Writing as a career seemed such a far-fetched thing at that time. It as only after taking a year away from university and traveling on a shoe-string budget to the West Indies and Europe that I finally settled on direction for my future. I would become a teacher and write in my spare time. During my first year teaching I saw immediately that there were no novels which had characters in them much like the junior high school students I was teaching, nor did any portray the way of life they knew. To try writing a novel from the viewpoint of a Newfoundland teenager seemed a natural

step. My first attempt failed to find a publisher. The second attempt was *Hold Fast* which was published in 1978. By that time I had given up teaching on a regular basis and was spending the bulk of my time writing.

''I didn't write either of my books for a specific audience. I knew they would have particular interest for teenagers because the central characters are young fellows of fourteen and fifteen. But they enjoy a wide adult readership as well. Neither do I consider them regional, in the sense that you would have be a Newfoundlander to appreciate them. I travel widely doing reading tours in school and public libraries and have seen by the audience reaction that the characters in the books have a lot in common with teenagers far removed from my home territory.

''I work in a small house in a very scenic part of Newfoundland. The view from my house is a beautiful one—a stretch of sandy beach and the Atlantic Ocean. Sometimes during the summer I can see whales off shore. But when I write I shut out all that I can, drawing the curtains and working at a table by the light of a desk lamp. Too long in one position I get restless and I often move to different parts of the house—to a favourite chair or to a couch. It seems I work best in concentrated spurts spread over the day.

''At this point in my career, my writing has two main objectives: to say something about growing up generally (the problems, joys, frustrations that are universal) and to portray life in present-day Newfoundland outport society, a society that has changed drastically in the space of the thirty years since Newfoundland joined Canada.

''In *Hold Fast* I wanted to capture the Newfoundland way of life, its way of speaking and manner of dealing with people, and I wanted to convey some of my pride in our traditions—fishing, hunting, and the general closeness to nature.''

FOR MORE INFORMATION SEE: Toronto Sun, June 29, 1978; *Saturday Night*, October, 1978; *In Review*, February, 1979; *Ottawa Journal*, June 19, 1979; *Maclean's* December 17, 1979.

MARTIN, Stefan   1936-

PERSONAL: Born January 10, 1936, in Elgin, Ill.; son of David Stone (an artist) and Thelma (a photographer; maiden name, Durkin) Martin; married Patricia Dancer, September 17, 1955 (divorced, 1975); married Elaine Stochel (an artist), July 20, 1982; children: Debra, Cheryl, Tanya, Christopher, Ian. *Education:* Art Institute of Chicago, 1958. *Home:* 48 Pine Dr., Roosevelt, N.J. 08555.

CAREER: Illustrator, wood engraver, artist. Sandor Wood Engraving Co., Chicago, Ill., apprentice, 1954-58. Lecturer, instructor at various places, including Beaver College, Pa., Summit Art Center, Summit, N.J., Printmaking Council, North Branch, N.J., Mercer County Community College, Trenton, N.J., Foundation of the Arts and Sciences, Love Ladies, N.J., and Princeton Art Association, Princeton, N.J.

EXHIBITIONS—One-man: ROKO Gallery, New York, N.Y., 1961, 1962, 1963, 1967, 1972, 1974; Gallery 100, Princeton, N.J., 1961, 1967; Dickson Gallery, Washington, D.C., 1964; McCarter Theater, Princeton, N.J., 1968; Old Queens Gallery, Highland Park, N.J., 1968, 1971, 1973; New Jersey State Museum, Trenton, N.J., 1968; Lillian Kornbluth Gallery, Fair Lawn, N.J., 1973; Discovery Gallery, Clifton, N.J., 1974; Reed House, Hightstown, N.J., 1975; Hamburg Museum, Germany, 1976, 1977; Mercer County Community College, Triangle Gallery, N.J., 1977; Gallery 500, Elkins Park, Pa., 1981, 1982; George School, Newtown, Pa., 1982.

Group: Washington Printmakers at Library of Congress, 1957, 1959, 1960; Art Student's League, Chicago, Ill., 1958; 12th Annual Boston Printmakers, Museum of Fine Arts, 1959; Boston Printmakers, 1960, 1962; Associated American Artists, 1960; Honolulu Printmakers, 1960; Invitation Annual Exhibition of Contemporary American, Bayonne, N.J., 1961; Terry Dintenfass Gallery, N.Y., 1962; 31st Annual New Jersey State Exhibition, Montclair Art Museum, 1962; Philadelphia Print Club, 1963, 1964, 1965, 1966, 1967, 1969; Brooklyn Museum National Print Exhibition, 1964, 1966; 24th and 26th National Print Exhibition, Jersey City Museum, 1965; World's Fair, N.Y., 1965; Hunterdon County Art Center, National Print Exhibition, 1965, 1966, 1967, 1968, 1969, 1970, 1975, 1981; National Print Exhibition, Kutztown, Pa., 1966; Potsdam Mu-

(From *Ronnie and the Chief's Son* by Elizabeth Coatsworth. Illustrated by Stefan Martin.)

seum, Potsdam, N.Y., 1966, 1967; New Jersey State Museum, 1966, 1967, 1968, 1969, 1970; 9th and 10th National Print Exhibition, New Jersey State Museum, 1966, 1967; 38th Northwest Printmakers, International Exhibition, 1967; Seattle Art Museum, Seattle, Wash., 1967; Portland Art Museum, Portland, Oregon, 1967; 20th National Print Exhibition, Library of Congress, 1967; 29th Annual Color Print Exhibition, New Jersey State Museum, 1968; Society of American Graphic Artists, 49th Annual, N.Y., 1968; Xylon's National Exhibitions, Geneva, Switzerland, 1969-71; Newark Museum, N.J., 1969; Selections from Fine Arts Collection of New Jersey State Museum, 1970; Monmouth Museum, N.J., 1970, 1971; American Academy of Art and Letters, New York, N.Y., 1971, 1972; USIS Brasilia, Brazil, 1973; Summit Art Center, New Jersey, 1974, 1975, 1976; International Print Society, Mexico, 1975; The Printmaking Council, N.J., 1976, 1977, 1978, 1979, 1980, 1981, 1982; Susuni Ltd., N.J., 1976; Somerset Art Association Museum, 1977; Mercer County Community College, 1977, 1978, 1979, 1980, 1981, 1982; Peter Rose Ball, 1977; New York Contemporary Graphics Art Exhibition, Taiwan, Republic of China.

Permanent collections: Philadelphia Museum of Fine Arts, Pa.; Library of Congress, Washington, D.C.; Mobil Oil Co., New York, N.Y.; Philadelphia Free Library, Pa.; Smithsonian Institute, Washington, D.C.; Metropolitan Museum of Art, New York, N.Y.; Museum of Modern Art, New York, N.Y.; Chicago Art Institute, Ill.; Princeton University, N.J.; Columbia University, New York, N.Y.; Charleton College, Minn.; Virginia Museum of Fine Arts, Va.; Seattle Museum, Wash.; Ben Shahn Foundation, N.J.; University of Pennsylvania, Dental College, Pa.; Rockefeller Collection, New York, N.Y.; Hirshhorn Museum, Washington, D.C.; Squibb Corporation Headquarters, Lawrenceville, N.J.; Johnson & Johnson Pharmaceutical, New Brunswick, N.J.; Playboy Magazine Enterprises, Chicago, Ill.; State Museum, Trenton, N.J.; Monmouth Museum, N.J.; Montclair Museum, N.J.; Jersey City Museum, N.J.; Newark Museum, N.J.; Brooklyn Museum, N.Y.; Firestone Library, Princeton, N.J.

MEMBER: Society of American Graphic Artists (vice-president, 1972-74), Visual Artist & Galleries Association, Associated American Artists in New York City, American Color Print Society, Philadelphia Print Club, International Graphic Arts Society, Associated Artists of New Jersey, Hunterdon County Art Center, Summit Art Center, Princeton Art Association, World Print Council, Printmaking Council. *Awards, honors:* First Prize, lithograph, Art Student League, Chicago, Ill., 1958; First Prize, etching, American Academy of Arts & Letters, N.Y., 1959; First Prize, oil painting, Metropolitan Young Artist, N.Y., 1960; First Prize, wood engraving, Philadelphia Print Club, Pa., 1960, 1963; Tiffany Fellowship, graphics, 1961-62, 1963-64; American Institute of Graphic Arts, Children's Book Show selection, 1962, for *Ronnie and the Chief's Son,* 1966, for *They Walk in the Night,* 1969, for *Small Pond;* engraving commissioned by International Graphic Art Society, 1964, 1965, 1968; Purchase Award, New Jersey Painters & Sculptures Society 26th National Exhibition, 1965; Best in Show, Atlantic City Boardwalk Art Show, N.J., 1965; Purchase Prize, 10th National Print Exhibition, New Jersey State Museum, 1966; Purchase Prize, Hunterdon County 10th National Print Exhibit, 1966; Purchase Award, New Jersey State Museum, 1968; Best in Show, Hunterdon Art Center, 1975; 18th Annual Award of Excellence, Art Directors Club of New Jersey, 1980.

ILLUSTRATOR—Of interest to young people: Elizabeth Coatsworth, *Ronnie and the Chief's Son,* Macmillan, 1962; Mary

STEFAN MARTIN

Elting and Franklin Folsom, *How the Animals Get to the Zoo,* Grosset, 1964; E. Coatsworth, *The Sparrow Bush: Rhymes* (*Horn Book* honor list), Norton, 1966; Marguerite Walters, *Small Pond,* Dutton, 1967; Raymond Sacks, *Magnets,* Coward, 1967; E. Coatsworth, *They Walk in the Night,* Norton, 1969; Robert Gannon, *What's under the Rock?,* Dutton, 1971; Anton Chekhov, *The Wolf and the Mutt,* translated by Guy Daniels, McGraw, 1971; Berniece Freschet, *The Ants Go Marching,* Scribner, 1973.

Other: Earl Schenck Miers, *Arctic Sun and Tropic Moon,* Curtis Paper, 1960; Adolph Murie, *A Naturalist in Alaska,* Doubleday, 1961; Paul M. Angle and E. S. Miers, *American Culture: Some Beginnings,* Kingsport Press, 1961; John Muir, *The Yosemite,* Doubleday, 1962; Farida A. Wiley, *Theodore Roosevelt's America,* Doubleday, 1962; Sienko and Blane, *Chemistry,* McGraw, 1966; Lorna Beers, *Wild Apples and North Wind,* Norton, 1966; Vernon Pizer, *The World Ocean—Man's Last Frontier,* World, 1967; May Sarton, *The Poet and the Donkey,* Norton, 1969; Iverson, McCarthy, and Sebesta, *Panoramas of Literature,* Random House, 1969; Lynn Hall, *Too Near the Sun,* Follett, 1970; Freya Littledale, editor, *Ghosts and Spirits of Many Lands,* Doubleday, 1970; Roget Lockard, *Glaciers,* Coward, 1970; Charles Fenn, *Journal of a Voyage to Nowhere,* Norton, 1971; John Hall Wheelock, *In Love and Song: Poems,* Scribner, 1971; Patrick D. Smith, *Forever Island,* Norton, 1973; J. Ernst, *Escape King: The Story of Harry Houdini,* Prentice-Hall, 1974; Kirchoff Wohlberg, *1976,* Kirchoff Wohlberg, 1976; New Jersey Arts Council, *Middle Jersey Writers,* Middlesex County, 1979; Bass, Bellias, and Lapsansky, *Our American Heritage,* Silver Burdett, 1979.

(From "The Lutin in the Barn" by Natalie Savage Carlson in *Ghosts and Spirits of Many Lands,* edited by Freya Littledale. Wood engraving by Stefan Martin.)

Garraty, *U.S. History,* Harcourt, 1982; Littell, *Literature 8,* McDougal, 1982. Also illustrator of cover, *Dog Town,* Prentice-Hall, in press. Contributor of drawings and engravings for periodicals, including *Scientific American, Mobil Oil, News from the Art World, Natural History* and *The Kenyon Review.*

WORK IN PROGRESS: Several large collages, demonstrations, lectures, and slide shows.

SIDELIGHTS: Born in Elgin, Illinois, on January 10, 1936. "As a child I lived and drew pictures in the environment of an artistic family. I am the son of David Stone Martin, a well-known illustrator and graphic artist. . . . Art was a day to day thing, as much a part of life as breathing and eating." [Lee Kingman and others, compilers, *Illustrators of Children's Books: 1957-1966,* Horn Book, 1968.¹]

"We moved to Knoxville, Tennessee where my father did a mural for the Tennessee Valley Authority at Norris Dam. I recall him working very hard on an important painting depicting the strength of the men putting in lines to bring electricity to the farms and towns of Tennessee. My brother Tony was born during this time.

"Soon we moved to Washington D.C. where I first met Ben Shahn who was to become a strong influence on my career. We lived on the outskirts of Washington, D.C. My father and Ben were working on WPA projects, including posters enlisting the men for the Second World War. I don't remember much about the artwork; my fascination at that time was the tame rabbit that lived in the yard as our pet. Nature was surely making her impression on me. I was four years old. There was a stream in the back of the house that kept overflowing and we had to move.

"I don't know what made my father move to Manhattan, perhaps he felt he could do his artwork better. He always liked the city. We moved to 4th Street and I started first grade at P.S. #41 in the Village. Living in New York was probably my first experience at seeing life. Everything is very grand through the eyes of young boy. I didn't like going to school in New York—there were bars on the windows which I remember very clearly. I had to chase away the kids who picked on my brother who was fifteen months younger than I.

"Roosevelt, a small country town in New Jersey, is where I finished my grade school. Ben Shahn lived a few houses away from us. This was a better environment for young boys and a better education for us in both nature and art. My father worked at his commercial drawings in a small bedroom. It was wonderful seeing him there, while playing marbles and riding my bike to school. I never realized how important art was till I was in the sixth grade and elected to do art projects in my classroom. Seven children were in my grade school graduating class. My whole life was centered around this very small town.

"It was at this time that music became important in my life. I almost thought I wanted to pursue a career in the field. My father was working for many record companies, designing album covers for folk singers, jazz and blues recording artists. Many of them came to our town. His career began to spiral and he built a studio in our backyard. This became a very festive time for everyone. In the late night hours the artists would put the drawing board aside and dance. My brother and I would watch them through the windows as they kept us awake till all hours of the night. The records played on the loudspeaker all day and all night. I wanted a career in music. I had no interest in money. My small town loved me. I was very happy all through high school.

"It was very difficult when I left Roosevelt and went to school in Chicago. Everyone encouraged me to take fine art classes at the Art Institute. I had learned the commercial end of art by watching my father. As a young adult I always dreamed of illustrating a book. My art school training helped me conquer the means. I studied printmaking and I worked for four years as an apprentice wood engraver for about $1.50 per hour.

"While attending the Chicago Art Institute I worked as an apprentice at the Sandor Wood Engraving Company. It was at this shop that I learned every aspect of wood engraving. I think that unless I had gone through this rigid work discipline I could not have mastered the techniques of wood engraving, the knowledge of how to hold the tools—the hand becoming almost the mind."[1]

"During this time I was married and had two small children. I thought my art was the *only one* in the world. 'What a combination that would be,' I thought, 'the ideas, to put them on a block of wood, take a print and then to be enthralled at the results.' My first book was a big success. I received the AIGA certificate and my dream came true. That was four years after completing art school. Just as my father took us to the country, I took my children and moved back to New Jersey."

Martin has lived most of his life in the Monmouth County section of New Jersey, because of "the acceptance of the arts in this community. In some towns you might not have this acceptance. Neighbors might wonder why you're home every day." [Michele Molnar, "Wood Engraving: Monmouth Artist Works in Rare Medium at Home Studio," *The Home News*, January 22, 1981.[2]]

An accomplished wood engraver, Martin is one of only four or five practicing this art in this country. About his work he writes: "I draw directly on the wood with an idea in mind, interpret what I draw with engraving tools and finally print the block."[1]

"I interpret the drawing or photo on wood using India ink, brushes, and pens. When I draw the picture on wood, I'm thinking in flopped image. Then I go to the engraving table and start cutting."[2] He will work for six to eight hours in his studio at a time and "will spend days, weeks, right there."[2]

"I keep my artwork personal, aesthetic and crisp. I feel that a medium I know well, wood engraving or woodcuts, would adapt nicely to artistic thoughts for book illustration. The editors let me be free to create. I feel that if you have a commercial job, you should treat it as if it is fine art. Learn your techniques, but don't let your techniques overpower what you really want to say. I think illustrating a book is a visual concept of the environment in which you live. For instance, if I'm confused about the shape of a certain tree, or the position of a person, I'll go outside. I look at that shape or individual and draw directly. When I illustrate a book, I think of a music composition, done visually. I still structure my artwork as if I was making a model airplane. I still play the harmonica and I think about when I was a Boy Scout. I know all these things have something to do with it. Of course, some distractions—such as growing up experiences, sports and maturing add texture."

Art is an intrinsic part of Martin's life. "Without the visual arts and music and the theatre, I have nothing. We're born with eyes and hands and senses and I feel it's important to keep these things going. They wouldn't know about (ancient) Greek culture if it weren't for the art that was left behind."[2]

Martin's works are included in the Kerlan Collection at the University of Minnesota.

HOBBIES AND OTHER INTERESTS: Skiing, tennis, pool, playing the clarinet.

FOR MORE INFORMATION SEE: Lee Kingman and others, compilers, *Illustrators of Children's Books: 1957-1966*, Horn Book, 1968; *The Home News*, January 22, 1981.

MASON, Edwin A. 1905-1979

OBITUARY NOTICE: Born April 25, 1905, in Nottingham, England; died July 9, 1979, in West Hartford, Conn. Wildlife manager and author of two books for children, *Robins* and *Swans and Wild Geese*. Mason began his career designing park systems in South Carolina during the 1920's. He became a professional wildlife manager, and from 1926-43 he was in charge of Wharton Bird Banding Station in Groton, Mass. In 1944 Mason founded Audubon's Arcadia Wildlife Sanctuary. He served as director of the sanctuary until 1962, when he was named director of the department of wildlife management for the Massachusetts Audubon Society. He received an honorary degree from Heidelberg University in Germany in recognition of his work with bird parasites. He was also made an honorary citizen of Argentina for his efforts relating to the organization of the first South American conservation movement. Mason was also a contributor to *The New York Times, Yankee Magazine,* and other publications. *For More Information See: Contemporary Authors Permanent Series*, Volume 2, Gale, 1978. *Obituaries: The New York Times*, July 11, 1979; *AB Bookman's Weekly*, August, 1979; *Contemporary Authors*, Volumes 89-92, Gale, 1980.

If wishes were horses,
  Beggars would ride;
If turnips were watches,
  I'd wear one by my side.

—Nursery rhyme

THE UNICORN AND THE LAKE

by MARIANNA MAYER
Pictures by MICHAEL HAGUE

The unicorn was pure white, as white as mountain snow, and his ivory horn was a magnificent spiral. Men believed the unicorn was immortal. . . . At last the unicorn was forced to flee high up into the mountains to escape the hunters' arrows. ■ (Cover illustration from *The Unicorn and the Lake* by Marianna Mayer. Illustrated by Michael Hague.)

"My poor beast, this is my fault for being so heartless. I have repaid your love with my own blindness and selfishness." ■ (From *Beauty and the Beast*, retold by Marianna Mayer. Illustrated by Mercer Mayer.)

MAYER, Marianna 1945-

PERSONAL; Born November 8, 1945, in Queens, N.Y.; married Mercer Mayer (an author and illustrator), now divorced. *Education:* Attended the Art Students League. *Home:* Roxbury, Conn.

CAREER: Author and illustrator. Previously employed as a commercial artist by an advertising agency, and as a copy writer; currently engaged as a free-lance writer and illustrator of children's books. *Awards, honors: A Boy, A Dog, a Frog, and a Friend* received the Brooklyn Art Books for Children Citation in 1973.

WRITINGS—Juveniles: (With Mercer Mayer) *Mine* (self-illustrated picture book), Simon & Schuster, 1970; (with M. Mayer) *A Boy, a Dog, a Frog, and a Friend* (illustrated by M. Mayer; picture book), Dial, 1971; (with M. Mayer) *Me and My Flying Machine* (illustrated by M. Mayer; fantasy), Parents' Magazine Press, 1971; (with M. Mayer) *One Frog Too Many* (illustrated by M. Mayer; picture book), Dial, 1975; *Beauty and the Beast* (a retelling of the French classic by Marie Leprince de Beau-

mont; illustrated by M. Mayer), Four Winds, 1978; (reteller) Carlo Collodi, *Pinocchio* (illustrated by Gerald McDermott), Four Winds, 1981; *The Unicorn and the Lake* (illustrated by Michael Hague), Dial, 1982.

SIDELIGHTS: Mayer was born and reared in New York City. Before she learned how to read, she spent a great deal of time drawing, making pictures for the stories her parents read to her or copying them from picture books. At an early age Mayer decided to become an artist. A lasting impression was made by an illustrator-friend of the family who encouraged her talent.

Mayer pursued her interest in drawing and painting throughout high school and college. After one year at college, Mayer enrolled in the Art Students League where she completed her art studies. She began her career as a commercial artist in an advertising agency and later as a copy-writer until she chose free-lance writing and illustrating children's books.

As an adult, she has retained her ingenuous appreciation for picture stories as evidenced in her own books for children. As *Horn Book* observed, the drawing in *A Boy, a Dog, a Frog,*

MARIANNA MAYER

and a Friend "convey a sense of childlike wonder and response to the unexpected in a manner which is neither stereotyped or sentimental. A small book, but one with potential for enlarging the 'reader's' sympathetic reactions to the human comedy."

One of Mayer's latest books is an adaptation of *Pinocchio.* "Fairy tales have given me a sense of optimism that I probably wouldn't have had. That's why working on them is wonderful—they are my friends." [Lis Bensley, "Well, Jimmy Cricket—Look Whose Age (100) Has Outgrown Even His Nose," *People,* December 21, 1981.[1]]

In her research of the project Mayer found "the original tale was not Disney's story at all! I was very impudent as a kid. Like Pinocchio, I was always in trouble. Nobody could tell me how to do things either. It's the conflict in Pinocchio that makes him wonderful."[1]

Mayer lives in a 1730 farmhouse on fifteen acres in Roxbury, Connecticut, with her dog, Max, a briard, and her horse, Lea.

FOR MORE INFORMATION SEE: Horn Book, June 1971; Doris de Montreville and Elizabeth D. Crawford, editors, *Fourth Book of Junior Authors and Illustrators,* H. W. Wilson, 1978.

Life being very short, and the quiet hours of it few, we ought to waste none of them in reading valueless books.

—John Ruskin

MAYER, Mercer   1943-

PERSONAL: Born in Little Rock, Ark.; married wife, Marianna (an author; divorced); married second wife, Jo; children: Len, Jessie. *Education:* Studied at the Honolulu Academy of Arts and the Art Students League. *Residence:* Bridgewater, Conn.

CAREER: Has been an art director in an advertising agency, but is presently a full-time author and illustrator of children's books.

AWARDS, HONORS: Winner of the Society of Illustrators Annual National Exhibit Citation of Merit for *A Boy, a Dog, and a Frog,* 1970, *What Do You Do with a Kangaroo?,* 1975, and *Frog Goes to Dinner,* 1976; Children's Book Award from the American Institute of Graphic Arts, 1970-71, for *A Special Trick;* illustrations for Jane Yolen's *The Bird of Time* and Jan Wahl's *Margaret's Birthday* were included in the American

Inside there was enough moonlight coming through the windows for them to see more religious statues, crates and boxes. But Tom was only interested in the ceiling. And in one corner of it he saw a trapdoor leading to the attic. ■ (From *The Great Brain at the Academy* by John D. Fitzgerald. Illustrated by Mercer Mayer.)

Mercer Mayer with two of his characters: "Little Monster" and "Professor Wormbog."

Institute of Graphic Arts Children's Book Show, 1971-72; *A Boy, a Dog, a Frog, and a Friend* received the Brooklyn Art Books for Children Citation, 1973, *What Do You Do with a Kangaroo?*, 1975, and *Frog Goes to Dinner*, 1977; *A Boy, a Dog, and a Frog, A Boy, a Dog, a Frog, and a Friend*, and *A Frog and a Friend* received the International Books for Children award from the Association for Childhood Education,

1974; *You're the Scaredy-Cat* was named by the Child Study Association as one of the best books of the year, 1974; *While the Horses Galloped to London* was selected as part of the Children's Book Showcase, 1974, *Beauty and the Beast*, 1979; *Everyone Knows What a Dragon Looks Like* was selected as one of the *New York Times* Choice of Best Illustrated Books of the Year, was selected as one of the year's ten best books by *Learning* magazine, and was part of the American Institute of Graphic Arts Book Show, 1976, and won the Irma Simonton Black Award, 1977.

WRITINGS—All self-illustrated, except as noted: *A Boy, a Dog, and a Frog* (picture book), Dial, 1967; *There's a Nightmare in My Closet*, Dial, 1968; *Terrible Troll*, Dial, 1968; *If I Had. . .*, Dial, 1968; *I Am a Hunter*, Dial, 1969; *Frog, Where Are You?*, Dial, 1969; *A Special Trick*, Dial, 1970; (with Marianna Mayer) *Mine*, Simon & Schuster, 1970; *The Queen Always Wanted to Dance* (Junior Literary Guild selection), Simon & Schuster, 1971; (with Marianna Mayer) *A Boy, a Dog, a Frog, and a Friend*, Dial, 1971; (with Marianna Mayer) *Me and My Flying Machine*, Parents' Magazine Press, 1971; *A Silly Story*, Parents' Magazine Press, 1972; *Frog on His Own*, Dial, 1973; *Bubble, Bubble*, Parents' Magazine Press, 1973; *Mrs. Beggs and the Wizard*, Parents' Magazine Press, 1973; *A Frog and a Friend*, Golden Press, 1974; *What Do You Do with a Kangaroo?*, Four Winds, 1974; *One Monster after Another*, Golden Press, 1974; *Two Moral Tales* (includes *The Bird's New Hat* and *Bear's New Clothes*), Four Winds, 1974; *Two More Moral Tales* (includes *Just a Pig at Heart* and *Sly Fox's Folly*), Four Winds, 1974; *Walk, Robot, Walk*, Ginn, 1974; *You're the Scaredy-Cat*, Parents' Magazine Press, 1974; *Frog Goes to Dinner*, Dial, 1974.

Just for You, Golden Press, 1975; (with M. Mayer) *One Frog Too Many*, Dial, 1975; *The Great Cat Chase: A Wordless Book*, Four Winds, 1975; *Professor Wormbog in Search for the Zipperump-a-Zoo*, Golden Press, 1976; *Liza Lou and the Great Yeller Belly Swamp*, Parents' Magazine Press, 1976; *Ah-Choo*,

Dial, 1976; *Four Frogs in a Box*, Dial, 1976; *Hiccup*, Dial, 1976; *There's a Nightmare in My Cupboard*, Dent, 1976; *Just Me and My Dad*, Western, 1977; *Little Monster's Word Book*, Western, 1977; *Oops*, Dial, 1977; *Professor Wormbog's Gloomy Kerploppus: A Book of Great Smells*, Western, 1977; (editor) *The Poison Tree, and Other Poems*, Scribner, 1977; *Mercer's Monsters*, Western, 1977; *Appelard and Liverwurst* (illustrated by Steven Kellogg), Four Winds, 1978; *Little Monster at Work*, Western, 1978; *Little Monster's You-Can-Make-It Book*, Western, 1978; *Little Monster's Bedtime Book*, Western, 1978; *Little Monster's Counting Book*, Western, 1978; *Little Monster's Neighborhood*, Western, 1978; *Mercer Mayer's Little Monster's Library* (set of six books), Western, 1978; *Little Monster's Mother Goose*, Western, 1979; *How the Trollusk Got His Hat*, Western, 1979; *Herbert, the Knightly Dragon*, Western, 1980; *East of the Sun and West of the Moon*, Four Winds, 1980; *Professor Wormbog's Cut It, Glue It, Tape It, Do-It Book*, Western, 1980; *Little Monster's Scratch and Sniff Mystery*, Western, 1980; *Professor Wormbog's Crazy Cut-Ups*, Western, 1980; *Herbert, the Timid Dragon*, Western, 1980; *Favorite Tales from Grimm*, Four Winds, 1982; *Liverwurst Is Missing*, Four Winds, 1982.

Illustrator: John D. Fitzgerald, *The Great Brain*, Dial, 1967; Liesel M. Skorpen, *Outside My Window*, Harper, 1968; George Mendoza, *The Gillygoofang*, Dial, 1968; Sidney Offit, *The Boy Who Made a Million*, St. Martin's, 1968; G. Mendoza, *The Crack in the Wall, and Other Terribly Weird Tales*, Dial, 1968; Sheila LaFarge, *Golden Butter*, Dial, 1969; J. D. Fitzgerald, *More Adventures of the Great Brain*, Dial, 1969; Kathryn Hitte, *Boy, Was I Mad!*, Parents' Magazine Press, 1969; Warren Fine, *The Mousechildren and the Famous Collector*, Harper, 1970; Jean R. Larson, *Jack Tar*, M. Smith, 1970; Barbara Wersba, *Let Me Fall before I Fly*, Atheneum, 1971; Jane H. Yolen, *The Bird of Time*, Crowell, 1971; Jan Wahl, *Margaret's Birthday*, Four Winds, 1971; J. D. Fitzgerald, *Me and My Little Brain*, Dial, 1971.

Candida Palmer, *Kim Ann and the Yellow Machine*, Ginn, 1972; Mildred Kantrowitz, *Good-Bye Kitchen*, Parents' Magazine Press, 1972; J. Wahl, *Grandmother Told Me*, Little, Brown, 1972; J. D. Fitzgerald, *The Great Brain at the Academy*, Dial, 1972; Mabel Watts, *While the Horses Galloped to London*, Parents' Magazine Press, 1973; J. D. Fitzgerald, *The Great Brain Reforms*, Dial, 1973; B. Wersba, *Amanda Dreaming*, Atheneum, 1973; J. D. Fitzgerald, *The Return of the Great Brain*, Dial, 1974; J. D. Fitzgerald, *The Great Brain Does It Again*, Dial, 1975; John Bellairs, *The Figure in the Shadows*, Dial, 1975; Jay Williams, *Everyone Knows What a Dragon Looks Like*, Four Winds, 1976; J. Williams, *The Reward Worth Having*, Four Winds, 1977; Marianna Mayer, reteller, *Beauty and the Beast*, Four Winds, 1978.

SIDELIGHTS: **1943.** Born in Little Rock, Arkansas. Attended elementary school in Camden, Arkansas. Traveled with his family throughout the United States before settling in Hawaii.

1961. Graduated from Theodore Roosevelt High School in Honolulu and attended the Honolulu Academy of Arts. Mayer and his mother were commissioned to decorate the Kahala Hilton Hotel with collage wall panels. He was also a political cartoonist for the International Brotherhood of Teamsters in Honolulu. "It's strange when you grew up in a place where people respect you because you're white, then get uprooted and find yourself in a place where the situation is reversed, especially when the change is abrupt and at the tender age of 13. It was a real shock to find out the world doesn't really

Birds could rest on the wings, if they were tired from flying around all day.

(From *Me and My Flying Machine* by Marianna and Mercer Mayer. Illustrated by the authors.)

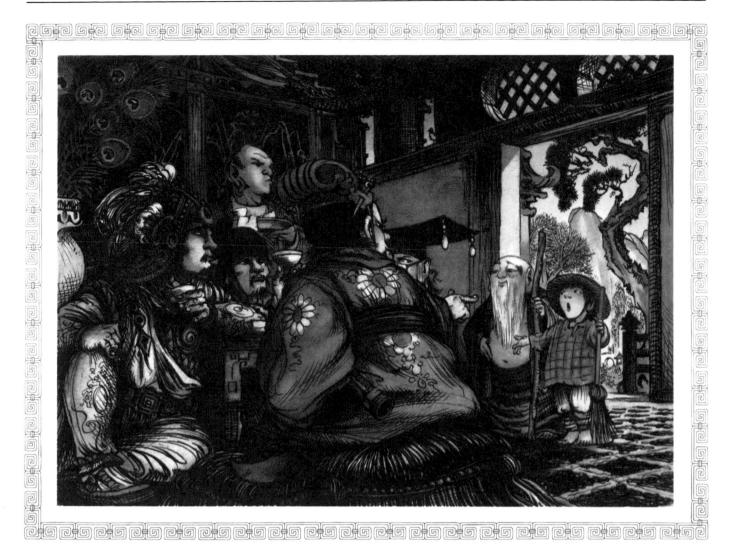

"Sir," said Han, "he is a dragon."

"Don't be ridiculous," said the Mandarin. "He's a fat man who is tracking dirt on my fine carpets. What do you want here, old man?"

"I have come to help you," said the little fat man. "But if you want a dragon to help you, you must treat him with courtesy." ■ (From *Everyone Knows What a Dragon Looks Like* by Jay Williams. Illustrated by Mercer Mayer.)

revolve around a particular race." [Betti Logan, "You Can Call Him a Monstrous Success," *Newsday*, December 21, 1978.]

1964. Left the Hawaiian Islands for New York. Mayer received additional art training at the Art Students League in New York City. "My one philosophy as an artist is to learn how to draw the human figure, which is the most complicated and delicately balanced form in nature. Once that is mastered, an artist can complete and succeed in any area of the arts he or she wishes. Without this mastery, the artist will limit himself tremendously. I have drawn all my life. One of my earliest memories is of looking at a book illustrated by N. C. Wyeth."

As a young man, Mayer began his career as a door-to-door salesman. "I always liked to draw, and one day I decided I had nothing to lose, so I made a lot of sketches and began to peddle them." His first book was a picture book, *A Boy, a*

Dog, and a Frog, which won the Brooklyn Art Books for Children Citation.

1968. *There's a Nightmare in My Closet* was published. "It was a true story. When I was a child I was afraid of the dark. Before I went to sleep at night, I would close the closet door. You have to hear the click of the latch catching or else you won't know if the googly monster's coming out. Then if you hear the latch click during the night you know the monster's coming out and that's when you know you have to run like hell.

". . . Critics compared it to Maurice Sendak's *Where the Wild Things Are*. They tore it to shreds, and turned 'My Nightmare' into a best seller. There was so much negative said about it, that it got enough people interested in taking a look at it.

(From *Beauty and the Beast,* retold by Marianna Mayer. Illustrated by Mercer Mayer.)

''Every book has its own formula. Sometimes the story comes first, the pictures later, in the case of 'My Nightmare,' the nightmare creature had been created years ago.

''The truth of it is I don't really do monsters. Children do love monsters, dinosaurs, bears and bunny rabbits—I do not do bunny rabbits. What I've really done are critters.

"I never think of it (the books) as being done in terms of children. My books are for the children in all of us really." [Susan Yim, "Lovable Monsters Between the Covers," *Star Bulletin* (Hawaii), October 8, 1979.[2]]

1974. *Frog Goes to Dinner,* the fifth book in Mayer's "Frog" series was published. The author-illustrator does not see himself as their creator. "They have not so much been created by me, but rather given to me. One day I will sit down and wonder, 'will I ever think of another frog book?' 'Oh, probably not,' comes the answer, and then a few days later, there it is. One, two, three, I have the theme and the plot. The time then goes into polishing the rough dummy. But try as I might I cannot deliberately think up one of those silly books. I've now come to the conclusion that I am Frog's creation, which is just fine with me. After all, the responsibility of thinking up new things to make books about is overwhelming."

1975. The sixth "Frog" book, *One Frog Too Many,* was published. "I had been trying for about a year to come up with a sixth 'Frog' book, making false starts and getting nowhere. Then Marianna heard Phyllis [Fogelman; his editor] talking about 'Frog in a Box,' said 'That's it!' and just reeled off the whole plot. I reached for pencil and paper and started working on the dummy right there."

1976. *Ah-Choo* and *Hiccup,* two almost wordless picture books for children, were published. *Ah-Choo* was created at a workshop for elementary school teachers in New Orleans when Mayer was asked how he creates a new book. The subject exploded from the sketches he drew for his audience. "The first picture I drew was an elephant, for no other reason than I thought elephants would show up best to a large crowd. I truly had no intention of actually creating a new book.

"Next I drew a picture of my elephant coming upon a small mouse selling flowers. 'What could possible happen next?' I asked my audience, and before anyone could answer I had an idea: of course, the elephant sneezes. Well, before I knew it, my demonstration turned into the actual creation of a new book, which delighted everyone, myself included. On the airplane coming home I sketched in the rest of the dummy, this time on Eastern Airlines' stationery."

On that same airplane trip *Hiccup* was created. "Sitting there a few thousand feet above the ground I thought, what about a hippopotamus with the hiccups, and a new project was born. This all may seem easy, and it is when it finally comes, but before I arrive at a publishable story there are stacks of dead ends."

That same year, Mayer illustrated *Everyone Knows What a Dragon Looks Like,* which was written by Jay Williams. The book was selected as one of the *New York Times* Choice of Best Illustrated Books of the Year for 1976 and won the Irma Simonton Black Award in 1977. "Being an author-illustrator has its problems because editors have a tendency not to ask if I would like to illustrate someone else's work. Usually I am very busy, but on rare occasions I would love to, and Jay Williams' manuscript was one of those rare occasions.

"I knew from the start I didn't want to draw a historical document. I wanted this book to come directly from me as if I lived in China. But I made no bones about being a Westerner. The China I drew is a China of the heart. I surrounded myself with Chinese art and books. I pored over everything Chinese I could find. I China-fied myself. Then I tried to forget it all

(From the short film "A Boy, a Dog and a Frog," produced by Phoenix Films, Inc., 1981.)

and began to sketch. It was wonderful fun, a very rich experience."

1978. Created the "Little Monster" books for Golden Press, which have been quite successful. Mayer claims that he does not know what makes a book popular with children. "If I knew, I'd make sure they were in all of my stuff. Kids like everything except what they don't like. When they don't like it they don't touch it. If they do, they read it over and over again." ["When He Beckons, Monsters Appear," *Detroit Free Press,* November 2, 1979.[3]]

Mayer, who has been writing books for about fifteen years, has received almost every prestigious award there is for children's literature. "It's nice when someone gives you an honor . . . but there's the danger of getting hung up on that saying, 'Oh, who's going to give me a prize next time.' You've got to get on with what you're doing."[3]

1982. Working from his home in Bridgewater, Connecticut, Mayer works a seven-hour day, five-day week. "You have to get yourself on a schedule, otherwise you'll find yourself doing nothing else but working. When I didn't have a schedule, I'd feel guilty if I took a break, went for a walk or even took time out to eat. But now everything is in it's place."[1]

Many of Mayer's books do not contain words, but tell a story through pictures. Most critics agree that in books such as *Frog, Where Are You?* and *A Boy, a Dog, a Frog and A Friend* words are not needed and that it is easy for children to follow the action through the pictures.

Mayer's drawing for *A Poison Tree and Other Poems* were critiqued in *Horn Book* by a reviewer who described the book as: "A new anthology for young people in which the illustration is fully as significant as the poetry but does not supersede it. For each poem a full-page drawing complements an emotion expressed by the poet, often from the point of view of a child. . . . With alternating misty grays and sepia—a strikingly different style for the artist—the full-page illuminations subtly project inspiration and ecstasy and other emotions. Some of the illustrations are executed brilliantly in chiaroscuro: a dark face with light in the eyes; a spider web in the moonlight; a crouching giant under a sickle moon and stars."

HOBBIES AND OTHER INTERESTS: Guitar playing, painting, walking in the woods, and sitting by the river.

FOR MORE INFORMATION SEE: Horn Book, December, 1969, June, 1971, October, 1973, December, 1974, February and April, 1975; *Newsday,* December 21, 1978; *The Commercial Appeal* (Memphis, Tenn.), February 25, 1979; *Star Bulletin* (Hawaii), October 8, 1979; *Detroit Free Press,* November 2, 1979.

McKINLEY, (Jennifer Carolyn) Robin

BRIEF ENTRY: Born in Warren, Ohio. An author of books for young readers, McKinley has gained a reputation as a versatile reteller of classic fairy tales. While adhering to the original stories, she develops deeper characterizations, broadens the plots, and creates fantastical imagery in a smooth prose style. *Horn Book* compares her writing to ". . . a musical theme and variations . . . arpeggios of ideas and of language. . . ." Her first book, *Beauty: A Retelling of the Story of Beauty and the Beast,* 1979, was praised by critics for its inventiveness and what the *English Journal* called "lush feminine fantasy." In *The Door in the Hedge,* a collection of four stories, McKinley borrowed from the Brothers Grimm while adding two originals, "The Stolen Princess" and "The Hunting of the Hind." Her third book, *The Blue Sword,* was a Newbery Honor Book, 1983. Also her own creation, it is a rendition of the heroic tale complete with forces of good and evil, kingdoms to defend, and high adventure. *Residence:* Boston, Mass.

McNAUGHT, Harry

PERSONAL: Born in Scotland; children: Four. *Education:* Attended Philadelphia Museum School of Art.

Piglets are baby pigs.

(From *Baby Animals* by Harry McNaught. Illustrated by the author.)

CAREER: Writer and illustrator of books for young people.

WRITINGS—All self-illustrated; all for children: *500 Words to Grow On*, Random House, 1973; *Baby Animals*, Random House, 1976; *Trucks*, Random House, 1976; *Animal Babies*, Random House, 1977; *Muppets in My Neighborhood*, Random House, 1977; *The Truck Book*, Random House, 1978.

Illustrator: (Illustrated with Hershel Wartik) Herbert Zim and others, *Photography*, Golden Press, 1964; Hedy Baklin-Landman and Edna Shapiro, *The Story of Porcelain*, Odyssey, 1965; Adelaide Holl and Seymour Reit, *Time and Measuring*, Golden Book Educational Services, 1966; Melvin Keene, *Beginners' Story of Minerals and Rocks*, Harper, 1966; Peter Farb, *Land, Wildlife, and Peoples of the Bible*, Harper, 1967; (illustrated with Charles J. Berger) Norman Lloyd, *Golden Encyclopedia of Music*, Golden Press, 1968; Eugene and Katherine Rachlis, *Our Fifty United States*, Golden Press, 1974; Sarah Riedman, *Heart*, Golden Press, 1974; B. G. Ford, *Do You Know?*, Random House, 1979; Dinah L. Moche, *Astronomy Today: Planets, Stars, Space Exploration*, Random House, 1982.

SIDELIGHTS: After graduating from high school, McNaught worked in a commercial art studio, first as an errand boy and later as an artist. World War II interrupted his art work, but at the end of the war he enrolled in illustration classes at the Philadelphia Museum School of Art as a G.I. student. After three years of art training, he resumed his art career as a free-lance illustrator.

As an illustrator, McNaught's techniques are varied. He is equally at home in black and white, limited, or full color. His subjects range from the contemporary scene to historical subjects; from modern science to fairyland.

In addition to illustrating numerous books for children, he has written and illustrated his own children's books, including *500 Words to Grow On*, a picture dictionary for young children.

FOR MORE INFORMATION SEE: American Artist, October, 1952.

McPHAIL, David M(ichael)   1940-

BRIEF ENTRY: Born June 30, 1940, in Newburyport, Mass. An author and illustrator of books for children, McPhail attended Vesper George University and Boston Museum of Fine Arts School. He has illustrated over ten books written by others, including *Sailing to Cythera, and Other Anatole Stories* by Nancy Willard, which was selected as one of the American Institute of Graphic Arts Fifty Books of the Year, 1974. He has also written and illustrated about twenty of his own books, among them *Captain Toad and the Motorbike*, 1979, and *Grandfather's Cake*, 1980, both of which were selected for the American Institute of Graphic Arts Book Show. McPhail utilizes pen-and-ink or washed, subdued coloring to produce pictures that are, according to *School Library Journal*, "... pleasantly reminiscent of Sendak's in both style and *fin de siècle* ambience." His other written works include *In the Summer I Go Fishing*, 1971, *Henry Bear's Park*, 1976, *The Magical Drawings of Moony B. Finch*, 1978, *Pig Pig Grows Up*, 1980, *That Grand Master Jumping Teacher, Bernard, Meets Jerome, the Giant Jumping Glump*, 1982, and *Snow Lion*, 1983. Among his illustrated works are Robert Brooks's *The Run, Jump, Bump Book*, Emily McLeod's *The Bear's Bicycle*, *Strangers' Bread* and *The Island Grass King: The Further*

Adventures of Anatole by Willard, and Genie Iverson's *I Want to Be Big. Home:* Granite St., Pigeon Cove, Mass. 01966. *For More Information See: Illustrators of Children's Books: 1967-1976*, Horn Book, 1978; *Contemporary Authors*, Volumes 85-88, Gale, 1980.

MERWIN, Decie   1894-1961

BRIEF ENTRY: Born October 20, 1894, in Middleboro, Ky.; died September 6, 1961. Author and illustrator of books for children. Merwin attended private schools, and a small art school in Boston, Mass. As a young adult, with encouragement from local Southern editors, she moved to the North to pursue her interest in book illustration. She was married to the late John Ernest Bechdolt, also an author of children's books. Together they wrote *John's Dragon*, 1937, and a series of books about a 19th century little girl named Dulcie. Inspired by her husband, Merwin began writing and illustrating her own works, including *Time for Tammie*, 1946, *Pink-Tails*, 1950, *Where's Teresa?*, 1956, *Somerhaze Farm*, 1958, *Scottish Treasure Mystery*, 1960, and others. She was also the illustrator of books by other authors, among them Rebecca Caudill's *Happy Little Family*, Margaret J. Baker's *Four Farthings and a Thimble*, *Wise House* by Robin Palmer, and Alvena Seckar's *Misko. For More Information See: Illustrators of Children's Books: 1946-1956*, Horn Book, 1958. *Obituaries: Publishers Weekly*, September 25, 1961.

MOLLOY, Anne Baker   1907-

PERSONAL: Born October 4, 1907, in Boston, Mass.; daughter of Lawrence Wills (an orthodontist) and Lila (Nichols) Baker; married Paul Edward Molloy, March 13, 1928 (deceased); children: John Stearns, Jane. *Education:* Attended Mount Holyoke College, 1925-28. *Religion:* Unitarian Universalist. *Home:* 3 Edward St., Portsmouth, N.H. 03801.

CAREER: Writer of books for children. Exeter (N.H.) Public Library, trustee, 1957.

WRITINGS: Coastguard to Greenland (illustrated by John L. Delano), Houghton, 1942; *Decky's Secret* (illustrated by D. Hauman), Houghton, 1944; *Bird in Hand*, Houghton, 1945; *Shooting Star Farm* (illustrated by Barbara Cooney), Houghton, 1946; *The Pigeoneers* (illustrated by Elizabeth Converse), Houghton, 1947; *Celia's Lighthouse* (illustrated by Ursula Koering), Houghton, 1949, Star Island Corporation, 1976; *Uncle Andy's Island*, Houghton, 1950; *Lucy's Christmas* (illustrated by John O'Hara Cosgrove II), Houghton, 1950; *Where Away?* (illustrated by Joshua Tolford), Houghton, 1952; *The Monkey's Fist* (illustrated J. Tolford), Houghton, 1953; *The Secret of the Old Salem Desk* (illustrated by Arline K. Thompson), Farrar, Straus & Cudahy, 1955; *Captain Waymouth's Indians*, Hastings, 1957, published as *Five Kidnapped Indians: A True Seventeenth Century Account of Five Early Americans* (illustrated by John Jacques), 1968; *The Tower Treasure* (illustrated by Artur Marokvia), Hastings, 1958; *The Christmas Rocker* (illustrated by A. Marokvia), Hastings, 1958; *Blanche of the Blueberry Barrens* (illustrated by A. K. Thomson), Hastings, 1959; *Three-Part Island* (illustrated by A. K. Thomson), Hastings, 1960; *A Proper Place for Chip*, Hastings, 1963; *The Mystery of the Pilgrim Trading Post* (illustrated by Floyd J. Torbert), Hastings, 1964; *Shaun and the Boat* (illustrated by B. Cooney), Hastings, 1965; *The Girl from Two Miles High* (illustrated by Polly Jackson), Hastings, 1967; *The Years before the Mayflower: The Pilgrims in Holland* (illustrated by Richard Cuffari), Hastings, 1972; *Wampum,* Hastings, 1977.

WORK IN PROGRESS: A picture book of Guatemala; a story of the California Gold Rush.

SIDELIGHTS: "Two prerequisites are needed, it seems to me, for writing for juveniles. One is never having quite grown up oneself, if indeed one ever is. The second is as true for any writer as it is for those who write for young people, the ability to sit at a typewriter even when spring arrives or your friends hold out tempting plans for you.

"The most common question asked at any gathering where writing for children is being discussed is 'How long does it take to write a book?' If the askers only knew how long! Should the author be paid only a cent an hour of thought and labor he must give, it seems to me that no publisher could afford to buy a book. This is an exaggeration, of course, but it's a thought that strikes when I'm sitting at the typewriter.

"First of all, we must tell the questioner there is the 'honeymoon' period when characters, scenery and plot float effortlessly and most pleasantly in one's mind. During this time characters become old friends, they look you in the eye and start to talk to you. Often they surprise you by the action they want to take. This can go on for a long time, even for years, and the characters by then have moved in and taken over.

"Of course, the time comes when scenes and characters must be corralled and put down in cold type, looking colder at first than the warm intimates of your mind. There will be a draft or two or three and then a fair copy with an extra carbon for the potential illustrator. Then the manuscript can be mailed off. This has all taken a long time, except for the rare book that almost walks from your head straight onto paper.

Shaun opened the red door alone.

At once his mother flew at him. "Aren't you the wicked boy now!" she cried. . . . Oh, she was angry, but she had been full of sorrow. ■ (From *Shaun and the Boat* by Anne Molloy. Pictures by Barbara Cooney.)

ANNE BAKER MOLLOY

"In the years since I've been writing (about forty) the sort of books being published have changed a great deal. Many more have urban settings. The author is now allowed to write about mothers and fathers without idealizing them. They can now be made quite mean. The author can write about the seamy side of life as he couldn't before. Publishers now want juveniles full of fast action because, they say, that is what a generation nourished upon TV wants.

"I, for one, wonder if young readers themselves have changed all that much. From their letters and conversations they sound the same. They still want books that make them laugh and those that point out (not too obviously) the difference between right and wrong. They still enjoy backgrounds unlike their own and like to identify with someone they admire or feel sorry for. And they still, if my grandchildren are indicators, like to stretch out on a bed or curl up in a chair and lose themselves in a book. The difference today is that no child is as innocent of the dangers around them.

"As a child I was lucky enough to spend long summers on the coast of Maine in spots not contaminated by development or industrial pollution. I wish that every child could have that same experience in spots as unchanged. Now oil refineries and nuclear plants threaten and military bases surround us. That is one reason that I write, to let young people know of the delights of the natural world and the need to not destroy them. That, and the fun of doing it."

MOORE, Jack (William) 1941-

BRIEF ENTRY: Born November 14, 1941, in Macon, Ga. Cartoonist. Moore attended both the University of Maryland and the Maryland Institute of Art. In 1964 he became the editor of the college edition of the *Baltimore (Morning) Sun*, a position he held for eleven years. He is the author and artist of the syndicated cartoon "Kelly and Duke," which he began producing in 1972. The characters of the cartoon were incorporated into a book for children entitled *What Is God's Area Code?*, published in 1974. Moore is also the author of *Furlong Deep*, 1977.

MORTON, Lee Jack, Jr. 1928-
(Lee Jac)

PERSONAL: Born April 20, 1928, in Detroit, Mich.; son of Lee Jack (a policeman) and Theresa (Leonard) Morton, Sr.; married Carlene Hatcher, February 18, 1950 (divorced, 1960); married Vivian Louise Sheperd (a secretary), August 25, 1962; children: Glynda Leslie, Jill Lee, Lee Jack III. *Education:* Wayne State University, Detroit, Mich., B.A., 1953; attended Detroit Society of Arts and Crafts, 1950-53. *Politics:* "Decidedly Democratic." *Religion:* Non-denominational. *Home:* 81 Hillside Ave., Hillside, N.J. 07205.

LEE JACK MORTON, JR.

"It's my tame mouse and I couldn't leave it home. There's too many people at my house that don't like mice." ■ (From *Leroy Oops* by Barbara Glasser. Illustrated by Lee Jack Morton.)

CAREER: Illustrator; designer. Detroit Historical Museum, Detroit, Mich., designer, 1950-51; United States Navy, Bayonne, N.J., technical illustrator, 1952-54; Norman Associates, New York, N.Y. designer, illustrator, 1955-59; free-lance graphic artist, New York, N.Y., 1960-80; City of Newark, Newark, N.J., art director, 1981—. *Exhibitions:* Henry O. Tanner Gallery, New York, N.Y. 1980. *Military service:* U.S. Navy, Seaman 1st Class, 1947-49.

ILLUSTRATOR: C. A. Russell, *A Birthday Present for Katheryn Kenyatta,* McGraw, 1970; Barbara Glasser, *Leroy, Opps,* Cowles, 1971; Louis Meriwether, *The Freedom Ship of Robert Smalls,* Prentice-Hall, 1971; Richard W. Bruner, *Black Politicians,* McKay, 1971; R. W. Bruner, *Pragmatic Humanist: The Whitney M. Young, Jr. Story,* McKay, 1971; Marguerite P. Dolch, *Animal Stories from Africa,* Garrard, 1975.

WORK IN PROGRESS: Several oils and two pastel portraits.

SIDELIGHTS: "Becoming an artist is a lifetime process. Those who choose it, find the highs can be very high, just as the lows, very low. But one thing is certain, life is never boring. That's the beauty of being an artist—you can never make the absolute statement, but the desire to do so as an approximation keeps you going."

HOBBIES AND OTHER INTERESTS: Baking, playing pool, and wood-working.

MOZLEY, Charles 1915-

BRIEF ENTRY: Born May 29, 1915, in Sheffield, England. A free-lance artist and illustrator, Mozley attended Sheffield School of Art and graduated from Royal College of Art in 1937. Although his main interest is in book illustration, he has executed various commissioned works including auto-lithographic posters, film posters and murals. He has also produced advertisements for business firms and drawings for television commercials. Mozley's work has appeared in various exhibitions, among them AIA Gallery, London, 1957, and a one-man show at Savage Gallery in 1960. Permanent collections of his work are located in the Klingspor Museum, Offenbach, West Germany, Victoria and Albert Museum, London, and Imperial War Museum. For children, he wrote and illustrated *The First Book of Tales of Ancient Araby* and *The First Book of Tales of Ancient Egypt,* 1960. He has illustrated over thirty books for children and young adults, including Lorenzini's *The Adventures of Pinocchio,* Perrault's *Famous Fairy Tales, Black Beauty* by Anna Sewell, Coleridge's *The Rime of the Ancient Mariner, Sonnets* by Shakespeare, *Sinbad the Sailor,* and *Oscar Wilde Fairy Tales.* For adults, he wrote and illustrated *Wolperiana: An Illustrated Guide to Berthold L. Wolpe,* 1960. His illustrated works for adults incude Defoe's *Moll Flanders* and Trollope's *The Dukes Children. For More Information See: Artists of a Certain Line,* Bodley Head, 1960; *Illustrators of Children's Books: 1957-1966,* Horn Book, 1968.

MURPHY, Jim 1947-

BRIEF ENTRY: Born September 25, 1947, in Newark, N.J. Author and editor. Murphy received his B.A. from Rutgers University in 1970 and continued his schooling with graduate study at Radcliffe College. From 1970 to 1977 he worked for Clarion Books in New York, beginning as editorial secretary and advancing to the position of managing editor. A free-lance author and editor since 1977, Murphy has done editing for numerous companies including Clarion Books, Crowell, Crown, Macmillan, and Farrar, Straus. His books for children include *Weird and Wacky Inventions,* 1978, *Rat's Christmas Party,* 1979, *Harold Thinks Big,* 1980, and, for young adults, *Death Run,* 1982. He has also written articles for *Cricket* magazine. *Home and Office:* 138 Wildwood Ave., Upper Montclair, N.J. 07043.

NATTI, Susanna 1948-

PERSONAL: Born October 19, 1948, in Gloucester, Mass.; daughter of Robert Henrik (a teacher and principal) and Lee (an author; maiden name, Kingman) Natti; married Alan S. Willsky (an associate professor of electrical engineering), May 25, 1980. *Education:* Smith College, Northhampton, Mass., B.A., 1970; attended Montserrat School of Visual Art, Beverly, Mass., 1972-73, and Rhode Island School of Design, 1973-75. *Home and office:* Arlington, Mass. 02174.

CAREER: Illustrator, 1977—. Worked as a secretary/technical typist at Massachusetts Institute of Technology, part- and full-time, between 1970-78. *Exhibitions:* Biennale of Illustrations, Bratislava, Czechoslovakia, 1981; Master Eagle Gallery, New York, N.Y., 1981, 1982. *Member:* Society of Children's Book Writers. *Awards, honors:* Christopher Award for *Frederick's Alligator,* 1979; *Today Was a Terrible Day* was chosen one of International Reading Association's Children's Choices, 1980.

ILLUSTRATOR: Charlotte Pomerantz, *The Downtown Fairy Godmother,* Addison-Wesley, 1978; Esther Allen Peterson, *Frederick's Alligator,* Crown, 1979; William Cole, editor, *Dinosaurs and Beasts of Yore,* Collins, 1979; Clyde Watson, *Midnight Moon,* Collins, 1979; Patricia Giff, *Today Was a Terrible Day,* Viking, 1980; Jim Murphy, *Harold Thinks Big* (Junior Literary Guild selection), Crown, 1980; William Hooks, *The Mystery on Bleeker Street,* Random House, 1980; Jane Yolen, *The Acorn Quest,* Crowell, 1981; Louise Fitzhugh, *I Am Three,* Delacorte, 1982; E. A. Peterson, *Penelope Gets Wheels,* Crown, 1982.

SUSANNA NATTI

"That black cat with the pale green eyes," she said longingly. "I want it more than anything in the world."

The fairy godmother sighed. A deep, unhappy sigh. Then, reaching into her pocketbook, she pulled out a handkerchief and blew her nose. ■ (From *The Downtown Fairy Godmother* by Charlotte Pomerantz. Illustrated by Susanna Natti.)

"Cam Jansen and the Mystery of" series; all written by David Adler; all published by Viking: *Cam Jansen and the Mystery of the Stolen Diamonds,* 1980; . . . *the U.F.O.,* 1980; . . . *the Dinosaur Bones,* 1981; . . . *the Television Dog,* 1981; . . . *the Gold Coins,* 1982; . . . *the Babe Ruth Baseball,* 1982.

WORK IN PROGRESS: Illustrations for *Cam Jansen and the Mystery of the Circus Clown* by David Adler; illustrations for *Helpful Hattie* by Janet Quin-Harkin; illustrations for *Today Is the Day of the Play* (tentative title) by Patricia Giff.

SIDELIGHTS: "By the time I was eight I knew I was going to be an illustrator. I'm not sure it ever occurred to me that I might do something else. I always liked to draw and at the age of five was making crude copies of paintings from one of my parents' large art books. My favorite cousin and I used to devise contests in which we'd pick a subject and both illustrate it. I don't think we ever compared our drawings—it was just the fun of drawing that we were after.

"I grew up in Gloucester, Massachusetts in a wonderfully varied community, including many artists and quite a few authors. Among the children's book authors and author/illustrators living on Cape Ann when I was growing up were Virginia Lee Burton, Ruth Holberg, Hetty Beatty, and Lee Kingman, who also happens to be my mother. The business of making books seemed at once very normal and very special. Besides

Frederick put his alligator in the box and carried it home. "I don't think I should keep you," he said. "When you get bigger, you might eat my hamster . . . or even my baby brother." ■ (From *Frederick's Alligator* by Esther Allen Peterson. Illustrated by Susanna Natti.)

the many authors on Cape Ann, there were other accomplished people in the arts who lived there. There were sculptors, painters, and craftsmen. A number of my relatives were and are artists. These many people influenced me in some important ways. The two most important principles I gleaned from them were these: that good art involves integrity and a solid knowledge of basic skills and that the history of art and illustration is a resource to be treasured.

"I started studying figure drawing when I was ten with George Demetrios (Virginia Lee Burton's husband). He taught me how to express motion and spontaneity in my drawings. I use the basic method he taught me every time I lay out a drawing, lightly and quickly sketching the whole shape with the pencil barely leaving the paper until all the proportions are laid out satisfactorily—and only then going back and laying in the detail. He gave me a solid foundation and, of all my teachers, I owe him the greatest debt.

"I studied with him for five summers, but then it was another nine years before I began to prepare seriously for a career in illustration when I attended art school for three years. It was an additional three years after that before I got my first book to illustrate, and since then I've had the good fortune to have a lot of work come my way.

"I generally use black and white line drawings with a technical pen. When I get a chance to do full-color illustrations I use watercolor as I did for *Midnight Moon* which was a wonderful opportunity to do a series of tiny watercolor paintings. If I were to pick my favorite of the books I've illustrated so far, I'd say it was *Dinosaurs and Beasts of Yore*. I was truly sad the day I packaged the finished art and sent it to the publisher because I had such a wonderful time working on it."

HOBBIES AND OTHER INTERESTS: Gardening, playing the piano, and crafts: hooking, knitting and sewing. "I do volunteer work at the high school in Cambridge, Mass., working in a sophomore English class with kids who have a variety of learning disabilities."

If all the world was apple-pie,
   And all the sea was ink,
And all the trees were bread and cheese,
   What should we have for drink?

            —Nursery rhyme

OLSON, Gene 1922-

PERSONAL: Born in 1922, in Montevideo, Minn. *Education:* University of Oregon, B.A.; Pacific University, M.A.

CAREER: Author of novels and histories for young people. Has worked as a teacher, newspaper editor, and television scriptwriter. *Military service:* Served in the U.S. Army during World War II.

WRITINGS—For young people: *Stampede at Blue Springs,* Dodd, 1956, adaptation published as *Between Me and the Marshall,* Dodd, 1964; *The Tall One: A Basketball Story,* Dodd, 1956; *Last Night at Black Hammer,* Dodd, 1957; *The Bucket of Thunderbolts,* Dodd, 1959; *The Ballhawks,* Westminster, 1960; *Sacramento Gold,* Macrae, 1961; *The Red, Red Roadster,* Macrae, 1962; *The Roaring Road,* Dodd, 1962; *The Tin Goose,* Westminster, 1962; *Bonus Boy: The Story of a Southpaw Pitcher,* Dodd, 1963; *Bailey and the Bearcat* (Junior Literary Guild selection), Westminster, 1964; *Fullback Fury,* Dodd, 1964.

(With Joan Olson) *Oregon Times and Trails,* Windyridge, 1965; *Three Men on Third,* Westminster, 1965; *Cross-Country Chaos,* Westminster, 1966; *Pistons and Powderpuffs,* Westminster, 1967; *The Iron Foxhole,* Westminster, 1968; *The Most Beautiful Girl in the World,* Westminster, 1968; *Drop into Hell,* Westminster, 1969; (with J. Olson) *Washington Times and*

GENE OLSON

Take it from me, it'll be a long season. Rule No. 1 in football coaching—don't burn yourself up in September and October. November's soon enough. ■ (Cover illustration from *Fullback Fury* by Gene Olson. Jacket illustrated by Morton Künstler.)

Trails, Windyridge, 1970; (with J. Olson) *California Times and Trails,* Windyridge, 1971; *Sweet Agony: A Writing Manual of Sorts,* Windyridge, 1972; (with J. Olson) *Silver Dust and Spanish Wine: A Bilingual History of Mexico,* Windyridge, 1978.

SIDELIGHTS: Olson was born in Montevideo, Minnesota in 1922, and has since lived in all sections of the United States, except New England. He holds a degree in journalism from the University of Oregon and an M.A. degree from Pacific University. He has written westerns for adults, several novels for young adults, television scripts, and articles for newspapers and magazines.

Besides a writing career which began in 1945, Olson has taught high school English in California and Oregon, thereby gaining vast experience in both writing and in teaching writing. "Writing is hard work. Teaching writing is at least as hard. Writers and teachers of writing need all the help they can get. . . .

"Writing is like falling in love in that we know it happens but no one is quite sure how it happens. Writing can be learned, but only the hard way, by doing it. You must make your own mistakes, learn what you can from them, then plunge on to make more mistakes.

"If you go about this properly, both in falling in love and in writing, you won't make the same mistake more than three times and your new mistakes will be bigger and better than your old ones and you will learn more from them.

"It's not that plenty of advice isn't available, both for writing and for falling in love. It's available in towering piles and the bulk of it isn't worth the powder to blow it to Stratford-on-Avon. I should know; I've sifted most of it through my brain. Through good luck or good sense, I've managed to ignore practically all of it, for a very good reason: *The advice simply didn't seem to work for me.*

"You are no more likely to get a writing blueprint that works for you from somebody else then you are to get a plan for an ostrich house from the 'Home & Garden' section of your local newspaper.

"At some time during your struggle to write, someone said or you read something like this:

"'Writing is FUN!'

"Or: 'Creative writing is good for you!'

"Or: 'A writing person is a happy person!'

"One, twice, three times—NONSENSE. Anyone who believes this can't have done much serious writing. Nothing saps human energy—mental, emotional and *physical*—like sustained writing.

"Even for a seasoned professional, the act is close to torture at times and he will often go to great lengths to avoid beginning it a moment sooner than necessary. A resourceful writer can postpone the beginning of writing for hours without really trying, for days with just a little effort and, if he is willing to strain a little, for months. I know of one writer who managed to avoid writing for two full years. (Anyone who achieves this kind of performance is entitled to refer to his difficulty as 'writer's block.')

"No one can write for you and there aren't any pat answers. . . . Facing a blank sheet of paper, you are so alone that only you and the paper exist on a tiny, barren island. And you can sometimes feel the sand shifting. . . .

"This is at once the great charm of it and the terrible affliction of it.

"*Sweet agony.* . . .

"I can give you a few pills for the pain but doubt not: The pain will always be there.

"So why does anybody write anything?

"I think I know. The fun is not in writing; the fun is in HAVING WRITTEN. I contend that few acts give human animals more and deeper emotional satisfaction than the act of writing. Those words spreading majestically over the paper are YOURS; they came out of YOUR teeming mind and no one else's. Your banner is unfurled before the world; you stand revealed, warts and all.

"Writing is thinking and everyone knows how difficult *that* is. This piece of paper trembling in your hands proves that you have accomplished this wondrous deed. Now you are entitled to take the rest of the day off to enjoy the plaudits of the multitude who didn't write but just sat around like clods, among the clover.

"There, friend, right there and only there, is the fun of writing.

"There is no more demanding task than writing. No matter how long one works at it, no matter how many words are produced, room for improvement will always remain. Herein lies the ultimate frustration of writing; herein also lies its bittersweet charm and challenge. It's like chasing butterflies in a world where there are always more butterflies, each new batch prettier than the last.

"My writing place has a spectacular view of southern Oregon and northern California—forests, mountains and long reaches of blue-gray sky, all of which is visible through large windows. Now and then someone sees my writing place and exclaims: 'Ah! I see where you get your Inspiration!'

"Big deal. When I'm writing, I'm not looking at the view. I am not even dimly conscious of the view; I am creating my own view in my brain and hoping that it is being transcribed to the paper in my typewriter. A writer who is writing is concentrating so intensely that he is only faintly aware of what goes on around him.

"Instead of a hilltop office, I could have one in a basement. I would probably accomplish just as much in the basement. I'm glad my writing room is on a hilltop, though, because I think I go more often to this pleasant place with the sweeping view than I would go to a basement. . . .

"Now and then someone asks: 'Do you enjoy writing?'

"In a fit of honesty, I answer: 'I enjoy the money I make from writing. Sometimes I enjoy reading my writing. I enjoy getting compliments on my writing. I enjoy knowing that having my writing published makes me just a little bit more than a face in the crowd. But do I enjoy the actual act of writing? No; most of the time, I don't. I enjoy *having written:* I enjoy that immensely, but that's another thing.'' [Gene Olson, *Sweet Agony: A Writing Manual of Sorts*, Windyridge Press, 1972.]

PALLADINI, David (Mario) 1946-

BRIEF ENTRY: Born April 1, 1946, in Roteglia, Italy. Illustrator and artist. Palladini came to the United States as a child, later attending Pratt Institute in New York. He worked as a photographer for the 1968 Olympic Games in Mexico City before establishing himself as a free-lance illustrator and artist. Palladini has illustrated eight books for children, including Jane Yolen's *The Girl Who Cried Flowers, and Other Tales* which was selected for the American Institute of Graphic Arts Book Show, 1973-74, was named one of the *New York Times* Best Illustrated Books of the Year, 1974, and received a National Book Award, 1975. His other works include Constance B. Hieatt's *The Sword and the Grail, The Moon Ribbon, and Other Tales* and *The Hundredth Dove, and Other Tales* by Yolen, Barbara Wersba's *Twenty-Six Starlings Will Fly Through Your Mind,* and Crescent Dragonwagon's *If You Call My Name. For More Information See: Illustrators of Children's Books: 1967-1976,* Horn Book, 1978.

PINKNEY, Jerry 1939-

BRIEF ENTRY: Born December 22, 1939, in Philadelphia, Pa. Illustrator and designer. Pinkney attended the Philadelphia Museum College of Art before moving to Boston where he was employed by a prominent design studio. After a year and a half, he and two other illustrators founded their own studio where he continues his work as both designer and illustrator. He has also done advertising and promotional projects for companies such as Sheraton Hotels, Borden, and Pan Am. Pinkney's work has been exhibited at various locations, including Brandeis University, the National Center of Afro-American Artists, and the Boston Museum of Fine Arts. He has received awards from the New York Illustrators and the New York, New Jersey, Providence and Boston Art Directors Shows. He has illustrated over thirty books for children, including *Song of the Trees* which was selected for the Children's Book Showcase, 1976, and *Childtimes: A Three-Generation Memoir* and *Tonweya and the Eagles, and Other Lakota Indian Tales,* both of which were selected for the American Institute of Graphic Arts Book Show, 1980. Among his other illustrated works are Joyce Cooper Arkhurst's *The Adventures of Spider,* 1964, Francine Jacob's *The King's Ditch: A Hawaiian Tale,* 1971, Verna Aardema's *Ji-Nongo-Nongo Means Riddles,* 1978, and William Wise's *Monster Myths of Ancient Greece,* 1981. *For More Information See: Illustrators of Children's Books: 1957-1966,* Horn Book, 1968; *Afro-American Artists: A Bio-Bibliographical Directory,* Boston Public Library, 1973.

PONTIFLET, Ted 1932-

PERSONAL: Surname is pronounced Pon-ti-fley; born June 19, 1932, in Oakland, Calif.; son of John W. (a legal recorder) and Victoria E. (a housewife) Pontiflet; married Addie Roberson (a hospital administrator), November 17, 1966; children: Pamela Denise. *Education:* California College of Arts and Crafts, B.F.A., 1962; Yale University, M.F.A. (with honors), 1971. *Home and office:* 1050 7th St., N. 1205, Oakland, Calif. 94607.

CAREER: Artist, writer, and photographer. Has worked as a teacher in Ghana, West Africa, at Medgar Evers College of the City University of New York, Brooklyn, N.Y., and as a teacher of Afro-American humanities and history, at Contra Costa College, San Pablo, Calif. Work has been exhibited on the East Coast, including a showing at the Smithsonian Institution. *Military service:* Paratrooper, 1952-55. *Member:* National Conference of Artists, International Black Photographers, West Oakland Writers Workshop (director and founder). *Awards, honors:* Travel grant from Yale University, 1967-70, for research of Afro-American art in Ghana; honors from Yale University for creative writing, 1971.

WRITINGS: Poochie (juvenile; illustrated by Mahiri Fufuka), Dial, 1978.

WORK IN PROGRESS: Other Poochie-related stories; *When Violence Dies,* a one-act play exploring physical and emotional violence by blacks from 1940 to 1970; *The Preacher's Son,* a two-act play about a talented son with a drug problem; *Home and Back,* a novel dealing with the emotional and psychological metamorphosis of Blacks in Africa.

SIDELIGHTS: "I was born in West Oakland, and after living in New York and Africa, I now live a few blocks from where I grew up. This neighborhood was once ethnically mixed, a kind of mini United Nations, and everyone was friendly. It was a neighborhood of small homes then.

"After I graduated from Arts and Crafts, where I was student government president, I worked for a year, saved my money, and took a freighter to Casablanca. I arrived in Africa with $45.00 in my pocket, and no job waiting. I was crazy and adventurous. I stayed and taught in Ghana for four years.

"I'm not sure if I was running to Africa or running from America. It was the height of the '60s, with political unrest all over, but what interested me was the beauty of the continent. It was a self-imposed exile, but I considered myself an apolitical artist. I was out of the country when Malcolm X and Kennedy were assassinated, and six months after I returned, Martin Luther King was assassinated. I felt a lot of anger, but the 'coming home' part of going to Africa was never part of my illusion.

"While there, I saw and lived an alternative to this country. By having the experience of seeing black men as doctors, lawyers, judges, policemen, clerks in stores, civil servants, in control of their own environment, I developed a belief in an alternative destiny.

"When I came back from Africa, I went to Yale on scholarship. I got a Master of Fine Arts degree and an Honors in Creative Writing. Surviving Yale was easy; surviving West Oakland and three years as a paratrooper was much more traumatic. You don't step out of an inner city and into an Ivy League college without being affected.

"I've had a lot of exhibits on the east coast, and I've shown at the Smithsonian. Some of my work is in textbooks. . . .

"I didn't start out to be a writer for children. When I came back from Africa, the expatriot experience was fresh in my mind. I wanted to write a novel about the emotional and psychological metamorphosis of Blacks during their self-imposed exile in Africa in the '60s. . . . I took two chapters to an editor at Dial Press, but he was a children's editor, and that's how I came to write *Poochie.*

"Right now I'm involved in the West Oakland Writer's Workshop, a group I started. There's no money and no politics involved, just craftsmanship. I also teach Afro-American humanities and history in Contra Costa. I wish I had more time to write, but I have to work so I can pay the rent. Even if I had money, I'd want to teach. I think it would be criminal to die with all this information locked in my head." [Ted Pontiflet, "Bay Area Writer and Photographer Ted Pontiflet," *Oakland Public Library Association Newsletter,* June, 1980.]

Pontiflet's self-expression has taken many forms. "I have always been motivated to create something or other; self-motivated mostly. I have gone from a deep passion for sculpture, to painting, to photography, to writing. I find writing to be the greater challenge because of the language factor. But for pure freedom, give me a torch and some metal, some concrete to pour, or a mural to create. More important than the work of art produced is the statement of the human condition that it must express."

A short film which looks at Pontiflet's life and work, entitled "Ponti," was produced in 1980 by Nebby Crawford Bello.

FOR MORE INFORMATION SEE: Oakland Public Library Association Newsletter, June, 1980.

"Wow, that's right," I said. "C'mon, you guys, let's take a look. It's real spooky down there, and we can have lots of fun." ■ (From *Poochie* by Ted Pontiflet. Illustrated by Mahiri Fufuka.)

RÉMI, Georges 1907-1983
(Hergé)

OBITUARY NOTICE—See sketch in *SATA* Volume 13: Surname listed in some sources as Remy; born May 5, 1907, in Brussels, Belgium; died in 1983, in Brussels. Cartoonist, author, and illustrator of books for children. Under the pseudonym Hergé, Rémi was the creator of the internationally known comic strip featuring the character, Tintin, and his companion dog Milou. The famous pair made their debut in the January 10, 1929, edition of *Le Petit Vingtieme*. Gaining worldwide exposure, the strip cartoons appeared in newspapers in Thailand, Egypt, Turkey, Australia, New Zealand, South Africa, and Ireland. The adventures of the youthful reporter were subsequently chronicled by Rémi in twenty-three books for children which were translated from their original French into English, German, Spanish, Japanese, and several other languages. The English titled series includes *Tintin in Tibet* and *Tintin and the Golden Fleece*, 1965, *Flight 714*, 1968, *The Land of the Black Gold*, 1972, *Tintin and the Broken Ear*, 1975, and *Tintin and the Picaros*, 1976. *For More Information See: Contemporary Authors*, Volumes 69-72, Gale, 1978. *Obituaries: Time*, March 14, 1983.

ROBBINS, Frank 1917-

BRIEF ENTRY: Born September 9, 1917, in Boston, Mass. Cartoonist and illustrator. Robbins displayed his artistic talent at an early age, winning scholarships at nine, painting murals in high school, and receiving a Rockefeller grant at fifteen. Due to the hardships of the Depression years, he was forced to sacrifice a college education, moving with his family to New York where he went to work as an errand boy for an advertising company. His career began to flourish when noted muralist Edward Trumbull hired him to draw mural sketches for a Radio City project. More work followed, including promotional and poster illustrations for RKO Pictures. In 1939, at the request of Associated Press, he took over the "Scorch Smith" daily comic strip, proving so successful that, in 1944, he began to produce his own original strip for King Features, "Johnny Hazard." In addition to strip cartoons, Robbins has written material for National Comic titles such as "Batman," "The Flash," and "The Unknown Soldier." His work has appeared in various exhibitions, including those at the Whitney Museum of Art, Toledo Museum of Art, Audubon Artists, and Corcoran Gallery of Art. He is the recipient of numerous awards and merits of distinction, among them the National Academy of Design Prize, 1935. For children, Robbins illustrated a series of "beginner" sports books written by Howard Liss, including *Football Talk for Beginners*, 1970, and *Skiing Talk for Beginners*, 1977. His illustrations have also appeared in periodicals such as *Look, Life, Saturday Evening Post,* and *Cosmopolitan*. *For More Information See: The World Encyclopedia of Comics,* Volume 2, Chelsea House, 1976.

ROBINSON, Marileta 1942-

PERSONAL: Born December 26, 1942, in Kansas City, Kan.; daughter of Thomas B. (employed by U.S. Department of Agriculture) and Rebecca (Hurt) Sawyer; married Patrick Leland Robinson (an attorney), March 21, 1973; children: John Leland, Bennett Nicholas. *Education:* Grinnell College, B.A., 1965; attended Northern Arizona University, 1969-70; University of New Mexico, M.A., 1973. *Home:* 4301 Sussex Dr., Montgomery, Ala. 36116.

MARILETA ROBINSON

CAREER: U.S. Peace Corps, Washington, D.C., volunteer teacher in Togo, 1965-67; Scott, Foresman & Co., Glenview, Ill., assistant editor, 1967-69; Rough Rock Demonstration School, Rough Rock, Ariz., teacher, 1970-72; writer, 1973—. *Member:* Creative Writers of Montgomery, Guild for Professional Writers for Children, Press and Authors Club. *Awards, honors:* First prize from Alabama Writers Conclave, 1979, for juvenile story, "Bessie, the Christmas Cow"; International Reading Association, Children's Choices for 1980, for *Mr. Goat's Bad Good Idea;* winning story in *Highlights for Children* "Talking Animal" contest, 1981, for "How Elephant Found Her Voice."

WRITINGS—Juvenile: *Mr. Goat's Bad Good Idea* (illustrated by Arthur Getz), Crowell, 1979.

WORK IN PROGRESS: How Elephant Found Her Voice, a collection of stories set in Africa.

SIDELIGHTS: "I feel very fortunate to be able to draw on my experiences among people of other cultures in my writing. While in Togo, I rented two rooms in the compound of a wonderful old gentleman who ran a small general store and palm wine bar. Besides having a constant supply of cold Cokes, I was able to share in the life of his family. He gave me a message to take back to the people of America: *O gbona vivi,* 'we can only draw one breath at a time.'

By the time Mr. Goat got home, sore and tired and covered with dust, the sun was just going down behind the hogan. ■ (From *Mr. Goat's Bad Good Idea* by Marileta Robinson. Illustrated by Arthur Getz.)

"Back in the United States, I spent two exciting years in the multi-ethnic city of Chicago. There was even a Japanese festival every year on my street. But I missed the close contact with another culture I had had in Togo, and I decided to get a job teaching on the Navajo reservation, at Rough Rock Demonstration School. Although teachers lived in 'regular' housing during the school year, I took advantage of the summers to rent a hogan from a family in the community. The first summer, I ate my meals in the school cafeteria and one of my small neighbors couldn't understand why I never had anything to cook when she came to visit. To my chagrin, she generously brought me some of her family's food.

"At Rough Rock, I discovered that I loved writing for children. Ann Nolan Clark, who has written such beautiful stories about Indian children, came to the school to help teachers (Navajo and Anglo) write stories that would motivate the children to read (in Navajo and English)—stories that would reflect the flavor of the desert and the Navajo culture. That is when I wrote the first version of *Mr. Goat's Bad Good Idea*. A little praise from a published author is a dangerous and heady thing, and having been encouraged by Mrs. Clark, I decided after leaving the school to become serious about writing.

"Lately, writing has had to work its way in between part-time teaching and raising two active boys, but I wouldn't have it any other way. As much as I sometimes desire unlimited time and quiet, I don't know if I could write if I had it.

"I still keep in touch with other cultures. Lately, through tutoring Saudi Arabian women here in Montgomery, I have glimpsed another world waiting to be explored.

"My goal when I write is to delight children. I hope that humor and love and truth come through in my stories. I enjoy the challenge of finding the simple word or sentence to take the place of a more complicated one. I write to satisfy my own ear, my own sense of humor and my own sense of values. I have learned from my own children that the difference between what they and I enjoy is very slight, and mainly a matter of degree. I try for a meeting of minds on a field of experiences common to us both—we can both laugh at ridiculous hats, be terrified of crabs, and yearn to fly with Santa's reindeer."

HOBBIES AND OTHER INTERESTS: Reading (science fiction, fantasy, natural history, anthropology), language.

There is no frigate like a book
To take us lands away,
Nor any coursers like a page
Of prancing poetry.

This traverse may the poorest take
Without oppress of toll;
How frugal is the chariot
That bears a human soul.

—Emily Dickinson

Books should to one of these four ends conduce,
For wisdom, piety, delight, or use.

—John Denham

When she came to the hedge in front of her house, she crouched down. Her mother would probably be in the kitchen, she thought. And from the kitchen window her mother might see her .... ■ (From *Wendy and the Bullies* by Nancy K. Robinson. Illustrated by Ingrid Fetz.)

ROBINSON, Nancy K(onheim) 1942-

PERSONAL: Born August 12, 1942, in New York, N.Y.; daughter of Norris David (in advertising) and Natalie (Barnett) Konheim; married Peter Beverley Robinson, May 6, 1966; children: Kenneth Beverley, Alice Natalie. *Education:* Vassar College, B.A., 1964. *Residence:* New York, N.Y.

CAREER: Free-lance writer and researcher, 1966—. *Member:* Authors Guild, Authors League of America, Writers Guild of America East, Inc., PEN American Center, American Society of Picture Professionals, Industrial Photographers Association of New York, Vassar Club of New York. *Awards, honors:* U.S. Customs Award, 1978, for an historical article, "New York's First Coast Guard Cutter, the *Vigilant*"; Four Leaf Clover Award, from Scholastic Book Services, 1981, for her contribution to the reading pleasure of seven and eight year olds.

WRITINGS—All for children: *Jungle Laboratory: The Story of Ray Carpenter and the Howling Monkeys* (nonfiction; illustrated by Bill Tinker), Hastings House, 1973; *Firefighters!* (nonfiction), Scholastic Book Services, 1979; *Wendy and the Bullies* (fiction; illustrated by Ingrid Fetz), Hastings House, 1980; *Just Plain Cat* (fiction), Scholastic Book Services, 1981, reprinted, Four Winds Press, 1983; *Mom, You're Fired* (fiction), Scholastic Book Services, 1981; *Veronica the Show-Off*, Scholastic Book Services, 1982, reprinted, Four Winds Press, 1983.

"Can You Solve It?" series; all with Marvin Miller; all published by Scholastic Book Services: *T*A*C*K to the Rescue*, 1982; *T*A*C*K Secret Service*, 1982; *T*A*C*K Into Danger*, 1983; *T*A*C*K Against Time!*, 1983.

Writer of "Men of Bronze," a PBS-TV documentary broadcast, February, 1978.

NANCY K. ROBINSON

ROBISON, Nancy L(ouise)   1934-
(Natalie Johnson)

PERSONAL: Born January 20, 1934, in Compton, Calif.; daughter of Iver and May (Ingersoll) Johnson; married Robert B. Robison, (a fire department administrator), August 14, 1954; children: Jeff, Todd, Eric, Glenn. *Education:* Attended University of California, Los Angeles, and Pasadena City College, 1951, 1972-75. *Home:* San Marino, Calif.

CAREER: Film and television actress and model in Los Angeles, Calif., 1954-74; full-time writer, 1974—. *Member:* International PEN, Society of Children's Book Writers, California Writers Club, Southern California Council on Writing for Children and Young People.

WRITINGS—All juveniles: *Where Is Zip?,* Ginn, 1974; *Hang Glider Mystery,* Lantern Press, 1976; *Department Store Model Mystery,* Scholastic Book Services, 1977; *Where Did My Little Fox Go?,* Garrard, 1977; *The Missing Ball of String,* Garrard, 1977; *Hang Gliding* (nonfiction), Harvey House, 1978; *Tracy Austin: Teen Tennis Champ* (nonfiction), Harvey House, 1978; *UFO Kidnap!* (illustrated by Edward Frascino), Lothrop, 1978;

The Other Place (science fiction; illustrated by Joan Drescher), Walker & Co., 1978; *On the Balance Beam* (edited by Kathy Pacini; illustrated by Rondi Anderson), A. Whitman, 1978; *Space Hijack!* (illustrated by E. Frascino), Lothrop, 1979; *The Lizard Hunt* (illustrated by Lynn Munsinger), Lothrop, 1979; *Baton Twirling* (nonfiction), Harvey House, 1979; *Nancy Lopez: Wonder Woman of Golf* (nonfiction), Childrens Press, 1979; *Janet Guthrie: Race Car Driver* (nonfiction), Childrens Press, 1979; *Mystery at Hilltop Camp,* Garrard, 1979.

Games to Play in the Pool, Lothrop, 1980; *Izoo* (illustrated by E. Frascino), Lothrop, 1980; *Kurt Thomas: International Winner,* Childrens Press, 1980; *U and Me* (edited by Howard Schroeder; illustrated by Paul Furan), Crestwood House, 1981; *Ballet Magic,* A. Whitman, 1981; *Cheerleading,* Harvey House, 1981; (under name, Natalie Johnson) *Jenny,* Tempo Books, 1981.

Young adult romances: *Love: Lost and Found,* Dutton, 1983; *One Kiss,* Dutton, 1984; *Julie and the Jogger,* Dutton, 1984; *Laughter in the Rain,* Dutton, 1984; *More than Just Friends,* Dutton, 1984.

The rings require him to twist and turn almost eight feet off the floor. ■ (From *Kurt Thomas, International Winner* by Nancy Robison. Photograph courtesy of Indiana State University.)

NANCY L. ROBISON

Contributor of more than fifty stories and articles to magazines, including *Jack and Jill, Christian Science Monitor, Young World,* and *Boston Research,* and to newspapers.

WORK IN PROGRESS: Fiction, nonfiction, and science fiction for children and young people.

SIDELIGHTS: "I come from a Scandinavian background. My grandmother on my mother's side was a vaudeville actress and later a motion picture and television actress. She also wrote plays, so I came by my acting and writing careers naturally. When I was three years old I was adopted from that family into another one—an experience I intended to write about someday.

"My first article was published when I was fifteen, and it had to do with my experiences as a television actress. At this time I couldn't choose between careers. I loved to act and I loved to write, but writing meant I had to sit still and I wasn't ready to do that. I pursued a career in the theatre.

"When my boys were small, I read books to them all the time and felt that someday I would write some. After the boys started school, I found more time to write, but it wasn't until 1974 that I got serious about writing children's books, and now I enjoy it so much I write every day.

"At this time I still haven't written the book I want to write or feel I am capable of writing. I suppose when I do write it my career will be over, so I'll just keep putting it off until I'm ready to retire.

"I enjoy travel and have been to Mexico, England, Scotland, Wales, Norway, Sweden, Denmark, France, Belgium, and Germany. I find travel educational and plan to do more."

HOBBIES AND OTHER INTERESTS: Tennis, skiing, sailing, swimming, photography, baton twirling, cheerleading, baking breads and pastries.

ROCK, Gail

BRIEF ENTRY: Author of books for young readers. Rock received her B.A. in Fine Arts from the University of Nebraska before moving to New York where she has worked as a film and television critic for *Women's Wear Daily* and as a freelance newspaper and magazine writer. She also writes both television scripts and screenplays for motion pictures. Rock has written four books for young readers, all centering on the character of Addie Mills, a young Nebraskan girl growing up in the 1940s. They include *The House Without a Christmas Tree,* 1974, *The Thanksgiving Treasure* (a Junior Literary Guild selection), 1974, *A Dream for Addie,* 1975, and *Addie and the King of Hearts,* 1976. The stories are full of sentimentalism and old-fashioned homespun into which Rock adeptly interjects a sense of realistic truth in both immediate surroundings and character portrayal. The *New York Times Book Review* credits her for having ". . . found a new way of handling a trite old scene." All four books were presented as critically acclaimed television specials under the same titles, with the exception of *A Dream for Addie* which was aired as "The Easter Promise." "The House Without a Christmas Tree" won both an Emmy and a Christopher Award.

ROSS, Dave   1949-

PERSONAL: Born April 2, 1949, in Scotia, N.Y.; son of Donald A. (a toolmaker) and Lois (a teacher; maiden name, Collier) Ross; married Cynthia Brugnetti, August 6, 1969 (divorced, 1977); children: Edward Alexander, Joel David. *Education:* State University College at Buffalo, B.S., 1971; State University of New York at Albany, M.S., 1976. *Religion:* Former Druid. *Residence:* Clifton Park, N.Y.

CAREER: Author and illustrator. Shenendehowa Central Schools, Clifton Park, N.Y., art teacher, 1971-82; Helping Hands School, Clifton Park, N.Y., co-founder and executive director, 1981—.

WRITINGS—All self-illustrated: *Mummy Madness,* Watts, 1979; *A Book of Hugs,* Crowell, 1980; *How to Keep Warm in Winter,* Crowell, 1980; *Making Robots,* Watts, 1980; *Making Space Puppets,* Watts, 1980; *Making UFOs,* Watts, 1980; *Space Monster,* Walker, 1980; (with Jeanne Wilson) *Mr. Terwilliger's Secret,* Watts, 1981; *A Book of Kisses,* Random House, 1982; *Gorp and the Jelly Sippers,* Walker, 1982.

Illustrator: James B. Gardner, *Illustrated Soccer Dictionary for Young People,* Harvey House, 1976; Marion Meade, *The Little Book of Big Riddles,* Harvey House, 1976; Foley Curtis, *The*

Little Book of Big Tongue Twisters, Harvey House, 1977; Sarah Ann Henry, *The Little Book of Big Knock Knock Jokes*, Harvey House, 1977; Gloria Milkowitz, *Ghastly Ghostly Riddles*, Scholastic, 1977; Ross R. Olney, *Illustrated Auto Racing Dictionary for Young People*, Harvey House, 1978; Arnold Madison, *Surfing: Basic Techniques*, McKay, 1979; Karen Sweeney, *Illustrated Tennis Dictionary for Young People*, Harvey House, 1979; Margaret and Jeanne Wallace, *Really Ridiculous Rabbit Riddles*, Walker, 1979; G. Milkowitz, *Win, Lose or Wear a Tie*, Random House, 1980; Elizabeth VanSteenwyck, *Illustrated Skating Dictionary for Young People*, Harvey House, 1980.

WORK IN PROGRESS: Gorp and the Space Pirates, for Walker; *How to Prevent Monster Attacks*, for Morrow.

SIDELIGHTS: "I know it sounds funny, but if I had been good at spelling, I don't think I would have become an artist or an author. You see, art was one of the few subjects I did well in. I was always terrible at spelling, English and math. Even if I failed a spelling test, or got a D on a math paper, I was usually one of the children picked to decorate the bulletin boards or design a hall display. These successful experiences early in my life motivated me to keep plugging in art. In fact, art has always been my favorite subject. Even so, I can't remember any art class from elementary school to college where I was the best artist. Most of the time I was either the second best or one of the best artists.

"In high school, when it was time to decide what my future education and career would be, my father gave me some good

TOASTY WINTER FASHION HINT #6

Train fuzzy caterpillars to sit on your ears. ■ (From *How to Keep Warm in Winter* by Dave Ross. Illustrated by the author.)

DAVE ROSS

advice. He said, 'I don't care what you choose to do, but make it something you enjoy.' At the time I thought I wanted to go to a fine arts school and become a painter. However my guidance counselor made a mistake in addressing my portfolio. It ended up going to Buffalo State University College where the course of study was how to be an art teacher, instead of going to the University at Buffalo.

"As a freshman at the State University College at Buffalo I had my first experience writing and illustrating a children's book. In a design class we had to layout and do color separations for a children's story. It was an enjoyable experience that I filed away in a back corner of my mind. I didn't think much more about illustrating children's stories until about seven years later. This was in 1974, and I had been an art teacher for three years. I was sitting in a very boring faculty meeting and doodling on a piece of paper. The faculty meeting happened to take place in the school's library. I'm not sure whether it

was the proximity of all those books, or just the boredom that jogged loose that memory of writing and illustrating children's books. Anyway, I wrote a story in about a half hour. I decided that I wanted to become a writer and illustrator. I sent the book out the next week. I was positive it would be purchased and I would be a professional author and illustrator within a month. It took me over a year and many, many rejections before I finally got my first job illustrating a children's book. In fact, I had enough rejection slips to wallpaper a wall in my bathroom. Although I have over twenty children's books to my credit today, I never sold that very first manuscript. I would have to say that the stick-to-itiveness that enabled me to succeed in my goal of getting published was to a large extent due to a college professor of mine—Dr. Hubler. The lesson he taught me was important. That is—any goal is attainable with a creative approach and hard work."

FOR MORE INFORMATION SEE: Schenectady Gazette (New York), February 23, 1982.

I'll tell you a story
  About Jack a Nory—
And now my story's begun;
  I'll tell you another
  About Johnny, his brother—
And now my story is done.

        —Mother Goose

Dreams, books, are each a world; and books,
  we know,
Are a substantial world, both pure and good:
Round these, with tendrils strong as flesh and blood,
Our pastime and our happiness will grow.
        —William Wordsworth

PETER RUSH

RUSH, Peter 1937-

PERSONAL: Born July 26, 1937, in London, England; son of Philip (a writer) and Geraldine (Gould) Rush; married; children: Frances, Joseph, Samual. *Education:* Attended St. Martin's School of Art, London, England. *Office:* 45 Gooth St., Canterbury, Kent, England.

CAREER: Free-lance illustrator.

WRITINGS: (Self-illustrated) *Papier Mâché,* Farrar, Straus, 1980; *Balloonatics,* Canongate, 1982; *Traveller's Tales,* Kaye & Ward, 1983.

Illustrator: Alan Spooner, *The Singers of the Field,* Kestrel, 1977; Philippa Pierce, *The Elm Street Lot,* Kestrel, 1979; Rosemary Manning, *Dragon in the Harbour,* Kestrel, 1980; Janet Smith, *The Wakeley Witch,* Kaye & Ward, 1980; John Fuller, *The Extraordinary Wool Mill and Other Stories,* Deutsch, 1980; Margaret Dunnett, *No Pets Allowed and Other Animal Stories,* Deutsch, 1981; Griselda Gifford, *Pete and the Doodlebug,* Macmillan, 1982; Joyce Stranger, *Marooned,* Kaye & Ward, 1982.

WORK IN PROGRESS: Writing and illustrating a book, *Transforming Furniture,* for Canongate.

SIDELIGHTS: "I worked twelve years as a free-lance illustrator for the BBC-TV 'Jackanory,' but recently I have concentrated on books. Presently I am working on a series of papier mâché models for children's television and am also working on books for the programme, which I also wrote.

"I work best when I am completely isolated and am happiest when I have complete control over the making of books or television programs."

SAUER, Julia (Lina) 1891-

PERSONAL: Born in 1891, in Rochester, N.Y. *Education:* Attended the University of Rochester, and New York State Library School. *Residence:* Rochester, N.Y. and North Mountain, Nova Scotia.

CAREER: Rochester Public Library, Rochester, N.Y., children's librarian; author. *Awards, honors:* Recipient of the Lillian Fairchild Prize from the University of Rochester, 1943; runner-up for the Newbery Medal, 1944, for *Fog Magic,* 1952, for *The Light at Tern Rock.*

WRITINGS: (Editor) *Radio Roads to Reading: Library Book Talks Broadcast to Girls and Boys,* H. W. Wilson, 1939; *Fog Magic* (ALA Notable Book), Viking, 1943, new edition, Pocket Books, 1977; *The Light at Tern Rock* (originally published in *Horn Book,* November, 1949, under the title, "The Light at Christmas"; illustrated by Georges Schreiber), Viking, 1951, reissued, 1966; *Mike's House* (illustrated by Don Freeman), Viking, 1954, new edition, 1970.

SIDELIGHTS: Sauer's career as head of the Work With Children department of the public library in Rochester, N.Y. led her to write her first book for children, *Fog Magic,* which was runner-up for the Newbery Medal in 1944 and is still a favorite children's book. "Sooner or later I suppose that every children's librarian sends a manuscript, and here is mine. . . . For years I have been obsessed by the cellar holes of the abandoned little village near our cabin in Nova Scotia, and by the tales the old people up there tell us. And . . . , when we couldn't get there, I finally got it into tangible form out of sheer homesickness for the place itself and for the fog that is so much a part of it." [Taken from the book jacket of *Fog Magic* by Julia Sauer, Viking Press, 1943.]

JULIA SAUER

Robert was quite sure that Mike was his best friend. ■ (From *Mike's House* by Julia L. Sauer. Illustrated by Don Freeman.)

Speaking of Sauer's *Fog Magic,* a *Book Week* critic commented, "This is not a book for every child, but to the right child it will bring beauty, magic, tenderness, and a brave philosophy of living. . . ." The *Christian Science Monitor* called it, "An exquisite book, one that has great rewards for the imaginative reader." Added *Saturday Review of Literature:* "Sometimes a book comes along that creates a sort of nostalgia in adults; a longing to go back to a time when it would have had free entry into their mind and imagination. Such a book is *Fog Magic.* . . . There is nothing about this book that is 'creepy' or unhealthy. Sauer's feeling for Nova Scotia and its people gives the past as well as the present warmth and humor and reality."

In a review of *The Light at Tern Rock,* a *New York Times* critic wrote, "This is a quiet story, lacking in action, and will be chiefly appreciated by thoughtful readers who are receptive to its poetic sense of the sea." Noted *Saturday Review of Lit-*

erature: "As in her *Fog Magic,* Miss Sauer's wording sets an atmosphere that is strongly reinforced here in Georges Schreiber's beautiful drawings."

Sauer was born in Rochester, N.Y., graduated from the University of Rochester, and spent her entire library career with the Rochester Public Library, but her name became widely known throughout the country in connection with library work for children and radio broadcasting book talks to school children, which she originated. She was a pioneer in preschool reading and an authority on children's reading.

FOR MORE INFORMATION SEE: Saturday Review of Literature, November 13, 1943, November 10, 1951; *Christian Science Monitor,* November 15, 1943; *Book Week,* November 21, 1943; *New York Times,* December 2, 1951; (for children) Muriel Fuller, editor, *More Junior Authors,* H. W. Wilson, 1963.

SCHINDELMAN, Joseph 1923-

BRIEF ENTRY: Born July 4, 1923, in New York, N.Y. Illustrator. Schindelman attended Art Students League and City College (now of the City University of New York) before the onset of World War II which forced an end to his formal training. Following his service, he worked for the Columbia Broadcasting System, Inc. and then as a promotion art director for an advertising agency. His career as an illustrator began when fellow illustrator Joseph Low showed one of his Christmas cards to a friend at Atheneum. Soon after, Schindelman illustrated his first book for children, Eve Merriam's *There Is No Rhyme for Silver.* In 1963, *The Great Picture Robbery* by Leon Harris was selected as one of the *New York Times* choice of best illustrated children's books of the year. His other works include two books by Roald Dahl, *Charlie and the Chocolate Factory,* 1964, and *Charlie and the Great Glass Elevator,* 1972, J. Allan Bosworth's *Voices in the Meadow* (a Junior Literary Guild selection), 1964, John F. Raymond's *The Marvelous March of Jean Francois,* 1965, and Padraic Colum's *The Six Who Were Left in a Shoe,* 1968. Also a designer of books, Schindelman has had his work exhibited at the American Institute of Graphic Arts. *For More Information See: Illustrators of Children's Books: 1957-1966,* Horn Book, 1968; *Third Book of Junior Authors,* Wilson, 1972.

SHAPIRO, Irwin 1911-1981

PERSONAL: Born May 19, 1911, in Pittsburgh, Pa.; died November 7, 1981. *Education:* Attended Carnegie Institute of Technology (now Carnegie-Mellon University); studied painting at the Art Students League.

CAREER: Early jobs included typist, shoe salesman, bookstore clerk, group worker in a country school, manuscript reader for motion picture companies, lathe hand in a machine shop, and seaman; national affairs editor, *Scholastic* magazine and *Facts on File;* was also on the staff of a theater and film magazine; author of books for children, movie scripts, and criticism. *Awards, honors:* Julia Ellsworth Ford Foundation award, 1947, for *Joe Magarac and His U.S.A. Citizen Papers.*

WRITINGS: How Old Stormalong Captured Mocha Dick (illustrated by Donald McKay), Messner, 1942; *The Gremlins of Lieut. Oggins* (illustrated by D. McKay), Messner, 1943; *Steamboat Bill and the Captain's Top Hat* (illustrated by D. McKay), Messner, 1943; *Yankee Thunder: The Legendary Life of Davy Crockett* (illustrated by James Daugherty), Messner, 1944; *Casey Jones and Locomotive No. 638* (illustrated by D. McKay), Messner, 1944; *John Henry and the Double Jointed Steam-Drill* (illustrated by J. Daugherty), Messner, 1945; *Joe Magarac and His U.S.A. Citizen Papers* (illustrated by J. Daugherty), Messner, 1948.

(Reteller) *Walt Disney's Davy Crockett, King of the Wild Frontier,* Simon & Schuster, 1955; *J. Fred Muggs* (illustrated by Edwin Schmidt), Simon & Schuster, 1955; *Presidents of the United States* (illustrated by Mel Crawford), Simon & Schuster, 1956; *Daniel Boone* (illustrated by Miriam S. Hurford), Simon & Schuster, 1956; (reteller with Margaret Soifer) *Golden Tales from the Arabian Nights* (illustrated by Gustaf Tenggren), Simon & Schuster, 1957; *Lassie Finds a Way: A New Story of the Famous Dog* (illustrated by Hamilton Greene), Simon & Schuster, 1957; *Cleo,* Simon & Schuster, 1957; *Circus Boy* (illustrated by Joan W. Anglund), Simon & Schuster, 1957; (reteller) *Walt Disney's Old Yeller* (illustrated by Edwin Schmidt

"I'll show you some real muscle!" shouted Andy Dembroski. With one hand he picked up a chair with Steve's missus sitting on it. ■ (From *Joe Magarac and His U.S.A. Citizen Papers* by Irwin Shapiro. Illustrated by James Daugherty.)

and E. Joseph Dreany), Simon & Schuster, 1957; *Walt Disney's Paul Revere,* Western, 1957; (adapter) *The Golden Book of America: Stories from Our Country's Past,* Simon & Schuster, 1957; *Tall Tales of America* (illustrated by Al Schmidt), Golden Press, 1958; (with John B. Lewellen) *The Story of Flight, from the Ancient Winged Gods to the Age of Space* (illustrated by Harry McNaught), Golden Press, 1959, a later edition published as *The Golden Book of Aviation, from the Ancient Winged Gods to the Age of Space,* 1961; *The Story of Yankee Whaling,* Golden Press, 1959.

The Golden Book of California from the Days of the Spanish Explorers to the Present, Golden Press, 1961; *Jonathan and the Dragon* (illustrated by Tom Vroman), Golden Press, 1962; *Heroes in American Folklore* (illustrated by J. Daugherty and D. McKay), Messner, 1962; (adapter) *The Golden Book of the Renaissance,* Golden Press, 1962; *Gretchen and the White Steed* (illustrated by Herman Vestal), Garrard, 1972; *Sam Patch, Champion Jumper* (illustrated by Ted Schroeder), Garrard, 1972; *Willie's Whizmobile* (illustrated by Paul Frame), Garrard, 1973; *Twice Upon a Time* (illustrated by Adrienne Adams), Scribner, 1973; *Uncle Sam's 200th Birthday Parade* (illustrated by Frank Brugos), Golden Press, 1974; *Dan McCann and His Fast Sooner*

Hound (illustrated by Mimi Korach), Garrard, 1975; *Paul Bunyan Tricks a Dragon* (illustrated by Raymond Burns), Garrard, 1975; *Smokey Bear's Camping Book* (illustrated by M. Crawford), Golden Press, 1976; *Darwin and the Enchanted Isles,* Coward, 1977; *The Hungry Ghost Mystery* (illustrated by R. Burns), Garrard, 1978; *The Gift of Magic Sleep: Early Experiments in Anesthesia* (illustrated by Pat Rotondo), Coward, 1979.

Editor: Anne Bailey and Seymour Reit, *The West in the Middle Ages,* Western, 1966; Stephen Crane, *The Red Badge of Courage* (illustrated by E. R. Cruz), Pendulum Press, 1973; Herman Melville, *Moby Dick* (illustrated by Alex Nino), Pendulum Press, 1973; Mark Twain, pseudonym of Samuel Langhorne Clemens, *Tom Sawyer* (illustrated by E. R. Cruz), Pendulum Press, 1973.

SIDELIGHTS. "As a boy, I had one ambition: to be a scientist. Though I puttered around with chemicals, it was really the imaginative and fantastic aspect of science that interested me most. My hobbies were magic and drawing. I did a little better with drawing than with magic for somehow my tricks never seemed to come off the way I thought they would.

"I read a great deal, a little of everything, though I especially liked Jules Verne, Edgar Allan Poe, and Mark Twain. As I grew older, my friends and I began to read mystery and detective stories. We devoured so many of these that we learned all the mannerisms of our favorite authors, and finally we attempted to write like them.

"Born in Pittsburgh, Pennsylvania, on May 19, 1911, I spent my childhood in the steel town of Braddock. It was in school there that, one day during lunch, I turned out a chapter in which a member of my class met his doom. After that, I wrote a chapter a day, my classmates reading over my shoulder, anxious to learn who would be the next victim in my tall tales. This went on for a month, until at last the entire class, including me, had been annihilated in fun.

"Shortly after this, I began to write in earnest, mainly poetry. I won several honorable mentions in the annual contests sponsored by *Scholastic Magazine,* and some of my poems were reprinted in newspapers. I still worked away at art, however, and also added two new interests—music and the theater.

"But art finally won out. After graduating from high school, I entered the Carnegie Institute of Technology. Later I went to New York, where I studied at the Art Students League. But eventually I discovered that I wasn't to be a painter. So I returned home and started to write again. When I had completed a novel, I went back to New York. In trying to find a publisher for it, I became interested in drama and motion picture criticism. I also collaborated on a motion picture story purchased by Metro-Goldwyn-Mayer, and on the translation of two novels.

"It was at this time that I began a series of American folklore stories for boys and girls. This was interrupted by a good cause—work in a war plant. [Later] I [was] happy teaching art at a children's school in the country."

Shapiro's interest in American folklore led him to writing. In one of his early books, *Yankee Thunder: The Legendary Life of Davy Crockett,* Shapiro retold the folk tales preserved in old almanacs and songs about this legendary American hero. "The biographer of Davy Crockett is immediately confronted with a problem: which Davy Crockett shall he write about?

Irwin Shapiro. Sketch by Donald McKay.

For if there ever was a man of multiple identity, that man was Davy Crockett.

"First of all there was—or at least there exists some fairly reliable evidence to that effect—the flesh-and-blood Crockett, the frontiersman and hunter of early Tennessee. There was the historical Crockett, with his heroic exploits at the Alamo duly recorded in history. There was the political Crockett, a figure alternately built up and deflated by the Jacksonites and anti-Jacksonites, according to the exigencies of the moment. And then there was the mythical Crockett, the Crockett of legend and folksay, of the tall tales and fireside yarns and almanac stories—the veritable yaller blossom of the forest, half horse, half alligator, with a little touch of snapping turtle, the ring-tailed roarer who could bring a coon out of a tree, ride a streak of lightning, wade the Mississippi, and come down off the Peak o' Day with a piece of sunrise in his pocket.

"It was to this last Crockett, in the grand American tradition of Paul Bunyan, John Henry, Old Stormalong, and Pecos Bill, that I turned as being obviously the most credible, authentic, significant, and true.

"Having made the obvious choice, I went to the Crockett almanacs. This series of anonymous pamphlets, published for a period of about fifty years beginning in 1836, justified the title of almanac by carrying a page or so of information on the phases of the moon and similar subjects. The almanacs' real reason for existence was their main text, a collection of tales, anecdotes, and plain and fancy whoppers that had grown up around the name of Davy Crockett. I found them so outrageous, so fantastic, so far-fetched and contrary to the laws of nature, that I knew I was on the trail of the real Crockett.

''The trouble was that the tales were too fragmentary for my purpose. Some were coarse, even brutal, and not consonant with the larger outlines of Davy's character. There were glaring discrepancies. We are told, for instance, that as a child Davy was as big as a mountain and weighed over three hundred pounds. But in later life his size is given as no larger than an ordinary man's. There were innumerable omissions, innumer-

"Does ether actually relieve pain?" he wondered. "Could it possibly be used in operations?"

One day he saw the chance to find the answer to these questions. ■ (From *The Gift of Magic Sleep* by Irwin Shapiro. Illustrated by Pat Rotondo.)

He got a hammer and nails.
He got his one skate.

■ (From *Willie's Whizmobile* by Irwin Shapiro. Illustrated by Paul Frame.)

able questions unanswered. How did Davy meet his wife, Sally Ann Thunder Ann Whirlwind? How did he acquire his famous pets, the bear Death Hug and the buffalo Mississip? How did he get to the South Seas and back again? As Constance Rourke has said, 'No effort is made to create a consistent mythology in the almanacs.'

"Faced with a problem within a problem, I had to read between the lines. I reconstructed, filled in, elaborated. I jumped to some conclusions. I guessed, reckoned, surmised, fabricated, concocted, and wound up with some whoppers of my own. I gathered a little information from books written about Davy and those purportedly written by him. And finally—I confess it with shame—I had to fall back on history.

"Let me assure you, however, that even here I did not rely on mere facts. I couldn't. Take Davy's relationship with Andy Jackson. The almanacs say practically nothing about it, and history says they differed on the land question, the Indians, the Bank of America. I knew it went deeper than that, because if Davy is the embodiment of our American democracy, Jackson was its exponent, and Old Hickory is by way of being a folk hero himself. I knew, too, that democracy and its exponents do not always move forward at the same speed. Democracy has a way of outdistancing its most fervent admirers; often it takes some time for us to catch up with forces we ourselves have put into motion. Pondering the hints and half-hints, the shadowy allusions of both history and legend, I caught a glimpse of what had come between Davy and Andy Jackson—the sinister figure of Slickerty Sam Patch Thimblerig Skippoweth Branch.

"This Slickerty Sam is a personage rather neglected, as such, by the historians, but I think they will agree that he left his mark on the American scene. He is a compound of the traditional slyness of the backwoods peddler, the chicanery of the professional gambler, and the brutality of those who seek personal gain at any cost. . . .

"Well, then, I took what I could from history, from the almanacs, from the books. In the end I had to more or less shift

for myself, with nothing to guide me but Davy's own motto: *Be sure you're right, then GO AHEAD!* I sat down and put my yarn on paper, writing it for younger readers because I felt they would be less biased against the true and the wonderful, the absurd and sublime story of the real Crockett. . . ." [Irwin Shapiro, "Author's Note," *Yankee Thunder: The Legendary Life of Davy Crockett,* Messner, 1944.[1]]

Shapiro's tales have filled more than forty books and have been translated into ten languages for children all over the world. They are a testimony to his belief that folklore expresses the spirit of American life. "Now more than ever, it is important not only to establish a continuity with our past, but to keep alive all that is best in the American tradition. Mere research is not enough—our folk heros must be revitalized and re-created in terms of our own times." [Taken from the book jacket of *Yankee Thunder: The Legendary Life of Davy Crockett* by Irwin Shapiro, Messner, 1944.[2]]

FOR MORE INFORMATION SEE: New York Times, November 15, 1942; Irwin Shapiro, *Yankee Thunder: The Legendary Life of Davy Crockett,* Messner, 1944; *Horn Book,* May, 1944, February, 1974; Stanley J. Kunitz and Howard Haycraft, editors, *Junior Book of Authors,* second revised edition, H. W. Wilson, 1951.

Piping down the valleys wild,
Piping songs of pleasant glee,
On a cloud I saw a child,
And he laughing said to me:

"Pipe a song about a Lamb."
So I piped with merry cheer;
"Piper, pipe that song again."
So I piped; he wept to hear.

—William Blake

MILTON J. SHAPIRO

SHAPIRO, Milton J. 1926-

PERSONAL: Born in 1926, in Brooklyn, N.Y. *Education:* Attended City College (now City College of the City University of New York). *Residence:* London, England.

CAREER: Sportswriter and movie critic for a New York newspaper; *National Enquirer,* sports editor; *Gunsport* magazine, executive editor; Warner Communications, Inc., publishing director; founder of a magazine publishing company; author of books for young people. *Military service:* Served in the U.S. Air Force during World War II.

WRITINGS—All published by Messner, except as noted: *The Sal Maglie Story,* 1957; *Jackie Robinson of the Brooklyn Dodgers,* 1957, reissued, 1973; *The Roy Campanella Story,* 1958; *The Warren Spahn Story,* 1958; *The Phil Rizzuto Story,* 1959; *The Mel Ott Story,* 1959; *The Willie Mays Story,* 1960; *The Gil Hodges Story,* 1960; *The Hank Aaron Story,* 1961; *A Beginner's Book of Sporting Guns and Hunting,* 1961; *The Whitey Ford Story,* 1962; *Mickey Mantle, Yankee Slugger,* 1962; *The Dizzy Dean Story,* 1963; *The Don Drysdale Story,* 1964; *Laughs from the Dugout,* 1966; *The Year They Won the Most Valuable Player Award,* 1966; *Champions of the Bat: Baseball's Greatest Sluggers,* 1967; *Heroes of the Bullpen: Baseball's Greatest Relief Pitchers,* 1967; *Heroes behind the Mask: America's Greatest Catchers,* 1968; *The Day They Made the Record Book,* 1968; *Baseball's Greatest Pitchers,* 1969; *All Stars of the Outfield,* 1970; *The Pro Quarterbacks,* 1971; *A Treasury of Sports Humor,* 1971; *The Screaming Eagles: The 101st Airborne Division in World War II,* 1976; *Behind Enemy Lines: American Spies and Saboteurs of World War II,* 1978; *Ranger Battalion: American Rangers in World War II,* 1979; *Undersea Raiders: U.S. Submarines in World War II,* McKay, 1979.

SIDELIGHTS: "I was born and raised in the Canarsie section of Brooklyn, in the days when every corner had its sandlot and its sandlot sports, from baseball to the vanishing art of marbles. At P.S. 115 and Boys High School, I played at all sports,

excelling at none, but from my earliest years I was sports minded and enjoyed playing at any game wherever I could. After high school I entered the Baruch School of Business at the City College of New York intending to major in economics, but the war interrupted my education and changed my thinking. I spent two years in the Air Force, part of it in the South Pacific, where I managed to find time for more sports, playing on basketball and football teams with the 13th Air Force.

"In the Army I first thought of writing as a career. On my return to civilian life, I re-entered City College as an advertising major, worked on *Ticker,* the undergraduate newspaper, as feature columnist and editor, and while still a senior I got a job as copy boy on a New York newspaper. On graduation I was promoted to the sports department, then switched to the entertainment desk as movie critic." [Taken from the book jacket of *Jackie Robinson of the Brooklyn Dodgers* by Milton J. Shapiro, Messner, 1957.]

"From newspaper work I moved on to free-lance writing and positions as book and magazine editor for various publishing companies. For a number of years I have been living in England where I was for a time publishing director for Warner Communications, Inc. I now have my own magazine publishing company and in my spare time I write books for young people, specializing in World War II history."

Shapiro's early books were all biographies of great baseball players. The *Christian Science Monitor* called *Jackie Robinson of the Brooklyn Dodgers,* "An excellent contribution. . . . The real heartwarming story in this book is the acceptance and the success with which Robinson himself met the challenge. In a review of *The Phil Rizzuto Story,* a *Kirkus* critic observed, "Milton Shapiro not only writes confidently of the man as an athlete, but, as in his previous books, portrays his subject with dramatic insight. . . . Of interest to fans and to all readers who are attracted by accounts of contemporary valor."

About *The Willie Mays Story,* a *Booklist* reviewer wrote, "The lively account shows the Giants' star as a natural-born ballplayer and as an individual whose good humor and engaging lack of sophistication have won the liking of teammates and fans."

In the latter 1960s, Shapiro's books concentrated on collective, rather than individual, biographies. Of *Heroes Behind the Mask: America's Greatest Catchers,* *Young Reader's Review* commented, "The book is interestingly written, fast-paced, and provides considerable action. The author does not try to force each of the capsule biographies into a set form but adapts the approach to the particular case. . . ." A *Young Reader's Review* critic, in writing about *The Day They Made the Record Book,* said, ". . . There is drama a plenty in these stories without need to dress up the facts, and the author sticks to the facts, and so enhances the drama. . . . Today's youngsters will enjoy reading about the 'legendary' feats here presented: Don Larsen's perfect series no-hitter, Roger Maris' home run hitting, Joe DiMaggio's hitting streak, and Maury Wills' one hundred four stolen bases. . . . The author emphasizes the record making feat, but also tells about the subsequent careers and the personalities of these players. . . ."

FOR MORE INFORMATION SEE: Christian Science Monitor, November 21, 1957; *Kirkus,* March 1, 1959; *Booklist,* June 15, 1959, November 1, 1960; *Young Reader's Review,* May, 1968, December, 1968.

SHTAINMETS, Leon

PERSONAL: Born in Siberia, U.S.S.R. *Education:* Attended Moscow Academy of Art. *Residence:* Philadelphia, Pa.

CAREER: Author and illustrator of books for young people, artist. Has held one-man shows in Moscow, Rome, and New York. *Member:* Artists Guild of the U.S.S.R. *Awards, honors:* Best Designed Art Book of the Year in U.S.S.R., 1968; Biennale of European Artists and Sculptors prize, 1973; Children's Reading Round Table Award, 1975; Breadloaf Writers' Conference (fellow), 1976.

WRITINGS—Self-illustrated: (Reteller) Hans Christian Andersen, *Hans Clodhopper,* Lippincott, 1975; *The Story of Ricky, the Royal Dwarf,* Harper, 1976.

Illustrator: Ruth Manning-Sanders, *Old Dog Sirko: A Ukrainian Tale,* Methuen, 1974; R. Manning-Sanders, *Stumpy: A Russian Tale,* Methuen, 1974; Gaile Bodwell, *The Long Day of the Giants,* McGraw, 1975; I. L. Peretz, *The Case against the Wind, and Other Stories,* translated and adapted by Esther Hautzig, Macmillan, 1975.

On a winter's night, Sarah sits by an oil lamp, darning socks. ■ (From "The East" in *The Case against the Wind and Other Stories* by I. L. Peretz. Translated and adapted by Esther Hautzig. Illustrated by Leon Shtainmets.)

SIDELIGHTS: "From the age of five I sculpted portraits of my relatives. Having sculpted them all, I gave up sculpture forever and occupied myself only with painting. At first I simply fantasized. Later when I began to study professionally, I drew a lot from life.

"In 1965 I received my first commission to do the illustrations for several children's poems for the largest children's book publisher in Russia. Since then I have illustrated many children's books for Russian, English, and American publishers. In 1970 I was accepted as a member of the Artists Guild of the U.S.S.R. Aside from working on books I took part in several group exhibitions in Russia and Europe and had one-man shows in Moscow, Rome, and New York." [Lee Kingman and others, compilers, *Illustrators of Children's Books, 1967-1976,* Horn Book, 1978.]

SIMON, Howard   1903-1979

PERSONAL: Born July 22, 1903, in New York, N.Y.; died October 15, 1979, in White Plains, N.Y.; son of Samuel and Bertha (Seide) Simon; married Charlie May Hogue (an author; divorced, 1936); married Mina Lewiton (an author), January 20, 1936 (died, 1969); married Pony M. Bouche, June 18, 1971; children: (second marriage) Bettina (Mrs. James Niederer). *Education:* Studied at National Academy of Art, New York, 1920-21, and Julien Academy, Paris, 1922-23. *Home and studio:* Lilac Hill, Stanfordville, N.Y. 12581.

CAREER: Artist, author, illustrator, educator, and designer of books; adjunct professor of art at New York University, New York, N.Y., 1946-64. Paintings, drawings, woodcuts and lithographs have been shown in a number of exhibits in America and at Victoria and Albert Museum, London; has had one-man shows at Art Center, New York, at Smithsonian Institution, and at Three Arts Gallery, Poughkeepsie, N.Y.; work included in collections of Metropolitan Museum, New York Public Library, New York University Gallery of Portraits, and other galleries. *Member:* American Institute of Graphic Arts, Dutchess County Art Association.

WRITINGS: *500 Years of Art and Illustration, from Albrecht Duerer to Rockwell Kent,* World Publishing, 1942, 2nd edition published as *500 Years of Art in Illustration, from Albrecht Duerer to Rockwell Kent,* 1945, and 3rd edition, revised, under same title, 1949; (editor) George B. Bridgman, *Complete Guide to Drawing from Life,* Sterling, 1952 (published in England as *Bridgman's Complete Guide to Drawing from Life,* Foulsham, 1955); *Primer of Drawing for Adults,* Sterling, 1953, revised edition published as *Primer of Drawing,* 1958, reprinted as *Techniques of Drawing,* Dover, 1963, revised edition, under same title, Dover, 1972; *Watercolor,* Pitman, 1963; (with wife, Mina Lewiton) *If You Were an Eel, How Would You Feel?* (Junior Literary Guild selection), Follett, 1963; (with M. Lewiton) *Who Knows Where Winter Goes?,* Follett, 1966; *Cabin on a Ridge* (autobiographical), Follett, 1970. Also author of *The Creation According to Genesis* (portfolio of wood engravings), 1977.

Illustrator: Eliot H. Paul, *La Rive Gauche,* McMullen (Paris), 1925; Voltaire, *Candide,* Washburn, 1929; Theophile Gautier, *Mademoiselle de Maupin,* Washburn, 1929.

Michael Gold, *Jews without Money,* Liveright, 1930; Harry E. Burroughs, *Tale of a Vanished Land,* Houghton, 1930;

HOWARD SIMON

Samuel Butler, *The Way of All Flesh*, Diehl, 1930; Francois Rabelais, *Gargantua and Pantagruel*, Washburn, 1930; Herman Melville, *Moby Dick*, A. & C. Boni, 1931; Wayman Hogue, *Back Yonder: An Ozark Chronicle*, Minton, Balch, 1932; Francois Villon, *Lyrics*, Spiral Press, 1933; Charlie May Hogue Simon, *Robin on the Mountain*, Dutton, 1934; Charlie May Hogue Simon, *Teeny Gay*, Dutton, 1936; John Ise, *Sod and Stubble . . .*, Wilson-Erickson, 1936; Maurice S. Sullivan, *Jedediah Smith: Trader and Trail Breaker*, Press of the Pioneers, 1936; Anton P. Chekhov, *Plays*, Diehl, 1936, also published as *The Cherry Orchard and Other Plays*, Grosset, 1936; Marjorie Knight, *Alexander's Christmas Eve*, Dutton, 1938; Hayyim Nahman Bialik, *And It Came to Pass: Legends and Stories about King David and King Solomon*, Hebrew Publishing, 1938; Charlie May Hogue Simon, *Bright Morning*, Dutton, 1939; Bob Barton, *Old Covered Wagon Days*, Dutton, 1939; Lorraine Beim and Jerrold Beim, *The Burro That Had a Name*, Harcourt, 1939.

Marjorie Knight, *Alexander's Birthday*, Dutton, 1940; May Justus, *Mr. Songcatcher and Company*, Doubleday, 1940; Ada Claire Darby, *Columbine Susan*, Stokes, 1940; Harry Levy, *The Dog That Wanted to Whistle*, Lothrop, 1940; Dorothy Cottrell, *Wilderness Orphan*, Messner, 1940; Lorraine Beim and Jerrold Beim, *Lucky Pierre*, Harcourt, 1940; Charlie May Hogue Simon, *Roundabout*, Dutton, 1941; Effie Louise Power, *Osceola Buddy*, Dutton, 1941; Lorraine Beim and Jerrold Beim, *The Little Igloo*, Harcourt, 1941; Harry Levy, *The Burro That Learned to Dance*, Knopf, 1942; Abraham Burstein, *West of the Nile: A Story of Saadia Gaon*, Hebrew Publishing, 1942; Charlie May Hogue Simon, *Younger Brother: A Cherokee Indian Tale*, Dutton, 1942; Harry Levy, *The Bombero: Tales from Latin America*, Knopf, 1943; Marjorie Knight, *Alexander's Vacation*, Dutton, 1943; David A. Boehm, *Stampography*, Printed Arts Co., 1945, revised edition, Sterling, 1951; Deborah Pessin, *The Aleph-bet Story Book*, Jewish Publication

Society, 1946; Charles Dickens, *Christmas Stories*, World Publishing, 1946; Mark Twain, *The Prince and the Pauper*, World Publishing, 1948; Moritz Jagendorf, *The Marvelous Adventures of Johnny Caesar Cicero Darling*, Vanguard, 1949; Moritz Jagendorf, *Upstate, Downstate: Folk Stories of the Middle Atlantic States*, Vanguard, 1949.

Vera M. Graham, *Treasure in the Covered Wagon*, Lippincott, 1952; David A. Boehm and Fred Reinfeld, *Blazer the Bear*, Sterling, 1953; Sofie Schieker, *House at the City Wall*, Follett, 1955; William Wise, *Jonathan Blake* (poems), Knopf, 1956; Eula M. Phillips, *Chucko: The Boy with the Good Name*, Follett, 1957; Katharine Carter, *Johnny of Johnnycake*, Lothrop, 1958.

Clarice Maizel, *Son of Condor*, Criterion, 1964; Elaine M. Ward, *A Big Book*, Abingdon, 1965; Betty Morrow, *A Great Miracle: The Story of Hanukkah*, Harvey House, 1968.

Bonnie Nims, *Always at Home: The Story of Sea Shells*, E. M. Hale, 1970; Lowell Swortzell, editor, *All the World's a Stage: Modern Plays for Young People*, Delacorte, 1972; William E. Keyser, *Days of the Week*, E. M. Hale, 1976.

Illustrator of Mina Lewiton's juvenile books: *The March King*, Didier, 1944; *Beasts of Burden*, Lothrop, 1954, reprinted, 1965; *Rachel*, F. Watts, 1954; *Rachel and Herman*, F. Watts, 1957; *Candita's Choice*, Harper, 1959; *Faces Looking Up*, Harper, 1960; *Animals of the Field and Forest*, Whitman Publishing, 1961; *Lighthouses of America*, Follett, 1963; *That Bad Carlos*, Harper, 1964; Samuel Taylor Coleridge, *The Rime of the Ancient Mariner*, edited by Mina Lewiton, Duell, Sloan & Pearce, 1966; Henry Wadsworth Longfellow, *Evangeline* and *The Song of Hiawatha*, both edited by Mina Lewiton, Duell, Sloan & Pearce, 1966; *Especially Humphrey*, Delacorte, 1967; *Is Anyone Here?*, Atheneum, 1967.

SIDELIGHTS: **July 22, 1903.** Born in New York City, Simon's childhood was spent there and in its suburbs. "As a child I lived in a pleasant suburb and, later, in upper Manhattan in New York City. I felt no insecurity growing up in these places. I knew, however, by the time I was fifteen, and going down daily to the National Academy of Design that I would spend the rest of my life in the almost certain poverty that was supposed to be the lot of a worker in the arts. I never did expect to make anything but a living at it, but I had decided to be a painter. I was unquestioning about taking the consequences, meaning the punishments, I had been warned about.

"I spent two years at the Academy on West 109th Street. During this time I did some apprentice drawings for New York newspapers. I saved enough money to take myself across the Atlantic on the *S.S. France* and celebrated my seventeenth birthday by myself in Paris. I lived and studied and worked there for the next five years.

". . . My own major interest then was drawing the people who slept under the Seine bridges at night and who were living in miserable ways that did not bear close examination. It had been a new and frightening experience for an American boy to find himself among people so poor and so without the opportunity of changing their status, or the hope of doing so. I saw them and I drew them with sympathy. I had no exactly defined social point of view.

"I remember an evening around a table with Grant Wood and some other friends in the Latin Quarter cafe, the *Dome*. We talked about where we were heading in art. Grant said, 'I've had enough of French Impressionism, enough of Paris. It doesn't seem to work for me. I am going back home, pick some small town in the west, and paint the people around me.'

"He did go back and somehow found his plan right for him and found wide acceptance too. Little of what he learned in Paris stuck to him. I think I never quite shook off the influence of the School of Paris. When I left Paris, Picasso, Braque, Matisse, and even Monet were still at work. Even more important for me was the impact of the Expressionists—Edvard Munch, Nolde, Marc, Kokoschka, and Max Beckmann.

"I had read about the magnificence of the western wilderness of America and I had been more and more attracted to it, reading about James Catlin and Prince Maximilian; the German, Bodmer; and the pioneer diaries of Jedediah Smith and the others, and especially Francis Parkman's *The Oregon Trail*. I studied the drawings of both Catlin and Bodmer. I decided to drive to California on my return from Paris and settled into a studio in San Francisco. I continued to illustrate books that came my way and the patterns of the working days in Paris were repeated in San Francisco. Painting now became as important to me as illustration and graphic work." [Howard Simon, *Cabin on a Ridge*, Follett, 1970.[1]]

1930. ". . . An unforgettable year. A bad year. One-third of the nation was ill-housed and ill-fed, as President Roosevelt said several years later. Some of this one-third lived in tin shacks and cabins made of packing crates along the Hudson River below Riverside Drive in the city of New York. I saw them as I walked along the Drive, sketch pad in my hand.

"Jobs were non-existent. Men were wearing clothes that came originally from good shops but by now they were barely wearable and these men were selling apples along the New York City streets. Life was hard and uncertain. All segments of the richest society that man had known were bewildered and floundering. Our country was overpopulated in the urban areas, yet vast forests and farmlands with small or no populations lay neglected. Farm products were sold at below the cost of raising them. More banks failed each day.

"Art at that moment was a luxury not many people could afford. Publishers produced few books, and these without illustrations. As a painter and book illustrator I considered my condition. I wanted to go on making pictures for books, even if I could not do so where the best market had been. So I thought to search for a place where living was possible and money scarcely needed. The idea of working close to nature in an environment of green silent beauty, and uninhabited, for the most part, except by animals of the fields and forests, appealed to me.

"Because of an early interest in pioneer life in America—I had already illustrated several books of the frontier—I knew about the Homestead Law of 1867. The possibility of finding out for myself the pattern of life in the sparsely-peopled hills of the Southwest presented itself strongly to my imagination. I never intended to spend the rest of my life there; even when I thought of it as a solution, it could only be a temporary one. Yet as it turned out, I spent the better part of five years there.

"I made no great preparations for my mountain adventure; the serious work involved in homesteading hardly played so important a part in my thoughts as the knowledge that I would have a remote place in which to think and work. What beckoned me most, I believe, was a completely new environment.

She looked at the faces of a crowd of children standing in a circle to watch two boys wrestling. The two who were wrestling rolled toward her. . . . ■ (From *Candita's Choice* by Mina Lewiton. Illustrated by Howard Simon.)

"I loaded into my car everything I thought I would need for my work: canvas and paint, wood blocks and tools—the essential and innumerable things of my craft. I took along books, clothing and whatever garden tools I owned, these left over from a Connecticut farm summer.

"In late spring I headed toward Arkansas and the Ozark Mountains. There were few states in which land could still be homesteaded under the federal law; Arkansas was one of these. It appealed because it was heavily forested, and in the hill country. What I had already learned of the mountain folk of the region interested me. It seemed they had not yet stepped into the twentieth century."[1]

Simon spent five years homesteading in the Ozark Mountains, where he continued painting. "The materials of art . . . were close to me in my new environment and in the people themselves. After my years in Paris I felt myself starting again with these new-old elements. It seemed important to me to record my impressions.

"To paint and draw the mountain people and to make murals of the indigenous subject matter, all of which I now hoped to do, was in a way returning to what had been done by Winslow

He put both feet on the fire hydrant, firmly, and slowly bent down, holding on to the knob of the hydrant with both hands. Then gradually he raised his feet in the air while standing on his hands. . . . ■ (From *That Bad Carlos* by Mina Lewiton. Illustrated by Howard Simon.)

Homer, Thomas Eakins, John Sloan, George Luks, and others of that earlier group, some of whom were still at work. Except for Homer, these American painters had confined themselves mainly to the cities for subject matter.

"I thought then and still think that storytelling composition is not the answer for me, although much of my work is in illustration. More important, I feel, are mood and design, the surface of the canvas, exploration of new, personal techniques, and my own way of expressing myself in my medium.

". . . During my homestead years . . . I was being paid for illustrating books sent me by publishers. The fees for illustration in the thirties were small, and when I sold a print outside the mountains, the price was never more than twenty-five dollars and often less, but it did happen occasionally that a collector would buy a print or two. Of course I had to buy materials and canvas and often several reference books.''[1]

Simon's five years in the Ozark Mountains were a major influence in his work as an illustrator and painter, and he frequently selected classics to illustrate, using his experiences in the mountains for his illustrations. "Those years were filled with observation of the woodlands, the flora and fauna, and the mountain people particularly. The interest I already had in early American life and its pioneers was confirmed and

strengthened by this experience, and it remains a source of inspiration to me.'' [Bertha Mahony Miller and others, compilers, *Illustrators of Children's Books: 1946-1956*, Horn Book, 1958.[2]]

1936. Married author, Mina Lewiton. During their thirty-three-year marriage Simon illustrated many of her juvenile books and the two collaborated on several books.

1972-1977. Joined the Barlow School, a co-educational boarding school in Amenia, New York, where he served as chairman of the art department until he became artist-in-residence. Simon wrote several books about drawing, painting and illustrating. "To learn to draw you must learn to see. All of us have experienced an inability to remember even approximately the shape of familiar objects. The essential shapes of things seem always to elude us. How to remember and how to set down these shapes in line and in form are learned by training the eye and hand. To see things as they are and not as you imagine or remember them requires a little unlearning and more learning, but this is basic and essential.

"Cézanne said that if you can draw the cylinder, sphere, and cube you can draw anything. At first sight this seems like a formula for reproducing the seen shapes of things. But Cézanne also said, 'I am always trying to *realize*.' Cézanne meant by this that to *understand* the form of things and to give dimension in space to these forms were his intentions. Only then can the reality of the form be felt even though the transcript from nature may not be exact. *The character and quality of a form are important rather than the superficial appearance.*

"We should understand this and make use of it not as a formula but as a means to the desired end. In this case the end is the simplification of form to enable us to carry expression of the seen into whatever medium we are using.

"To learn to draw you must learn to feel. The tactile or '*felt*' approach to drawing is not new.

"We must recognize at once that drawing is an abstract device. The most naturalistic of drawings is still in no sense a copy from nature. In drawing we are constantly transferring into symbols the object seen and remembered. *There is no line in nature.* When we *feel* the shape of an object we know that it is three-dimensional, and only by translation into terms of linear edge and by systems of light and dark values can we convey the feeling of form to paper.

"Today more people are interested in learning to draw then even a few years ago. The renascence of interest in learning to draw proves among other things that the impulse and desire to draw cannot and should not be suppressed by our mechanized and so-called atom-age civilization. It is perhaps deeply significant that this is so. Indicative of this aspect of drawing is the fact that the terms of psychopathology often are used in connection with art and art criticism today. Drawing itself, for example, is often referred to as therapy.'' [Howard Simon, *Techniques of Drawing*, Dover, 1963.[3]]

In **June, 1979,** the Simon Art Studio at the Barlow School was dedicated.

October 15, 1979. Died of a stroke at the White Plains Medical Center in New York. During his lifetime, Simon illustrated over 100 books of which his favorite was Mark Twain's *The Prince and the Pauper*. His work was exhibited in numerous

Stretch then proved how correctly he was named for he grew swiftly and soon was taller than the pine tree.
■(From "Stretch, Puff and Blazer: A Russian Tale" in *Eurasian Folk and Fairy Tales* by I. F. Bulatkin. Illustrated by Howard Simon.)

museums and private collections, and he was also a teacher of art at New York University for eighteen years.

FOR MORE INFORMATION SEE: Bertha Mahony Miller and others, compilers, *Illustrators of Children's Books: 1946-1956*, Horn Book, 1958; Howard Simon, *Techniques of Drawing*, Dover, 1963; H. Simon, *Cabin on a Ridge*, Follett, 1970; Martha E. Ward and Dorothy A. Marquardt, editors, *Illustrators of Books for Young People*, Scarecrow, 1975; *Obituary: New York Times*, October 17, 1979.

SMITH, Lillian H(elena)   1887-1983

OBITUARY NOTICE: Born in 1887, in London, Ontario; died January 5, 1983. Children's librarian, lecturer, author, teacher, and consultant in children's services. Smith began her career as a children's librarian in 1911, working in the children's department of the New York Public Library. After only three weeks at the library, she was put in charge of the children's

department of the Washington Heights Branch Library. About 1912, she accepted an invitation from Dr. George H. Locke, chief librarian of the Toronto Public Library, to organize a children's book department there, consequently becoming the first children's librarian in the British Empire. By the end of her stay there in 1952, Smith saw the Toronto Public Library establish 16 children's rooms in branch libraries, and in 30 public library branches in elementary schools and two settlement houses. She was also a lecturer at the University of Toronto's Library school from 1913 to 1952. During her career, Smith also served on the Executive Board of the American Library Association (ALA) from 1932 to 1936, and was the chairman of the Children's Services Division of the ALA during the 1920s and 1940s. In 1962 she won the Clarence Day Award for her book *The Unreluctant Years: A Critical Approach to Children's Literature* (American Library Association, 1953). Commenting about children's literature, in her book, she wrote: "The impact of even one good book on a child's mind is surely an end in itself, a valid experience which helps him to form standards of judgment and taste at the time when his mind is most sensitive to impressions of every kind." Smith also edited *Books for Boys and Girls* (Ryerson, 1927). *For More Information See: The Horn Book Magazine*, June, 1982. *Obituaries: School Library Journal*, February, 1983.

SPICER, Dorothy (Gladys)   (?)-1975

PERSONAL: Born in New York, N.Y.; died in January, 1975; daughter of J. Lindley (a minister) and Phoebe Bryan (Washburn) Spicer; married Malcolm Fraser, September 14, 1925. *Education:* Vassar College, A.B., 1916; Radcliffe College, A.M., 1918; additional studies at Columbia University, New York University, City College (now City College of the City University of New York), and in various European and Asian countries. *Politics:* Republican. *Religion:* Society of Friends. *Residence:* White Plains, N.Y.

CAREER: Free-lance writer and folklorist. Assistant in Oriental department, Boston Museum of Fine Arts, art department, Vassar College, and department of education, Metropolitan Museum of Art, 1918; folklore and folk arts specialist, national board of Young Women's Christian Association (Y.W.C.A.), 1919-29; Y.W.C.A., Brooklyn, N.Y., director of foreign communities department, 1945-47; American Federation of International Institutes, New York, N.Y., research consultant, 1947-50; free-lance editor, information service, Grolier Society, 1951-59.

*WRITINGS—*For young readers: *Children's Prayers from Other Lands*, Association Press, 1955; *Forty-Six Days of Christmas: A Cycle of Old World Songs, Legends, and Customs* (illustrated by Anne M. Jauss), Coward, 1960; *13 Witches, Two Wizards, the Devil, and a Pack of Goblins* (illustrated by Sofia), Coward, 1963; *13 Monsters* (illustrated by Sofia), Coward, 1964; *13 Ghosts* (illustrated by Sofia), Coward, 1965; *13 Giants* (illustrated by Sofia), Coward, 1966; *13 Devils* (illustrated by Sofia), Coward, 1967; *Desert Adventure*, Bouregy, 1968; *The Humming Top*, S. G. Phillips, 1968; *Long Ago in Serbia* (illustrated by Linda Ominsky), Westminster, 1968; *The Owl's Nest: Folktales from Friesland* (illustrated by Alice Wadowski-Bak), Coward, 1968; *13 Goblins* (illustrated by Sofia), Coward, 1969; *13 Jolly Saints* (illustrated by Sofia), Coward, 1970; *The Kneeling Tree, and Other Folktales from the Middle East*, Coward, 1971; *13 Rascals* (illustrated by Sofia), Coward, 1971; *13 Dragons* (illustrated by Sofia), Coward, 1974.

Feet planted wide apart, Juri laughed. "Well? Has the cat got your tongue? Am I stronger than you or not?" he demanded.

"Y-yes," stammered the Giant, fear creeping into his eyes. ■(From *13 Dragons* by Dorothy Gladys Spicer. Illustrated by Sofia.)

Other writings: *Folk Festivals and the Foreign Community,* Womans Press, 1923, reprinted, Gale, 1976; *The Book of Festivals,* Womans Press, 1937, reprinted, Gale, 1969; *Holiday Parties,* Womans Press, 1939; *Parties for Young Americans,* Womans Press, 1940; *Latin American Costumes,* Hyperion Press, 1941; *Windows Open to the World: A Handbook of World Fellowship Projects,* Womans Press, 1946; *From an English Oven: Cakes, Buns, and Breads of County Tradition,* Womans Press, 1948; *Folk Party Fun* (illustrated by June Kirkpatrick), Association Press, 1954; *Yearbook of English Festivals,* H. W. Wilson, 1954, reprinted, Greenwood Press, 1972; *Festivals of Western Europe,* H. W. Wilson, 1958; *Feast-Day Cakes from Many Lands* (illustrated by Tim Lofton), Holt, 1960.

Contributor of articles on folk customs, festivals, and foods to magazines and newspapers.

SIDELIGHTS: During her lifetime, Spicer studied and traveled in numerous countries. Her books for children and adults reflected her interest in international customs and folktales. She had a special interest in the Middle East, resulting in her collection of folktales, *The Kneeling Tree.* "The area we call the Middle East is vast. . . . These mysterious lands have fascinated me since early childhood. I listened avidly to marvelous tales of wise talking birds and Middle Eastern potentates, patriarchs and prophets through whom God spoke. I cherished the treasures my parents gave me, such as tinkling camel bells and a silver charm fashioned into a hand—'the hand of the Prophet's daughter, Fatimah.' Then there was a ring, handwrought in brass, set with white onyx and incised with an Arabic legend. Best of all were the olive wood beads, carved

in Jerusalem, to help one pray; the smooth dark-red 'fidget' beads from who knows where, to help one think, and amber beads to wear and to touch. But most precious to me were the strings of flat round blue-green beads, with a staring eye in the center. *They* once hung between a Syrian donkey's ears, to protect the beast from harm and the Evil Eye!

"As I grew up, I made many friends from the countries of my treasures. While I ate exotic foods, nibbled strange sweets, and sipped thick sweet coffee—'black as night and strong as love'—I heard the tales from their homelands. . . .

"When at last I visited the Middle East to gather material for . . . [my] collection [*The Kneeling Tree*], many things I heard and saw were already familiar. The task of selecting so few stories from so great an area was awesome.

"In the preparation of *The Kneeling Tree,* I read much, consulted aged folk wise in village lore, and talked with scholars, priests, and rabbis. Then I wrote in my own way the stories from their marvelous lands, where anything may happen—and does—as in my tales.'' [Dorothy Gladys Spicer, *The Kneeling Tree, and Other Folktales from the Middle East,* Coward, 1971.[1]]

In all of Spicer's books great attention was given to research, but the retelling of the folktales was in her own style, with her personal interpretation. "As always, the telling of the stories is entirely my own. For as with all tales that have been told and retold for hundreds of years, precious details have been forgotten, omitted through carelessness, or entirely lost. To make the stories more appealing to present-day readers, I have filled in such gaps, imagined *what really might have happened,* and written it down." [Taken from the preface of *13 Rascals* by Dorothy Spicer, Coward, 1971.[2]]

HOBBIES AND OTHER INTERESTS: Walking, gardening, bird watching, and cooking.

SPIELBERG, Steven 1947-

PERSONAL: Born December 18, 1947, in Cincinnati, Ohio; son of Arnold Spielberg (an electrical engineer and computer specialist) and Leah (Posner) Spielberg Adler. *Education:* California State College (now University), Long Beach, B.A., 1970. *Residence:* Beverly Hills, Calif. *Office:* Steven Spielberg Productions, Warner Brothers Studios, 400 Warner Blvd., Burbank, Calif. 91522.

CAREER: Universal City Studios, Inc., Universal City, Calif., director of television series episodes, television films, and motion pictures, 1968-75; director of motion pictures, 1975—; writer, 1977—. Director of television series episodes of "Marcus Welby, M.D.," "Owen Marshall," "The Name of the Game," "The Psychiatrist," and "Columbo," of television films including "Night Gallery," "Something Evil," and "Duel," and of motion pictures including "The Sugarland Express," "Jaws," "Close Encounters of the Third Kind," "1941," "Raiders of the Lost Ark," and "E.T.: The Extra-Terrestrial." Producer of motion pictures including "I Wanna Hold Your Hand," "Used Cars," "Poltergeist" (partially directed), and "The Twilight Zone." *Awards, honors:* Won film contest for "Escape to Nowhere"; won prizes at Atlanta Film Festival and Venice Film Festival for "Amblin'"; Grand Prix de Festival at the Festival de Cinéma Fantastique, Avoriaz, France, 1971, for ''Duel''; nominated by Academy of Motion Picture Arts and Sciences for Oscar for best director, 1977, for ''Close Encounters of the Third Kind,'' 1982, for ''Raiders of the Lost Ark,'' 1983, for ''E.T.: The Extra-Terrestrial''; won the Hollywood Foreign Press Association Golden Globe Award for best director, 1983, for ''E.T.''

WRITINGS: Close Encounters of the Third Kind, Dell, 1977. Also author and director of the screenplay ''Close Encounters of the Third Kind,'' and author and director of amateur films including ''Escape to Nowhere,'' ''Firelight,'' and ''Amblin.''

SIDELIGHTS: **December 18, 1947.** Born in Cincinnati, Ohio.

''I get along very well with my parents. I'm proud of them too. My father was always in electronics. He was a radio operator on a B-25 over Burma in World War II, in a squadron called the Burma Bridgebusters. It's funny, our careers are very similar in two different fields. I've been obsessed with films since I was 12, he with electronics since he was 8 or 9.'' [Jerry Tallmer, ''Jawing with Steven Spielberg,'' *New York Post,* June 25, 1975.[1]]

1954. Family moved to Arizona. ''. . . I lived in Scottsdale from about the age of 7 to 17. Then a burgeoning cow town on the outskirts of Phoenix. You lump them all together, Scottsdale and Phoenix.

''One year my father got a movie camera from my mother for Father's Day, an 8-mm. Kodak. We were very much an outdoor family. I called my parents professional campers. But my father just couldn't seem to shoot good family films. So I took the camera away from him.

''That's how it all began, me directing, setting up, moving them around. Films of our camping trips. Telling stories. Like: Father Chopping Wood. Mother Digging Latrine. Young Sister Removing Fishook from Right Eye—my first horror film. And a scary little picture called 'Bear in the Bushes.'''[1]

''Most of what I've learned about cinema—and this sounds so pretentious—has been self-taught. My parents would not let me see movies when I was very young. I couldn't get into a movie theater to see the cartoons. And I had all my TV viewing censored. . . . I came from a strict Jewish family and they didn't believe in my 'wasting' an afternoon in the movie theater eating popcorn.'' [Rochelle Reed, editor, ''Steven Spielberg Seminar,'' *Dialogue on Film,* 1974.[2]]

''Then I began to think that staging real life was much more exciting that just recording it. So I'd do things like forcing my parents to let me out of the car 100 yards before we reached the campgrounds when we went on trips. I'd run ahead and film them arriving and unpacking and pitching camp. Then I began cutting the films together, speeding the camera up, slowing it down, experimenting with time-lapse photography. I also played the bully brother, dressing my sisters up as German soldiers, blasting at them with toy submachine guns, and filming them tumbling down a hill—they died four or five times in each picture. But I never really thought I would make movies for a living. Mainly, it was something fun to do, to keep me away from studying algebra and French.'' [''Penthouse Interview: Steven Spielberg,'' *Penthouse* magazine, February, 1978.[3]]

Spielberg's mother, Leah Adler, recalls: ''Steven always had a highly developed imagination. He was afraid of everything. When he was little he would insist that I lift the top of the

Steven Spielberg. Drawing by Steven Muller.

baby grand so he could see the strings while I played. Then he would fall on the floor, screaming in fear.'' [Sue Reilly, ''By Raiding Hollywood Lore and His Childhood Fantasies, Steven Spielberg Rediscovers an Ark That's Pure Gold,'' *People,* July 20, 1981.[4]]

Spielberg confirms: ''My biggest fear was a clown doll. Also the tree I could see outside my room. Also anything that might be under the bed or in the closet. Also 'Dragnet' on TV. Also a crack in the bedroom wall—I thought ghosts might come from it.'' [''Steve's Summer Magic,'' *Time,* May 31, 1982.[5]]

''I remember lying there, trying to go to sleep, and I used to always imagine little Hieronymus Bosch-like creatures inside, peeking out and whispering to me to come into the playground of the crack and be drawn into the unknown there, inside the wall of my home in New Jersey.'' [Michiko Kakutami, ''The Two Faces of Spielberg—Horror Vs. Hope,'' *New York Times,* May, 1982.[6]]

''I used to tell my sisters bedtime horror stories all the time, and make them up as I go along. I could feel them twisting under the sheets and wanting to escape the room, and I'd make them more horrible. The more they squirmed, the more horrible the stories would get. And I'd usually cap off the story by letting them fall off to sleep and going to the window with a flashlight and prowling around.

''I remember one day a famous movie came on TV, a very famous William Cameron Menzies film called 'Invaders from Mars.' The brains behind the bad guys is a severed head with tentacles coming out of the neck, and in a fishbowl. So I had

(From the television movie "Duel," starring Dennis Weaver. Directed by Steven Spielberg. Released by Universal Pictures, 1971.)

a skull, a plastic skull, and it was in my room, and I put an Air Force flak cap on the skull with some red lights under it, and I stuck it in a long walk-in closet we had. I blindfolded my sisters, put them in the closet with this thing and locked them in. They were screaming for hours." [Chris Hodenfield, *Rolling Stone*, January 26, 1978.⁷]

"Movies took the place of crayons and charcoal and I was able to represent my life at 24 frames a second."⁶

"I was probably the only student director at Arcadia High School in Arizona who was allowed to control and put together a show. I did 'Guys and Dolls' and brought the action, especially the brawl in the Hot Box, into the audience. I guess that's kind of commonplace in today's theater, but then it was very strange to have people running up and down the aisles singing and acting. I got killed for it! Every critic in Arizona who could write said, 'How dare he open up the proscenium and do this drivel in the audience. "Guys and Dolls" is meant to be on stage.' I did the standards—'Arsenic and Old Lace,' 'I Remember Mama'—everything you were allowed to do then." [Hollis Alpert, editor, "Dialogue on Film: Steven Spielberg," *American Film,* September, 1978.⁸]

1965. Spielberg's family moved to San Francisco where he continued making short films to the detriment of his high school grades. "I saw a shrink—primarily to get out of the Army—

when I was eighteen. I really didn't have a problem that I could articulate, I didn't have a central dilemma that I was trying to get the psychiatrist to help me with. So I would just talk, and I felt at times that the psychiatrist disapproved of the long lapses in conversation, because he would sit there smoking his pipe and I'd sit there with nothing to say. So I remember feeling, even though I was paying the fifty dollars an hour, that I should entertain him.

"So I would go in, once a week, and for those fifty-five minutes make up stories. And sometimes the stream of consciousness, on the chair in his office, gave me great movie ideas. I would test all these scenarios on him. If he put down his pipe, or if he looked at me and began nodding his head, I'd realize I'd be getting to him. I determined after six months of this that he was human like the rest of us, and he was responding to exciting tales, or he was getting bored at the slow parts. And I was able, during those sessions, to go home and write some of the ideas down. And I got a feeling that, in all my movies, there's something that came out of those extemporaneous bullshit sessions."⁷

1966. Entered California State College at Long Beach, not having been accepted in the major film schools because of his poor grades. Spielberg recalls that during his college years in the '60s: "I was never part of the drug culture. I never took LSD, mescaline, coke or anything like that. In my entire life

(From the movie "The Sugarland Express," starring Goldie Hawn. Co-written and directed by Steven Spielberg. Copyright © 1974 by Universal Pictures.)

I've probably smoked three joints. But I went through the entire drug period, several of my friends were heavily into it. I would sit in a room and watch TV while people climbed the walls. . . .

"I've always been afraid of taking drugs. I've always been afraid of losing control of myself. That's one of the things I found when I was bouncing stories off the shrinks. I found that I could never lose control: I felt I would never regain it. One of the reasons I never got into drugs is that I felt it would overpower me. Take over me."[7]

1967. Seeking filmmaking experience, Spielberg made his way into Universal Studios. "When . . . my mom and dad split, and there was no longer a routine to follow. My life changed radically. I left home and went to L.A. I lived with my second cousins for a summer. One day I went to the Frey Line tour of Universal Studios. I was fascinated by it all; so when the bus made a rest stop, I got out and hid behind one of the sound stages. So the bus left without me, and I spent the day walking around the lot. I watched the television shows being shot. It was my first exposure to the clapper sticks, the ringing bells, all the great nonsense and shouting.

"For about the next three months, I returned to the lot every day and got in by dressing up in a suit, waving to the guards, and bluffing my way around. I suspect that the guards were

afraid to kick me off the lot because they thought I might have been related to somebody in the black tower."[3]

"I took over an office and was there for three months. But it never helped me. Sid Sheinberg, who got me the contract at Universal, had no idea that I had been in residence for so long, watching. I watched movies and television shows being made; I watched editing and dubbing. But I couldn't learn from watching filmmakers direct. Today a lot of new filmmakers want to watch me direct, but I usually say no, because it didn't much help me to watch others when I was coming along. The excitement of watching the 'push-in' of a camera or hearing actors converse wears off in about two weeks. After that, watching a movie being made is boring. Observers soon get tired and go home. I think the best way into the movie business is by writing scripts; at some point, a writer can hold out to direct his own work. The total filmmaker, anyway, is one who writes and directs, even if he collaborates with other writers."[8]

1968. "I made a film about a man being chased by someone trying to kill him. But running becomes such a spiritual pleasure for him that he forgets who is after him. I did a picture about dreams—how disjointed they are. I made one about what happens to rain when it hits dirt. They were personal little films that represented who I was. And then I made a slick, very professional-looking film, although it had as much soul and content as a piece of driftwood. And that was the film that got

Universal to sign me to a seven-year contract.''[Jack Kroll, ''Close Encounters with Spielberg,'' *Newsweek,* November 21, 1977.⁹]

''Amblin''''began Spielberg's television career. ''TV taught me to think on my feet. You have six days to shoot 50 pages of script. TV is a well-oiled machine. Either you roll with it or it rolls over you.''⁵

''I think television is the best place to start because it disciplines the hell out of you. Television has taught me to imagine the finished product and then just before shooting retrace my thoughts and follow that imaginary blueprint. TV taught me that because you're making an hour show in six days, you better know line for line, shot for shot exactly what you're doing. The minute you dissemble, you're behind schedule a day. I mean the minute you fall down you also fall behind schedule. You pace yourself according to the ten hour working day.''²

''I was convinced there was a way to produce quality TV in sausage factory time. They said to me, 'Do a TV show and it'll be on in three weeks.' I dug that. It taught me how to prepare. Now I get all kinds of kids who come to me because they hear I was on the Universal lot when I was 20. They get indignant. But I had made 15 short films by that time. No film school. No AFI [American Film Institute]. Just work. You can't sell people chutzpah. You've got to have films to show them.'' [Tom Zito, ''Steven Spielberg, Child of the Movies,'' *Washington Post,* May 31, 1975.¹⁰]

''I was 21 when I was directing Joan Crawford on 'Night Gallery.' She treated me like I had been directing for 50 years. She was great. But I did an awful job.''⁹

''. . . For my first two years in television I ran scared. I wanted to be good at meeting the schedule and please the producers. I did about four or five *bad* shows. Then I decided to risk getting fired in order to do something brave. I gave in to my own impulses, and the shows got better. I began to shoot everything in master shots, to give the actors off-the-wall directions—little behavioral points of interest that weren't in the script. It wasn't a story point to have a character suddenly pull the phone off the wall and throw it through the window. I began having fun, enjoying myself. But I worked on only eleven shows, including three television movies. That was it.''⁸

(From the movie "Jaws," starring Richard Dreyfuss. Directed by Steven Spielberg. Released by Universal Pictures, 1975.)

1970. Graduated with a B.A. in English.

1971. Spielberg made his first feature film for television. "Duel" won the Grand Prix de Festival at the Festival de Cinéma Fantastique in Avoriaz, France. Its plot: "A mild-mannered businessman on a trip in his rented car takes a short-cut through the desert—and is engaged, pursued, and harassed by a gasoline trailer truck."[1]

". . . I had the entire picture planned on IBM cards, the first time I've done that. Every sequence was plotted on the cards and I had them mounted on a bulletin board in the motel room in Lancaster, rather than taking the script and opening it to a page, I would select, let's say, ten cards. That would be the day's work and when the cards were finished, I'd tear them up; I saved the pieces but that's the way the picture was shot."[2]

1974. "Duel's" success led to the making of "Sugarland Express," which established Spielberg as a major filmmaker.

1975. Spielberg directed the film "Jaws," based on Peter Benchley's novel of the same name. In its first two years it grossed approximately 410 million dollars. "It's essentially a horror film, a sociological study about a town being victimized by an unknown element in the sea. I want to get in some humor, which the book doesn't have. And you won't see any blood and guts when the shark attacks. I'm going to get the sense of shock into the minds of the audience and not on the screen." [Wayne Warga, "Spielberg Keeps His Touch in Transition," *Los Angeles Times,* April 3, 1974.[11]]

"My feeling about sharks is that they've had 80 million years to get their act together. My vision for 'Jaws' began with my reading of the book. Parts of the book terrorized me. I tried to translate my fear into visual language. It became a picture book of fear, phobias and anxieties." [Joseph Gelmis, "Turning Fear into Fame," *Newsday,* July 6, 1975.[12]]

Despite its enormous success, "Jaws" did not receive an Oscar nomination, much to Spielberg's disappointment. "It hurt me because I felt it was a director's movie. But there was a 'Jaws' backlash. The same people who had raved about it began to doubt its artistic value as soon as it began to bring in so much money."[9]

1977. Directed "Close Encounters of the Third Kind" which enjoyed international success, soon grossing over 250 million dollars. "The difference between 'Jaws' and 'Close Encoun-

Spielberg on the set of "Close Encounters," 1976.

(From "Close Encounters of the Third Kind," written and directed by Steven Spielberg. Produced by Columbia Pictures, 1977.)

ters' is that 'Jaws' was a physical effects movie and 'Close Encounters' was an optical effects movie."[8]

"I wrote the screen play from eleven to eight o'clock in the morning because I was editing 'Jaws' in the daytime. I'd come home, have dinner, rest for a few hours, and start writing 'Close Encounters.' Subconsciously you begin writing about your environment while you're behind the typewriter. I expect if I had written the film in daylight, there would be more daylight scenes, and perhaps some daylight encounters.

"I'm a night person, basically. I always stay up late, I sleep late in the mornings. I love the night."[7]

Before its release, Spielberg said: "This film will only be successful if, when people see it, they come out of the theater looking up at the sky. If they come out looking for their car keys, we're in big trouble.

"My whole thing about taking special effects to the limit—where there is nothing to criticize because you can't see how it was done—it stems from being in school and hearing the word 'fakey.' You know, you could go back to class on Mon-

day after everyone's seen a movie over the weekend. 'How'd you like the film?' '_Ah,_ that was kind of _fakey._ Those weren't dinosaurs, those were big lizards with things glued on their backs. That wasn't a brontosaur, that was a Gila monster.'

"I really do think that kids notice flaws in films more than adults. I get a lot of letters from kids who say, 'I love _Jaws_ even though the shark was only mechanical.'"[7]

"I do most of the original sketches myself. I can't draw, but I do stick figures and perspectives. I can give a sketch artist an idea of what I want. I designed all the ships in 'Close Encounters' by doing them in black-and-white, then drawing arrows, indicating an orange light, a yellow light. . . . I spend maybe two-and-a-half years per film, so I have the luxury of spending six months to conceive and six months to sit with the sketch artist and just draw pictures and throw them away.

"But once I committed myself to the last four hundred sketches for 'Jaws' and the last fifteen hundred sketches for 'Close Encounters,' I didn't just stop and say that's all I'm going to shoot. I changed things and threw things out as I went along, partially because the film was too expensive. There was a whole

(From the movie "Close Encounters of the Third Kind," starring Richard Dreyfuss. Produced by Columbia Pictures, 1977.)

sequence in the original storyboard for 'Close Encounters' in which ten thousand little cuboids, each about the size of your fist and too bright to look at, flow out of the ship. They perform like little tugboats and ferry the mother ship across the base of operations in order to coordinate a safe landing. But I still would be shooting today if I had attempted that.

"My first concept of the mother ship was terrible. It was completely limiting. It was a black, pie-shaped wedge, with a little tip on the end; a phantom shape that blotted out the stars. All you knew was that something darker than the sky was moving out from behind the mountain. For me, that was going to be very terrifying, to see something so huge that it just blacked out the sky. No bulkhead, no rivets, nothing! Then, at the last minute, it would turn on its lights and land. That was the concept, and the wedge was built. Then I said to myself, What am I leading up to, a Sara Lee pie tin in the third act of my movie? After all that's gone before, a black wedge is going to offer cosmic bliss?

"The catharsis came in Bombay, India. On the way to and from the Bombay location, I passed a huge oil refinery with about ten thousand lights inside pipes and tubes. It was amazing

to see at night. I made a sketch of it. When I came back to Los Angeles, I was up on Mulholland Drive, and I said, 'Wouldn't it be neat to take the lights of the San Fernando Valley and invert them beneath the oil refinery concept from Bombay.'. . . It's a distillation of both of those thoughts. The mother ship was the last four weeks of effects photography. Otherwise you would have seen a frozen-food tray landing on Devils Tower.[10]

"[For 'Close Encounters'] I really wanted to take a child's point of view. The uneducated innocence that allows a person to take this kind of quantum jump and . . . go abroad, if you will. A conscientious, responsible adult human being probably wouldn't. Especially if his life had a lot of equilibrium, he certainly would turn down the chance to go that far abroad. As opposed to someone like Neary, [character in 'Close Encounters'; a telephone lineman, played by Richard Dreyfuss] whose life sprouted out of model trains. His den-workshop. Because, for me, Neary was not so much the father of the family of four, but a member of that family, no different than any of the kids.

"I think in order to want to go on that journey, you'd have to have that naive wonderment. He was, for me, in my mind, a prime candidate. He was ready even before anything happened to him."[7]

1979. Spielberg filmed "1941," a World War II farce taking place in Los Angeles. "We're taking history and bending it like a pretzel. I would use the words stupidly outrageous to describe this movie. It's really a celebration of paranoia. I hope that you'll come away saying that hypertension is fun.

"Comedy is not my forte. I don't know how this movie will come out. And yes, I'm scared. I'm like the Cowardly Lion, and two successes back to back have not strengthened my belief in my ability to deliver." ["Animal House Goes to War," *Time*, April 16, 1979.[13]]

Spielberg admits: "Until then I thought I was immune to failure. But I couldn't come down from the power high of making big films on large canvases. I threw everything in, and it killed the soup. '1941' was my encounter with economic reality."[5]

1981. Directed "Raiders of the Lost Ark," produced by George Lucas. "The film's like popcorn, it doesn't fill you up and it's easy to digest and it melts in your mouth and it's the kind of thing that you can just go back and chow down over and over again. It's a rather superficial story of heroics and deeds and great last-minute saves; but it puts people in the same place

that made me want to make movies as a child, which is wanting to enthrall, entertain, take people out of their seats to get them involved—through showmanship—in a kind of dialogue with the picture you've made. I love making movies like that. I mean, I'd really still like to do my 'Annie Hall,' but I love making films that are stimulus-response, stimulus-response." [Todd McCarthy, "Sand Castles," *Film Comment*, May-June, 1982.[14]]

1982. "E.T.: The Extra-Terrestrial" produced and directed by Spielberg, and "Poltergeist" produced and partially directed by Spielberg, came out almost simultaneously in the summer of 1982, confirming Spielberg as one of the most successful modern moviemakers. "'Poltergeist' is what I fear and 'E.T.' is what I love. One is about suburban evil and the other is about suburban good. I had different motivations in both instances: in 'Poltergeist,' I wanted to terrify and I also wanted to amuse—I tried to mix the laughs and screams together. 'Poltergeist' is the darker side of my nature—it's me when I was scaring my younger sisters half to death when we were growing up—and 'E.T.' is my optimism about the future and my optimism about what it was like to grow up in Arizona and New Jersey."[6]

"I essentially wrote the idea [for 'E.T.']. I was on location with Harrison [Ford] and Harrison's lady, Melissa Mathison, who had co-written 'The Black Stallion' and 'Escape Artist.'

(From the movie "Raiders of the Lost Ark," starring Harrison Ford. Directed by Steven Spielberg. Released by Paramount Pictures, 1981).

She was working on another project. I kept thinking about 'E.T.' and where the story was going, and I asked Melissa if she would care to sit with me and let me test this on her.

"So we sat down, and I told her the story, and she wept. I thought, 'Gee, she has a tear in her eye. Was it the way I told the story? Was it my performance or was it the story?' And I realized that it was not my performance at all; so I asked Melissa if she would write it. She said absolutely, and dropped everything. We began working on the outline right in the middle of the Sahara Desert. When we returned to civilization, Melissa wrote the screenplay in about ten weeks."[14]

"Melissa is 80% heart and 20% story logic. It took her sensitivity and my know-how to make 'E.T.' Besides, I work better with women. I claim no profound understanding of women, but have an agreeable faith in them."[5]

Said Mathison: "None of us is afraid to tell Steven he is wrong. He's a softy, as big a sap as anyone. But he rarely lets that show in his movies. He kept fretting that E.T. was too soft, until finally he stopped worrying about pleasing the men in the audience."[5]

Spielberg admits: "I've always wanted to do something about kids because *I'm* still a kid. I'm still waiting to get out of my Peter Pan shoes and into my loafers. I think it's easier for me to have a complete conversation from Pac-Man to exobiology with an 11-year-old than it is to sit down with an adult and discuss Nietzsche and the Falklands. Why? I guess because I'm probably socially irresponsible and way down deep I don't want to look the world in the eye. Actually, I don't mind looking the world in the eye, as long as there's a movie camera between us.

"I always thought of the adult world as being symbolized by tall people who cast giant shadows, people who don't think like kids, but think like professionals. That's dangerous—they might understand E.T. biologically and scientifically, but they'd never ever understand that he had a heart.

"'E.T.' really expresses how I feel this year about a lot of things. Five years ago, I think I would probably have been too embarrassed about what people might think of me to make 'E.T.' or even respond to an idea like this. I had to essentially get over my fear of running through the world naked and say, 'take me or leave me.' I guess my priorities have shifted over the last half a decade, and in a nice way I think it's come back around through my films. That's what I mean about running around naked for the first time—I'm saying I'm going to deal with people, with what makes them happy and what makes them cry."[6]

Referring to the creature in "E.T." which cost 1.5 million dollars to make, Spielberg noted: "He's fat and he's not pretty. I really wanted E.T. to sneak up on you—not in the easy way

(From the movie "1941," starring Penny Marshall, Dan Aykroyd, and John Belushi. Directed by Steven Spielberg. Copyright © 1979 by Universal City Studios, Inc.)

(From the movie "Poltergeist," starring Heather O'Rourke. This science-fiction horror film was produced by Spielberg who also collaborated on the screenplay. Copyright © 1982 by Metro-Goldwyn-Mayer Film Co.)

of an F.A.O. Schwarz doll on the shelf. The story is the beauty of his character." [Charles Michener, "A Summer Double Punch," *Newsweek,* May 31, 1982.[15]]

"I wanted a creature that only a mother could love. I didn't want him to be sublime or beatific, or there would be no place to go in the relationship."[5]

Spielberg interviewed some 300 children for the principal roles. "Many of them were remarkable, but they weren't real. They thought before they felt. Then, just a few weeks before we were to start shooting, Henry Thomas walked in. He gave a dreadful reading. I could see he was petrified. But when I asked him to improvise a scene with our casting director, he transformed immediately into Elliott. He can act and react. He's gifted and malleable. He gave an incredible controlled performance."[5]

"I felt the best way to work with Henry in 'E.T.' was not to be his director but his buddy. It was easy because we both like Pac-Man. But Henry is going to be a man at an earlier age than I became one. He's a much better kid than I was.

"... [Children's] inexperience allows the honesty to come out—they *can't* censor. And I *am* a kid. . . ."[15]

"I probably enjoyed myself more making 'E.T.' than I have any movie I've ever made. I like to call it a four-wall experience. The entire movie takes place in a house, in the front yard and back yard. With the exception of the end of the picture, which is rather dramatic and adventurous—where there's a chase and a rescue—the movie really takes place in a home right under the nose of many adults and parents."[14]

"I put myself on the line with this film, and it wasn't easy. But I'm proud of it. It's been a long time since any movie gave me an 'up' cry."[5]

"'Poltergeist' reflects a lot of the fears I had at night—scary shadows that could simply be bunched-up dirty clothes or a shadow like Godzilla cast by the hall light."[15]

"Movies are a reflection of the times we live in, and today's audiences like to react—and react strongly—to what they see. A lot of movies seem to come at you from the screen and wreak havoc on your body. You walk out of the theater vibrating,

(From the movie "E.T.: The Extra-Terrestrial," starring Drew Barrymore. Produced and directed by Steven Spielberg. Released by Universal Pictures, 1982.)

not quite sure what you have experienced until you see it the second or third time.

"My own experience indicates that people want their imaginations stirred, like we tried to do in 'Jaws' and my . . . movie, 'Close Encounters of the Third Kind.'

"I grew interested in that subject matter because I have always been fascinated with the possibility of extraterrestrial contact. More and more people are developing a curiosity about the possibility of life in space, a yearning that the sky isn't as lonely as it seems." [Steven Spielberg, "TV's Impact on the Movies as a Noted Director Sees It," *U.S. News and World Report,* November 21, 1977.[16]]

"*Every* filmmaker is a commanding officer. Even the directors most noteworthy for their rapport and expertise with the actor. I mean, don't kid yourself. [Elia] Kazan was just as much a general on the set of 'On the Waterfront' as Coppola ['Apocalypse Now'] was in the Philippines. It's a war. The only real winners are the public. The only real losers, often, are the filmmakers. It's an unnatural act to make a movie." [Chris Hodenfield, "'1941.' Bombs Away," *Rolling Stone,* January 24, 1980.[17]]

HOBBIES AND OTHER INTERESTS: Audio-visual gimmicks, custard pies, skeet shooting.

FOR MORE INFORMATION SEE: Rochelle Reed, editor, "Steven Spielberg Seminar," *Dialogue on Film,* 1974; *New Yorker,* March 18, 1974, November 28, 1977; Wayne Warga, "Spielberg Keeps His Touch in Transition," *Los Angeles Times,* April 3, 1974; *Newsweek,* April 8, 1974, June 23, 1975, November 21, 1977, June 15, 1981; Tom Zito, "Steven Spielberg, Child of the Movies," *Washington Post,* May 31, 1975; Joseph Gelmis, "Turning Fear Into Fame," *Newsday,* July 6, 1975; *Time,* June 23, 1975, April 16, 1979, May 31, 1982; Jerry Tallmer, "Jawing with Steven Spielberg," *New York Post,* June 25, 1975; *New York,* November 7, 1977; *New York Times,* November 13, 1977, May, 1982; *Current Biography Yearbook 1978; Rolling Stone,* January 26, 1978, July 22, 1982; *Film Comment,* January, 1978, May-June, 1982; Hollis Alpert, editor, "Dialogue on Film: Steven Spielberg," *American Film,* September, 1978; *Film Commentary,* July-August, 1981; *People,* July 20, 1981, August 23, 1982; *Saturday Review,* June 1981; *Commonweal,* August 13, 1982; *Contemporary Literary Criticism,* Volume 20, Gale, 1982; *New York Times Biographical Service,* May, 1982.

E.T. gazing at Spielberg.

(Elliott and E.T. sail over the forest on their way to the landing site in the movie "E.T.: The Extra-Terrestrial," Universal Pictures, 1982.)

STANLEY, Diane 1943-
(Diane Zuromskis)

BRIEF ENTRY: Born December 27, 1943, in Abilene, Tex. An author and illustrator of books for children, Stanley received her B.A. in 1965 from Trinity University. Deciding upon a career in medical illustration, she spent a year of special study in Scotland at Edinburgh College of Art and went on to receive her M.A. from Johns Hopkins University in 1970. From 1970 to 1974, she worked as a free-lance medical illustrator in Boston, Mass. and Norfolk, Va. It was while visiting libraries with her children that Stanley discovered the varied opportunities available in the field of children's book illustration. Desiring to express her creativity along with her artistic ability, she began a career as an illustrator and has since illustrated about ten books for children. She uses mainly soft pastels to produce pictures that are delicate yet lavish in detail.

Her works include her own adapted version of an old verse, *The Farmer in the Dell,* which was a 1979 children's choice in a selection sponsored by the American Reading Association. Another book, *Fiddle-I-Fee,* 1979, was a Junior Literary Guild selection. She also illustrated Giambattista Basile's *Petrosinella: A Neopolitan Rapunzel,* 1981, Jane Yolen's *Sleeping Ugly,* 1981, and *Robin of Bray,* 1982, by Jean and Claudio Marzollo. In addition to her work as an illustrator, she has been a graphic designer for Dell Publishing and served as art director of children's books for G. P. Putnam's Sons from 1978 to 1979. Among her anticipated works is her first self-written and illustrated book, *The Conversation Club,* with publication by Macmillan. She is also illustrating the James Whitcomb Riley poem "Little Orphant Annie" for Putnam, *The Month Brothers,* a Russian folktale, for Morrow, and *The Rainy Day* for Harper. Several of Stanley's books appear under the surname of her first husband, Zuromskis. *Home:* 2120 Tangley, Houston, Tex.

RALPH STEADMAN

STEADMAN, Ralph (Idris) 1936-

PERSONAL: Born May 15, 1936, in Wallasey, Cheshire, England; son of Lionel Raphael (a commercial traveler, now retired) and Gwendoline (Welsh) Steadman; married Sheila Thwaite, September 5, 1959 (divorced, 1972), married Anna Deverson (a teacher), December 8, 1972; children: (first marriage) Suzannah, Genevieve, Theo, Henry; (second marriage) Sadie. *Education:* Attended East Ham Technical College, 1957-64, and London College of Printing and Graphic Arts, 1958-64. *Politics:* "Apolitical." *Religion:* Church of England. *Agent:* Abner Stein, The Vicarage, 54 Studley Villa, Lyndhurst Grove, Camberwell, London SE15 5AH, England; Nat Sobel Associates, Inc., 128 East 56th St., New York, N.Y. 10022.

CAREER: Free-lance cartoonist and illustrator. Early in career worked at odd jobs, including trainee manager, F.W. Woolworth Co., apprentice aircraft engineer, De Havilland Aircraft Co., 1952, cartoonist, Kemsley (Thomson) Newspapers, 1956-59, and pool attendant. Did free-lance work for *Punch, Private Eye,* and *Telegraph* during the 1960s. Exhibited his work at the National Theatre, 1977. *Military service:* Served in the Royal Air Force, 1954-56. *Member:* Chelsea Arts Club. *Awards, honors:* Recipient of Francis Williams Book Illustration Award, 1972, for *Alice in Wonderland;* Gold Award from Designers and Art Directors Association, 1977, for outstanding contribution to illustration; Silver Award from Designers and Art Directors Association, 1977, for outstanding editorial illustra-

tion; recipient of Merit Award and voted Illustrator of the Year, American Institute of Graphic Arts, 1979; Silver Pencil Award (Holland) for children's book illustrations, 1982, for *Inspector Mouse.*

WRITINGS—All self-illustrated: *Ralph Steadman's Jelly Book* (juvenile), Dobson, 1967, published as *Jelly Book,* Scroll Press, 1970; (with Fiona Saint) *The Yellow Flowers,* Dobson, 1968, Southwest Book Service, 1974; *The Little Red Computer* (juvenile), McGraw, 1969; *Still Life with Raspberry; or, The Bumper Book of Steadman* (collected drawings), Rapp & Whiting, 1969; (with Richard Ingrams) *The Tale of Driver Grope* (juvenile), Dobson, 1969; *Dogs Bodies,* Abelard-Schuman, 1970, Grosset, 1977; *Ralph Steadman's Bumper to Bumper Book for Children,* Pan Books, 1973; *Bumper Book of Boobs,* Deutsch, 1973; *Flowers for the Moon,* Nord-Süd, 1974; *Two Donkeys and the Bridge,* Collins, 1974; *The Bridge* (juvenile), Collins (London), 1974, Collins (Cleveland), 1975; *America* (drawings), Straight Arrow Books, 1974; *Cherrywood Cannon* (juvenile; based on story told by Dimitri Sidjanski-Hanhart), Paddington, 1978; *Charlie's Angels: Ralph Steadman's Royal Series,* Steam Press, 1978; *Sigmund Freud,* Paddington, 1979, Simon & Schuster, 1980; *A Leg in the Wind and Other Canine Curses,* Arrow Books, 1982; *Life of Leonardo da Vinci,* J. Cape, 1983; (with Hunter S. Thompson) *The Curse of Lono,* Bantam, 1983.

The early dawn sunlight was shining through the avenue of trees outside the bay windows . . . a nurse came toward him pushing the early morning breakfast cart. ■ (From *Emergency Mouse* by Bernard Stone. Illustrated by Ralph Steadman.)

Illustrator: Frank Dickens, *Fly Away Peter* (juvenile), Dobson, 1963, Scroll Press, 1970; Mischa Damjan (pseudonym of Dimitri Sidjanski-Hanhart), *Das Eichhorn und das Nashörnchen,* Mönchaltorf, 1964, published as *The Big Squirrel and the Little Rhinoceros,* Norton, 1965; Daisy Ashford and Angela Ashford, *Love and Marriage,* Hart-Davis, 1965; D. Ashford, *Where Love Lies Deepest,* Hart-Davis, 1966; M. Damjan, *Die Falschen Flamingos* (juvenile), Mönchaltorf, 1967, published as *The False Flamingoes,* Scroll Press, 1960; Charles L. Dodgson, *Lewis Carroll's Alice in Wonderland* (juvenile), Dobson, 1967, C. N. Potter, 1973; Harold Wilson, *The Thoughts of Chairman Harold* (compiled by Tariq Ali), Gnome Press, 1967; M. Damjan, *The Little Prince and the Tiger Cat,* McGraw, 1968.

Tony Palmer, *Born Under a Bad Sign,* Kimber, 1970; Randolph Stow, *Midnite,* Penguin, 1970; M. Damjan, *Two Cats in America,* Longman Young Books, 1970; Patricia Mann, *150 Careers in Advertising: With Equal Opportunity for Men and Women,* Longman, 1971; Brian Patten, *And Sometimes It Happens,* Steam Press, 1972; John Fuller, *Boys in a Pie: Broadsheet,* Steam Press, 1972; Charles Causley, *Contemporary Poets Set to Music,* Turret Books, 1972; Kurt Baumann, *Der Schlafhund und der Wachhund,* Mönchaltorf, 1972; H. S. Thompson, *Fear and Loathing in Las Vegas: A Savage Journey to the Heart of the American Dream,* Paladin Press, 1972; Ted Hughes, *In the Little Girl's Angel Gaze,* Steam Press, 1972;

Edward Lucie-Smith, *Two Poems of Night* (cover), Turret Books, 1972; E. Lucie-Smith, *The Rabbit,* Turret Books, 1973; John Letts, *A Little Treasury of Limericks Fair and Foul,* Deutsch, 1973; Jane Deverson, *Night Edge* (poems), Bettiscombe Press, 1973; K. Baumann, *Dozy and Hawkeye,* Hutchinson, 1974; Flann O'Brien, *The Poor Mouth—an Beal Bacht: A Bad Story about the Hard Life,* Hart-Davis, 1974.

H. S. Thompson, *Fear and Loathing: On the Campaign Trail,* Allison & Busby, 1975; C. L. Dodgson, *The Hunting of the Snark: An Agony in Eight Fits,* Studio Vista, 1975, C. N. Potter, 1976; Bernard Stone, *Emergency Mouse: A Story* (juvenile), Prentice-Hall, 1978; B. Stone, *Inspector Mouse,* Anderson Press, 1980; T. Hughes, *The Threshold,* Steam Press, 1980; H. S. Thompson, *The Great Shark Hunt* (adult), Paladin, 1980.

Author of frontispiece of *Portfolio Poets* published by Putney, 1978. Also illustrator of covers including *The Common Millionaire* by Robert Heller; *The Best of Myles, The Third Policeman,* and *The Dalkey Archive,* all by Flann O'Brien.

ADAPTATIONS—Filmstrip: "The Bridge" (with cassette), Listening Library, 1976.

SIDELIGHTS: "I am motivated by a need to be noticed and a desire to shock. I started my drawing career more as a cause than a business. I thought I could change the world, but now I realize that it is a hopeless dream. But, I still try. Man is still an idiot with aspiration.

"My biggest work to date and most challenging [is] *Life of Leonardo da Vinci*—drawings of incidents and events in his life which may have conceivably happened just as I drew them. [It is] a humorous/serious attempt to make the man human without denigration."

HOBBIES AND OTHER INTERESTS: Gardening, collecting, writing, fishing, and astronomy.

FOR MORE INFORMATION SEE: Economist, December 23, 1973; *Graphis,* 1973-74; *Book World,* April 3, 1977; *The New Review,* March, 1977; Doris de Montreville and Elizabeth D. Crawford, *Fourth Book of Junior Authors and Illustrators,* H. W. Wilson, 1978; *Listener,* September 27, 1979; *Viz* magazine, No. 5, 1979; *Illustrators,* January/February, 1980.

STEINER-PRAG, Hugo   1880-1945

BRIEF ENTRY: Born in 1880, in Prague, Czechoslovakia; died in 1945. Book designer, illustrator, artist, and teacher. Steiner-Prag was an innovator and master of book design whose distinctive style and philosophy have influenced generations of artists in his field. His impact as an illustrator was felt as early as 1907 when he was summoned to the Leipzig Academy for Book and Graphic Arts as a result of illustrations executed for a Hoffman novel. There he became a full professor at the age of twenty-eight. An instructor in book design in Czechoslovakia and Germany prior to World War I, he gained international renown in 1916 with the publication of his lithographs in Gustaf Meyrink's *The Golem.* In 1918 he became advisor, designer, and illustrator for Propylaen-Verlag, a subsidiary of the House of Ullstein publishers in Germany. In an effort to escape the Nazis during World War II, he traveled to Stockholm where the School of Book and Advertising Artists was founded in his name. From Sweden, he eventually found his way to the United States with the aid of George Macy, founder of the Limited Editions Club for which Steiner-Prag illustrated a number of books, including Shakepeare's *Measure for Measure,* Byron's *Don Juan,* and Moliere's *Tartuffe.*

Steiner-Prag was the founder of the Guild of German Book Artists which, in 1927, sponsored the International Exhibition of Modern Book Arts. The exhibition catalogue is considered by many to be the best reference work on fine books of the 1920s, marking the first time Russian book illustrations, especially those of children's books, were seen by the Western world. Throughout his long and prolific career, he produced more than 1400 books and illustrated more than sixty. He was a firm believer in the fact that book design has both a usefulness and a purpose, that of reflecting a sense of high quality in decorative appeal. In 1981, the Leo Baeck Institute, New York, N.Y., held a commemorative exhibition of Steiner-Prag's work, honoring the 100th anniversary of his birth. *For More Information See:* Richard W. Ellis, *Book Illustration,* Kingsport Press, 1952; *Publishers Weekly,* May 1, 1981.

STOCKTON, Frank R(ichard)   1834-1902

BRIEF ENTRY: Born April 5, 1834, in Philadelphia, Pa.; died of a brain hemorrhage April 16, 1902, in Washington, D.C.

Wood engraver, editor, and author of short stories and novels for children and adults. Known for his humorous and ironic style of writing, Stockton spent several years as a wood engraver before entering the journalistic field as a free-lance short story writer for numerous publications. He served as a staff member on *Hearth and Home,* in 1869, and *Century,* and then as assistant editor on the newly established *Scribner's Monthly* in 1873. From 1873 to 1881, he worked as assistant editor under Mary Mapes Dodge on *St. Nicholas* while at the same time cultivating his career as a writer. Stockton's first publications were for children, including *Ting-A-Ling,* 1870, *Round-About Rambles in Lands of Fact and Fancy,* 1872, *What Might Have Been Expected,* 1874, and *Tales Out of School,* 1876.

In 1879 he published a humorous adult novel, *Rudder Grange,* which met with such success that it was later followed by two sequels, *The Rudder Grangers Abroad,* 1891, and *Pomona's Travels,* 1894. Following the publication of *Rudder Grange,* he turned more toward writing for an older audience although he continued to produce works for children. One of his most humorous novels is *The Casting Away of Mrs. Lecks and Mrs. Aleshine,* published in 1886. A forerunner of O. Henry, Stockton is widely remembered for his short story "The Lady, or the Tiger?" which utilizes the technique of a trick ending to cause a dilemma for the reader. The story created a sensation when it first appeared in the November, 1882 edition of *Century,* and was subsequently adapted into several motion pictures and an operetta. *Residence:* Harper's Ferry, W.Va. *For More Information See: The Junior Book of Authors,* H. W. Wilson, 1934; Martin I. Griffin, *Frank R. Stockton: A Critical Biography,* Kennikat, 1939, reprinted, 1965; Elizabeth R. Montgomery, *Story Behind Great Stories,* McBride, 1947; Laura Benét, *Famous American Humorists,* Dodd, 1959; Benét, *Famous Storytellers for Young People,* Dodd, 1968.

STOKES, Olivia Pearl   1916-

PERSONAL: Born January 11, 1916, in Middlesex, N.C.; daughter of William Harmon and Bessie (Thomas) Stokes. *Education:* New York University, B.S., 1947, M.S., 1948; Columbia University, Ed.D., 1952. *Home:* 2050 Seward Ave., Bronx, N.Y. 10473. *Office:* The G.H.C. Guidance Center, Inc., 180 West 135th St., New York, N.Y. 10030.

CAREER: Young Women's Christian Association, Uptown Branch, New York City, contact interviewer, 1935-41; Baptist Educational Center, New York City, director, 1941-52; Girl Scouts of America, New York City, program consultant, 1952; Massachusetts Council of Churches, Boston, director of department of religious education, 1953-66; National Council of Churches of Christ in the U.S.A., New York City, staff associate in urban education, Division of Christian Education, 1966-73, consultant to Education and Ministry Division, 1975-76, developed Black Curriculum Resource Center; Herbert H. Lehman College of the City University of New York, New York City, associate professor of education, 1973-76, chairperson for development of a multi-ethnic, multi-cultural teacher education program, developed a graduate teacher education study abroad-ethnic-heritage-African program in conjunction with five Nigerian universities; educational consultant, 1976—.

New York University, New York, N.Y., associate professor, 1978—; The G.H.C. Guidance Center, Inc., New York, N.Y., executive director, 1979—. Ordained minister, American Baptist Church. Adjunct professor, City College of the City of New York, 1970-71, Colgate Rochester and Andover Newton Theological Seminary, 1973-76. Leader of delegates to White

OLIVIA PEARL STOKES

House Conference on Education, 1955, and Youth, 1960, 1970. Consultant, Princeton and Drew Theological Seminaries, Roxbury-North Dorchester Comprehensive Health Center (Boston), and Columbia University Sickle Cell Comprehensive Health Center, 1974-77. Lecturer for African Studies Association, Educational Studies Association, National Association for Study of Afro-American Life and History, 1965-74. Trustee, Berea College (Berea, Ky.). Member of the board, Bronx Council of the Arts; also member of World Council Ecumenical Study Program, Bossey, Switzerland, 1978-80.

Volunteer posts as secretary with National Council of Churches: Department of Racial and Cultural Relations, 1950-60, program board, Division of Christian Education, 1962-74, and Department of Educational Development, 1964-66.

MEMBER: National Education Association, American Educational Studies Association, American Association for Higher Education, Adult Education Association, American Federation of Teachers, National Association for Public and Continuing Adult Education (life member), Council of National Organizations for Adult Education (first vice-president, 1969-71), Religious Education U.S.A., American Association of University Professors, American Association of University Women, Afro-American Association for the Study of Life and History, African-American Institute's Educators to Africa Association,

National Association for the Advancement of Colored People (life member), National Council of Negro Women, National Council of Women of the United States, Delta Kappa Delta, Pi Lambda Theta, Alpha Kappa Delta, Delta Sigma Theta, League of Women Voters, Friends of City University and Bronx Community College.

AWARDS, HONORS: Guidance citation, Vocational Guidance Center (New York City), 1964; Christian Education Leadership Tribute from Massachusetts Council of Churches, 1966; Leadership Award from the National Urban League, 1966; Reconciliation Award of Ministerial Interfaith Association, 1969; Mary McLeod Bethune Bicentennial Achievement Award from the National Council of Negro Women, 1975, 1976; certificate of appreciation, Committee on Social Justice, National Association for Public and Adult Education, 1975; Fulbright-Hays fellowship, 1976; International Award from Business and Professional Women's Association, 1979.

WRITINGS—Juvenile, except as noted: *Why the Spider Lives in Corners: African Facts and Fun*, edited by Louise Crane, Friendship, 1971; *The Beauty of Being Black: Folktales, Poems, and Art from Africa*, edited by L. Crane, Friendship, 1971; (contributor) *If Teaching Is Your Job* (adult), National Baptist Publishing Board of America, 1974. Also contributor to a book on values published by United Presbyterian Program Agency. Contributor to religious education journals. Special issue editor, *Church Woman*, November, 1969; member of editorial board, *Colloquy*, 1969-71; special issue editor, *Spectrum*, July-August, 1971.

WORK IN PROGRESS: Emerging Role of African Women; a study on the life of Roland Hayes, an Afro-American tenor.

SIDELIGHTS: Stokes has visited Africa nineteen times since 1958 for educational seminars and as leader of the World Christian Education Institute in Nairobi in 1967. In 1976, she led sixteen graduate students in a six-week study of the Yourba civilization at the University of Ife and University of Ibadan, Nigeria. She has also traveled in a number of countries of Asia, Europe, and Central America.

In the course of her travels, Stokes has acquired an extensive collection of African art which has had two major exhibits in New York City galleries. "Nearly all African art is religious growing out of African traditional religions; thus African art is of a religio-mythological nature. The tribal and social structure is marked by a complex of authority; kings, secret societies, medicine men, etc. Thus every act in the life of the people is expressed in a ritual. And every rite has its sculptured image appropriate for the ceremonial occasions. . . . Two of the striking characteristics of African art are its feeling for the material and the fact that its carvings are done out of the mass of ivory, wood, bronze, and clay. Through these media, African artists express the clan's outlook on the world, combined with the intensity of the people's religious feelings."

Stokes was one of seventy black women included in a book that Radcliff College compiled as part of their "Oral History of Black Women, 1980-1982" program.

HOBBIES AND OTHER INTERESTS: Plants, music appreciation, collecting fine art and international dolls.

STONG, Phil(ip Duffield) 1899-1957

PERSONAL: Born January 27, 1899, in Keosauqua, Iowa; died April 26, 1957, in Washington, Conn.; buried in Keosauqua, Iowa; son of Benjamin J. (a merchant) and Ada Evesta (Duffield) Stong; married Virginia Maude Swain (a newspaper reporter), 1925. *Education:* Drake University, A.B., 1919; graduate study, Columbia University, 1920-21, and University of Kansas, 1923-24. *Politics:* Independent. *Home:* Washington, Conn.

CAREER: Novelist and journalist. Began as teacher of debating and journalism and athletic director in Minnesota and Kansas high schools, 1919-23; editorial writer for the Des Moines *Register* and instructor in journalism at Drake University, 1923-25; journalist in New York City, variously employed by the Associated Press, North American Newspaper Alliance, *Liberty, Editor and Publisher,* and the New York *World,* 1925-31; full-time creative writer, beginning 1931. *Member:* Society of American Historians, American Geographical Society (fellow), Masons (32nd degree; Knight Templar), P.E.N., Authors' Club (president, 1935-56). *Awards, honors:* Runner-up for the Newbery Medal, 1936, for *Honk, the Moose; New York Herald Tribune* Spring Festival Award, 1939, for *The Hired Man's Elephant;* Litt.D., Parsons College, 1939; LL.D., Drake University, 1947.

*WRITINGS—*For children: *Farm Boy: A Hunt for Indian Treasure* (illustrated by Kurt Wiese), Doubleday, Doran, 1934; *Honk, the Moose* (illustrated by Wiese), Dodd, 1935, reprinted, 1966; *No-Stitch, the Hound* (illustrated by Wiese), Dodd, 1936; *High Water* (illustrated by Wiese), Dodd, 1937; *Edgar, the 7:58* (illustrated by Lois Lenski), Farrar & Rinehart, 1938;

PHIL STONG

Young Settler (illustrated by Wiese), Dodd, 1938; *The Hired Man's Elephant* (illustrated by Doris Lee), Dodd, 1939; *Cowhand Goes to Town* (illustrated by Wiese), Dodd, 1939.

Captain Kidd's Cow (illustrated by Wiese), Dodd, 1941; *Way Down Cellar* (illustrated by Wiese), Dodd, 1942; *Missouri Canary* (illustrated by Wiese), Dodd, 1943; *Censored, the Goat* (illustrated by Wiese), Dodd, 1945; *Positive Pete!* (illustrated by Wiese), Dodd, 1947; *The Prince and the Porker* (illustrated by Wiese), Dodd, 1950; *Hirum, the Hillbilly* (illustrated by Wiese), Dodd, 1951; *A Beast Called an Elephant* (illustrated by Wiese), Dodd, 1955; *Mike: The Story of a Young Circus Acrobat,* Dodd, 1957; *Phil Stong's Big Book* (illustrated by Wiese), Dodd, 1961 (contains *Farm Boy, High Water,* and *No Stitch, the Hound*).

Adult novels, except as noted: *State Fair,* Century, 1932, reprinted, Tom Stacey Reprints, 1972; *Stranger's Return,* Harcourt, 1933; *Village Tale,* Harcourt, 1934; *The Farmer in the Dell,* Harcourt, 1935; *Week-End,* Harcourt, 1935; *Career,* Harcourt, 1936; *The Rebellion of Lennie Barlow,* Farrar & Rinehart, 1937; *Buckskin Breeches,* Farrar & Rinehart, 1937; *The Long Lane,* Farrar & Rinehart, 1939; *Ivanhoe Keeler,* Farrar & Rinehart, 1939; *The Princess,* Farrar & Rinehart, 1941 (also published as *Miss Edeson,* 1941); (editor and author of introduction) *The Other Worlds* (short story collection), Funk, 1941 (also published as *Twenty-Five Stories of Mystery and Imagination,* Garden City Publishing, 1942); *The Iron Mountain,* Farrar & Rinehart, 1942; *One Destiny,* Reynal & Hitchock, 1942; *Jessamy John,* Doubleday, 1947; *Forty Pounds of Gold* (illustrated by Arthur Shilstone), Doubleday, 1951; *Return in August* (sequel to *State Fair*), Doubleday, 1953; *Mississippi Pilot: With Mark Twain on the Great River,* Doubleday, 1954; *Blizzard,* Doubleday, 1955; *Adventures of "Horse" Barnsby,* Doubleday, 1956; *Gold in Them Hills: Being an Irreverent History of the Great 1849 Gold Rush,* Doubleday, 1957.

(From *The Hired Man's Elephant* by Phil Stong. Illustrated by Doris Lee.)

And he ate so much that he went to sleep. He knew he had gone to sleep because he had several dreams about People, but, young as he was—he had just reached his full growth—he knew they were just dreams and only honked at them once or twice. ■ (From *Honk the Moose* by Phil Stong. Illustrated by Kurt Wiese.)

Nonfiction: (Author of text) *County Fair* (book of photographs by Josephine von Miklos and others), Stackpole Sons, 1938; *Horses and Americans* (illustrated by Wiese), Stokes, 1939; *Hawkeyes: A Biography of the State of Iowa,* Dodd, 1940; *If School Keeps* (autobiography), Stokes, 1940; *Marta of Muscovy: The Fabulous Life of Russia's First Empress,* Doubleday, Doran, 1945.

ADAPTATIONS—Motion pictures: ''State Fair,'' (starring Will Rogers, Janet Gaynor, Lew Ayers; directed by Henry King), Fox Film, 1933; ''Farmer in the Dell,'' RKO Radio Pictures, Inc., 1936; ''Career,'' RKO, 1939; ''State Fair,'' (musical; starring Jeanne Crain, Dana Andrews, Charles Winninger; music by Richard Rodgers and Oscar Hammerstein II, directed

by Walter Lang), Twentieth Century-Fox Film, 1945; ''State Fair,'' (starring Pat Boone, Ann Margaret, Bobby Darin, Alice Faye, Tom Ewell; directed by José Ferrer), Twentieth Century-Fox Film, 1962.

Recordings: ''State Fair,'' starring Ann Blyth, American Forces Radio and Television Service, 1974.

SIDELIGHTS: **January 27, 1899.** Born in Keosauqua, Iowa. ''On a September day in 1904 my mother kissed me goodby, and I went stumbling off with a slate, a 'Big Chief' tablet and a ten-cent pencil-box to the old two-storey brick school on the hill. Father had moved to town from the farm particularly for the sake of my education, and except for Brown Manning and

George ('Pot') Kittle, who were across-the-street neighbors, I was as much a stranger as if I had just dropped in from Mars.

"Mother had taught me to read in my third year; I was a consummate introvert and a sissy of high degree—an oldest child brought up in a virtually boyless village, till we moved to town—but my literary abilities frequently saved my life from the large roughnecks of the hooky-playing classes.

"Dad had run a village store and I had the fundamentals of very simple mathematics; I watched the Second Grade struggling with short division with profound contempt. . . .

"This was the day of the Four R's, Reading, Writing, 'Rithmetic and Writhing. The teacher of the Fifth and Sixth Grades had a notable paddle with holes bored in it; the Superintendent of the whole school had a section of rubber hose; anywhere from the Third Grade up one might hear the fateful command, 'Go out and get me a switch.' It was like making Joan of Arc furnish her own fuel.

". . . I took my first seven grades in a year under par and spent the whole time in a good deal of suffering, for various reasons. As if I had not already been sufficiently introverted, I spent my fourth school year in a state of almost total deafness without having sense enough to realize that there was anything wrong with me. The world about me had curious gaps in its causes and effects; somebody would punch me in the eye without my knowing of any prior conversation. We used the 'head-mark' system—a very stupid one; a sure breeder of inferiority and rebellion at one end of the 'turn-down-line' and of stupid egotism at the other—and I who had been running win, place and show for three years, suddenly found myself turned down regularly without any audible question having been addressed to me.

"My consummate idiocy kept me from associating these unanticipated disasters with their cause and naturally made me more egocentric than ever, and bitter at an unpredictable universe. The fortunate revelation came through my being yanked by the collar up on the podium of the Third Room and placed in a seat of disgrace and later 'kept after school.'

"What I had not suspected for myself, a good teacher, Mary Day, was able to figure out for me in the subsequent hour. She had spoken to me several times during the day and I had paid no attention and kept on with whatever crime I was committing—drawing in one of my books, probably, for 'whispering' was out as a sport as far as I was concerned. I had never been defiant because I was one of the leading cowards

(From the movie "Farmer in the Dell," starring Jean Parker. Copyright 1936 by RKO Radio Pictures, Inc.)

(From the movie "State Fair," starring Janet Gaynor and Will Rogers. Copyright 1933 by Fox Film Corp.)

of my time; my grades had been consistently high till I had suddenly quit answering questions completely. Miss Day asked me if I were hard of hearing; I did not know that I was but it sounded like as good a way out as any so I answered with a fifty-cent word, 'Slightly.'

"My parents had suspected this, too, but the phases of even pre-adolescent childhood are such that they had waited awhile to see if this sudden moodiness might not pass. Consulted by Miss Day they took me to a specialist, who removed some large adenoids. I heard normally as soon as I came out from under the ether, but I had had a hell of a year.

"Another misfortune was physical precociousness. Clear up to late adolescence my size kept well ahead of my strength; when I was eight I was an easy scalp for smaller and stronger ten-year-olds; when I was ten, kids who were sprouting fuzz on their lips knocked my block off and were applauded because I was bigger than they were; up to my high-school years I could be and was regularly whipped by any number of young pickles whom I could have handled in lots of three five years later. That didn't do me any good while the pugilists of the Second, Third, Fourth, Fifth, Sixth and Seventh Grades were using me regularly as an emblem of glory.

"The psychological factors in the maladjustment are too painful to discuss. My fortuitous facility at reading made most school subjects, especially in the grades, comparatively and sometimes ridiculously simple for me, so that I spent about equal amounts of time in whining about how I lost a fight and bragging about how I made a headmark. The circumstances of my first five years, too, had been such that my mother and an easygoing cousin had been almost my only playmates. I did, and still do, throw with the inept, overhand gesture of a woman; I had to be taught every mass game and, what was more important, every regulation of juvenile mass behavior, and almost every detail of juvenile psychology.

"College was not much of a factor in my childhood and even youth. It was extraordinary education reserved for prospective lawyers, doctors, and preachers. My family had more educational background than the average; but almost to the day of my graduation from high school there was a serious question about whether I should be sent on to college or down to a jobbing house which had promised Father to make a new Marshall Field or John Wanamaker of me." [Phil Stong, *If School Keeps*, Frederick A. Stokes, 1940.[1]]

(From the movie "State Fair," starring Jeanne Crain and Dana Andrews. Copyright 1945 by Twentieth Century Fox-Film Corp.)

1915. "I began at Drake University with an eagerness that amounted to avidity. I wanted to acquire Greek, Philosophy, Chemistry, French, and Short Story. Astronomy, Calculus, and College Physics, I regretfully recognized, were beyond me because of my helplessness in mathematics. I accepted this fact with resignation—few people have ever beaten me in a long run at poker, and no person has ever lost to me at chess, though I like the game almost as much as poker. A man had best take his mind the way he finds it, and enjoy whatever uses there are in it."[1]

1919. Graduated from Duke University. ". . . We all assembled with our relatives in the University Christian Church, to receive the document which attested that we were bachelors of this and that; I have never seen my scroll since that time but I guess that somebody has it somewhere. I have had more jobs than most B.A.'s—I suppose that I have been fired from more jobs than most B.A.'s have held—but no one ever wanted to see my diploma and except for my teaching years no one was ever very curious about whether I had ever been to college, let alone whether I had a degree.

"The question is whether I got more practice going through the academic routine than I would have had raising bunions for the newspaper. The answer is doubtful—some of my courses were invaluable for my purposes and would not have been supplied in the ordinary fun of reportorial work; on the other hand, there was a lot of waste time that would have been much better spent in the newspaper curriculum: Night Police, City Hall, General Feature, State House, the Rim, Make-Up, Editorials and so on. By eliminating twenty or thirty useless term hours from my studies, I could have had a year or so of this kind of study and experience. . . .

"The days of easy and lucrative summer jobs had crashed with the War and I went home for the summer to try to find a teaching job—which was all I was fit for with a general education in the arts—and to work desperately at getting my writing into some sort of salable shape. I was no Marlowe or Chatterton or Bryant; fortunately, I was aware of this—Professor Smith had been quite specific on the subject of the literature written by twenty-year-old children. I hammered away on my old Oliver, which weighed a little less than a parlor grand piano and operated with a touch like that of a carillon. Occasionally I got odd jobs on farms, but I was chiefly concerned about getting a steady winter income. I wanted to go to New York, study short story and see the town.

(From the musical film "State Fair," starring Pat Boone. Copyright © 1962 by Twentieth Century-Fox.)

". . . I offered my splendid talents to American education again and signed with Biwabik High School, in Minnesota. . . .

"A good teacher does not teach children; he discusses with them the matters on which it is conceded he has an advantage; an advantage which they are supposed to eliminate, in some part, during their course. In all other matters all men are equal, and the sooner that equality is established the more agreeable the relations between class and preceptor are likely to be.

"I did odd jobs again that summer after my return to Iowa in late July; early in September I went to New York to get a little of the feel of the town before I entered for an M.A. at Columbia. . . .

"There were three good courses in my whole Master's course: Peter Trent on the Georgian satirists, and those of Queen Anne's time; Carl Van Doren, with lucid and amusing and even exciting comments on American literature; Dorothy Scarborough, the backstop of the Short Story course, with her fine critical method and gentle soul—God rest it.

"I spent about eight hundred dollars with the University and I got nothing at all from it, aside from the instruction of the

persons mentioned and the use of the gymnasium. It was money well spent and I have no objection, but I presently began to drop all classes except Van Doren's and Trent's.

"As the year went on I neglected the place more and more, and took my education from the Brooklyn docks, where a friend of mine was a paymaster of stevedores, and a club, where I had managed an appointment as Night Superintendent of Service, and my casual wanderings around New York.

"It is appalling to consider the pedantry and misinformation and stodginess that can come off of the belts of a graduate school in the course of nine months. The system was completely formalized—I say nothing against the undergraduate school because I know nothing about it—but the graduate school wearily passed out dreary lectures (with exceptions noted) in order to supply high-school principals and small-college instructors with documents attesting that they were Masters or Doctors of Arts because they had heard of John Skelton and John Donne.

"I learned a great deal more about what I wanted to know—writing—from Harry Stephen Keeler, the editor of *Ten Story Book*, that year than I did from my eight-hundred-dollar investment; in addition to his extravagantly generous critiques, H.S.K. frequently bought a story. The rate was flat, six dollars a story, long or short, good or bad, but it is wonderful how six dollars will fit into a student budget at times. I did him a trick which he has undoubtedly forgotten, but which I have not forgotten possibly on account of my hypertrophied capacity for remorse. He rejected a story but sent a text on possible repairs that was about half the length of the story.

"I made the repairs and then, like a dirty dog, sent it to *Top-Notch*, a Street and Smith magazine which paid a good deal more than six dollars. They rejected it. I thought it over and decided that *Top-Notch* ought to buy it. They rejected it again. This filled me with righteous anger because it was obviously a story that they ought to buy. I sent it back by return mail and with their famous and commendable promptness they sent me forty dollars within the week. I should have sent this to Keeler for his document on the reconstruction of the story, but I bought a planked steak and my first bottle of champagne instead.

"This seemed to me to be the consummation of my academic career, so I did not bother any more about classes or studies but gave my time to seeing New York. I still believe that this was the best thing to do in the circumstances but not for the reason I gave myself; to me it was evident that since I had sold a story for forty dollars I was well launched on a writing career. It was ten years before I sold any more fiction for as much as forty dollars.

"Some day some school will give credit for a course in New York museums, theaters and libraries. I certainly profited more from them than I could have from the sterile halls of King's College, though it did have a useful gymnasium and pool which I visited two or three times a week."[1]

1921. Returned to teaching. ". . . I was considerably surprised when the Board of Neodesha, Kansas, offered me $2100 a term to utter a few things about English, coach debate and run the school publications. . . .

". . . I had exerted a small effort at the last moment to earn an M.A., for completely practical reasons, and failed; I was twenty-two and down to my last hundred dollars, and I was not sufficiently sophisticated to regard my parents' goods as my own; no magazine had sent me another forty dollars after the first strike; I doubted that I had the stability or background to be a good teacher; I couldn't see a good gutter in any direction."[1]

Taught for approximately another four years. "These were pleasant years, but I knew that a change must come. I was teaching about as well as I could and though the school was generous with me in the matter of salary increases, I was near the end of my string.

". . . I subsequently accepted twenty dollars a week at newspaper work in preference to twice or three times that amount for teaching.

"No one should ever teach for more than four or five consecutive years. It was after two and half years of Neodesha and another year and a half of Drake that I discovered that I was becoming authoritative and that this trait was slowing my own education to what might very easily become a dead halt. I pulled out hastily and ever since then I have been learning things with hot intensity, for the night cometh and I have capacious curiosities."[1]

1925-1931. Worked for various newspapers and magazines in New York City. The success of his first novel, *State Fair*, took him to Hollywood to work with Will Rogers, the famous cowboy, in a movie version of this work.

1931. Became a full-time writer. Stong drew upon his Iowa farm background for his stories. "When I was in college there was a plague of midwest 'regional' writing in which the principal characters were all committing suicide with sheep-dip or being eaten by the hogs. This did not seem reasonable to me in view of my early farm experiences when we ate the hogs and virtually everything else, but not sheep-dip. It was a fairly full life, and I had vague ideas of correcting the 'regional' impression. Since then I have had a consciousness of the horrors that always stalk the world and of the duty of a man to enjoy as much pleasantry and pleasure as he can in his brief time." [Harry R. Warfel, *American Novelists of Today*, American Book Co., 1951.[2]]

Due to the popularity of one of Stong's children's stories, *Honk: The Moose*, the phrase "just a moose" became a popular byword for quite some time. "Novel writing is necessarily almost wholly self-taught; there is a first essential. . . . 'You have the proper chromosomes, or you haven't' . . . good steady practice, reflection, self-criticism and any obtainable borrowed criticism, and above all things a perceptive and, if possible, active life will not hurt any hopeful writer. Too many people break their hearts and annoy professional writers by working on the pure chromosome theory. It is quite true that once in a blue moon some one turns up who writes without any preliminary labor—any *apparent* preliminary labor, for no one can say what reading, reflection and instinctive appreciation of design may lie behind these apparently spontaneous performances.

"Literature is supposed to look better in print; my stories, when they are baldly and brutally represented in print usually give me indigestion, and yet you have to keep them on your stomach till you feel just what feature of the dish made you sick. It is the only way to keep from being sicker still the next time.

"I suppose there are a million people in the United States who write, try to write or plan to write. I would guess that ninety-nine and a fraction percent of them come to grief through impatience and inapplication, amounting to indolence, as much as they do through straight fundamental incapacity. . . ."[1]

April 26, 1967. Collapsed and died of a heart attack in the workroom of his home in Washington, Connecticut.

FOR MORE INFORMATION SEE: Phil Stong, *If School Keeps*, Stokes, 1940; Elizabeth R. Montgomery, *Story behind Modern Books*, Dodd, 1949; Harry R. Warfel, *American Novelists of Today*, American Book Co., 1951; *Junior Authors*, Wilson, 1963; D. L. Kirkpatrick, editor, *Twentieth Century Children's Writers*, St. Martin's, 1978.

Obituaries: New York Times, April 27, 1957; *Newsweek*, May 6, 1957; *Publishers Weekly*, May 6, 1957; *Wilson Library Bulletin*, June, 1957; *Britannica Book of the Year 1958*.

The love of learning, the sequestered nooks,
And all the sweet serenity of books.
         —Henry Wadsworth Longfellow

STUART-CLARK, Christopher   1940-

PERSONAL: Born December 1, 1940, in Steyning, Sussex, England; son of Arthur (a schoolmaster) and Peggy (Anthony) Stuart-Clark; married Jill Price, April 15, 1967; children: Michael Philip, Nicola Clare. *Education:* Attended Tonbridge School, 1954-59; Pembroke College, Cambridge, B.A., 1963, M.A., 1967. *Religion:* Church of England. *Home:* 26 Bardwell Rd., Oxford OX2 6SR, England. *Office:* Dragon School, Oxford OX2 6SS, England.

CAREER: Cheam School, Newbury, Berkshire, England, teacher, 1963-68; Dragon School, Oxford, teacher of senior English, head of classics, housemaster, 1968—. *Member:* Schools Council of the United Kingdom, National Association for Gifted Children.

WRITINGS—For young people; editor with Michael Harrison: *The New Dragon Book of Verse,* Oxford University Press, 1977; *Poems,* Oxford University Press, 1980; *Poems 2,* Oxford University Press, 1980; *Narrative Poems,* Oxford University Press, 1981; *The Oxford Book of Christmas Poems,* Oxford University Press, 1983.

WORK IN PROGRESS: An anthology of prose and poetry on the theme of Noah's Ark, with Michael Harrison, to be published by Oxford University Press.

SIDELIGHTS: "Our aim with the poetry anthologies has been to present a mixture of modern and earlier poetry in an attractive combination to children of nine to fifteen years. *Poems* and *Poems 2* present anthologies to the pupils without any comment, while the teacher's books contain suggestions for follow-up work of a centripetal rather than centrifugal nature. Thus, we avoid having pupils regard poems as writing 'with questions on it afterwards.'

"*The New Dragon Book of Verse* and *Narrative Poems* are both anthologies of new and early poems, chosen by both of us from our experiences of teaching English to nine-to-thirteen-year-old children. The illustrations, which in both books were commissioned from artists for the book, aim to give further stimulus to the child's imagination."

(From the "War," in *The New Dragon Book of Verse,* edited by Michael Harrison and Christopher Stuart-Clark. Illustrated by Johnny Ross.)

CHRISTOPHER STUART-CLARK

TAYLOR, Mark 1927-

PERSONAL: Born August 15, 1927, in Linden, Mich.; *Education:* Attended Tufts College (now Tufts University), 1945-47; University of Michigan, B.A., 1950, M.A.L.S., 1952; University of Southern California, M.S., 1970, Ph.D., 1976. *Residence:* Los Angeles, Calif. *Agent:* Jane Jordan Browne, Multimedia Product Development, Inc., Room 828, Fine Arts Building, 410 South Michigan Ave., Chicago, Ill. 60605.

CAREER: University of Michigan Elementary School, Ann Arbor, children's librarian, 1950-56; University of Michigan Broadcasting Service, Ann Arbor, radio producer and performer, "Tales of a Talking Stone," 1950-56, and "Books and Around," 1952-56; Dayton and Montgomery County Public Library, Dayton, Ohio, head of young adult services, 1957-60; University of Southern California, Los Angeles, professor of library science, 1960-69; Columbia Broadcasting System, Inc., Hollywood, Calif., television producer and performer, "Tell It Again, Children," 1962-64; *Los Angeles Times,* Los Angeles, Calif., children's book columnist, 1962-70; free-lance writer, lecturer, counselor, and literary, library, and educational consultant, 1970—. Storyteller and balladeer, 1950—; guest lecturer and instructor at San Francisco State University, the University of Nebraska, Wittenberg University, and the University of California at Berkeley, Irvine, Los Angeles, Riverside and numerous private colleges; conductor of workshops and seminars for professional groups and associations such as the Association of Childhood Education, The Children's Book Council, and the Society of Children's Book Writers; author-in-residence for various school districts all over the U.S., in-

cluding Boston, Atlanta, Dallas, Seattle, Sacramento, Santa Barbara, San Diego, and Fresno.

MEMBER: P.E.N. International, International Reading Association, Association of Childhood Education International, National Council of Teachers of English, American Library Association, ASCAP, California Library Association, Ohio Library Association, Michigan Library Association, Society of Children's Book Writers, Southern California Council on Literature for Children and Young People (founding member; past vice-president), American Federation of Television and Radio Artists, American Federation of Musicians, American Institute of Graphic Arts, International Folk Music Council, Harp Society of America, Computer-Using Educators. *Awards, honors:* Dutton-Macrae Award for distinguished library work with children and young people, 1956; the National Association for Better Radio and Television cited "Tell It Again, Children" as the best children's television series of 1963-64; the *Library Journal* cited *The Bold Fisherman* as one of the forty best books of the year, 1967; National Defense Education Act fellowship for graduate study in media, 1969-71; Newbery Award consideration for *Jennie Jenkins,* 1975; the Southern California Council on Literature for Children and Young People recognized the "Henry" series as a significant contribution of excellence, 1976.

WRITINGS—All for young people: *Henry, the Explorer* (illustrated by Graham Booth; Junior Literary Guild selection), Atheneum, 1966; *The Bold Fisherman* (illustrated by G. Booth), Golden Gate Junior Books, 1967; *A Time for Flowers* (illustrated by G. Booth), Golden Gate Junior Books, 1967; *Henry Explores the Jungle* (illustrated by G. Booth; Junior Literary Guild selection), Atheneum, 1968; *Composition Through Literature: Understanding Your Language* (textbooks), three volumes, American Book Co., 1968; *The Old Woman and the Pedlar* (illustrated by G. Booth), Golden Gate Junior Books, 1969; *Bobby Shafto's Gone to Sea* (illustrated by G. Booth), Golden Gate Junior Books, 1970; *Old Blue, You Good Dog, You* (illustrated by Gene Holtan), Golden Gate Junior Books, 1970; (compiler with May H. Arbuthnot) *Time for Old Magic,* Scott, Foresman, 1970; *Wind in My Hand,* Golden Gate Junior Books, 1970.

The Fisherman and the Goblet: A Vietnamese Folk Talk (illustrated by Taro Yashima), Golden Gate Junior Books, 1971; *Lamb, Said the Lion, I Am Here* (illustrated by Anne Siberell), Golden Gate Junior Books, 1971; (compiler with Arbuthnot) *Time for New Magic,* Scott, Foresman, 1971; *Henry, the Castaway* (illustrated by G. Booth; Junior Literary Guild selection), Atheneum, 1972; *The Wind's Child* (illustrated by Erik Blegvad), Atheneum, 1973; *Henry Explores the Mountains* (illustrated by G. Booth, Junior Literary Guild selection), Atheneum, 1975; *Jennie Jenkins* (illustrated by Glen Rounds), Little, Brown, 1975; (contributor) Arbuthnot and others, compilers, *The Arbuthnot Anthology of Children's Literature,* 2nd edition (Taylor was not associated with earlier editions), Scott, Foresman, 1971, 4th edition, 1976; *The Case of the Missing Kittens* (illustrated by G. Booth), Atheneum, 1978; *Young Melvin and the Bulger,* Doubleday, 1981. Author of numerous textbook readers in the "Pathfinders" series, Allyn & Bacon, 1978.

"Double Scoop Books"; three sets of six titles each; all co-authored with P. Adams and E. Hartson: *The Troll Family,* Follett, 1982; *Cora Cow,* Follett, 1982; *Pippin,* Follett, 1983.

Writer of educational filmstrips for Pied Piper Productions and Bailey Films, and writer and editor for "Law in a Free Society"

(From *Old Blue, You Good Dog, You* by Mark Taylor. Illustrated by Gene Holtan.)

series of filmstrips and workbooks for the National Endowment for the Humanities. Writer of television scripts. Contributor of professional articles and reviews to *Library Journal, Book Talk, Elementary English, The Reading Teacher*, and *Psychology Today*.

ADAPTATIONS: "Henry the Explorer" (filmstrip), Weston Woods Studios, 1977.

WORK IN PROGRESS: Four books in the "Alphonse" series; an adult biography about Eula McClaney; another adult biography; television film script about two famous Russian ballet dancers; adult romances; books for children; a syndicated column; a play; computer software.

SIDELIGHTS: Reared in Michigan, Taylor attended schools in Ann Arbor and Plymouth. He studied international law on scholarship for two years at Tufts College before earning a B.A. degree in journalism and an M.A. in library service from the University of Michigan. He earned his M.S. and Ph.D. in

education at the University of Southern California in 1970 and 1976, respectively.

Taylor's professional career has focused on related fields of education, children's literature and children's entertainment. "For a number of years I have had the privilege and awesome responsibility of writing about children's books in a newspaper column for adults. Equally challenging has been the continuing opportunity to 'teach' children's literature in the graduate school of a large university and to lecture across the country to various groups and professional associations interested in and committed to good books for children.

". . . Children and books are among the great mysteries of creation. Through a process of transformation and growth, as yet little understood because it is so complex, the unique entity known as a child becomes the unique entity called an adult. And through a process of recognition and assimilation, still little understood though much studied, the reading of a book can trigger in the reader a complex of responses which we might call the *experience of literature*.

". . . We define literature in many ways . . . [one is] that it is writings whose value lies in beauty of form and emotional effect, whose excellence lies in the superior quality of its content. (Oral literature, of course, as imparted through tradition, is a part of this excellence.) And we speak of education as the striving for excellence in the human individual and in society. Through learning to read and write, through concourse with good and great books of all kinds, and especially through literature and the other arts, we hope to help young people grow up to be excellent persons.

". . . To be literate, I think, is to be something more than capable of spelling, writing memos and letters, and reading the daily newspaper; it is to be involved with literature. Primitive peoples, with their tribal myths and storytelling, are far more literate than many children of more advanced cultures. The peasant child who sat enthralled as he listened to the telling of a tale about Robin Hood or *The Fisherman's Wife* had far more literary exposure and experience than the modern child in a sophisticated society whose only exposure is to television's low comedy and to Bugs Bunny cartoon strips and various

But he couldn't leave the kittens. There was only one thing Detective Angus could do. He began to howl for help. ■ (From *The Case of the Missing Kittens* by Mark Taylor. Illustrated by Graham Booth.)

Jennie and Brute danced like crazy. They twirled and stomped and shuffled and jumped and kicked....■ (From *Jennie Jenkins* by Mark Taylor. Illustrated by Glen Rounds.)

filmed vulgarizations of the classics.'' [Mark Taylor, ''A Call to Excellence,'' *The Reading Teachers*, January, 1967.[1]]

Taylor is highly critical of the way television can distort children's literature and folktales, and has written several children's television scripts. ''Ours is a society which is greatly concerned for the education, welfare, and amusement of children. In fact it has become a hallmark of this century. However, in spite of experts on every side telling us how and what to do for our offspring, one can view only with dismay an injustice of increasing import which is being subtly wrought upon children. I refer to the distortion and vulgarization which occur almost invariably whenever folktales and children's books are adapted to television and motion pictures. Were not an important consumer market represented by children, and were not the calculated enticements of television and films so widely influential, this injustice might not seem as appalling as it does.

''It is the folktale which most often suffers distortion, since there are no authors and agents to protect its integrity. Our oral literary heritage of folktales is threatened by mass media which in one or two generations could easily weaken, perhaps destroy, for scores of children the long and enriching associations folktales have had with countless generations. Admittedly, there is always a tendency to lose the original quality and flavor of an artistic work in the process of translation from one medium to another, but it need not be inevitable.

''Folktales are the result of uncountable centuries of telling, sharing, polishing, until they came to us in near perfect form. They embody the wisdom, the experience, and the emotions of mankind. In them we have great symbols of truth, which, like seeds, are planted in the minds and hearts of children to grow in meaning with the maturing of the adult. Who has not known what it is like to be unappreciated as was Cinderella, to have an all-consuming desire like the fisherman's wife, to have to call upon all one's courage and wits like the maiden in 'East o' the Sun and West o' the Moon?' If all this is to be turned into something very like drivel, something cliched and commonplace, simply because producers, writers, and directors know no better, are we to say nothing?

''So many producers and performers in television studios understand little about the finer aspects of children. If boys and girls laugh at their neurotic clowns and squeal at their frenzied productions of science fiction, adventure, and fantasy, they think they know what their audience wants. They repeat the same worn materials over and over. They forget a very important point, however; it is that children, when not offered a choice between an ordinary mystery and a darned good mystery, between an announcer who makes a poor clown on Saturday mornings and a clown who is an artist, will accept what is at hand, with all the appropriate squeals, laughter, and applause. They also forget that children will get by on a sameness of diet for want of variety and quality. Children are more discriminating than widely believed, but they are also more long-suffering and will put up with foolsgold for want of real treasure.

"Adults should know when they are not receiving the best in their entertainment and do what they will about it. Children cannot. They take what is offered, until someone sees to it that better material is presented. Let us never stop fulfilling the ages old request. Tell me a story. Let us do it in books, magazines, movies, plays, and television enchantments. But let us do everything possible to make sure that the story, when we tell it, is worthy of the response and good faith children are so ready to give it." [Mark Taylor, "Television Is Ruining Our Folktales," *Library Journal,* December, 1959.[2]]

Along with his involvement in the television media, Taylor has written educational filmstrips and numerous books and textbooks for children. He is widely known as a storyteller and a balladeer and is a frequent lecturer and instructor to numerous colleges and children's educational associations. "Since books are in competition with other communication media these days, it is more imperative than ever that we devote ourselves to finding the best and in setting it before children. The day can and must come when books are not in competition with television and films and tape recorders, when literature can be successfully translated into the terms of other media in such a way that one is led back to the book. But until that day arrives, we must demand and promote excellence in children's books. We must not only obtain excellence, we must give children every opportunity to come in contact with it. Only an immersion in literature, reading and being read to, will help most children discover and hold on to excellence in written words."[1]

"In a world whose problems seem to multiply and grow complex beyond measure, one great aim for most of us is to help children grow up whole and happy on a rapidly shrinking planet in a rapidly expanding universe. We believe that through books we can help children find their way to the very thresholds of this universe, ready to face its dazzling facts and accept its awesome challenges. In one way or another, we try to see that children are given not only factual knowledge and technical know-how, but, even more importantly, the small store of man's dearly gained wisdom, and a sufficiency of aesthetic and spiritual insight and ideals. Books for children, besides providing delight, can open children's eyes to the splendors of the world and fill out their minds with great ideas and strengthen their hearts with great feelings.

". . . Children's books must meet certain standards and bring to children our best thinking and writing, whether in fact or fantasy. In children's books we look for *entertaining* products of the written word and graphic arts which are also contributions to art, literature and knowledge.

"Writing for young minds is a challenge because it is based on a vision of wonder, adventure, beauty, and knowledge, often threatened by economics. . . ." [Mark Taylor, "Writing for

Children: A Challenge and a Vision," *Elementary English,* December, 1962.[3]]

"... I think it quite possible that we can create for children a world in which books and television live in fruitful harmony. I think we can find ways in which to make children avid readers and pursuers of literature while they are also consumers of the other media." [Mark Taylor, "An Accumulation of Excellence," *The Reading Teacher,* February, 1967.[4]]

". . . A children's book is one not necessarily written *for* children but one which is inevitably read *by* children."[1]

One of Taylor's most popular literary creations is *Henry, the Explorer.* The series began in 1966. "Henry does the kind of things I think about doing. . . . I always know what he thinks and what he will do in any situation. Henry is a very real part of me, and that is why I understand him. But he is also a very real part of Graham Booth, his illustrator, and that is why Henry always has a surprise or two for me. I know the kind of adventures Henry will have, how they will begin and how they will end. But I am not always sure what interesting things Henry will do until Mr. Booth shows them to me in a drawing. So you see, I share Henry with Graham Booth, which is why we can work together to tell boys and girls about Henry's adventures.

"After Henry had found a cave full of bears and after he had caught a tiger when he explored the 'jungle,' I was pretty certain that Henry would next become a castaway. So I waited until one day, deep in my thoughts, Henry began to have his adventure looking for the 'uncharted seas.' And deep in my thoughts I followed along with him to see how it would all turn out. The result, after talking it over with Mr. Booth, [was] *Henry the Castaway.*

"Two things are very important to me as a writer: to produce humor and comedy. I feel a sense of comedy is one of man's great achievements. To me, laughter is divine, liberating, and therapeutic. Laughter heals; laughter expands life. Through humor in my writing, I communicate ideas that break conventional restrictions on man's vision and experience. Humor serves as bridge from the old to the new."

HOBBIES AND OTHER INTERESTS: Folklore, linguistics, ballet; plays guitar and harp. "I adore computers and their promise."

FOR MORE INFORMATION SEE: Library Journal, December, 1959; *Elementary English,* December, 1962; *The Reading Teacher,* January, 1967, February, 1967.

Thanks to my friends for their care in my breeding,
Who taught me betimes to love working and reading.
—Isaac Watts

Multiplication is vexation,
Division is as bad;
The Rule of Three perplexes me,
And practice drives me mad.

—Anonymous

Bob Teague at the news desk, 1969.

TEAGUE, Robert   1929-
  ### (Bob Teague)

PERSONAL: Born January 2, 1929, in Milwaukee, Wis.; married Matt Turney (a dancer), divorced; children: Adam. *Education:* University of Wisconsin, B.S., 1950.

CAREER: Journalist and author. *Milwaukee Journal,* Milwaukee, Wis., reporter, 1950-56; *New York Times,* New York, N.Y., reporter, 1956-62; National Broadcasting Company, Inc., New York, N.Y., newscaster, 1962—. *Awards, honors:* Recipient of Amistad Award from American Missionary Association for "his dignity and journalistic skill."

WRITINGS—All juvenile, except as noted: *The Climate of Candor* (adult novel), Pageant Press, 1962; *Letters to a Black Boy* (biographical civil rights protest), Walker & Co., 1968; *Adam in Blunderland* (illustrated by Floyd Sowell), Doubleday, 1971; *Agent K-Thirteen the Super-Spy,* Doubleday, 1974; *Super-Spy K-Thirteen in Outer Space* (illustrated by Sammis McLean), Doubleday, 1980; *Live and Off Color: News Biz* (adult), A & W Publishers, 1982. Contributor of articles to periodicals, including *High Fidelity and Musical America, TV Guide, New York Times Magazine, Look, Reader's Digest,* and *Redbook.*

SIDELIGHTS: Teague was born on **January 2, 1929** in Milwaukee, Wisconsin to Robert and Nancy Teague. After his mother's death, Teague's aunt came to live with him and his father. "Aunt Letty," who raised him until he was seventeen and off to college, became the only mother Teague knew.

"When my real mother died giving birth to me, Aunt Letty, her sister, dropped whatever she was doing in Detroit and came to live with my daddy and me in Milwaukee. I never did find out what it was she left behind. She stayed with us until I went away to college at 17.

"By then she had taught me what I still regard as the most important lesson a black boy has to learn. She convinced me that life is much larger than the limits imposed on us for the color of our skins; that I must keep in mind that my world is bigger than the boundaries of the ghetto; that it is a world of different pains and pleasures, beauty and ugliness, victories and defeats that all men everywhere come to know. She taught me to dream beyond my blackness." [Bob Teague, "Excerpts from *Letters to a Black Boy,*" taken from an article in *Redbook* magazine, January, 1969.[1]]

Teague's earliest memories were tainted by bigotry. At the age of six he suffered his first personal rejection because of his color. "While I flatter myself that I was able to recover in a sawed-off jiffy, the experience is still vivid [many] years later.

"The news came to my block that the Clarion Theater, the most elegant movie house on the white fringe of the ghetto, planned an amateur contest in connection with the latest Shirley Temple movie. First prize would be $500 in cash and a trip to Hollywood for a screen test.

"All my friends urged me to enter the contest, saying I might wind up being a black boy Shirley Temple.

"Me? In the movies? Singing and dancing like Shirley Temple? Wow! It was the kind of dream that would keep any child awake through the night. To my friends I pretended indifference, but secretly I practiced my favorite song, the one that begins, 'I think that I shall never see a poem lovely as a tree.' And a few days later, with the contest only a week away, I sneaked off to enter.

"There was a tall white usher in a dashing blue uniform—gold braid and brass buttons—standing under the Clarion Theater marquee. When I asked him where I should go to enter the contest, he said gruffly: 'Go home, boy. It's for whites only.'

"I had been warned that there were places and things in the world strictly out of bounds for Negroes, but I had never faced any of them personally, all alone. The shock was indescribable. I turned and ran as fast as my legs would carry me.

"I was spurred by an overpowering jumble of emotions that I identified years later as shame, frustration and rage. As I ran toward the safety of home, bawling and weeping through the streets, I remember thinking that I could have accepted losing the contest, or even not being allowed to compete, if only they had waited to make up their minds until I had had a chance to sing 'Trees.'"[1]

This bitter taste of prejudice was again experienced when he was eight, but this experience affected his entire family. "My Aunt Letty . . . helped my daddy study for a written test for a white union. An avid learner, Aunt Letty knew where to find books on almost anything. Finally, a few days before the test, she said Daddy knew enough to pass. The three of us talked about the things we'd buy when my daddy got his union card and began making more money. My dream was a Lone Ranger cowboy suit like the ones I had seen white boys wearing just a few blocks beyond the ghetto.

Happily, the secret agent ate the sandwich as he climbed the rope ladder to the whirlybird's cockpit. ■ (From *Super-Spy K-13 in Outer Space* by Bob Teague. Illustrated by Sammis McLean.)

A dozen hidden springs popped out from the bottom of each shoe.

So instead of crashing with a painful thud, he bounced across the floor like a runaway kangaroo.
■(From *Agent K-13, the Super-Spy* by Bob Teague. Illustrated by Geoffrey Moss.)

"However, on the day of the test, my daddy returned home sputtering and cursing, 'The man said I passed,' he told us. 'Then the sonofabitch tore up the papers and dropped 'em on the floor. He claims he seen me cheating. The lying bastard. I never done no such a thing.'

"My daddy crumpled into a chair at the kitchen table. He hid his eyes and cried. Aunt Letty left the room. I had never seen my daddy cry; within seconds I was crying too. He hugged me to his chest and between his sobs tried to tell me to hush, that everything would be all right, that he would still buy me that cowboy suit somehow.

"My fears had nothing to do with a cowboy suit. I had the feeling—though not the words to explain it—that my daddy would never again be the same. I was crying for what had been stolen from him and for the hurt I knew he would feel for the rest of his tomorrows.

"What they stole from my daddy they later stole from me, a little piece at a time, when I became a man. In self-defense, trying to hang on to what I thought was the real me, I replaced the stolen pieces with bitterness, suspicion and rage. These are not satisfactory substitutes; they cannot help me to become the person I might have been. Mainly they serve to keep me on guard against further losses to the enemy. Which means that there is still enough of the real me left to reject their notion of what I am, what I can do, what I deserve and where they think I belong. In other words, I am at odds with the main theme of this society. And I still dream of the man I could have been if they had let me alone."[1]

In high school Teague did so well on the football team that he was awarded an athletic scholarship to the University of Wisconsin. He played football in college and was selected as an "All-Big Ten" player in his junior year. In 1950 he graduated from the University with a B.S. in journalism. At that time there were less than a half-dozen black reporters in the U.S.; nevertheless, Teague opted for journalism instead of a pro-football career.

He was hired as a sports writer on *The Milwaukee Journal,* where he worked for six years. After much perseverance, Teague got the *New York Times* to hire him as a sports writer. ". . . I filed my fifty-first application. . . . They called me two weeks later." [James J. Flynn, *Negroes of Achievement in Modern America,* Dodd, 1980.[2]]

For the next six and one-half years Teague covered sports for the *Times* and wrote special articles on integration, politics, and economics. In 1955 he married a professional dancer, Matt Turney, whom he had met years before while they were both undergraduates at the University of Wisconsin. Finding their first apartment was yet another struggle against racial oppression. Several times the couple were 'rejected' as tenants by city landlords because of their color until they finally found a suitable apartment with a fair landlord. "We lived in his building quite happily ever after for five and a half years, until we bought the cooperative apartment. . . . Our landlord proved to be not only a fair man, but a good friend as well."[2]

In **1962** Teague's journalistic talents were recognized by NBC who offered him a job as a radio news writer. "As a matter of fact, I had been hired before they knew the color of my skin. . . . Furthermore, once I accepted the job, they treated me no differently from white writers hired about the same time."[2]

Teague wrote radio scripts until he was promoted to a television writer. From writing for television, Teague advanced to a full-time street reporter, working on news reporting assignments for NBC-TV. "In the spring of 1967, I covered a story that seemed a reply of a bitter moment I had lived with my daddy nearly 30 years earlier. What happened here in New York . . . was that an all-white union in the building trades—under pressure from civil rights pickets—gave a written test to . . . several . . . black men who said they were qualified for membership and the well-paying jobs they couldn't get without the union. All of them passed easily. However, the union decided—that is, some white men decided—that those black men couldn't have got those high scores without cheating.

"I couldn't say so in my television newscast, but that story brought back vividly the summer of 1937 in Milwaukee, when I was eight years old."[1]

After two years and nine months with NBC-TV, Teague was assigned a fifteen-minute newscast, which required study in elocution, breathing exercises and memory tests. His television exposure increased with his own weekly television program.

In **1968** he wrote *Letters to a Black Boy,* a book intended as a gift for his son, Adam. The book consisted of a series of letters written to his two-year old son about growing up black in a white society. "In the event of my death, it is my wish that these letters to my son Adam be held for him until he is 13 years old.

"I live in a time and place threatened by deliberate or accidental incineration. I am a black man in a society that alternates between denying that I exist and confirming that the quality of my existence shall be less than its laws, its churches and its leading citizens say I have every right to expect. Also I am at once a central figure, a pawn, a target and an important bystander in the Black Revolution.

"Besides those hazards, I deliberately expose my life to other caprices of my time. I drive a car. I breathe polluted air. I smoke a pack of cigarettes every day. Worst of all, I often tell my fellow human beings—including tyrants, madmen and men in power—exactly what I think.

"Clearly the odds against tomorrow are long. It is possible that I may not be around when my infant son has grown up enough to hear some sensible things he ought to know."[1]

His second book for young people incorporated his son's name in its title, *Adam in Blunderland.* He has since written two more juveniles.

FOR MORE INFORMATION SEE: Ebony, November, 1955; *Newsweek,* October 14, 1968; Robert Teague, *Letters to a Black Boy,* Walker & Co., 1968; *Redbook,* January, 1969; *New York Times Book Review,* March 2, 1969; *Selected Black American Authors: An Illustrated Bio-Bibliography,* G. K. Hall, 1977; James J. Flynn, *Negroes of Achievement in Modern America,* Dodd, 1980.

When at home alone I sit
And am very tired of it,
I have just to shut my eyes
To go sailing through the skies—
To go sailing far away
To the pleasant Land of Play;
To the fairy land afar
Where the little people are;
Where the clover-tops are trees,
And the rain-pools are the seas,
And the leaves, like little ships,
Sail about on tiny trips;
And above the daisy tree
   Through the grasses,
High o'erhead the Bumble Bee
   Hums and passes.

—Robert Louis Stevenson

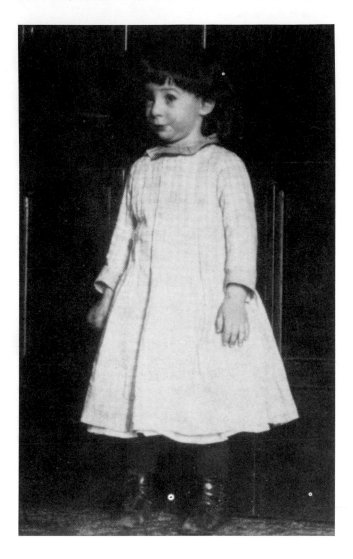

Sara Teasdale, about five years old.

TEASDALE, Sara   1884-1933

PERSONAL: Born August 8, 1884, in St. Louis, Mo.; died January 29, 1933, by her own hand, in New York, N.Y.; buried in Bellefontaine Cemetery, St. Louis, Mo.; daughter of John Warren (a merchant) and Mary Elizabeth (Willard) Teasdale; married Ernst B. Filsinger (a businessman), December 19, 1914 (divorced, 1929). *Education:* Educated at home until she was nine years old; attended private schools in St. Louis, beginning about 1893; attended Mary Institute, 1898-99; graduated from Hosmer Hall, 1903. *Home:* St. Louis, Mo.; New York, N.Y.

CAREER: Poet. Joined with a group of her friends to publish the *Potter's Wheel,* a monthly manuscript magazine, 1904-07; toured Europe and the Middle East, 1905-07; first published poem, ''Guenevere,'' appeared in the St. Louis weekly, *Reedy's Mirror,* 1907; author of verse and editor of anthologies, 1907-33. *Member:* Poetry Society of America, American Women's Club (London), The Author's Club (New York), St. Louis Artists' Guild. *Awards, honors:* Awarded the annual prize of the Poetry Society of America and the Columbia University Poetry Society Prize, forerunner of the Pulitzer Prize for poetry, 1918, for *Love Songs.*

*WRITINGS—*Of interest to young readers: (Compiler) *Rainbow Gold: Poems Old and New Selected for Boys and Girls* (illustrated by Dugald Walker), Macmillan, 1922, reprinted, Granger, 1979; *Stars Tonight: Verses New and Old for Boys and Girls* (illustrated by Dorothy P. Lathrop), Macmillan, 1930.

Other principal poems; all published by Macmillan, except as indicated: *Sonnets to Duse, And Other Poems,* Poet Lore, 1907; *Helen of Troy, and Other Poems,* Putnam, 1911, revised edition, Macmillan, 1922; *Rivers to the Sea,* 1915; *Love Songs,* 1917, new edition with photographs by Eric Bauer, 1975; (compiler) *The Answering Voice: One Hundred Love Lyrics by Women,* Houghton, 1917, revised edition published as *The Answering Voice: Love Lyrics by Women,* Macmillan, 1928, reprinted, Books for Libraries, 1971; *Flame and Shadow,* 1920; *Dark of the Moon,* 1926; *A Country House,* Knopf, 1932; *Strange Victory,* 1933; *The Collected Poems,* 1937, revised edition (edited by Marya Zaturenska), 1967; *Those Who Love: Love Poems* (edited by Arthur Wortman; illustrated by Bill Greer), Hallmark, 1969.

Also contributor of poems to numerous periodicals including *Harper's, Scribner's, Century, Forum, Lippincott's, Putnam's, Bookman,* and *New Republic.*

*ADAPTATIONS—*Recordings: ''The Poetry of Sara Teasdale,'' read by Esther Benson (selected from *The Collected Poems of Sara Teasdale,* Macmillan, 1937), Listening Library, c.1970.

Some of her verses were set to music such as: ''Vignettes of Italy,'' music by Wintter Watts, Ditson, 1919; ''Joy,'' music by Watts, 1922; ''I Shall Not Care,'' music by McNair Ilgenfritz, 1934; and ''Peace,'' piano accompaniment by May Sabeston Walker, 1936.

SIDELIGHTS: **August 8, 1884.** Born in St. Louis, Missouri. ''My earliest recollections are of . . . story-spinning to myself when I was a baby. I have always put myself to sleep with it, and I can remember the funny little tales I used to tell myself when I was a wee tot. A good many of them had to do with a lame boy who lived across the street and was about twelve or fifteen years older than I. It was long before I knew how to read, so you see I fell in love very early. I don't know why he had such a fascination for me unless it was that he played several instruments. I used to hear him on summer evenings. They had a beautiful lawn . . . and he used to play out under the trees. Sometimes the sheet-lightning would be shining fitfully—it always used to frighten me—but still he kept playing.'' [William Drake, *Sara Teasdale: Woman and Poet,* Harper, 1979.[1]]

1893-1899. Attended Mrs. Lockwood's school and the Mary Institute (founded by T. S. Eliot's grandfather).

1899-1903. Graduated from Hosmer Hall. ''I wrote my first verses when I was a schoolgirl, and they were very bad indeed. They were the result of an unhappy affair du coeur. I was fifteen. One of the bad rhymes, 'dusk' and 'trust,' haunts me to this day. I remember that all my verses at the age of sixteen were parodies and attempts at humor.''[1]

1904-1907. With a group of friends, published a monthly literary magazine, *The Potter's Wheel.* Considering the age of the girls and the fact that it was done principally for amusement, it met with surprising success in St. Louis.

1905. First trip abroad with her mother. In her diary she wrote of an experience at the Louvre: ''We went down-stairs next, and when we got to the door, I looked to the end of the long, long corridor and way at the end of it, against a dark red curtain, beautifully lighted, stood the most beautiful thing in the world—the Venus de Milo. Oh, I could hardly contain myself, her beauty made me so happy. She is far, far more lovely than any reproduction that I ever saw. The nearer I came to her, the more I loved her. Yes, I really love her—almost as one loves a real person. I can understand how Pygmalion loved Galatea. I cannot express the pleasure one has in being near this glorious woman. You are glad, as was Theophile Gautier, that her arms are gone, because they might hide her body. I have never seen so noble and pure and unconscious a woman as this Venus. The marble is so magnificently carved that it looks like flesh. I have left the loveliest thing until the last. It is her mouth. In no reproduction is it at all like the original. It is so very near a smile, and yet so full of repose. I don't believe that the exact reproduction of it will ever be caught by anyone. The lips are the most beautiful shape—you can tell from them that she is the goddess of love, but it is a spiritual love.'''[1]

1907. *Sonnets to Duse and Other Poems* published. Teasdale, whose attitude was typical of her times and of a well-to-do upbringing, expressed a view that seems unliberated by today's standards. "I am glad that I am a woman. I have sometimes thought that if I ever had to support myself, I should commit suicide. It is so hard for a woman to make even enough to keep soul and body together—and if one is hampered by ill health one might about as well give it up altogether. . . . I sometimes wonder if there is *any* hope for me as a poet since I am neat and terribly punctual and care for clothes. . . . I don't want to a 'literary woman.'. . .

"Maybe it is at bottom a wish that nobody would ever think of me as 'a woman who writes.' I *know* I'm not like most of the 'women who write,' for they love to argue and I don't, and they are never afraid of people, and I always am, and they know all about the subconscious mind and food-values and politics. . . . As for my own poetry, it is far too weak and plaintive to please me. It is only incidental to my life. Art can never mean to a woman what it does to a man. Love means that.

"If I were only beautiful and a genius, what fun life would be. It seems to me I should always be happy if I were somewhere else."

"[I am] in a very blue mood in regard to my poetry. It seems to me that it is almost utterly worthless. I have never hated it so before."[1]

1911. Teasdale, whose frail health would later become something of an obsession, wrote to a friend: "I am ill and very much in the dumps generally. It seems to me as tho' the whole creation, and myself in particular, were pretty much of a failure. My mother who is a sort of super-woman, nearly drives me mad. I ought not to say this, but sometimes I feel that I *must* tell somebody. Since her accident she is more terrible than ever. You have no idea how utterly selfish and restless and jealous she is. I keep saying to myself, 'You must not grow like her, you must not grow like her.' I don't know what is to become of her. She is sixty-seven and has as much strength in her little finger as I have in my whole body. She has nothing to do in the world but to worry and fret people. There, do you think me horrible and unnatural to speak so? You must forgive it. If it were not for my father I should—Oh I *will* stop. I have no right to bore you."[1]

(From *Stars Tonight: Verses New and Old for Boys and Girls* by Sara Teasdale. Illustrated by Dorothy P. Lathrop.)

1914. Courted by Vachel Lindsay, the poet, and Ernst Filsinger, a businessman. "And I must marry, for at the bottom I am a mother more intensely than I am a lover. . . . I realize either that I am not as passionate as I have always believed myself, or else that with all of his fire and tenderness Vachel cannot stir me to the depths. . . . He still feels that he can support me after a year or so. But if I must wait a year or so for him, I cannot ask Ernst [Filsinger] to do the same thing. [I'll] give Vachel until the end of the month to see if he can make me *desperately* in love. If he can, of course I suppose that I will marry him regardless of finances. If he can not, I will go up to Charlevoix and see if I love Ernst. . . . My room is filled with flowers. . . . How I should have adored four years ago some of this love that is going to waste now. . . . I have told Ernst everything very frankly. I do not know how he will feel about it. But it is all a part of me and he must take me as I am. I do not love him now, but probably I shall in a month! I am suddenly grown beyond my own forecasting."[1] Married Ernst Filsinger.

1916. Moved to New York. Filsinger travelled a great deal and Teasdale wrote to him during a business trip: ". . . After all, a life of action is the happy life. A life like mine which consists almost wholly of meditation is damned gloomy. If only I had

(From *Rainbow Gold: Poems Old and New Selected for Boys and Girls* by Sara Teasdale. Illustrated by Dugald Walker.)

better health I would have no cause for complaint. I could go with you and that would be jolly all around. . . . I truly envy you your travels. How I long for bodily health to take them!''¹

1918. During World War I Teasdale published several war poems in magazines. ''The war has made me hideously unhappy these last months. How much of this is bona fide patriotism, I don't know. It all makes me heart-sick, for it represents such terrible loads of sorrow to be borne later when our men are maimed and killed by the thousands. It is staggering when one thinks of the four thousand years of so-called civilization on this planet—that it culminates now in the most brutal and tremendous bloodshed that the world has ever seen. If I were strong and unmarried I'd be . . . doing something more vital just now than poetry.''¹

1919. Although her husband's prolonged and frequent absences were a strain on the marriage, they gave Teasdale a sense of self-reliance and the privacy she so cherished. ''Men are never rocks. *I've* never found one. Women are less likely to turn out un-rock-like than men. Women are solider than men—less likely to get all worked up and light-headed. A man is almost always light-headed and somehow you don't mind it after you've learned you have to put up with it. By that I don't mean emotional instability any more than any other kind. Ernst, for instance, is emotionally, so far as likelihood of falling in love with any other woman goes, very stable, but in a general way, more excitable than I—and that's going some.

''. . . No highly developed, thoroughly self-conscious modern woman can really give her soul and be proud of it. I used to always think that I wanted to lose myself in the man I loved. I see now that I can never do that, and that I was foolish to wish that I could. The man who wants a woman's brain, soul and body wants really only a slave. And the woman who wants to give *all* of herself, spirit and intellect and flesh, really doesn't want a lover but a master—and that isn't beautiful except in books, and not *really* beautiful then. I am saying all this for myself, just to put on paper some random thoughts that have come to me as a sort of shock since my marriage.

''. . . It is easier to talk through veils, after all. I take great pains to keep veils between myself and most people. . . . It is too terribly exhausting to talk without veils, to be ones own self and as purely ones self as one may be. I suppose that most people count on their fingers the ones to whom they have been willing to be their whole selves. Usually a very small piece of oneself is quite enough to give even close friends. And it is much simpler so, all around. . . .''¹

October, 1920. *Flame and Shadow* published. ''The planning of the pattern of a poem is largely subconscious with me. Naturally the idea needs more or less space according to whether it is simply a statement of an emotion, or whether added to the statement, a deduction is made. The patterns of most of my lyrics are a matter of balance and speed rather than a matter of design which can be perceived by the eye. The pattern of 'The Unchanging' in *Flame and Shadow* is necessarily very simple for the poem is only eight lines long. It consists of the balancing of a picture of the sea shore against the mood of the maker of the poem. The poem rises swiftly for the first three lines and subsides on the slower fourth line. It rises again for two lines and subsides finally on the slow last two lines. The short and very slow last line is an emotional echo of the fourth line.

''The better the lyric is the less I consciously plan it. The best modern poets can not be pinned down to regular and exact metres for very long. Often I am seeking not so much communication with my reader as a better understanding of myself.

''My theory is that poems are written because of a state of emotional irritation. It may be present for some time before the poet is conscious of what is tormenting him. The emotional irritation springs, probably, from subconscious combinations of partly forgotten thoughts and feelings. Coming together, like electrical currents in a thunder story, they produce a poem. A poem springs from emotions produced by an actual experience or, almost as forcefully, from those produced by an imaginary experience. In either case, the poem is written to free the poet from an emotional burden. Any poem not so written is only a piece of craftsmanship.

''Out of the fog of emotional restlessness from which a poem springs, the basic idea emerges sometimes slowly, sometimes in a flash. This idea is known at once to be the light toward which the poet is groping. He now walks round and round it, so to speak, looking at it from all sides, trying to see which aspect of it is most vivid. When he has hit upon what he believes is his peculiar angle of vision, the poem is fairly begun.

''If a poet has a great gift, he may be able to speak for a whole race, creed, or class simply by speaking for himself. But for a poet consciously to appoint himself the mouthpiece of a certain class or creed *en masse* is dangerous business.

". . . Of course the subconscious plays a predominant part in the making of lyrics. . . . But with me the conscious mind is on the job at the same time as a sort of governess to the child. For instance, that song of mine that begins 'Let it be forgotten as a flower is forgotten' was written almost entirely without intervention by my brains. It simply was in my mind. But I was broad awake all the time and could not be said to be in a subconscious state.

"Maybe a poem comes to me at night, maybe not. . . . I've dreamed lines many a time, and some of them aren't bad, but the context had always faded into nothingness when I woke up. I had a full remembrance that there *was* a poem (or what seemed to be one) all composed, but by the time I was fully awake it had gone. Nothing is left usually but a phrase or a line. . . .''[1]

September, 1922. *Rainbow Gold: Poems Old and New Selected for Girls and Boys,* a collection of poems for children between the ages of ten and fourteen, published. *Rainbow Gold* was dedicated "To the beautiful memory of my father John Warren Teasdale" who had died the year before. She chose the poems according to what she and her friends read as children, especially poems "with highly accented rhythms. . . . They enjoyed certain sad poems as much as merry ones, but meditative, moralistic and gloomy poems were never read but once, if they were read at all. And I am glad to say that poems full of sentimentality fared no better.

"I shall try to avoid poems teaching a moral lesson, I shall use 'La Belle Dame Sans Merci,' in spite of Miss Lawlor's telling me that she feels such an inclusion will damn the book in the eyes of some virtuous parents."[1]

Teasdale had hoped that this anthology would bring in some "real money," and was not very excited about her own work. "I am writing very little, and I begin to wonder if I shall ever publish another book. At the rate I am writing I shall not have enough material until ten years from now!"[1]

Of her own poetry she wrote: ". . . I avoid, not from malice aforethought, but simply because I dislike them, all words that are not met with a common speech and all inversions of words and phrases. My poems aren't written in the literal sense of the word. They sometimes never meet pen and paper until they have been complete for days in my mind. Perhaps that habit of composition is partly responsible for the fact that I never use intricate stanzas—it would be too hard to compose them in my usual way. For me one of the greatest joys of poetry is to know it by heart—perhaps that is why the simple song-like poems appeal to me most—they are the easiest to learn." [Margaret Haley Carpenter, *Sara Teasdale: A Biography,* Schulte Publishing, 1960.[2]]

Teasdale became widely read, but avoided public appearances and large parties, going to the extent of writing her own interviews. She had "a growing shyness, and a positive horror of hearing any well-meaning soul try to read my poetry in public. My lyrics were never meant for reading aloud—or, if they are read so, for being listened to by more than two or three people. . . . Of course not all of my stuff is bang out of my own life (thank the kind gods!)—but it is tinged so deeply and directly with my own feelings that the idea of its being read or recited to a roomful of people (especially if I have to be present) gives me a longing to die at once."[1]

September 4, 1929. Divorced Filsinger. She wrote to him in Africa: ". . . During these last few months, while I have been

I Stood Upon a Star

**I stretched my mind until I stood
Out in space, upon a star;
I looked, and saw the flying earth . . . .**

■ (From *Stars Tonight* by Sara Teasdale. Illustrated by Dorothy P. Lathrop.)

coming to the decision which is now absolutely irrevocable, I have wept often.

"I do not forget our early happy years together, nor all of the beautiful hours that I owe to you. I am very grateful for them and I want always to keep the remembrance unhurt. The only way we can keep it so is the way I am taking. It is the way that, but for the fact that you are a man, and must try to oppose, you would very likely choose.

"Both of us are too high spirited to tolerate a patched-up relationship. I can not even consider it for a moment. There must be a clean break. I shall make it here and as quickly as possible. . . .

"I suppose no one in the world realizes the depression I am fighting—but there is no use to talk about it."[1]

1932. Her old friend and suitor, Vachel Lindsay, committed suicide. "To me it was a tragedy, for he was one of the half dozen people who meant anything real to me. So far as he

SARA TEASDALE, 1932

himself is concerned, I suppose it was a deep sleep for a man needing sleep. I do not quarrel with the fate that willed it, but my private sorrow in missing my friend is not lessened by these thoughts. He will be remembered with more acclaim by the next generation but one than by his own."[1]

January 29, 1933. Died in her bath, of an overdose of sleeping pills, in her apartment in New York. She had been increasingly depressed and reclusive, excluding practically all visits save that of her close friend, Margaret Conklin. Always fearful of catching a cold or exhausting herself, she had developed a morbid fear of having a stroke—she was convinced her blood vessels were ready to burst, despite her doctors' reassurances. Many years earlier, she had written: ". . . Oh how I should love to make one really fine poem before there is no more *me*. Isn't it *terrible* to think of stopping, of being nothing but a little heap of —oh dear, death is so full of horror. I sometimes think if I ever went mad, it would be from the terror of death."[1]

Buried in St. Louis, Missouri.

> ". . . since at the end
> 　My body will be utterly destroyed. . . .
> Since there is no escape even for me
> 　Who love life with a love too sharp to bear. . . .
> Let me go down as waves sweep to the shore
> 　In pride; and let me sing with my last breath."[1]

FOR MORE INFORMATION SEE: Margaret Haley Carpenter, *Sara Teasdale: A Biography,* Schulte, 1960, reprinted, Pentelic, 1977; Rosemary Sprague, *Imaginary Gardens,* Chilton, 1969; William Drake, *Sara Teasdale: Women and Poetry,* Harper, 1979. Obituaries—"Literature Mourns," *Commonweal,* February 15, 1933; *Publishers Weekly,* February 4, 1933.

Movies and filmstrips: "Sara Teasdale, a Poet of Loneliness" (filmstrip), RMI Film Productions, 1967.

THANE, Elswyth　1900-

PERSONAL: Born May 16, 1900, in Burlington, Iowa; married William Beebe a (naturalist and writer), September 22, 1927 (deceased). *Residence:* Wilmington, Vt. 05363. *Agent:* Jo Stewart, 201 East 66th St., New York, N.Y. 10021.

CAREER: Free-lance author beginning in 1925. Formerly a newspaper-woman and writer of films.

*WRITINGS—*Nonfiction: *The Tudor Wench,* Harcourt, 1932; *Young Mr. Disraeli,* Harcourt, 1936; *England Was an Island Once,* Harcourt, 1940; *The Bird Who Made Good,* Duell, Sloan & Pearce, 1947; *Reluctant Farmer,* Duell, Sloan & Pearce, 1950, published as *Strength of the Hills,* Christian Herald House, 1976; *The Family Quarrel,* Duell, Sloan & Pearce, 1959; *Washington's Lady,* Duell, Sloan & Pearce, 1960; *Potomac*

Elswyth Thane with husband, William Beebe.

The spokesman for this first colonial resistance to taxation by Parliament was a young backwoods lawyer named Patrick Henry. His fiery oratory in the Virginia Assembly was interrupted by shocked cries of "Treason!"... ■ (From *The Virginia Colony* by Elswyth Thane. Illustration courtesy of Virginia State Library.)

Squire, Duell, Sloan & Pearce, 1963; *Mount Vernon Is Ours*, Duell, Sloan & Pearce, 1966; *Mount Vernon: The Legacy*, Lippincott, 1967; *Mount Vernon Family*, Macmillan, 1968; *Virginia Colony*, Macmillan, 1969; *Dolly Madison: Her Life and Times*, Macmillan, 1970; *Fighting Quaker: Nathaniel Greene*, Hawthorn, 1972.

Fiction: *Riders of the Wind*, Stokes, 1926; *Echo Answers*, Stokes, 1927; *His Elizabeth*, Stokes, 1928; *Cloth of Gold*, Stokes, 1929; *Bound to Happen*, Putnam, 1939; *Remember Today*, Duell, Sloan, & Pearce, 1941; *Melody*, Duell, Sloan & Pearce, 1950; *The Lost General*, Duell, Sloan & Pearce, 1953; *Letter to a Stranger*, Duell, Sloan & Pearce, 1954.

Williamsburg novels; all published by Duell, Sloan & Pearce: *Dawn's Early Light*, 1943; *Yankee Stranger*, 1944; *Ever After*, 1945; *The Last Heart*, 1947; *Kissing Kin*, 1948; *This Was Tomorrow*, 1951; *Homing*, 1957.

Plays: "The Tudor Wench," produced in 1934; "Young Mr. Disraeli," produced in London, 1935, in New York, 1937.

SIDELIGHTS: "When I read the sometimes lyrical accounts of how other people have written their books, I am always skeptical, if not worse. I only know I never wanted to do anything else and can not remember learning to read. I served a brief apprenticeship on a newspaper as the 'youngest' reviewer of books and films. I worked for a time at a film studio just as the 'silents' were turning into the 'talkies' and the scenario problems taught me something about economy of words and not over-writing. I began with several short stories which promptly came back from several magazines. Then I began and finished my first booklength script (*Riders of the Wind*), although there was nothing I wanted less for myself than adventure like that which drove that heroine to the Himalayas. It was accepted by the first publisher who saw it and was not mauled about by any so-called publisher's 'editor' in the office but was printed straight from the original script with few alterations. I was at that time influenced by Kipling and Talbot Mundy, and though I had never been to India and had no desire to go there myself, I was told by one who knew it well that I had somehow made no mistakes in the settings or atmosphere. The publishers wanted another book just like it so I wrote that (*Cloth of Gold*).

"Then some inherent love of England, where I had never been either, and a lot of reading by preference of English authors took charge, and I began to write books laid in England and on the Continent. When I finally got to London in the 1920s, a couple of years after my marriage, my husband, who already knew England well himself—and even knew Kipling!—was astonished and delighted with my apparent instinctive knowledge of what I wanted to see and where it was, and his wide acquaintance in England opened many impressive doors. Then I discovered the Reading-Room of the British Museum, to which I was given immediate access. It was there that I got the background for the account of Elizabeth I's girlhood *(The Tudor Wench)* and Disraeli's youth *(Young Mr. Disraeli)*. I was at work on Charles II's boyhood exile on the Continent when the Hitler war ended my annual trips to the British Museum Reading Room *(England Was an Island Once)*.

"After a couple of modern novels, I discovered the Williamsburg, Virginia restoration project and a book laid in Williamsburg's early period before the Revolution *(Dawn's Early Light)* was turned by the encouragement of Dr. Beebe [her husband] and my publisher, Sam Sloan, into the series of seven Williamsburg novels tracing the generations of two families from there till 1941 of another war. I wrote some modern novels between those seven volumes while I worked on the research necessary for the Civil War, the action in Cuba after the *Maine* was sunk, etc.

"Altogether, I seem to have written some thirty-odd books, fiction and non-fiction, some of which required travel to the actual scene—such as the delightful trip through the Francis Marion country of South Carolina *(Family Quarrel)*. Then came the privilege of actually living inside the gates at Mount Vernon in the Regent's quarters while I made free use of their closely guarded files and correspondence since the 1860s when the house was acquired by the Association. Mount Vernon was the most impressive and touching experience I ever encountered while researching a book.

"I can almost never pinpoint the origin of an idea for another book, especially the novels, but I can guarantee that none of them—especially that one about a woman who married an explorer *(From This Day Forward)*—was in any way autobiographical! The sole exception being *Reluctant Farmer* (recently reprinted under the title *Strength of the Hills*.) I am still living in that house.

"I suppose I might add, as it is apparently unusual, that no manuscript of mine is ever worked on by any hand but mine before it goes to the printer. I write the first draft in longhand in ruled notebooks from Woolworth's and I type and retype every page myself through the final copy. I have no 'secretary' or researcher, I do it *all*. And I never read bits of it aloud to my family or friends, seeking encouragement or criticism. How I have got as many books written as there seem to be now, I shall never know, as I have never had a regular working schedule nor any temperamental 'seclusion' to work in. I wrote when, where, and if I could find a chance to sit at a desk, often late at night and sometimes still wearing the evening dress in which I had returned from theaters or parties or dances with my husband, for I never allowed 'my work' to interfere with our crowded social calendar. We were often separated for months at a time, he at his jungle field stations or oceanographic work, I at the British Museum or somewhere like Mount Vernon on my own job. This sort of schedule, if you can call it that, never did our over thirty-year marriage any harm and on the contrary, we always had something to talk about! There was no boredom or staleness and very little silence in the Beebe household, which was based at a duplex apartment in the West Sixties in New York. Later when we acquired the country place in Vermont, he came there or I went to New York, whenever it got lonesome where either of us happened to be.

"I confess that I have no patience and no sympathy with the agony and the ecstasy many writers seem to brag about. It was something nobody else could do for me and I enjoyed doing it, but I never gave myself airs about it as a 'calling.' I never made an outline before beginning a book, believing that if you lock yourself into a pattern before you begin, you have created a handicap. Things just developed as I went along and yet I never wrote myself into a corner and had to throw away chunks of superfluities as so many say they do. I always enjoy reading about other authors, either in their autobiographies or in biographies carefully fashioned from their letters or diaries—I never kept a diary—by some dedicated stranger after their death. But while reading about other and more famous writers, I often wonder if I haven't always done it all wrong!"

TINER, John Hudson 1944-

PERSONAL: Born October 8, 1944, in Pocahontas, Ark.; son of John A. (a pipeline construction inspector) and Martha (a clerk; maiden name, Hudson) Tiner; married Delma Jeanene Watson (an elementary school teacher), May 5, 1962; children: John Watson, Lambda Jeanene. *Education:* Harding College, B.S. 1965; Duke University, M.A.T., 1968; graduate study at Arkansas State University, 1965-68, College of the Holy Cross, 1971, Sam Houston State University, 1973, University of Missouri, 1975, National College of Education, 1977, St. Louis Community College, 1979. *Politics:* Independent. *Religion:* Church of Christ. *Home:* 6440 Kathy Lane, High Ridge, Mo., 63049. *Office: Bible Truth,* P.O. Box 38, House Springs, Mo. 63051.

CAREER: Pipeline construction worker, 1960-62; high school teacher of mathematics and science in Harrisburg, Ark., 1965-68, head of mathematics department, 1968; junior high school mathematics teacher in High Ridge, Mo., 1968-72; high school teacher of physics, astronomy, and science in House Springs, Mo., 1972-77; Defense Mapping Agency, Aerospace Center, St. Louis, Mo., photogrammetric cartographer, 1977-80; mathematician, 1980—. Photographer for *Harrisburg Modern News,* 1966-68. Instructor at Jefferson College, Hillsboro, Mo., 1972-77. *Member:* Missouri Association for Creation, Missouri Writers Guild, Jefferson County Writers Guild, Mystery Writers of America, Jefferson County Teachers Association (chairman of mathematics chapter, 1969). *Awards, honors:* Plaque from Missouri Writers Guild, 1977, for *Johannes Kepler;* National Science Foundation grants.

WRITINGS: When Science Fails, Baker Book, 1974; *Isaac Newton: The True Story of His Life* (juvenile; illustrated by Bill Biel), Mott Media, 1976; *Johannes Kepler: Giant of Faith and Science* (juvenile; illustrated by Rod Burke), Mott Media, 1977; *How to Earn Extra Income as a Free-Lance Writer,* Pamphlet Publications, 1977; *Evolution Versus Creation,* Pamphlet Publications, 1978; *Space Colonies,* Pamphlet Publications, 1978; *College Physical Science,* Accelerated Christian Education, 1980; *Seven Day Mystery* (young adult), Baker Book, 1981; *Word Search: Jesus the Teacher,* Standard, 1982; *Science Bulletin Boards with a Bible Background,* Quality Publications, 1983; *Word Search: Favorite Bible Stories from Acts,* Standard, 1983; *Bible Word Search Puzzles,* Broadman, 1983; *College Algebra I,* Accelerated Christian Education, 1983; *Word Search: They Followed Jesus,* Standard, 1984.

Contributor of more than four hundred articles, stories, and poems for children and adults to religious periodicals. Editor of *Castor,* 1965. Editor and publisher of *Bible Truth,* 1978—.

WORK IN PROGRESS: Louis Agassiz, a biography; *Survival Handbook for Planet Earth,* Christian devotions and essays; *Seven Mile Island Mystery* for teens; *The 1000 Year Voyage,* science fiction for teens.

SIDELIGHTS: Tiner's writings have covered a wide variety of subjects and styles. He has written mysteries and science fiction, articles on such hobbies as coin collecting, photography, and astronomy, and scientific papers. His religious writing has been published by most Christian denominations.

''I like to write, especially biographies of historical characters. After the research is finished and the outline complete, a magic moment occurs, when the story takes over and the characters come alive. No longer am I a writer, but a time traveler who stands unobserved in the shadows and reports the events as they occur. The time traveling goes forward in time as well as backward. What is committed to paper today will speak to readers who are not yet born.

''Writing gives a person leverage. The relatively simple action of putting words on paper has the potential to produce far-reaching and longlasting results. Because of this potential I believe a writer should feel strongly about his subject and express himself clearly and forcefully. And the writer has the responsibility to state the truth as he understands it.

''My background in science and strong Christian faith has attracted me to write about the interaction of science and religion. In a sense the two activities, science and religion, are closely related because both scientists and Christians have a relentless dedication to truth.''

Tiner's book, *Johannes Kepler: Giant of Faith and Science,* demonstrates this interaction. ''Many people find it strange that science and religion can be combined. But Kepler showed it could be done. He considered his scientific studies to be merely another way of looking into God's creation. In fact, in some of his most important books, Kepler became so excited about the universe, he broke into song and wrote poems of praise to God—right on the same page as his scientific laws. But Johannes Kepler lead an exciting life, too. His mother was tried for a witch, and his father disappeared into the dark smoke of war. In Kepler's case, no fiction is really as exciting as his personal life story.

''Despite the seriousness with which I approach my writing for children the final test is this: Would I enjoy reading it? If I cannot see myself as a young person reading the book and enjoying it, then the project is dumped. Books should be entertaining, even books that are intended to educate the reader in some way.''

TOLKIEN, J(ohn) R(onald) R(euel) 1892-1973

PERSONAL: Surname pronounced *Tohl*-keen; born January 3, 1892, in Bloemfontein, South Africa; brought to England in 1895; died September 2, 1973, in Bournemouth, England; son of Arthur Reuel (a bank manager) and Mabel (Suffield) Tolkien; married Edith Mary Bratt, March 22, 1916 (died, 1971); children: John Francis Joseph Reuel, Michael Hilary Reuel, Christopher John Reuel, Priscilla Mary Reuel. *Education:* Exeter College, Oxford, B.A., 1915, M.A., 1919. *Religion:* Christian. *Home:* 76 Sandfield Rd., Headington, Oxford, England.

J. R. R. TOLKIEN

CAREER: Assistant on *Oxford English Dictionary,* 1918-20; University of Leeds, Leeds, England, reader in English, 1920, professor of English, 1924-25; Oxford University, Oxford England, Rawlinson and Bosworth Professor of Anglo-Saxon, 1925-45, Merton Professor of English Language and Literature, 1945-59, fellow emeritus of Merton College. Fellow of Pembroke College, 1926-45; Leverhulme research fellow, 1934-36; Andrew Lang Lecturer, St. Andrews University, 1939; W. P. Ker Lecturer, University of Glasgow, 1953. *Military service:* Served in the British Army, Lancashire Fusiliers, 1915-18. *Member:* Royal Society of Literature (fellow), Science Fiction Writers of America (honorary), Philological Society (vice-president), Hid Islenzka Bokmenntafelag (honorary). *Awards, honors: New York Herald Tribune* Children's Spring Book Festival award, 1938, for *The Hobbit;* International Fantasy Award, 1957, for *The Lord of the Rings;* Benson Medal, Royal Society of Literature, 1966; made Commander, Order of the British Empire, 1972; Gandalf Award, 1974; D. en Phil. et Lettres, Liege, 1954; D. Litt, University College, Dublin, 1954, University of Nottingham, 1970.

WRITINGS—Of interest to young people: *The Hobbit; or, There and Back Again* (self-illustrated), Allen & Unwin, 1937, Houghton, 1938, reprinted (with illustrations from the film by Arthur Rankin, Jr. and Jules Bass), Abrams, 1977; *Farmer Giles of Ham* (illustrated by Pauline Diana Baynes), Allen &

(From "The Hoard," in *The Adventures of Tom Bombadil* by J.R.R. Tolkien. Illustrated by Pauline Baynes.)

Unwin, 1949, Houghton, 1950, reprinted, Allen & Unwin, 1976; *The Lord of the Rings*, Houghton, Volume I: *The Fellowship of the Ring*, 1954, Volume II: *The Two Towers*, 1954, Volume III: *The Return of the King*, 1955, with new foreword by author, Ballantine, 1965, 3rd edition, in three parts, Allen & Unwin, 1979, silver anniversary edition, Houghton, 1981; *The Adventures of Tom Bombadil, and Other Verses from the Red Book* (illustrated by Baynes), Allen & Unwin, 1962, Houghton, 1963; also published in *Farmer Giles of Ham* [*and*] *The Adventures of Tom Bombadil*, Unwin Books, 1975; *The Road Goes Ever On: A Song Cycle* (piano music; illustrated by Tolkien and Samuel H. Bryant; music by Donald Swann), Houghton, 1967, 2nd edition, revised, 1978; *Smith of Wootton Major* (illustrated by Baynes), Houghton, 1967, 2nd edition, Allen & Unwin, 1975; also published in *Smith of Wootton Major and Farmer Giles of Ham* (illustrated by Baynes), Ballantime, 1970; *Bilbo's Last Song* (poem; illustrated by Baynes), Houghton, 1974; *The Father Christmas Letters* (self-illustrated), edited by daughter-in-law Baillie Tolkien, Houghton, 1976, revised edition, 1979; *The Silmarillion*, edited by son, Christopher Tolkien, Houghton, 1977; *Poems and Stories* (illustrated by Baynes), Allen & Unwin, 1980; *Unfinished Tales of Númenor and Middle-Earth*, edited by C. Tolkien, Houghton, 1980; *Mr. Bliss*, Houghton, 1982.

Other writings: *A Middle English Vocabulary*, Milford, 1922; (editor with Eric V. Gordon) *Sir Gawain and the Green Knight*, Oxford University Press, 1925, 2nd edition, revised by Norman Davis, 1967; *Selections from Chaucer*, Clarendon Press, 1925; *Chaucer as a Philologist*, Philological Society, 1934; *Beowulf: The Monsters and the Critics*, British Academy, 1936, reprinted, Arden Library, 1978; *Songs for Philologists*, privately printed, 1936; (contributor) *Essays Presented to Charles Williams* (essay entitled "On Fairy-Stories"), Oxford University Press, 1947; (editor) *Ancrene Wisse*, Oxford University Press, 1962; *Tree and Leaf* (reprint of "On Fairy-Stories" and "Leaf by Niggle," the latter originally published in *The Dublin Review*, 1945), Allen & Unwin, 1964, Houghton, 1965, revised edition, Allen & Unwin, 1975; also published in *Tree and Leaf; Smith of Wooton Major; The Homecoming of Beorhtnoth, Beorhthelm's Son*, Unwin Books, 1975; *The Tolkien Reader*, introduction by Peter S. Beagle, Ballantine, 1966; (translator) *Sir Gawain and the Green Knight, Pearl, and Sir Orfeo*, Houghton, 1975; *The Letters of J.R.R. Tolkien*, edited by Humphrey Carpenter and C. Tolkien, Houghton, 1981; *The Old English Exodus: Text, Translation and Commentary*, edited by Joan Turville-Petre, Clarendon Press, 1981; *Finn and Hengest: The Fragment and the Episode*, Allen & Unwin, 1982.

Contributor to various periodicals, including *Shenandoah*, *Times Literary Supplement*, *Microcosm*, and *Oxford Magazine*.

ADAPTATIONS—Movies and filmstrips: "The Hobbit" (animated motion picture), with voices by Orson Bean and Richard Boone, Xerox Films, 1978; "The Hobbit" (filmstrip; with teacher's guide), Xerox Films, 1978.

Plays: *The Hobbit: A Musical Play* (music by Allan J. Friedman; lyrics by David Rogers), Dramatic Publishing, 1972.

Recordings: "Poems and Songs of Middle Earth," read by Tolkien, sung by William Elvin, music by Donald Swann, Caedmon, 1967; "The Hobbit," dramatic narration by Nicol Williamson, Argo, 1974; "Lord of the Rings," EMI EMC, 1975; "J.R.R. Tolkien Reads His 'The Hobbit' and Reads and Sings His 'The Fellowship of the Ring,'" Caedmon, 1975; "J.R.R. Tolkien Reads and Sings from His 'The Lord of the Rings," Caedmon, 1975; "The Silmarillion: Of Beren and Luthien," read by Christopher Tolkien, Caedmon, 1977; "Of The Darkening of Valinor and of The Flight of the Noldor from the Silmarillion," read by C. Tolkien, Caedmon, 1978; "J.R.R. Tolkien Songbook" (boxed set), Caedmon, 1978; "The Hobbit" (with 12 page illustrated book), Disneyland Records, 1979.

SIDELIGHTS: **January 3, 1892.** Born in Bloemfontein, South Africa. "My name is TOLKIEN (*not-kein*). It is a German name (from Saxony), an anglicization of *Tollkiehn*, i.e. *tollkühn*. But, except as a guide to spelling, this fact is as fallacious as all facts in the raw. For I am neither 'foolhardy' nor German, whatever some remote ancestors may have been. They migrated to England more than 200 years ago, and became quickly intensely English (not British), though remaining musical—a talent that unfortunately did not descend to me.

"I am a West-midlander by blood (and took to early west-midland Middle English as a known tongue as soon as I set eyes on it), but perhaps a fact of my personal history may partly explain why the 'North-western air' appeals to me both as 'home' and as something discovered. I was actually born in Bloemfontein, and so those deeply implanted impressions, underlying memories that are still pictorially available for inspection, of first childhood are for me those of a hot parched country. My first Christmas memory is of a blazing sun, drawn

Gandalf and Bilbo. ▪ (From *The Tolkien Scrapbook*, edited by Alida Becker. Illustrated by Tim Kirk.)

curtains and a drooping eucalyptus.'' [Christopher Tolkien and Humphrey Carpenter, editors, *The Letters of J.R.R. Tolkien*, Houghton, 1981.[1]]

Tolkien was kidnapped, while still a baby, by the Tolkien's native servant who wanted to show him off to his peers. ''It was typical native psychology but it upset everybody very much, of course. I knew he called me his son Isaac after himself. Mister Tolkien after my father and Victor—ha! ha!—after Queen Victoria.

''I was nearly bitten by a snake and I was stung by a tarantula, I believe. In my garden. All I can remember is a very hot day, long, dead grass and running. I don't even remember screaming. I remember being rather horrified at seeing the Archdeacon eat mealies [Indian corn] in the proper fashion [with his fingers].'' [Philip Norman, ''The Prevalence of Hobbits,'' *The New York Times Magazine*, January 15, 1967.[2]]

1895. Tolkien's mother returned to England with Tolkien and his brother, Hilary. ''. . . My own rather sharp memory is probably due to the dislocation of all my childhood 'pictures' between 3 and 4 by leaving Africa: I was engaged in a constant attention and adjustment. Some of my actual visual memories I now recognize as beautiful blends of African and English details.''[1]

''[I had a] . . . vivid child's view, which was the result of being taken away from one country and put in another hemisphere—the place where I belonged but which was totally novel and strange. After the barren, arid heat a Christmas tree. But no, it was not an unhappy childhood. It was full of tragedies but it didn't tot up to an unhappy childhood.''[2]

''I found I had for the countryside of England both the native feeling and the personal wonder of somebody who comes to it.'' [Henry Resnik, ''The Hobbit-Forming World of J.R.R. Tolkien,'' *Saturday Evening Post*, July 2, 1966.[3]]

1896. Tolkien's father, Arthur, died. Tolkien, his mother and brother, rented a cottage at Sarehole Mill, Birmingham, where they stayed for ''four years, but the longest-seeming and most formative part of my life.

''We spent lovely summers just picking flowers and trespassing. The Black Ogre used to take people's shoes and stockings from the bank where they'd left them to paddle, and run away with them, make them go and ask for them. And then he'd thrash them! The White Ogre wasn't quite so bad. But in order to get to the place where we used to blackberry (called the Dell) we had to go through the white one's land, and he didn't like us very much because the path was narrow through his field, and we traipsed off after corn-cockles and other pretty things. My mother got us lunch to have in this lovely place, but when she arrived she made a deep voice, and we both ran!'' [Humphrey Carpenter, *Tolkien: A Biography*, Houghton, 1977.[4]]

1899. At the age of seven Tolkien wrote a story about a dragon. ''I desired dragons with a profound desire. Of course, I in my timid body did not wish to have them in the neighbourhood. But the world that contained even the imagination of Fafnir was richer and more beautiful, at whatever cost of peril.

''I remember nothing about it except a philological fact. My mother said nothing about the dragon, but pointed out that one could not say 'a green great dragon,' but had to say 'a great green dragon.' I wondered why, and still do. The fact that I remember this is possibly significant, as I do not think I ever

tried to write a story again for many years, and was taken up with language.''[4]

1900. ''. . . I went to King Edward's School and spent most of my time learning Latin and Greek; but I also learned English. Not English Literature! Except Shakespeare (which I disliked cordially), the chief contacts with poetry were when one was made to try and translate it into Latin. Not a bad mode of introduction, if a bit casual. I mean something of the English language and its history. I learned Anglo-Saxon at school (also Gothic, but that was an accident quite unconnected with the curriculum though decisive—I discovered in it not only modern historical philology, which appealed to the historical and scientific side, but for the first time the study of a language out of mere love: I mean for the acute aesthetic pleasure derived from a language for its own sake, not only free from being useful but free even from being the 'vehicle of a literature').''[1]

''The fluidity of Greek, punctuated by hardness, and with its surface glitter captivated me. But part of the attraction was antiquity and alien remoteness (from me): it did not touch home.''[4]

While at King Edwards, Tolkien began inventing his own languages. ''It's not that uncommon, you know. An enormously greater number of children have what you might call a creative element in them than is usually supposed, and it isn't necessarily limited to certain things: they may not want to paint or draw, or have much music, but they nevertheless want to create something. And if the main mass of education takes a linguistic form, their creation will take a linguistic form. It's so extraordinarily common, I once did think that there ought to be some organised research into it.''[4]

A strong love of trees started early in youth when he would draw them and talk to them. ''There was a willow hanging over the mill-pool and I learned to climb it. It belonged to a butcher on the Stratford Road, I think. One day they cut it down. They didn't do anything with it: the log just lay there. I never forgot that.

''[Because of] the bitter disappointment and disgust from schooldays with the shabby use made in Shakespeare of the coming of 'Great Birnam Wood to high Dunsinane hill': I longed to devise a setting by which the trees might really march to war.''[4] Tolkien did in fact offer trees their revenge by creating the ''Ents'' in his later writings.

November, 1904. Mother died of diabetes. ''My own dear mother was a martyr indeed, and it is not to everybody that God grants so easy a way to his great gifts as he did to Hilary and myself, giving us a mother who killed herself with labour and trouble to ensure us keeping the faith.''[4] Father Francis Morgan became Tolkien's guardian.

1908. Met Edith Bratt. ''Her hair was raven, her skin clear, her eyes bright, and she could sing—and *dance*.''[4]

Writing to her later, Tolkien recalled: ''My first kiss to you and your first kiss to me (which was almost accidental)—and our goodnights when sometimes you were in your little white nightgown, and our absurd long window talks; and how we watched the sun come up over town through the mist and Big Ben toll hour after hour, and the moths almost used to frighten you away—and our whistle-call—and our cycle-rides—and the fire talks—and the three great kisses.''[4]

Two Orcs. ■(From *The Tolkien Scrapbook*, edited by Alida Becker. Illustrated by Tim Kirk.)

Father Morgan discovered their secret romance and forbade further communication between Edith and Tolkien. ''. . . Trouble arose: and I had to choose between disobeying and grieving (or deceiving) a guardian who had been a father to me, more than most real fathers, but without any obligation, and 'dropping' the love-affair until I was 21. I don't regret my decision, though it was very hard on my lover. But that was not my fault. She was perfectly free and under no vow to me, and I should have had no just complaint (except according to the unreal romantic code) if she had got married to someone else. For very nearly *three* years I did not see or write to my lover. It was extremely hard, painful and bitter, especially at first. The effects were not wholly good: I fell back into folly and slackness and misspent a good deal of my first year at College. But I don't think anything else would have justified marriage on the basis of a boy's affair; and probably nothing else would have hardened the will enough to give such an affair (however genuine a case of true love) permanence. . . .''[1]

1911. Poem, ''The Battle of the Eastern Fields,'' published in *The King Edward's School Chronicle*. Left King Edwards. ''The school-porter was sent by waiting relatives to find me. He reported that my appearance might be delayed. 'Just now he's the life and soul of the party.' Tactful. In fact, having just taken part in a Greek play, I was clad in a himation and sandals, and was giving what I thought a fair imitation of a frenzied Bacchic dance.

''[Now that it was over] I felt like a young sparrow kicked out of a high nest.''[4]

Began first term at Oxford University. ''A good few bills unaccounted for. Money matters are not very cheerful.''[4]

While an undergraduate at Oxford, Tolkien read the *Kalevala,* Finnish myths which were to become a source of inspiration. ''This strange people and these new gods, this race of unhypocritical low-brow scandalous heroes. The more I read of it, the more I felt at home and enjoyed myself.''[4]

After learning enough Finnish to read the *Kalevala* in the original version he claimed that ''it was like discovering a wine-cellar filled with bottles of amazing wine of a kind and flavour never tasted before.'' [Katharyn F. Crabbe, *J.R.R. Tolkien*, Frederick Ungar, 1981.[5]]

January 3, 1913. ''On the night of my 21st birthday I wrote again to . . . [Edith]. On Jan. 8th I went back to her, and became engaged, and informed an astonished family. I picked up my socks and did a spot of work . . . and then war broke out the next year, while I still had a year to go at college. In those days chaps joined up, or were scorned publicly. It was a nasty cleft to be in, especially for a young man with too much imagination and little physical courage. No degree: no money: financée. I endured the obloquy, and hints becoming

(From the animated movie ''The Lord of the Rings.'' Produced by United Artists, 1978.)

outspoken from relatives, stayed up, and produced a First in Finals in 1915. Bolted into the army: January 1915. . . .''[1]

While training for the Lancashire Fusiliers he wrote: "These grey days wasted in warily going over, and over and over again, the dreary topics, the dull backwaters of the art of killing, are not enjoyable.''[4]

March 22, 1916. ''I found the situation intolerable and married. . . . May found me crossing the Channel (I still have the verse I wrote on the occasion!) for the carnage of the Somme.''[1]

November, 1916. Returned to England to recover from ''trench fever.''

January and February, 1917. Began writing *The Book of Lost Tales,* which was to become *Silmarillion.*

November, 1917. Son, John, born.

1918-1920. Worked on the staff of the *Oxford English Dictionary.* ''I learned more in those two years than in any other equal period of my life.''[4]

Said one of his superiors, Dr. Bradley: ''His work gives evidence of an unusally thorough mastery of Anglo-Saxon and of the facts and principles of the comparative grammar of the Germanic languages. Indeed, I have no hesitation in saying that I have never known a man of his age who was in these respects his equal.''[4]

1920. Appointed Reader in English Language at Leeds University. Birth of second son, Michael.

Many of the students at Leeds were from Yorkshire and had the reputation of being unsophisticated. ''I am wholly in favour of the 'dull stodges.' A surprisingly large proportion prove 'educable': for which a primary qualification is the willingness *to do some work.*''[4]

1924. Birth of son, Christopher.

1925. Appointed professor of Anglo-Saxon at Oxford University.

Beginning in 1920 and lasting twenty years, Tolkien wrote the ''Father Christmas Letters'' to his children. ''I am dreadfully busy this year—it makes my hand more shaky than ever when I think of it—and not very rich. In fact, awful things have been happening, and some of the presents have got spoilt and I haven't got the North Polar Bear to help me and I have had to move house just before Christmas so you can imagine what a state everything is in. It all happened like this: One very windy day last November my hood blew off and went and stuck on the top of the North Pole. I told him not to, but the North Polar Bear climbed up to the thin top to get it down— and he did. The pole broke in the middle and fell on the roof of my house, and the North Polar Bear fell through the hole it made into the dining room with my hood over his nose, and all the snow fell off the roof into the house. . .'' [J.R.R. Tolkien, ''The Father Christmas Letters,'' *McCall's,* December, 1976.[6]]

1926. Befriended C. S. Lewis. Formation of ''The Coalbiters,'' [later called ''The Inklings''] a small group of Oxford professors who met periodically for discussion and to read one another's works in progress.

. . . He was the ruin of roads and the desolation of gardens. . . . If he stumbled into a house, that was the end of it. ■ (From *Farmer Giles of Ham* by J.R.R. Tolkien. Illustrated by Pauline Baynes.)

1929. Daughter, Priscilla, born.

1936. Finished writing *The Hobbit,* a work he had begun in 1930. Said Lewis of Tolkien: ''He has only two reactions to criticism. Either he begins the whole work over again from the beginning or else takes no notice at all.''[4]

1937. *The Hobbit; or, There and Back Again* published by Allen & Unwin. ''The Hobbits are just rustic English people, made small in size because it reflects the generally small reach of their imagination—not the small reach of their courage or latent power.''[4]

Hobbits are ''little people, smaller than the bearded dwarves. Hobbits have no beards. There is little or no magic about them, except the ordinary everyday sort which helps them to disappear quietly and quickly when large stupid folks like you and me come blundering along, making a noise like elephants which they can hear a mile off. They are inclined to be fat in the stomach: they dress in bright colors (chiefly green and yellow); wear no shoes, because their feet grow natural leathery soles and thick warm brown hair like the stuff on their heads (which is curly); have long clever brown fingers, good-natured faces and laugh deep fruity laughs (especially after dinner which they have twice a day when they can get it).'' [*New York Times,* September 3, 1973.[7]]

''I am in fact a hobbit in all but size. I like gardens, trees, and unmechanized farmlands; I smoke a pipe, and like good plain food (unrefrigerated), but detest French cooking; I like, and even dare to wear in these dull days, ornamental waistcoats. I am fond of mushrooms (out of a field); have a very simple sense of humour (which even my appreciative critics find tiresome); I go to bed late and get up late (when possible). I do not travel much.''[4]

It was believed that Tolkien wrote *The Hobbit* for his own children. ''That's all sob stuff. No, of course, I didn't. If you're a youngish man and you don't want to be made fun of, you say you're writing for children. At any rate, children are your immediate audience and you write or tell them stories, for which they are mildly grateful: long rambling stories at bed-time.

"*The Hobbit* was written in what I should now regard as bad style, as if one were talking to children. There's nothing my children loathed more. They taught me a lesson. Anything that in any way marked out *The Hobbit* as for children instead of just for people, they disliked—instinctively. I did too, now that I think about it. All this 'I won't tell you any more, you think about it' stuff. Oh no, they loathe it; it's awful.

"Children aren't a class. They are merely human beings at different stages of maturity. All of them have a human intelligence which even at its lowest is a pretty wonderful thing, and the entire world in front of them. It remains to be seen if they rise above that."[2]

"I am not interested in the 'child' as such, modern or otherwise, and certainly have no intention of meeting him/her half way, or a quarter of the way. It is a mistaken thing to do anyway, either useless (when applied to the stupid) or pernicious (when inflected on the gifted).

"My eldest boy was thirteen when he heard the serial. It did not appeal to the younger ones who had to grow up to it successively."[4]

"It's not even very good for children. I wrote some of it in a style for children, but that's what they loathe. If I hadn't done that, people would have thought I was loony."

In creating *The Hobbit,* his ambition was to start "to make a body of more or less connected legend, ranging from the large and cosmogonic to the level of the romantic fairy-story . . . which I could dedicate simply: to England; to my country." [Deborah Webster Rogers and Ivor A. Rogers, *J.R.R. Tolkien,* Twayne, 1980.[8]]

Tolkien defended the fairy-story. "If fairy-story as a kind is worth reading at all it is worthy to be written for and read by adults. They will, of course, put more in and get more out than children can. Then, as a branch of a genuine art, children may hope to get fairy-stories fit for them to read and yet within their measure; as they may hope to get suitable introductions to poetry, history, and the sciences.

"First of all: if written with art, the prime value of fairy-stories will simply be that value, which, as literature, they share with

(From *Smith of Wootten Major* by J.R.R. Tolkien. Illustrated by Pauline Baynes.)

The hall at Bag-End, residence of B. Baggins Esquire. ■(From *The Hobbit; or, There and Back Again* by J.R.R. Tolkien. Illustrated by the author.)

other literary forms. But fairy-stories offer also, in a peculiar degree or mode, these things: Fantasy, Recovery, Escape, Consolation, all things of which children have, as a rule, less need than older people." [J.R.R. Tolkien, "On Fairy-Stories," *Horn Book*, October, 1963.⁹]

Urged by publisher, Allen & Unwin to write a sequel, Tolkien began *The Lord of the Rings*. "... Mr. Baggins began as a comic tale among conventional and inconsistent Grimm's fairy-tale dwarves, and got drawn into the edge of it—so that even Sauron the terrible peeped over the edge. And what more can hobbits do? They can be comic, but their comedy is suburban unless it is set against things more elemental. . . .

"I find it only too easy to write opening chapters—and at the moment the story is not unfolding. I squandered so much on the original *Hobbit* (which was not meant to have a sequel) that it is difficult to find anything new in the world."⁴

"I think *The Lord of the Rings* is in itself a good deal better than *The Hobbit*, but it may not prove a very fit sequel. It is more grown up—but the audience for which *The Hobbit* was written has done that also. The readers young and old who clamoured for 'more about the Necromancer' are to blame. . . . The writing of *The Lord of the Rings* is laborious, because I

have been doing it as well as I know how, and considering every word. The story, too, has (I fondly imagine) some significance. In spare time it would be easier and quicker to write up the plots already composed of the more lighthearted stories of the Little Kingdom to go with *Farmer Giles* [*Farmer Giles of Ham*, published, 1949]. But I would rather finish the long tale, and not let it go cold.

"It is not possible even at great length to 'pot' *The Lord of the Rings* in a papagraph to two. . . . It was begun in 1936, and every part has been written many times. Hardly a word in its 600,000 or more has been unconsidered. And the placing, size, style, and contribution to the whole of all the features, incidents, and chapters has been laboriously pondered. I do not say this in recommendation. It is, I feel, only too likely that I am deluded, lost in a web of vain imaginings of not much value to others—in spite of the fact that a few readers have found it good, on the whole. What I intend to say is this: I cannot substantially alter the thing. I have finished it, it is 'off my mind': the labour has been colossal; and it must stand or fall, practically as it is."¹

Of the principal character in *The Lord of the Rings*, Tolkien said: "My 'Sam Gamgee' is indeed a reflection of the English soldier, of the privates and batmen I knew in the 1914 war, and recognised as so far superior to myself."⁴

1959. Retired from his professorship at Oxford, and soon felt bored and occasionally depressed. "Life is grey and grim. I can get nothing done, between staleness and boredom (confined to quarters), and anxiety and distraction. What am I going to do? Be sucked down into residence in a hotel or old-people's home or club, without books or contacts or talk with men? God help me!"[4]

1965. Unauthorized edition of *The Lord of the Rings* published by Ace Books in the United States. Tolkien expressed his irritation in the foreword of the authorized Ballantine edition. "I hope that those who have read *The Lord of the Rings* with pleasure will not think me ungrateful: to please readers was my main object, and to be assured of this has been a great reward. Nonetheless, for all its defects of omission and inclusion, it was the product of long labour, and like a simple-minded hobbit I feel that it is, while I am still alive, my property in justice unaffected by copyright laws. It seems to me a grave discourtesy, to say no more, to issue my book without even a polite note informing me of the project: dealings one might expect of Saruman in his decay rather than from the defenders of the West." [J.R.R. Tolkien, foreword to *The Fellowship of the Ring: Being the First Part of The Lord of the Rings,* Ballantine, 1965.[10]]

The American editions were enormously popular, and the object of a veritable cult on college campuses in the sixties. "Being a cult figure in one's own lifetime I am afraid is not at all pleasant. However I do not find that it tends to puff one up; in my case at any rate it makes me feel extremely small and inadequate. But even the nose of a very modest idol cannot remain entirely untickled by the sweet smell of incense.

"It is an astonishing situation, and I hope I am sufficently grateful to God. Only a little while ago I was wondering if we should be able to go on living here, on my inadequate pension. But saving universal catastrophe, I am not likely to be hard up again in my time."[4]

Tolkien, who rose at 8:30 a.m. and stayed up late, spent most of his day "Working like hell. A pen is to me as a beak is to a hen."[2]

But he noted that ". . . Most of the time I'm fighting against the natural inertia of the lazy human being. The same old university don who warned me about being useful around the house once said, 'It's not only interruptions, my boy; it's the fear of interruptions.'"[2]

1971. Wife, Edith, died at the age of eighty-two. He wrote to son, Christopher: "She was (and knew she was) my Lúthien. I will say no more now. But I should like ere long to have a long talk with you. For if as seems probable I shall never write any ordered biography—it is against my nature, which expresses itself about things deepest felt in tales and myths—someone close in heart to me should know something about things that records do not record: the dreadful sufferings of our childhoods, from which we rescued one another, but could not wholly heal wounds that later often proved disabling; the sufferings that we endured after our love began—all of which (over and above personal weaknesses) might help to make pardonable, or understandable, the lapses and darknesses which at times marred our lives—and to explain how these never touched our depths not dimmed the memories of our youthful love. For ever (especially when alone) we still met in the woodland glade and went hand in hand many times to escape the shadow of imminent death before our last parting."[4]

September 2, 1973. Died of perforated ulcer at the age of eighty-one, in Bournemouth, England.

1977. *The Silmarillion,* edited by son, Christopher, published posthumously. "I first began to write [*The Silmarillion*] in army huts, crowded, filled with the noise of gramophones." [J.R.R. Tolkien, *Unfinished Tales of Númenor and Middle Earth,* edited by Christopher Tolkien, Allen & Unwin Ltd., 1980.[11]]

(From *The Tolkien Scrapbook,* edited by Alida Becker. Illustrated by Michael Green.)

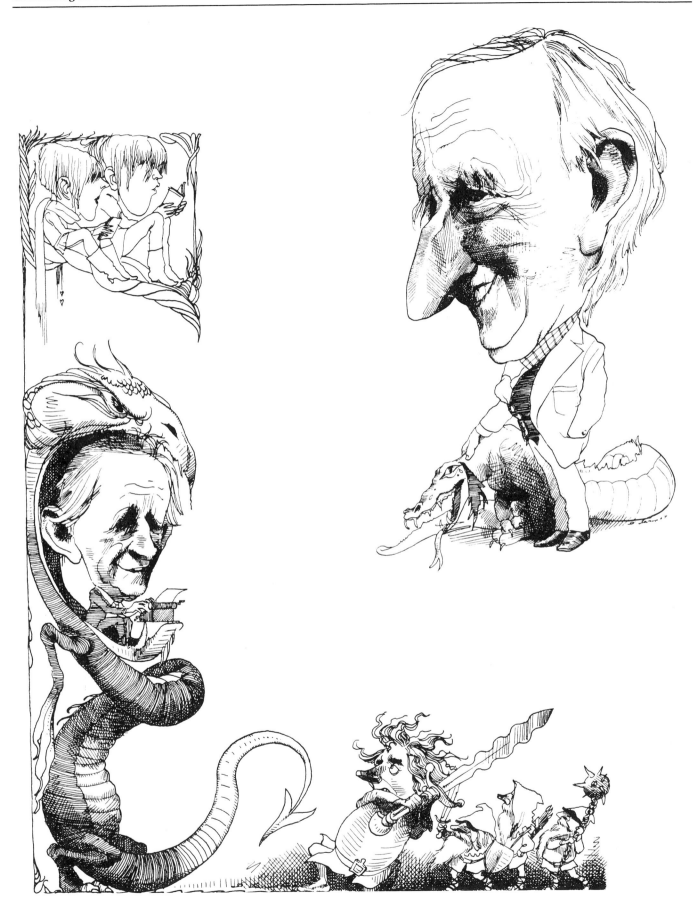

Caricatures of Tolkien.

The stories that made up the book ". . . arose in mind as 'given' things, and as they came, separately, so too the links grew. An absorbing, though continually interrupted labour (especially, even apart from the necessities of life, since the mind would wing to the other pole and spread itself on the linguistics): yet always I had the sense of recording what was already 'there,' somewhere: not of 'inventing.'"[4]

FOR MORE INFORMATION SEE—Books: J.R.R. Tolkien, *The Fellowship of the Ring: Being the First Part of the Lord of the Rings*, Ballantine, 1965; Neil D. Isaacs and Rose A. Zimbardo, editors, *Tolkien and the Critics*, University of Notre Dame Press, 1968; William B. Ready, *The Tolkien Relation: A Personal Inquiry*, Regnery, 1968; Catherine R. Stimpson, *J.R.R. Tolkien*, Columbia University Press, 1969; Lin Carter, *A Look behind "The Lord of the Rings,"* Ballantine, 1969; Mark R. Hillegas, editor, *Shadows of the Imagination: The Fantasies of C. S. Lewis, J.R.R. Tolkien, and Charles Williams*, Southern Illinois University Press, 1969, 2nd edition, 1979; Richard C. West, compiler, *Tolkien Criticism: An Annotated Checklist*, Kent State University Press, 1970, revised edition, 1981; Garcia F. Ellwood, *Good News from Tolkien's Middle Earth: Two Essays on the Applicability of "The Lord of the Rings,"* Eerdmans, 1970; Robert Foster, *A Guide to Middle Earth*, Mirage Press, 1971; Paul H. Kocher, *Master of Middle-Earth: The Fiction of J.R.R. Tolkien*, Houghton, 1972; Kocher, *Master of Middle-Earth: The Achievement of J.R.R. Tolkien*, Thames & Hudson, 1973; *Contemporary Literary Criticism*, Gale, Volume I, 1973, Volume 2, 1974, Volume 3, 1975, Volume 12, 1980; Richard L. Purtill, *Lord of the Elves and Eldils: Fantasy and Philosophy in C. S. Lewis and J.R.R. Tolkien*, Zondervan, 1974; Randel Helms, *Tolkien's World*, Houghton, 1974; Jared Lobdell, editor, *A Tolkien Compass*, Open Court, 1975; C. N. Manlove, "J.R.R. Tolkien (1892-1973) and 'The Lord of the Rings,'" in his *Modern Fantasy: Five Studies*, Cambridge University Press, 1975.

Daniel Grotta, *Biography of J.R.R. Tolkien, Architect of Middle-Earth*, Running Press, 1976, revised edition, 1978; J.E.A. Tyler, *The Tolkien Companion*, edited by S. A. Tyler, St. Martin's, 1976, 2nd edition, revised, Macmillan (London), 1979; Clyde Kilby, *Tolkien and "The Silmarillion"*, Harold Shaw, 1976; Humphrey Carpenter, *Tolkien: A Biography*, Houghton, 1977; Ruth S. Noel, *The Mythology of Middle Earth*, Houghton, 1977; Richard Mathews, *Lightning from a Clear Sky: Tolkien, the Trilogy and "The Silmarillion"*, Borgo, 1978; Alida Becker, editor, *The Tolkien Scrapbook*, Grosset, 1978; *Contemporary Authors*, Permanent Series, Volume 2, Gale, 1978; David Day, editor, *Tolkien Bestiary*, Mitchell Beazley, 1979; Mary Salu and Robert T. Farrell, editors, *J.R.R. Tolkien, Scholar and Storyteller: Essays in Memoriam*, Cornell University Press, 1979; J.R.R. Tolkien, *The Pictures of J.R.R. Tolkien* (with foreword and notes by Christopher Tolkien), Houghton, 1979; J.E.A. Tyler, *The New Tolkien Companion*, St. Martin's, 1979.

P. H. Kocher, *A Reader's Guide to the Silmarillion*, Houghton, 1980; R. S. Noel, *The Languages of Tolkien's Middle-Earth*, Houghton, 1980; Deborah W. Rogers and Ivor A. Rogers, *J.R.R. Tolkien*, Twayne, 1980; J.R.R. Tolkien, *Unfinished Tales of Númenor and Middle Earth*, edited by C. Tolkien, Allen & Unwin, 1980; H. Carpenter and C. Tolkien, editors, *The Letters of J.R.R. Tolkien*, Houghton 1981; Katharyn F. Crabbe, *J.R.R. Tolkien*, Ungar, 1981; Karen W. Fonstad, *The Atlas of the Middle-Earth*, Houghton, 1981; Robert Giddings and Elizabeth Holland, *J.R.R. Tolkien: The Shores of the Middle-Earth*, Aletheia Books, 1981; T. E. Little, *The Fantasts: Studies of J.R.R. Tolkien, Lewis Carroll, Mervyn Peake, Ni-*

kolay Gogol and Kenneth Grahame, Avebury Publishing (Amersham, England), 1981; Neil D. Isaacs and Rose A. Zimbardo, *Tolkien: New Critical Perspectives*, University Press of Kentucky, 1981; Randel Helms, *Tolkien and the Silmarils*, Houghton, 1981; Barbara Strachey, *Journeys of Frodo: An Atlas of J.R.R. Tolkien's "The Lord of the Rings,"* Ballantine, 1981; Geoffrey M. Ridden, *The Hobbit: Notes*, Longman, 1981; T. A. Shippey, *The Road to Middle-Earth*, Allen & Unwin, 1982.

Periodicals: *Time and Tide*, October 22, 1955; *New Republic*, January 16, 1956; *Nation*, April 14, 1956; *Hudson Review*, IX (1956-57); *South Atlantic Quarterly*, summer, 1959; *Critique*, spring-fall, 1959; *Sewannee Review*, fall, 1961; *Thought*, spring, 1963; *Horn Book*, October, 1963; *Atlantic*, March, 1965; *New York Times Book Review*, March 14, 1965, October 31, 1965; *National Review*, April 20, 1965; *Kenyon Review*, summer, 1965; *Commonweal*, December 3, 1965; *Holiday Magazine*, 1966; *Saturday Evening Post*, July 2, 1966; *Esquire*, September, 1966; *New York Times Magazine*, January 15, 1967; *Commentary*, February, 1967; *Book Week*, February 26, 1967; *New Society*, March 27, 1969; *South Atlantic Quarterly*, spring, 1970; *Signal*, September, 1971; *Times Literary Supplement*, March 12, 1976; *McCall's*, December, 1976; *New Republic*, October 1, 1977; *New York Times Book Review*, October 23, 1977; *New Statesman*, September 23, 1977; *Harper's Magazine*, November, 1977; *America*, November 4, 1977; *New York Review of Books*, November 24, 1977; *National Review*, December 9, 1977; *London Sunday Times* (magazine section), September 19, 1982.

Obituaries: *Washington Post*, September 3, 1973; *New York Times*, September 3, 1973; *Newsweek*, September, 17, 1973; *Publishers Weekly*, September 17, 1973; *Time*, September 17, 1973; *Library Journal*, October 15, 1973; *AB Bookman's Weekly*, October 15, 1973; *Contemporary Authors*, Volumes 45-48, Gale, 1974.

TRNKA, Jiri   1912-1969

BRIEF ENTRY: Name is pronounced *jeer*-ee *trink*-a; born February 24, 1912, in Pilsen, Czechoslovakia; died of a heart ailment December 30, 1969, in Prague, Czechoslovakia. Puppet film producer, animator, stage designer, artist, and illustrator of books for children. A multi-faceted artist, Trnka began his involvement with puppetry at an early age as an apprentice to noted puppeteer Josef Skupa. After graduating from the Prague Academy of Art in 1935, he became a successful illustrator of children's books, illustrating over fifty Czechoslovakian titles many of which were translated into English. These include several he wrote in collaboration with Frantisek Hrubin and his own *Zahrada*, 1962, translated as *Through the Magic Gate*. Among his other illustrated works are Josef Menzel's *Misa Kulicka v rodnem lese*, 1939, translated in 1957 as *Bruin Furryball in His Forest Home*, Jan Karafiat's *Broucci*, 1940, translated in 1970 as *The Fireflies*, Hrubin's *Pohadka o Kvetusce a jeji zahradce*, 1955, translated in 1965 as *Primrose and the Winter Witch*, and Alois Jirasek's *Stare povesti ceske*, 1960, translated in 1963 as *Legends of Old Bohemia*. In 1968 Trnka was awarded the Hans Christian Andersen Medal for his entire body of illustrated work.

In 1945, having also gained a reputation as an accomplished artist in both stage design and oil painting, Trnka began to develop his talents in yet another medium—animated film. In a field that had long been dominated by Walt Disney, Trnka proved himself an innovator by creating award-winning films such as "The Chimney Sweep" and "The Animals and the Brigands." By 1946 he was ready to return to his first and best-loved talent, that of puppetry. Considered by many to be a revolutionist in the art of the puppet film, Trnka endowed his puppets with life-like movement, deep emotion, and a sense of poetry. He produced about thirty films, including "The Czech Year" and "The Emperor's Nightingale." Recipient of innumerable awards for his puppet films, he also received the Czechoslovak Honour of Merited Artist in 1955, the Czechoslovak Peace Prize in 1958, and was awarded the title of National Artist of Czechoslovakia in 1963. *Residence:* Prague, Czechoslovakia. *For More Information See:* Jaroslov Bocek, *Jiri Trnka: Artist and Puppet Master,* Artia, 1965; Bettina Hurlimann, *Picture Book World,* Oxford University Press, 1968; *Third Book of Junior Authors,* Wilson, 1972. *Obituaries: New York Times,* December 31, 1969.

WATANABE, Shigeo 1928-

BRIEF ENTRY: Born March 20, 1928, in Shizuoka, Japan. Author, translator, and critic of books for children. Watanabe received his B.A. from Keio University, Tokyo, in 1953. As an exchange student in the United States, he attended Case Western Reserve University where he received his M.S. in library science in 1955. From 1955 to 1957 he worked as the only male librarian in the New York Public Library system during which time he gained recognition as an outstanding storyteller. In 1956 he participated in the Storytelling Festival held at the American Library Association Miami Beach Conference. Returning to Japan, he was associate professor at Keio University from 1957 to 1969, becoming professor from 1970 to 1975. Beginning in 1976, he served two years as vice-president of the International Board of Books for Young People. In 1977 he was chosen as the May Hill Arbuthnot Honor Lecturer by the American Library Association, and, in 1980, was the recipient of the Fifteenth Mobil Children's Culture Award.

A noted author of children's books in Japan, Watanabe has written a few dozen books several of which have been translated into English. Among them are *How Do I Put It On?* (Philomel, 1979), *Hallo! How Are You?* (Bodley Head, 1980), *Get Set! Go!* (Philomel, 1981), and *Where's My Daddy?* (Philomel, 1982). He has also translated a number of books from English to Japanese, including Clement Moore's *A Visit from St. Nicholas,* Madeleine L'Engle's *A Wrinkle in Time,* Eleanor Estes's *The Moffats,* and several by Dr. Seuss. Recognized as a school media specialist, he has been a visiting lecturer at various institutions both in the United States and abroad and has written several scholarly works on children's literature and library services for children. *Home:* 2-40-8 Sakuragaoka, Tamashi, Tokyo 206, Japan. *For More Information See: Top of the News,* April, 1976, Spring, 1977.

WATSON, Nancy Dingman

PERSONAL: Born in Paterson, N.J.; daughter of Norman McLeod and Ann (Bauer) Dingman; married Aldren A. Watson (an art editor, illustrator, and writer), August 9, 1941 (divorced); children: Wendy Watson Harrah, Peter, Clyde Watson

**Suspended in the summer air
With sparrow hawks and crows
But then the vines swing back to earth
And pebbles escape my toes.**

■ (From "Monkey Vines" in *Blueberries Lavender* by Nancy Dingman Watson. Illustrated by Erik Blegvad.)

Devlin, Linda Watson Wright, Ann Watson Blagden, Nancy Watson Cameron, Caitlin, Thomas. *Education:* Attended Wheaton College, Norton, Mass.; Smith College, B.A., 1965. *Home:* Truro, Mass. 02666. *Agent:* Marilyn Marlowe, Curtis Brown Ltd., 575 Madison Ave., New York, N.Y. 10022.

CAREER: Writer. Teacher, Castle Hill Center for the Arts; field worker, American Friends Service Committee. *Member:* Authors League (New York), Massachusetts Council for the Arts.

WRITINGS—Juvenile books; illustrated by Aldren A. Watson, except as indicated: *What Is One?,* Knopf, 1954; *Whose Birthday Is It?,* Knopf, 1954; *Toby and Doll,* Bobbs-Merrill, 1955; *When Is Tomorrow?* Knopf, 1955; *What Does A Begin With?* Knopf, 1956; *Anne's Spending Spree,* Viking, 1957; *The Fairy Tale Picture Book,* Garden City Books, 1957; *The Arabian Nights Picture Book,* Garden City Books, 1959; *Cat Tales,* Doubleday, 1961; *Pig Tales from Old English Nursery Rhymes,* Doubleday, 1961; *Pony Tales from Old English Nursery Rhymes,* Doubleday, 1961; *Puppy Dog Tales,* Doubleday, 1961; *Sugar on Snow,* Viking, 1964; *Katie's Chickens,* Knopf, 1963; *Carol to a Child* (music by daughter, Clyde Watson), World Publishing, 1969; *New under the Stars,* Little, Brown, 1970; *Tommy's Mommy's Fish,* Viking, 1971; *The Birthday Goat* (illustrated by daughter, Wendy Watson), Crowell, 1974; *Muncus Agruncus: A Bad Little Mouse* (illustrated by W. Watson), Golden Press, 1976; *Blueberries Lavender: Songs of the Farmers' Children* (poems; illustrated by Erik Blegvad), Addison-Wesley, 1977.

Author of column "One Woman's View," *Brattleboro Daily Reformer,* 1960—.

Something was pulling and jerking and splashing and I began to reel in. I reeled and I reeled....
■ (From *Tommy's Mommy's Fish* by Nancy Dingman Watson. Illustrated by Aldren A. Watson.)

SIDELIGHTS: For many years Watson lived on a farm in Vermont. Besides raising dogs, canaries, and enjoying her horses, she also wrote a great deal during her growing-up years, and started several enterprises, including making candy and selling sarsaparilla. "[My candy-making] ended in mountains of fudge, cooked in the barn and bought by my Uncle Fred, who had a sweet tooth, up to a point. I tried taxidermy, too, but this was not a success—I forget why—and my father wrote a hot letter to the school of taxidermy and told them to stop sending me lessons. My cousin and I thought we might dig sassafras roots and make sarsaparilla to sell—nothing cliché like lemonade for me—but the stuff tasted like mud." [Taken from the book jacket of *Blueberries Lavender: Songs of the Farmer's Children* by Nancy Watson, Addison-Wesley, 1977.]

Watson has written many children's books using her surroundings as story material. From the activities of the children, the many farm animals, and the countryside have come many of her books, including *Sugar on Snow, What Is One?,* and *Toby and Doll.* Her oldest daughter, Wendy, provided the idea for *The Birthday Goat,* and her youngest son, Thomas, helped her with *Muncus Agruncus.* Many of Watson's books are illustrated by her former husband, Aldren, and her daughter, Wendy.

FOR MORE INFORMATION SEE: New York Times Book Review, March 13, 1977.

WAYNE, (Anne) Jenifer   1917-1982

PERSONAL: Born August 1, 1917, in London, England; died December 10, 1982; daughter of Philip (headmaster of Marylebone Grammar School) and Dorrit Wayne; married C. Rolph Hewitt in 1948; children: two daughters, one son. *Education:* Somerville College, Oxford, England, B.A. (with honors), 1939. *Home:* Rushett Edge, Bramley, Guildford, Surrey GU5 OLH, England.

CAREER: London (war-time) Ambulance Service, London, England, employee, 1939; Newark High School, Nottinghamshire, England, instructor in English, 1940-41; British Broadcasting Corp. (BBC), London, scriptwriter, and producer in radio features department, 1941-48; writer, 1948-82.

WRITINGS—For children; all published by Heinemann, except as noted: *Clemence and Ginger* (illustrated by Patricia Humphreys), 1960; *The Day the Ceiling Fell Down* (illustrated by Dodie Masterman), 1961, second edition (illustrated by Jill Bennett), Puffin, 1978; *Kitchen People* (illustrated by Margaret Palmer), 1963, American edition (illustrated by Leonard Shortall), Bobbs-Merrill, 1964; *The Night the Rain Came In* (illustrated by D. Masterman), 1963; *Merry by Name* (illustrated by M. Palmer), 1964; *The Ghost Next Door* (illustrated by M. Palmer), 1965; *Saturday and the Irish Aunt* (illustrated by M. Palmer), 1966; *Someone in the Attic* (illustrated by M. Palmer), 1967; *Ollie* (illustrated by M. Palmer), 1969.

Sprout (illustrated by M. Palmer), 1970, American edition (illustrated by G. Owens), McGraw, 1976; *Something in the Barn* (illustrated by M. Palmer), 1971; *Sprout's Window-Cleaner* (illustrated by M. Palmer), 1971, American edition (illustrated by G. Owens), McGraw, 1976; *Sprout and the Dogsitter* (illustrated by M. Palmer), 1972, American edition (illustrated by G. Owens), McGraw, 1977; *The Smoke in Albert's Garden* (illustrated by M. Palmer), 1974; *Sprout and the Helicopter* (illustrated by M. Palmer), 1974, American edition (illustrated by G. Owens), McGraw, 1977; *Sprout and the Conjuror* (illustrated by M. Palmer), 1976, published in America as *Sprout and the Magician* (illustrated by G. Owens), McGraw, 1977; *John Brown, Rose and the Midnight Cat,* Kestrel, 1978.

Adults: *This Is the Law: Stories of Wrongdoers by Fault or Folly,* Sylvan Press, 1948; *The Shadows, and Other Poems* (verse), Secker & Warburg, 1959; *Brown Bread and Butter in the Basement: A Twenties Childhood,* Gollancz, 1973; *The Purple Dress: Growing Up in the Thirties,* Gollancz, 1979. Also author of the radio play, "The Queen of the Castle," 1969.

Slowly he grinned at the elephant, and slowly, with even more creases in its skin, it smiled back. Other people might not have seen this, but Sprout did. ■ (From *Sprout* by Jenifer Wayne. Illustrated by Gail Owens.)

The only ones who didn't say anything at all were Sprout and the dog. ■ (From *Sprout and the Dogsitter* by Jenifer Wayne. Illustrated by Gail Owens.)

SIDELIGHTS: Wayne was born in 1917 in London, England. ". . . My mother was not inclined to be 'fantastical.' She was a doer; much more shy than my father, but in some ways more doggedly adventurous." [Jenifer Wayne, *The Purple Dress: Growing Up in the Thirties*, Gollancz, 1979.[1]]

In the 1930s she was a student at Oxford University where she graduated with honors in 1939. ". . . I never really got over a feeling of awe at actually being there. Things seem to have gone to the other extreme now; there are so many universities where to be a student is not a particularly interesting condition. All the same, undergraduates shouldn't go about being awe-stricken for three years."[1]

Following graduation, Wayne worked briefly as an English teacher at Newark High School in England. "The headmistress was a youngish, pale mathematician with thick lenses; she seemed affable in a nervous way, but rather lost as to what to ask me. Senior English [teacher] naturally had more to tell me, and was very kind though I thought I sensed a little well-suppressed agitation. I realized, afterwards, that there may have been two reasons for this. One, that I was young and untrained; two, that I had been to Oxford. They had never had anyone from Oxford before; I was regarded with a mixture of respect and suspicion. They were afraid I should be highbrow. . . . All the same, I'm inclined to think it was the 'Oxford' that got me the job. Or perhaps they just didn't have any other candidates.

"As for school itself: by the end of the first week I had decided, grimly and secretly, that I would leave in exactly fifteen months' time. At the end, that is, of the next summer term, when the next year's public exams were over. I dared not confide this decision to anyone: it would have been almost scandalous. One was expected to stay in one's first job for three years, or, at the very least, two. I knew in a few days that four terms would be my utmost limit.

"What was wrong? Really, just myself. It irked me a little to be called 'Wayne' in the staff room; but I could have swallowed that. It worried me more to find myself teaching Kinglake's *Eöthen* to an O-level-standard fifth form who were bored stiff; and so was I. Scott, with the lower sixth, was even worse: crikey, I hadn't even *read* Scott! Addison and Steele with the fourth forms were rock-bottom end. The fourth forms were bad enough anyway, without having to shamble through *The Spectator*. They spent most of the time winding their hair round pencils—curls were still desirable. They were not so much naughty as apathetic, which is far worse. The only teaching I ever came near to enjoying was at the extreme ends of the school: the upper sixth, a small class doing Lamb, Hazlitt, Shakespeare, the Metaphysicals and some modern poetry; and the eight-year-olds, riotously acting ballads. They would push back their desks with deafening enthusiasm and stamp around being Lochinvar, or Lord Ullin, or Fair Helen of Kirkonnel, with their socks falling down; 'extras' cheering or hissing on the radiators. That was fun; though not for the person trying to teach geography in the next room.

"Let's face it, I was a rotten teacher. Partly, perhaps, because I was in a constant state of terror. This never wore off. I would wake up every morning under my pink eiderdown, terrified. I would walk down Lime Grove full of poached eggs, but laden-hearted and weak at the knees. I faced every class with a stage-fright which I tried to conceal; but they must have seen through it. Yet there were no disciplinary problems: if there had been, I might have sparked into defiance—or, more probably, I should have sunk without trace. But they were very different from London children; and different from most children today. They were not naughty; not cheeky; not malevolent; not inventive. Just more or less amiable; more or less respectful; more or less bored; more or less without ambition."[1]

After leaving the teaching profession, Wayne found her career niche working for the BBC radio in London. "It really was a pleasant place to be, even in war time. I was specially lucky because my job demanded some regional travelling: to Wiltshire, Devon, the Mendips, Bath, Cornwall. . . . I had no car, but you can see more of the country from train or bus."[1]

Following her marriage to C. Rolph Hewitt and the birth of her first child, Wayne resigned from her seven-year career in radio. She turned to free-lance writing, producing her first book for adults in 1948.

In 1960 her first children's book, *Clemence and Ginger,* was published, and eight more children's books quickly followed in the decade of the sixties. Her most loveable and popular children's books, about the loveable young scamp, Sprout, were written in the 1970s.

The "Sprout" books were drawn from her own family experiences. The background for the "Sprout" books was a 400-year-old cottage in Surrey, England, where Wayne lived with her husband and three children. "The characters of the children [are] based roughly on my own; most of the happenings [are] based *very* roughly on fact," Wayne commented.

Besides writing, Wayne was interested in gardening, playing the piano, and directing the village choir.

FOR MORE INFORMATION SEE: Publishers Weekly, February 28, 1977; Jenifer Wayne, *The Purple Dress: Growing Up in the Thirties,* Gollancz, 1979.

WIKLAND, Ilon 1930-

BRIEF ENTRY: Born February 5, 1930, in Dorpat, Estonia; emigrated to Sweden in 1944. An author and illustrator of books for children, Wilkand studied art in Stockholm at Skolan fuer Bok-Och Relkamkonst and Signe Barth's Painting School. After working for two years in a decorating studio, she spent a six-month hiatus furthering her art studies in England. Returning to Stockholm, she was employed as a lay-out artist for a large publishing firm, and in 1951, began a career as a free-lance artist. Three years later, she befriended Swedish children's author Astrid Lindgren and subsequently decided to concentrate all her efforts in illustrating books for children. In 1966 she was the recipient of a government scholarship and, in 1969, was awarded Sweden's highest award for an illustrator, the Elsa Beskow Plaque.

Wikland has illustrated over forty-five children's books, particularly those by Lindgren and Hans Peterson. Many of the titles, all originally written in Swedish, have been translated into English. They include Lindgren's *Mio, My Son* (Viking, 1962), *The Mischievous Martens* (Methuen, 1968), and *I Want a Brother or Sister* (Harcourt, 1981), Peterson's *Manus and the Squirrel* (Viking, 1959) and *Erik and the Christmas Horse* (Lothrop, 1970), Gunnel Linde's *Chimney Top Lane* (Harcourt, 1965), *The Pip-Larssons Go Sailing* (Macmillan, 1966) by Edith Unnerstad, and Viola Wahlstedt's *Ann and Susie Picks Berries* (Burke, 1972). In addition to illustrating the works of others, Wikland has written and self-illustrated two of her own picture books, *See What I Can Do!* and *I Can Help Too!* (both Random House, 1974). *Residence:* Sundlyberg, Sweden. *For More Information See: Illustrators of Children's Books: 1957-1966,* Horn Book, 1968; *Fourth Book of Junior Authors and Illustrators,* H. W. Wilson, 1978.

WILKINSON, (Thomas) Barry 1923-

BRIEF ENTRY: Born April 29, 1923, in Dewsbury, Yorkshire, England. A free-lance artist, author, and illustrator of books for children, Wilkinson attended Dewsbury Art School and Royal College of Art. He spent five years in the Royal Air Force and worked as both a designer and instructor in stained-glass before becoming a free-lance artist about 1960. His work has encompassed a variety of media—book publishing, television, magazines, and advertising. He has illustrated over thirty-five children's books including three of his own picture books. They are *The Diverting Adventures of Tom Thumb,* 1967, *Jonathan Just,* 1971, and *What Can You Do with a Dithery-Doo?,* 1971. Among his other works are Griselda Gifford's *The Mystery of the Wooden Legs,* 1964, Naomi Lewis's *The Story of Aladdin,* 1970, Charles Dickens's *A Tale of Two Cities,* 1973, Ursula Moray Williams's *The Line,* 1974, four "Paddington" books by Michael Bond, and Sheila Mc-Cullagh's *The Little Fox,* 1982. *Home:* Sevenoaks, Kent, England. *For More Information See: Fourth Book of Junior Authors and Illustrators,* H. W. Wilson, 1978; *Illustrators of Children's Books: 1967-1976,* Horn Book, 1978.

WILSON, Eric H. 1940-

BRIEF ENTRY: Born November 24, 1940, in Ottawa, Ontario, Canada. Author of mystery novels for young readers. Wilson received his B.A. from the University of British Columbia in 1963. Since 1967, he has been a remedial teacher of English and mathematics at the junior high level in various locations of British Columbia. Throughout his teaching career, he has periodically taken a year or two hiatus to devote his time to writing. He is the author of five novels, including *Murder on The Canadian,* 1976, *Vancouver Nightmare,* 1978, *Susie-Q,* 1978, *Terror in Winnipeg,* 1979, and *The Lost Treasure of Casa Loma,* 1980. With contemporary Canadians as characters, his books are filled with fast-paced action and excitement especially aimed at holding the interest of young readers with little inclination for reading. *Home:* 610 Third St., Nelson, British Columbia, Canada V1L 2P9. *For More Information See: Contemporary Authors,* Volume 101, Gale, 1981.

WULFFSON, Don L. 1943-

PERSONAL: Born August 21, 1943, in Los Angeles, Calif.; son of Charles Robin (an engineer) and Corinne (a real estate broker; maiden name, Lockwood) Wulffson; married wife, Pamela (a teacher), June 29, 1969; children: Jennifer, Gwendolyn. *Education:* University of California, Los Angeles, B.A., 1965, Teaching Credential, 1967. *Politics:* "Indifferent." *Religion:* "Confused." *Home:* 18718 Kirkcolm Lane, Northridge, Calif. 91326. *Office:* 11133 O'Melveny, San Fernando, Calif.

CAREER: San Fernando High School, Los Angeles, Calif., teacher of English, 1967—. *Member:* United Teachers of Los Angeles. *Awards, honors:* Leather Medal from New Directions Publishing Corp., 1971, for "You Too Can Be a Floorwax That Even Your Husband Could Apply"; distinguished achievement award from Educational Press Association of America, 1978, for *Writing You'll Enjoy.*

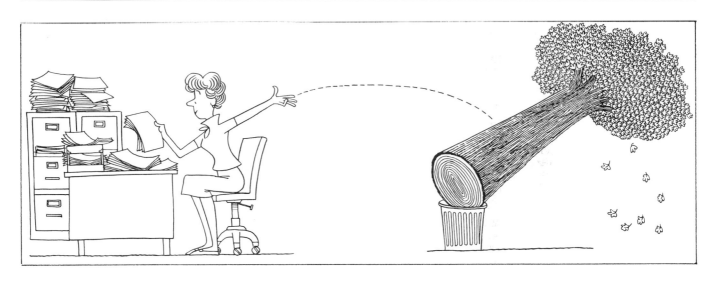

. . . The average clerk produces 4.4 pounds of waste paper a day. Roughly figured, this means that every clerk in this country throws away the equivalent of a thousand-pound tree every year! ■ (From *Extraordinary Stories Behind the Invention of Ordinary Things* by Don L. Wulffson. Illustrated by Roy Doty.)

WRITINGS—Juveniles: *Themes and Writers*, McGraw, 1973; *Eyebrowse* (stories and essays), Economy Co., 1976; *Building Vocabulary* (workbook), Xerox Education Publications, 1976; *Writing You'll Enjoy* (workbook), Xerox Education Publications, 1977; *The Touchstone Series* (workbooks), three volumes, Steck-Vaughn, 1977; *Punctuation Errors You Hate to Make* (workbook), Xerox Education Publications, 1978; *The Wonderful Word Book* (workbook), Xerox Education Publications, 1978; *Strange, Extraordinary Stories Behind How Sports Came to Be*, Lothrop, 1980; *True Stories You Won't Believe*, Xerox Education Publications, 1980; *Supergrammar* (workbook), Pruett, 1980; *Mindgame: Experiences in Creative Writing* (workbook), Xerox Educational Publications, 1980; *Visions* (stories and essays), Globe Book, 1980, published as *Facts and Fantasies*, Globe Book, 1982; *Extraordinary Stories Behind the Invention of Ordinary Things*, Lothrop, 1981. Also author of "Skillmaster Series," Xerox Education Publications. Contributor to *Isaac Asimov's Book of Facts*.

Plays for young people: "Heartbreak on the Beach" (one-act), published in *Read Magazine*, November 29, 1978; "Herbie's Comeuppance" (one-act), published in *Read Magazine*, April 11, 1979.

Work represented in anthologies, including *New Directions Twenty-Three*, New Directions, 1971; *Words and Beyond*, Ginn, 1973; *National Poetry Anthology*, National Poetry Press, 1975. Contributor of articles, poems, plays, and stories to magazines and to journals, including *Hyperion, Tangent Poetry Quarterly, Journal of Reading, Boys' Life, Cricket, Child Life,* and *Read*.

WORK IN PROGRESS: Twisted Visions, a book of science-fiction stories for teenagers; *Amazing Moments in History*, a nonfiction work for teenagers; *U.S.—S.R.*, a feature film screenplay.

SIDELIGHTS: "While in college I wanted to grow up to be Lawrence Ferlinghetti or a psychiatrist. Much to my dismay I ended up as an English teacher. In 1971 I published a surrealistic poem, 'You Too Can Be a Floorwax That Even Your

Husband Could Apply.' It appeared in the New Directions annual that included works by Ferlinghetti. I was so impressed by my achievement that I decided to quit writing poetry. Over the last few years most of my writing has been for children—educational workbooks, short stories, and nonfiction books.

"I have always been intrigued by both the past and the future. With my readers, I greatly enjoy exploring how the world came to be, what it is today, and trying to anticipate what it might someday become."

DON L. WULFFSON

CUMULATIVE INDEX TO ILLUSTRATIONS AND AUTHORS

Illustrations Index

(In the following index, the number of the volume in which an illustrator's work appears is given *before* the colon, and the page on which it appears is given *after* the colon. For example, a drawing by Adams, Adrienne appears in Volume 2 on page 6, another drawing by her appears in Volume 3 on page 80, another drawing in Volume 8 on page 1, and another drawing in Volume 15 on page 107.)

YABC

Index citations including this abbreviation refer to listings appearing in *Yesterday's Authors of Books for Children,* also published by the Gale Research Company, which covers authors who died prior to 1960.

Author Index

(The following index gives the number of the volume in which an author's biographical sketch, Brief Entry, or Obituary appears.)

YABC

Index citations including this abbreviation refer to listings appearing in *Yesterday's Authors of Books for Children,* also published by the Gale Research Company, which covers authors who died prior to 1960.